Expressions

An Introduction to Writing, Reading, and Critical Thinking

Megan C. Rainey

Cosumnes River College

Longman

New York   San Francisco   Boston
London   Toronto   Sydney   Tokyo   Singapore   Madrid
Mexico City   Munich   Paris   Cape Town   Hong Kong   Montreal

This book is dedicated to
My students at
Cosumnes River College
John, Brienna, Keely, Ann
and
Mom and Dad

Vice President/Editor-in-Chief: Joe Terry
Senior Acquisitions Editor: Steven Rigolosi
Development Manager: Janet Lanphier
Development Editor: Janice Wiggins-Clarke
Senior Marketing Manager: Melanie Craig
Supplements Editor: Donna Campion
Production Manager: Denise Phillip
Project Coordination, Text Design, and Electronic Page Makeup: WestWords, Inc.
Cover Designer/Manager: Wendy Ann Fredericks
Cover Illustrations: ©Romy Ragan/Brand X Pictures/Picture Quest
Manufacturing Buyer: Al Dorsey
Printer and Binder: Courier Corporation
Cover Printer: Coral Graphics

For permission to use copyrighted material, grateful acknowledgment is made to the copyright holders on p. 458, which is hereby made part of this copyright page.

Library of Congress Cataloging-in-Publication Data

Rainey, Megan
   Expressions: an introduction to writing, reading, and critical thinking / Megan C. Rainey.
      p. cm.
   Includes bibliographical references and indexes.
   ISBN 0-321-08355-5
      1. English language—Rhetoric. 2. English language—Grammar. 3. Critical thinking. 4.
   College readers. 5. Report writing. I. Title.

PE1408.R166 2002
808'.042—dc21

                                                                2002070214

Please visit our website at http://www.ablongman.com

ISBN 0-321-08355-5

1 2 3 4 5 6 7 8 9 10—CRW—05 04 03 02

Brief Contents

Detailed Contents

v

Readings by Theme

Preface for Instructors

Expressions is the first book in a three-book developmental writing series (*Expressions, Connections,* and *Interpretations*). The series was written to help instructors deal with the paradox we face in the developmental writing class. Our students are adult college students who need to be challenged as such. However, offering them the same full curriculum that freshman composition students have—reading, critical thinking, writing—can seem a daunting task for the instructor because of the unique needs developmental writers bring to the classroom.

Some students who come to us are highly oral/aural and have had little exposure to written language. They may have been inundated over the years with grammar and sentence exercises, yet their writing skills have not progressed. Others may speak English as their second language and will have varying degrees of education in their first language. Still others will come to us after having been out of school for many years.

The result is that we have students who have been frustrated and discouraged by previous classroom experiences, students who may have had no experience in an academic setting, students who have earned degrees in other languages, and students who are mature and bring a wealth of experiences and ideas to the classroom but need to strengthen their writing skills. Working with this complex mix of students, we must also consider that some of these students have learning disabilities.

My goal, then, in creating *Expressions* was threefold:

- Embrace developmental writing students as adult college students who deserve the richness of a class that offers interesting reading, critical thinking, and writing assignments.
- Offer significant supportive materials to make it possible for students with a variety of needs and backgrounds to succeed.
- Supply the developmental writing instructor with the textual support to make such a dynamic class manageable and rewarding.

Created for an introductory developmental writing class, *Expressions* takes the first crucial step with the adult developmental writer: building sensitivity to the rhetorical aspects of written texts. The "body" chapters (Chapters 6–11) of *Expressions* are divided by genre. The chapters on diaries, letters, academic paragraphs, autobiographies, fairy tales, and essays help developmental writers build awareness of a reading audience. Students learn that writers must adjust their writing to fit different purposes, messages, and audiences. Developing this flexibility as reader, writer, and thinker is critical to the developmental writer's progress. To help students meet these challenging goals, *Expressions* leads students step by step through the reading process and the writing process with *every* reading and writing assignment.

The readings in *Expressions* are longer than those in most developmental writing texts because I believe students need genuine readings that capture ideas worthy of discussion and full engagement. The writing assignments challenge students to move beyond strictly reflective pieces and into analysis. Again, *Expressions* offers substantial support to both student and instructor. In the margins, students find prompts and guides that encourage them to interact with and analyze their readings, use computers effectively, and participate in their own educations. Recognizing different learning styles, I encourage students to use note cards, their oral skills, highlighters, and so forth. Within these body chapters, **Skill Spotlights** and **Sentence Style** exercises offer students writing, reading and sentence strategies in manageable doses.

The extensive sentence work in *Expressions* is thematically connected to the reading and writing assignments. Students complete fill-in-the-blank warm-ups but then move on to revising paragraphs, creating original sentences, and applying their new knowledge to formal writing assignments. Finally, *Expressions* offers additional support to the student by addressing basic college survival skills: reading aloud, making the most of learning styles, taking notes, and writing in-class paragraphs.

Expressions aims to lift developmental writers out of the doldrums of curricula that focus almost exclusively on rote grammar drills. *Expressions* welcomes developmental students as adults into the world of academia where reading, critical thinking, and clear written expressions are the focus.

Goals of This Text

Expressions aims to prepare students for their collegiate and workplace tasks by inviting them into academia as adults and strengthening their reading, critical thinking, writing, and study skills.

Engage Developmental Writing Students as Adult Participants in College   Lack of skill and confidence often leads developmental writers to withdraw from the dynamics of learning. Chapters 1 and 2 aim to abolish myths about reading and writing so that students can see themselves as people capable of reading and writing well.

The adult tone of the text, readings, critical thinking work, and challenging analytical writing assignments speak to the students as adult college students. The questions in the reading margins, critical thinking questions that follow readings, **Express Yourself** assignments, and journal assignments require students to step forward, engage with the ideas, and express their responses. In addition, the **Get Involved!** activities in the body chapters and progress charts in the appendices encourage students to be less passive and more active in their own educations.

Strengthen Reading and Critical Thinking Skills   Although *Expressions* is a writing text with a writing emphasis, reading and critical thinking are major components. Better readers and thinkers are also better writers. Students who use *Expressions* will learn how to approach their readings (through an effective process); deal with new vocabulary; mark, discuss, and wrestle meaning out of difficult texts; and finally, imitate the readings by studying audience, purpose, development, focus, organization, and sentences.

Sharpen Writing Skills   *Expressions* emphasizes the writing process as key to generating meaningful text. Researchers such as Mina Shaughnessy (see "Beyond the Sentence" in *Errors and Expectations*) have shown that as inexperienced writers learn an effective process for completing writing assignments, they are able to create paragraphs with improved focus, development, organization, and clarity. Chapter 4 is dedicated to teaching students to use productive writing processes. All writing assignments in Chapters 7–11 lead the students step by step through this process.

Sentence Style exercises follow each reading in Chapters 7–11. These exercises ask students to study and then imitate the structures that professional writers use. The sentence exercises in Chapters 12–34 include the traditional fill-in-the-blank work but then move on to ask students to work with paragraphs and to create sentences of their own that connect to the themes in their reading and writing assignments.

Sharpen Study Skills   Because basic study skills can be a tremendous stumbling block for developmental writers, *Expressions* includes a section on college survival skills. Chapters 35–38 cover reading aloud, discovering and using learning styles, taking notes, and writing in-class paragraphs.

Content Overview

Designed to give instructors flexibility in planning their classes, *Expressions* offers 38 chapters in eight sections of instruction. *Expressions* can be adapted easily to classes from the lower end of skill development to classes at the higher end of skill development. A collection of syllabi in the *Instructor's Manual* addresses different approaches and how to make the most of the carefully designed interconnecting chapters.

Section I: The Power of Written Expression   Chapters 1 and 2 help to demystify writing and reading, offering the arguments that writing, reading, and critical thinking are integrally related skills and that all people can become competent readers and writers. These chapters also show students how to start off on the right foot—setting up their notebooks, seeking resources on campus, and creating a schedule that includes study time.

Section II: Strategies for Expression   Chapters 3, 4, and 5 introduce the student to key components in *Expressions:* the reading process, the writing process, and handling new vocabulary. Chapter 3 explains how experienced readers read and then offers the students a reading to which they can apply this process. This reading process is then repeated with every reading assignment in Chapters 6–11 and in Section VIII, "The Reader."

Chapter 4 introduces the student to the writing process and then offers the student a paragraph assignment for practice. Chapters 7–11 lead students through this writing process with every writing assignment.

Chapter 5 teaches students how to use the dictionary and methods for dealing with new vocabulary. After each reading in Chapters 8–11, students will find a list of vocabulary words that the class can work on together.

Section III: Variety in Expression   Section III emphasizes that people express ideas in a variety of ways, and in each instance, writers adjust the form of their writing, their vocabulary, and their style. Chapter 6 "Diaries and Journals," begins by showing students that private expressions are casual in style, but quite valuable to the writer (and, in rare cases, to the reading public.)

Chapter 7, "Academic Paragraphs," explains the form and function of this critical unit of academic expression. Though later chapters offer opportunities for students to write letters and stories, each chapter also includes a paragraph assignment since academic writing is the focus of this text.

Chapter 8, "Letters and E-mail," gives students the opportunity to think about writing in a very practical manner. Everyone has to write letters, and students see letter writing as a clear example of when writing can be a powerful tool toward achieving goals and solving problems. Here again, students focus on who is in the reading audience and what adjustments the writer must make.

In Chapter 9, "Autobiographies," students experiment with narration as a tool they can use in their own paragraphs and, later, essays. In studying Alice Walker's essay, students think critically about the choices she made as a writer. Then students write their own autobiographical piece or choose one of the other paragraph assignments.

In Chapter 10, "Fairy Tales," students are formally introduced to analyzing. Students first look at fairy tales written for significantly different audiences and then practice taking them apart as they write analytical responses. The chapter also offers the option of writing an original modern fairy tale.

Finally, Chapter 11, "Essays," serves as a bridge chapter to the next developmental writing class. This chapter reviews the qualities of effective writing first discussed in Chapter 7, "Academic Paragraphs." Then students look at a student essay before writing their own.

Section IV: Sentence Basics and Avoiding Sentence Errors   This section introduces students to basic sentence terminology: verbs, subjects, prepositional phrases, infinitives, phrases, clauses, and so on. Then students use these terms as they learn how to identify, correct, and avoid verb errors, fragments, run-ons, and comma splices.

Section V: Beyond the Basics—Creating Expressive Sentences   This section inspires students as they see that they can manipulate sentences in a number of ways to express more sophisticated ideas.

Section VI: Editing Essentials   Chapters in this section might be assigned on an individual basis when the instructor sees which errors a student tends to make.

Section VII: College Survival Skills   Designed to help students strengthen critical study skills, the chapters in this section can be assigned on an individual or group basis. Each chapter offers a writing or speaking assignment so the chapters can take a prominent position in class curriculum. Chapter 35 explains to students that reading aloud can be a terrific aid as they seek to develop an "ear" for written language. Chapter 36 helps students discover and strengthen their learning styles. Chapter 37 focuses on note-taking strategies to help the developmental writer who, hampered by weak spelling skills and a poor academic vocabulary, may be overwhelmed by lecture courses. Finally, Chapter 38, "In-Class Writing," offers strategies for preparing for in-class writing and then offers some practice prompts.

Section VIII: The Reader   This section offers readings that can supplement or replace the readings found in Chapters 6–11. Instructors might also assign these readings and the corresponding critical thinking questions to students who need additional reading and thinking practice.

Features

The following features of *Expressions* help instructors build dynamic learning environments and give students the necessary support as they strengthen their reading, writing, and critical thinking skills.

Academic Focus   Students engage in the kinds of critical reading and writing activities—summarizing, discussing, and analyzing—they'll encounter in college classes.

Flexibility   Eight sections and 38 chapters allow instructors to select class materials according to skill level, subject matter, and student needs.

Step-by-Step Guides through Readings   Students are guided through a productive reading process with each reading in this text.

Step-by-Step Guides through Writing Assignments   *Expressions* breaks each writing assignment into manageable steps for the developmental writer.

Chapter Title Pages with Journal Assignments   Chapter title pages offer interesting alternative forms of expression: paintings, sculptures, poetry, cartoons, and so on. Journal assignments on these pages ask students to think about these forms for expression and the themes that will follow in the chapter.

Study Skill Chapters   These informative chapters help sharpen study skills and can be woven into writing instruction since each includes either a writing assignment or speaking assignment.

Visual, Auditory, and Kinesthetic Assignments Because students will vary in their learning styles, *Expressions* offers charts, speaking activities, research activities (including viewing films and working on a computer), and index card activities. Throughout the text, students are also encouraged to highlight and write while reading—helping both the visual and kinesthetic learners.

Thematic Connections between Readings, Writing Assignments, and Sentence Work To assist students in seeing the applicability of their work, *Expressions* ties together the reading, writing, and sentence work by theme.

Notes Margin To encourage students to interact with their texts, *Expressions* provides not only wide margins labeled "Notes" but also questions in the text and margins that ask students to respond in writing in the margins.

Level-Appropriate, High-Interest Readings *Expressions* includes fiction and nonfiction readings that represent a number of accessible themes: dreams, survival, goals, personal and social change, lessons, values, and morals.

Supplemental Readings An additional set of readings in Section VIII, "The Reader," provides supplemental or alternative readings to those in Chapters 6–11. These readings come complete with reading process prompts and discussion questions.

Student Writing Samples Examples of successful student writing appear as models throughout the text.

Vocabulary Lists Following each reading in Chapters 8–11 are vocabulary lists that allow students to work in groups to learn new words. A comprehensive list of vocabulary words precedes the appendices.

Get Involved! Assignments Boxed activities encourage students to contribute to the class by seeing films, visiting websites, finding additional readings, and so on.

Computer Notes Boxed marginal notes encourage the novice computer user to become more adept at using computers.

Skill Spotlights   These mini-lessons offer students manageable lessons on key study and writing skills.

Sentence Style   After each reading in Chapters 7–11, students are asked to analyze and then imitate the sophisticated sentence structures found in their readings.

Reference and Progress Charts   Appendices A, B, and C provide students with reference charts on sentence terms, editing errors, and punctuation rules. Appendices D and E ask the students to keep track of their own writing progress.

The Other Texts in This Series

Expressions is the first book in a three-book developmental writing series.

Book Two, *Connections,* introduces the developmental writing student to the essay. Covering summaries and the reading and writing processes early in the text, body chapters in *Connections* each focus on a different theme and writing skill. Chapter 5 discusses heroes and focus; Chapter 6 explores television and development; Chapter 7 focuses on technology and organization; Chapter 8 covers music, poetry, and analysis. As with *Expressions, Connections* connects reading, writing, and critical thinking as skills that should be dealt with simultaneously. Sentence work appears at the end of each body chapter and is thematically and stylistically connected to both the reading and writing assignments. The last three sections of the text offer supplemental readings, skill building work (discovering learning styles, using the dictionary, building vocabulary, etc.), and easy reference rules (punctuation, using outside sources, etc.)

Book Three in this series, *Interpretations* (scheduled for publication in 2004), is for the most advanced developmental writer. This essay-level book challenges students to read, write, and think critically as they study, summarize, and interpret current controversial issues, literature, and film. These more complex reading, writing, and thinking tasks are accompanied by more complex sentence work that teaches not only sophisticated sentence structure but also punctuation and usage rules.

Teaching and Learning Package

The *Instructor's Manual* offers a discussion of the underlying pedagogy and an overview of features in *Expressions.* The manual also offers sample syllabi, teaching hints for each chapter, sentence work answers (including masters for duplication), sentence quizzes with answer keys, vocabulary quizzes with answer keys, word-form activities, vocabulary game suggestions, and overhead transparencies for class discussion activities.

In addition to the book-specific supplements discussed above, many other skills-based supplements are available for both instructors and students. All of these supplements are available either free or at greatly reduced prices.

For Additional Reading and Reference

The Dictionary Deal.   Two dictionaries can be shrinkwrapped with this text at a nominal fee. *The New American Webster Handy College Dictionary* is a paperback reference text with more than 100,000 entries. *Merriam Webster's Collegiate Dictionary,* tenth edition, is a hardback reference with a citation file of more than 14.5 million examples of English words drawn from actual use. For more information on how to shrinkwrap a dictionary with your text, please contact your Longman sales representative.

Penguin Quality Paperback Titles.   A series of Penguin paperbacks is available at a significant discount when shrinkwrapped with this text. Some titles available are Toni Morrison's *Beloved,* Julia Alvarez's *How the Garcia Girls Lost Their Accents,* Mark Twain's *Huckleberry Finn, Narrative of the Life of Frederick Douglass,* Harriet Beecher Stowe's *Uncle Tom's Cabin,* Dr. Martin Luther King, Jr.'s *Why We Can't Wait,* and plays by Shakespeare, Miller, and Albee. For a complete list of titles or more information, please contact your Longman sales consultant.

Penguin Academics: Twenty-Five Great Essays, Fifty Great Essays, and One Hundred Great Essays, edited by Robert DiYanni.   These alphabetically organized essay collections are published as part of the "Penguin Academics" series of low-cost, high-quality offerings intended for use in introductory college courses. All essays were selected for their teachability, both as models for writing and for their usefulness as springboards for student writing. For more information on how to shrinkwrap one of these anthologies with your text, please contact your Longman sales consultant.

100 Things to Write About.   This 100-page book contains 100 individual assignments for writing on a variety of topics and in a wide range of formats, from expressive to analytical. Ask your Longman sales representative for a sample copy. 0-673-98239-4

Newsweek Alliance. Instructors may choose to shrinkwrap a 12-week subscription to *Newsweek* with any Longman text. The price of the subscription is 59 cents per issue (a total of $7.08 for the subscription). Available with the subscription is a free "Interactive Guide to *Newsweek*"— a workbook for students who are using the text. In addition, Newsweek provides a wide variety of instructor supplements free to teachers, including maps, Skills Builders, and weekly quizzes. For more information on the Newsweek program, please contact your Longman sales representative.

Electronic and Online Offerings

The Longman Writer's Warehouse. The innovative and exciting online supplement is the perfect accompaniment to any developmental writing course. Developed by developmental English instructors specially for developing writers, The Writer's Warehouse covers every part of the writing process. Also included are journaling capabilities, multimedia activities, diagnostic tests, an interactive handbook, and a complete instructor's manual. The Writer's Warehouse requires no space on your school's server; rather, students complete and store their work on the Longman server, and are able to access it, revise it, and continue working at any time. For more details about how to shrinkwrap a free subscription to The Writer's Warehouse with this text, please consult your Longman sales representative. For a free guided tour of the site, visit **http://longmanwriterswarehouse.com.**

The Writer's ToolKit Plus. This CD-ROM offers a wealth of tutorial, exercise, and reference material for writers. It is compatible with either a PC or Macintosh platform, and is flexible enough to be used either occasionally for practice or regularly in class lab sessions. For information on how to bundle this CD-ROM FREE with your text, please contact your Longman sales representative.

GrammarCoach Software. This interactive tutorial helps students practice the basics of grammar and punctuation through 600 self-grading exercises in such problems areas as fragments, run-ons, and agreement. IBM only. 0-205-26509-X

The Longman Electronic Newsletter — Twice a month during the spring and fall, instructors who have subscribed receive a free copy of the Longman Developmental English Newsletter in their e-mailbox. Written by experienced classroom instructors, the newsletter offers teaching tips, classroom activities, book reviews, and more. To subscribe, visit the Longman Basic Skills Website at **http://www.ablongman.com/basicskills**, or send an e-mail to **BasicSkills@ablongman.com.**

iSearch Guide for English, by H. Eric Branscomb and Doug Gotthoffer. A guide to online research. Featuring the Longman Internet Guide and access to the Research Navigator Database, the iSearch guide gives students and instructors instant access to thousands of academic journals and periodicals any time from any computer with an Internet connection. With helpful tips on the writing process, online research, and finding and citing valid sources, starting the research process has never been easier! Free when packaged with this textbook.   0-321-12411-1

For Instructors

Electronic Test Bank for Writing. This electronic test bank features more than 5,000 questions in all areas of writing, from grammar to paragraphing, through essay writing, research, and documentation. With this easy-to-use CD-ROM, instructors simply choose questions from the electronic test bank, then print out the completed test for distribution. CD-ROM: 0-321-08117-X Print version: 0-321-08486-1

Competency Profile Test Bank, Second Edition. This series of 60 objective tests covers ten general areas of English competency, including fragments; comma splices and run-ons; pronouns; commas; and capitalization. Each test is available in remedial, standard, and advanced versions. Available as reproducible sheets or in computerized versions. Free to instructors. Paper version: 0-321-02224-6. Computerized IBM: 0-321-02633-0. Computerized MAC: 0-321-02632-2.

Diagnostic and Editing Tests and Exercises, Fifth Edition. This collection of diagnostic tests helps instructors assess students' competence in Standard Written English for purpose of placement or to gauge progress. Available as reproducible sheets or in computerized versions, and free to instructors. Paper: 0-321-11730-1. CD-ROM: 0-321-11731-X.

ESL Worksheets, Third Edition. These reproducible worksheets provide ESL students with extra practice in areas they find the most troublesome. A diagnostic test and post-test are provided, along with answer keys and suggested topics for writing. Free to adopters. 0-321-07765-2

Longman Editing Exercises. 54 pages of paragraph editing exercises give students extra practice using grammar skills in the context of longer passages. Free when packaged with any Longman title.   0-205-31792-8 Answer key: 0-205-31797-9

80 Practices. A collection of reproducible, ten-item exercises that provide additional practices for specific grammatical usage problems, such as comma splices, capitalization, and pronouns. Includes an answer key, and free to adopters. 0-673-53422-7

CLAST Test Package, Fourth Edition. These two 40-item objective tests evaluate students' readiness for the CLAST exams. Strategies for teaching CLAST preparedness are included. Free with any Longman English title. Reproducible sheets: 0-321-01950-4 Computerized IBM version: 0-321-01982-2 Computerized MAC version: 0-321-01983-0

TASP Test Package, Third Edition. These 12 practice pre-tests and post-tests assess the same reading and writing skills covered in the TASP examination. Free with any Longman English title. Reproducible sheets: 0-321-01959-8 Computerized IBM version: 0-321-01985-7 Computerized MAC version: 0-321-01984-9

Teaching Online: Internet Research, Conversation, and Composition, Second Edition. Ideal for instructors who have never surfed the Net, this easy-to-follow guide offers basic definitions, numerous examples, and step-by-step information about finding and using Internet sources. Free to adopters. 0-321-01957-1

Using Portfolios. This supplement offers teachers a brief introduction to teaching with portfolios in composition courses. This essential guide addresses the pedagogical and evaluative use of portfolios, and offers practical suggestions for implementing a portfolio evaluation system in a writing class. 0-321-08412-8

The Longman Instructor Planner. This all-in-one resource for instructors includes monthly and weekly planning sheets, to-do lists, student contact forms, attendance rosters, a gradebook, an address/phone book, and a mini almanac. Ask your Longman sales representative for a free copy. 0-321-09247-3.

For Students

Researching Online, Fifth Edition.   A perfect companion for a new age, this indispensable new supplement helps students navigate the Internet. Adapted from Teaching Online, the instructor's Internet guide, Researching Online speaks directly to students, giving them detailed, step-by-step instructions for performing electronic searches.   Available free when shrinkwrapped with this text. 0-321-09277-5

Learning Together: An Introduction to Collaborative Theory.   This brief guide to the fundamentals of collaborative learning teaches students how to work effectively in groups, how to revise with peer response, and how to co-author a paper or report. Shrinkwrapped free with this text. 0-673-46848-8

A Guide for Peer Response, Second Edition.   This guide offers students forms for peer critiques, including general guidelines and specific forms for different stages in the writing process. Also appropriate for freshman-level course. Free to adopters. 0-321-01948-2

Ten Practices of Highly Successful Students.   This popular supplement helps students learn crucial study skills, offering concise tips for a successful career in college. Topics include time management, test-taking, reading critically, stress, and motivation. 0-205-30769-8

FOR FLORIDA ADOPTIONS Thinking Through the Test, by D.J. Henry. This special workbook, prepared especially for students in Florida, offers ample skill and practice exercises to help student prep for the Florida State Exit Exam. To shrinkwrap this workbook free with your textbook, please contact your Longman sales representative. Available in two versions: with answers and without answers. Also available: Two laminated grids (one for reading, one for writing) that can serve as handy references for students preparing for the Florida State Exit Exam.

The Longman Student Planner. This daily planner for students includes daily, weekly, and monthly calendars, as well as class schedules and a mini-almanac of useful information. It is the perfect accompaniment to a Longman reading or study skills textbook, and is available free to students when shrinkwrapped with this text. 0-321-04573-4

The Longman Writer's Journal. This journal for writers, free with any Longman English text, offers students a place to think, write, and react. For an examination copy, contact your Longman sales consultant. 0-321-08639-2

The Longman Researcher's Journal. This journal for writers and researchers, free with this text, helps students plan, schedule, write, and revise their research project. An all-in-one resource for first-time researchers, the journal guides students gently through the research process. 0-321-09530-8.

NEW *The Longman Writer's Portfolio.* This unique supplement provides students with a space to plan, think about, and present their work. The portfolio includes an assessing/organizing area (including a grammar diagnostic test, a spelling quiz, and project planning worksheets), a before and during writing area (including peer review sheets, editing checklists, writing self-evaluations, and a personal editing profile), and an after-writing area (including a progress chart, a final table of contents, and a final assessment). Ask your Longman sales representative for ISBN 0-321-10765-9.

THE LONGMAN SERIES OF MONOGRAPHS FOR DEVELOPMENTAL EDUCATORS

Ask your Longman sales consultant for a free copy of these monographs written by experts in their fields.

#1: The Longman Guide to Classroom Management. Written by Joannis Flatley of St. Philip's College, the first in Longman's new series of monographs for developmental English instructors focuses on issues of classroom etiquette, providing guidance on dealing with unruly, unengaged, disruptive, or uncooperative students. Ask your Longman sales representative for a free copy. 0-321-09246-5

#2: The Longman Guide to Community Service-Learning in the English Classroom and Beyond. Written by Elizabeth Rodriguez Kessler of California State University-Northridge, this is the second monograph in Longman's series for developmental educators. It provides a definition and history of service-learning, as well as an overview of how service-learning can be integrated effectively into the college classroom. 0-321-12749-8

Acknowledgment

I'd like to acknowledge those who have contributed to the writing of *Expressions*. To Longman Publishers and, specifically, Steven Rigolosi, senior editor for Developmental English, I offer sincere thanks for believing in this project, offering great ideas, and supporting the three-book series. I am also grateful for the honest, thoughtful insight of my development editor, Janice Wiggins, who helped me reorganize and shape this text into a much more efficient, user-friendly book. My colleague Tammy Boeck-Montgomery has continued to offer her support and ideas, and I am grateful for her input. I also want to thank my colleague-reviewers for their indispensable responses to the manuscript:

Robert D. Angus, California State University, Fullerton
Chris Barkley, Palomar College
Brenda Bruno, Saddleback College
Marilyn L. Edwards, Athens Technical College
Rebecca Hewett, California State University, Bakersfield
David K. Himber, St. Petersburg Junior College
Timothy J. Jones, Oklahoma City Community College
Carol Myers, Athens Technical College
Amy F. Penne, Parkland College

Their comments have improved this book and my teaching.

I also extend my appreciation to Melanie Craig, marketing manager for Developmental English, and Alison Main, marketing assistant, Developmental English. Thank you for all you've done and continue to do to ignite interest in *Expressions*. Thanks go to Meegan Thompson for responding to a myriad of questions and to Melanie Becker of Write-Source for securing permissions. I am also grateful to Patrick Burt, the project manager at WestWords Inc., and to his staff for paying such close attention to detail as they saw *Expressions* through the production process.

Thank you to my mom, my great organizer, permissions and index compiler, proofreader, and friend. Of course, my heartfelt thanks extend to my students, whose honesty and encouragement have helped shape and improve this text. Thank you in particular to the students who gave me permission to use their work: Gloria Ayala-Partida, Judy Hudson, Lucky Le, Calvin Mak, Theresa Michelini, Francis Vessigault, Elizabeth Villars, and Ayanna Williams.

Finally, I thank John, Brienna, Keely, and Ann for each making their own distinct sacrifices as they supported me in this endeavor. And thanks go to Vesela Peneva for keeping my office organized and, most importantly, for taking care of and loving my babies when I couldn't be there.

Megan Rainey

A Note to Students

Dear Student,

If you are used to English textbooks that focus mainly on grammar and sentences, you'll be surprised by what you find here. *Expressions* is a book that looks at writing a little differently.

- First, good ideas are the basis of good writing.
- Good ideas come from keeping an open mind, reading, and discussing.
- To express your ideas effectively in writing, you need to take the right steps—read, think, discuss, draft, revise, edit.
- Everyone can be a good writer—with practice.

The Topics and Assignments in This Book

Since reading and thinking are so important to improving your writing skills, *Expressions* will help you develop a productive reading process, strengthen your critical thinking skills, and learn new vocabulary words. *Expressions* will also help you develop a productive writing process that you'll use with every writing assignment.

While practicing your new approaches to reading, vocabulary, and writing, you'll be introduced to many different types—or genres—of writing. Chapters 6–11 cover diaries, paragraphs, letters, autobiographies, fairy tales, and essays. In these chapters, you'll learn that writers change their tone and style when they write to different audiences and have different messages. In between your paragraph assignments, you may get the opportunity to write your own diary, letter, autobiography, or fairy tale. In all of these writing situations, you too will have to think about who is in your audience and what your message is. Being flexible as a writer (and as a reader and thinker) is important to your success in college and at work.

Finally, what about the sentence work? Well, there's plenty here! Chapters 12–34 are dedicated to sentence and grammar work. In those chapters, you'll find that the topics you see in your reading and writing assignments are also covered in your sentence work. You'll be asked to fill in some blanks as you warm up, but then you'll be challenged to work with paragraphs and to create sentences of your own. The key is to think about how your sentence practice can be applied to your own writing.

Special Features in Expressions

In this text, you'll find several opportunities to be in the driver's seat. Periodically, you'll see **Get Involved!** assignments. These assignments will ask you to watch a movie, go to a website, or perform some other type of research. Then you'll bring new information into your classroom—thus taking a more active part in your own education.

In Appendices D and E at the end of the book, you'll find charts that will help you keep track of your writing weaknesses and strengths. These charts may show you patterns that you have to break in order to improve your writing.

Also notice the wide margins in this book—use them to make notes about what you are reading. When you are reading, imagine that the writer is speaking to you. If you have questions, write them down in the margin. If you particularly like something or want to make sure you remember it, make a note in the margin.

The more active you are as a learner, the more you will learn.

I hope that this textbook helps you strengthen your reading, critical thinking, and writing skills. Work hard and you'll not only discover ideas worth writing about, but you'll develop the ability to express those ideas clearly. Good luck!

Megan Rainey

The Power of Written Expression

In this section of *Expressions,* you'll explore how writing, reading, and critical thinking are interrelated skills, and you'll consider how strong language skills can improve many aspects of your life. Then you'll be introduced to the methods this book will use to help strengthen your writing, reading, and critical thinking skills.

Written Expressions

1

Humans express their ideas, feelings, and needs many different ways. We use speech, music, gestures, facial expressions, and other methods.

Writing, of course, is one of our most common tools for expression. Being able to clearly express ourselves through writing gives us freedom and power.

Unfortunately, many people don't feel comfortable expressing themselves through writing. They fear that they will be unclear, that their audience may misunderstand or be uninterested, or that they will look "dumb" if they misspell a word. People often say, "I can express my thoughts just fine when I speak, but when I write, I can't seem to get my thoughts down."

Probably the greatest challenge in writing is dealing with the fact that your audience is not right in front of you. If you are unclear, your audience cannot interrupt you as if you were speaking. And you cannot then go back and further explain your idea.

Yet even with all these concerns, people do learn to write well and to enjoy writing. We learn to write because it is necessary in order to grow and fulfill the many complicated tasks in our lives. Writing lets us make a record of our thoughts. It lets us communicate to many people we might otherwise never meet. It lets us reach people without having to be there in person. Writing is a powerful tool, and it is a tool that everyone can use.

Notes

Written Language Is a Tool for Expression

Expressions is a textbook about written expression. With this book, you'll explore many different forms of writing. You'll read diaries, letters, e-mails, autobiographies, fairy tales, and essays. You'll see how writers adjust their writing to fit certain audiences and purposes, and you'll see that there are many ways you can use writing to express your concerns, plans, goals, and ideas.

As you investigate these different types of writing, you'll practice some of them yourself, and you'll sharpen your paragraph skills as you write analytical paragraphs about these forms of expression.

Expressions offers you the following:

- **Reading Assignments** To help you improve your comprehension and critical thinking skills, you'll be guided step by step through each reading.

- **Journal Assignments** These writing assignments ask you to explore ideas and express yourself freely. You do not have to be concerned about grammar and punctuation.

- **Express Yourself** assignments These assignments ask you to analyze what you are reading and discussing in class, and they require some polishing. You'll want to reread and improve your answers before turning your work in.

- Formal **Writing Assignments** You'll write paragraphs and perhaps a letter, a story, and an essay. Using the writing process explained in Chapter 4, you will be showing off your best writing in these assignments.

- **Skill Spotlights** These short lessons offer you a variety of strategies for working through writing, reading, and speaking assignments. See the inside cover of this book for a list of Skill Spotlights.

- **Computer Notes** Now and then you'll see these computer tips in the margins of this book. They will help you with everything from using spell check on your computer to learning how to italicize titles when typing.

- **Get Involved!** These assignments offer you opportunities to bring new information to your class—by watching films, researching on the Internet, and so on.

- **Sentence Style** These assignments ask you to study and then imitate especially effective sentences from the readings in this book.

You will also find

- Dictionary and vocabulary work.
- Sentence exercises.
- Reading process instruction.
- Writing process instruction.

All of these elements are blended together—around the topic of expression—to help you develop stronger paragraph-writing skills. One key to success in college and the work world is writing strong paragraphs.

Frequently, college instructors and employers will ask you to express yourself through paragraphs. Paragraphs allow you to demonstrate your

Notes

Use this "Notes" margin to write your comments.

Notes knowledge and communicate your ideas and proposals. And, when you use the reading and writing processes taught in this book, you'll find that you use your critical thinking skills and actually *learn* new information while you are writing. This is when writing is most interesting.

Of course, learning to write effective paragraphs will help you do more than just fulfill college and work assignments. Paragraph writing helps you become a stronger thinker and reader which, in turn, can help you reach many educational, professional, and personal goals in your life.

Writing Strengthens Thinking Skills

To write a clear, effective paragraph, a person must *think* logically and apply rules of focus, development, and organization to his or her ideas.

Such activities as playing chess and writing computer programs help people develop their thinking skills. For example, the chess player must consider his or her options and then think ahead and guess what the other player might do next. A computer programmer must consider the different paths to a desired result. He or she must think in a linear, organized fashion and carefully write down all the signals the computer will need, revising the program until it communicates effectively with the computer.

Writing is similar. As a writer, you take many ideas, sort through them, focus them, organize them, develop them, and express them in a

way your audience can understand. Writing paragraphs is a challenging mental activity, an activity that will build brain muscles—so to speak.

Notes

Writing Strengthens Reading Skills

Also, as you begin to better understand the requirements of paragraph writing, you'll find your reading comprehension improves. For example, *as a writer* you'll learn about focusing your ideas and stating your main point in a topic sentence. You'll learn where the topic sentence should be in a paragraph and how your other thoughts should be organized around this topic sentence.

Then, *as a reader,* you will be better able to find the main point in your college and work readings because most nonfiction writers follow the same basic set of rules. (Of course, it works the other way too. *Through reading, you learn from other writers. Reading can teach you writing skills.*)

Writing, Thinking, and Reading in Your Life

As you improve your academic writing skills and sharpen your thinking and reading skills, you'll be better prepared to do all sorts of things in life that call for written language skills and even speaking skills. (Yes, as you improve your written language skills, you'll find that your formal spoken language is strengthened, too.)

You'll be better able to communicate in your personal life—writing to and talking with family and friends. You'll be more confident when dealing with all the people and organizations that have power over your life—insurance companies, utility companies, landlords, and so on. At work, you'll have an easier time communicating your ideas and concerns. That's what it is all about—communicating. Developing your writing skills is one powerful way of coming closer to personal and professional enjoyment.

On the Most Personal Level

Writing, thinking, and reading well can help you discover truths about the human condition, science, art, this planet, your religious beliefs, and so on. Consider this quote from Anne Frank, a fourteen-year-old Jewish girl who wrote these words in her diary as she and her family hid in an attic from the Nazis during World War II.

Notes

What thoughts, ideals, or fantasies would you like to explore through writing?

I want to go on living even after my death! And therefore I am grateful to God for giving me this gift, this possibility of developing myself and of writing, of expressing all that is in me.

I can shake off everything if I write; my sorrows disappear, my courage is reborn. But, and that is the great question, will I ever be able to write anything great, will I ever become a journalist or a writer? I hope so oh, I hope so very much, for I can recapture everything when I write, my thoughts, my ideals and my fantasies.

Remember How Strong Writing Skills Can Help You

It is easier to attain a skill, if you remember why the skill is important to you. You will see in the readings in this textbook that people write for many different reasons.

Some people write in journals to express private thoughts. Some write letters and e-mail—casual ones to friends, formal ones to business acquaintances. Others write autobiographies, fairy tales, or essays. Some of these writers want to inform. Some want to entertain. Some have a powerful message that needs to be shared. Writing can help you do these same things. Writing can also help you to

- Remember special times and events.
- Think through or explore a topic or problem.
- Demonstrate your knowledge.
- Learn as you put ideas into words.
- Communicate feelings, needs, and ideas.

Express Yourself
How Can You Use Writing in Your Life?

Warm-Up

To warm up before writing your response, work with your classmates to create and complete a chart that is similar to the one shown here. Record what each classmate says. Your classmates may remind you of some ways you plan to use writing. (It is okay in this warm-up to just jot down words and phrases. You'll write complete sentences in your paragraph in the next step.)

I could use writing *to remember* in these situations:
(Examples: my first date, the birth of my child)

I could use writing *to think through or explore a topic or problem* in these situations: (Examples: an argument with my sister, a loud neighbor)
I could use writing *to demonstrate my knowledge* in these situations: (Examples: a report to my boss, a cover letter to my résumé)
I could use writing *to learn as I put ideas into words* in these situations: (Examples: research notes for a paper, observation notes at work)
I could use writing *to communicate feelings, needs, and ideas* in these situations: (Examples: a love letter, a complaint letter)

Write It Out

Now review your chart and explain to your classmates and instructor (in a paragraph) how you have been using—and will continue to use—writing as a form of expression in your life. Remember to consider your personal, college, and professional lives.

(**Express Yourself** assignments should be written carefully. The audience for your assignments includes your instructor and your classmates. These assignments are a chance to communicate your ideas and strengthen your writing skills. Take the time to plan your response. Then reread it and improve it by adding information and maybe recopying it. Always edit—check spelling and sentences.)

Becoming a Good Writer

People often believe that writers have some special skill they were born with. Perhaps some people *are* born feeling more at ease with language, while others are naturally more interested in music, science, or sports. But even people who want professional lives that focus more on the arts, science, or physical movement can be (and are) good writers.

Notes

How Do People Become Good Writers?

Writing is a skill. It is acquired through guided practice. This means that you need a more experienced writer (your instructor and maybe a tutor) to instruct you and respond to your writing.

Of course, one key to your success is practice. A tennis instructor does not simply talk about how to serve the ball. A music instructor does not simply ask you to listen to music. Talking and listening may be part of the instructional plan, but *practice* is the key to learning a skill.

Your Path to Good Writing Skills

Just as the tennis coach wouldn't ask you to focus only on serving, this textbook doesn't ask you simply to sit down and write a paragraph each day. To develop good writing skills, you must work on a number of areas. This book weaves them together so that you strengthen all of your writing muscles.

Reading

The first step to writing clearly is improving your reading skills. The reading assignments in *Expressions* will help you

- Strengthen your vocabulary skills.
- Understand the techniques other writers use.
- Strengthen your critical thinking skills.
- Gather ideas for you to use in your own writing.

Any additional reading you do in your free time will also help you improve your reading and writing skills.

You will use the reading process described in Chapter 3 of this book to help you improve your reading comprehension, speed, and enjoyment. At the end of Chapters 6 through 11 are "Additional Readings" lists. The readings listed there can be found in the back of this book. These readings offer you more opportunities to read about the subjects covered in class.

Writing

Writing, of course, is the second step toward improving your writing skills. This book will guide you through different types of writing assignments. Each type of assignment builds different writing muscles.

This textbook, for example, asks you to write private Journal Assignments so that you'll have the opportunity to explore your ideas and

Notes

express thoughts without anyone responding or criticizing. Sometimes these journal activities will help you discover some of your best ideas to use in your paragraph assignments. Sometimes these journal activities will be an opportunity to write freely about your life beyond the classroom.

The **Express Yourself** assignments in this book will give you frequent practice in a more public type of writing. Your responses will not require as much polishing as the paragraph assignments, but they will require you to think of your instructor and classmates as your audience and focus on communicating to this audience effectively. You'll want to plan your response and then reread and improve your response before turning it in.

Finally the *paragraph, letter, story,* and *essay assignments* will require you to use a writing process as you create formal pieces of writing that will represent your best writing skills. The *writing process* discussed in Chapter 4 and practiced throughout *Expressions* is probably the most important element in this textbook. By following the stages of the writing process, you'll complete your writing assignments more easily, and your final product will be better.

Critical Thinking

The third step toward becoming a good writer is improving your critical thinking skills. When you are writing your paragraphs, you will need to think critically about your ideas, who your audience is, what information you should include, and how you should present that information.

The *reading assignments* and *critical thinking questions* in this book will also help develop your critical thinking skills. **Reading Assignment** questions will ask you to think about the author's purpose and intended audience. You will think about why the writer used the vocabulary he chose and how he focused, developed, and organized his ideas. Finally, you'll question and discuss the message the author is expressing. Then, as a writer, you will be better prepared to think critically about your own work.

Sentence Work

Writing clear sentences is crucial to expressing yourself effectively. The fourth step in the instructional plan in *Expressions* includes sentence work.

In Chapters 7 through 11, you'll complete **Sentence Style** exercises that encourage you to imitate sentences by professional writers. In

Chapters 12 through 34, you'll learn some basic terms, how to avoid common errors, how to apply rules of punctuation and capitalization, and so on. You'll also experiment with writing sentences using sophisticated structure. At the ends of Chapters 6 through 11, you'll find lists of chapters that focus on grammar, sentence structure, and editing rules. The chapters in these lists connect to the reading topics presented in each chapter and to the editing suggestions in each chapter.

Notes

Express Yourself

What Are Your Strengths and Weaknesses as a Reader and Writer?

Warm-Up

Before writing, discuss with your classmates some of your strengths and weaknesses as a reader and writer. What do you do well? What do you like about reading and writing? You may want to consider these questions:

- What skills does a good reader need?
- Which of these skills do you have?
- Which reading skills do you want to focus on this semester?
- What have you read?
- What do you enjoy reading?
- What have you enjoyed writing in the past (such as poetry, letters, or essays)?
- What can you do well as a writer?
- What do you wish you could do better?

Write It Out

Imagine you are a writing instructor, and it is your job to write a paragraph about the "real you" as a student reader and writer. You must describe your reading and writing skills. (Use the questions listed in the warm-up to help you think of information to include. Be sure to cover both reading *and* writing skills.) For example, if your name is Mary Smith, your paragraph might begin like this:

> Mary Smith is an average reader and writer. She reads the newspaper every day, but she doesn't enjoy reading novels. Her favorite parts of the newspaper are the sports section and the front page. She is concerned that she reads slowly, and she would like to improve her vocabulary. . . . As a writer . . .

Notes

Campus Resources

Acquiring good writing skills is something you can do. It will take time, patience, and effort, but you don't have to do it alone. To help you in your learning process, you should investigate the resources on your campus. Here are some people and places to investigate:

- **Your instructor** Does he or she have office hours? When can you seek additional private help from him or her?
- **Tutoring services and reading and writing centers** Where are these located? What are the hours, costs, and requirements?
- **Computer labs** Where are these on campus? What are the hours?
- **Learning disability specialists** Are you concerned that you may have a learning disability? Who can help you on campus?
- **Financial aid** Where is this office? Can you get some financial support?
- **Day care services** Do you have children? Are there day care services offered on your campus?
- **Counseling office** Do you need to see a counselor to review your class schedule?

Time Management and Organization

Writing classes generally require a lot of time. Reading, thinking, and writing are time-consuming tasks. It is important to be honest with yourself and your family and friends about the time you will have to devote to your writing class. Is your class schedule manageable? Are your day care and work schedules manageable? Do your family and friends understand that your writing class will require significant time? Many colleges state that for every hour in class you must spend 2 hours on homework. What are the expectations at your college? To get a realistic look at your schedule and to organize your time, create a calendar that shows the hours you must work (include time spent caring for children), attend class, and study. First, review the sample calendar on the next page.

On the blank calendar on page 14, mark the hours you are at work and in class. Then mark your studying hours.

Being organized will also make you a more successful student. One key to succeeding in your writing class is keeping an organized notebook. For this class, you'll need a three-ring binder (1 1/2 inch width), a package of dividers, loose-leaf paper, and three-by-five inch index

	Monday	Tuesday	Wednesday	Thursday	Friday	Saturday	Sunday
7:00 a.m.							
8:00	Math	Psych	Math	Psych	Math		
9:00	English	Psych	English	Psych	English		
10:00	Study	Study	Study	Study	Work	Study	
11:00	Lunch	Lunch	Lunch	Lunch	Work	Study	
12:00 p.m.	Work	Work	Work	Work	Work	Study	
1:00	Work	Work	Work	Work	Work	Study	
2:00	Work	Work	Work	Work	Work		
3:00	Work	Work	Work	Work	Work		
4:00	Work	Work	Work	Work	Work		
5:00 p.m.							
6:00							
7:00	Study	Study	Study	Study			
8:00	Study	Study	Study	Study			
9:00	Study	Study	Study	Study			
10:00							

cards. (Check with your writing instructor to see if he or she wants to make any changes to this list of materials.)

You may want to organize your binder by using dividers to create these sections:

- Class/Lecture Notes
- Express Yourself

	Monday	Tuesday	Wednesday	Thursday	Friday	Saturday	Sunday
7:00 a.m.							
8:00							
9:00							
10:00							
11:00							
12:00 p.m.							
1:00							
2:00							
3:00							
4:00							
5:00 p.m.							
6:00							
7:00							
8:00							
9:00							
10:00							

- Journals
- Sentence Work
- Paragraph Assignment _____
  Complete the title for this divider when you are given a specific assignment.

Add more dividers, creating new sections, for each paragraph, summary, and essay assignment you are given.
Include all brainstorms, drafts, and revisions.

Another way to organize your binder would be to create a divider for each chapter that is assigned. In each chapter section you would keep your lecture notes, Express Yourself assignments, journals, sentence work, and formal writing assignments (including brainstorms, drafts, and revisions).

Note: When turning in your homework, put the chapter number and the page number on your work. Then it will be easier to keep your work organized.

Express Yourself
What Is Your Plan for Success?

Warm-Up

Discuss with your classmates the specific things you will do this semester to succeed in your writing class.

Consider these items:

- How many hours each week will you devote to your writing class?
- When (and how often) will you seek assistance from your instructor?
- Will you seek tutorial help?
- Are there any campus resources that you will use? When? How often?
- Do you need to adjust your personal or work schedule? How?
- Will you do any additional reading besides what is assigned? (You may want to take a look at Section VIII p.397 to see the extra readings offered in this text.)
- Will you do any additional writing besides what is assigned? For example, will you keep your own private journal?

Write It Out

Explain to your instructor and classmates what your plan for success is in this writing class. Using the questions listed in the warm-up to guide your writing, write this response with a strong, positive tone. Say, "I will . . ." Avoid sounding indecisive with such phrases as "Maybe . . ." or "I might . . ."

Strategies for Expression

In this section of *Expressions,* you'll be introduced to a reading process that you'll use with all the readings in this book. This process will help you read more efficiently and enjoy reading more. Next in this section, Chapter 4 introduces a writing process that you'll use with all of your formal paragraph assignments. This writing process will help you break down your writing tasks into manageable steps. Finally, Chapter 5 introduces you to methods for increasing your vocabulary.

Using the Reading Process

Do you believe these statements?

- ✦ Good readers always read fast.
- ✦ Good readers remember everything they read.
- ✦ Good readers read things only once.

The preceding statements are myths about reading. A *myth* is a false belief.

Here are the myths again—followed by some *truths* about reading.

Myth: Good readers always read fast.
Truth: Good readers often read quickly, but they don't read everything quickly. You can improve your reading speed by normal reading practice. You can also be a good reader without being really fast.

Myth: Good readers remember everything they read.
Truth: Good readers generally remember the *main points* of their readings and therefore may *appear* to remember everything. However, few people can remember everything they read, and the good news is that you don't need to remember everything.

Myth: Good readers read things only once.
Truth: Good readers can read some things just once if the information is already familiar to them. However, good readers usually reread things that are new, difficult, or important to them.

The message here is that everyone can be a good reader. The key is to engage with your reading and to read efficiently and productively. Experienced readers do a number of things that help them not only to enjoy their reading but also to read quickly and remember the main points. This chapter will explain these techniques before asking you to practice them.

The Reading Process

An effective **reading process** can be broken into five steps. You can re-member the five steps by thinking of this word:

PARTS

Step 1 **Preview**

In this step, **preview** the title, author's name, and any pictures or graphs. You might also read the introduction and the first sentence of each paragraph. This work helps prepare your mind to accept the in-formation that is in the reading.

Step 2 **Anticipate**

In this step, try to **anticipate** (or guess) what the reading will be about. This helps you focus your attention on the reading. As you read, con-tinue to make guesses about what will come next. Anticipating helps you to stay interested in your reading, and to stay awake.

Step 3 **Read and Reread**

There are two parts to the **read and reread** step. In the first part, quickly read the selection, marking any unknown words, but do not stop to look up any words. (Interrupting yourself may cause you to lose track of the main ideas.) In the second part, reread the selection more slowly, looking up unknown words, marking important points, and writing comments and questions in the margins.

As you'll notice, this book gives you a *Notes* margin to write com-ments in. When you write in the margin, you can carry on a conversa-tion with yourself and the author. You'll find some questions and directions in the margin to get you started. Answer the questions at the rereading step, and follow the directions. Then add your own ques-tions and comments in the margin. You can express confusion, sur-prise, agreement, and so on. You can also ask questions and record any other reactions. Through these comments you are interacting with the text—you are no longer a passive reader.

In the margins, you'll also find some definitions for difficult words. You can add your own definitions for other unfamiliar words and for the vocabulary words that are assigned after the readings.

This book has a glossary (p. 455) where you can find definitions for bold face terms like *reading process.* Refer to the glossary when you need to review a new term. After the definition in the glossary, you'll see the number of the page where the term first appears. Now, for practice, look up *reading process* in the glossary.

Step 4 *Think Critically*

In the **think critically** step, think about the techniques used in the reading, the message expressed, and your own reaction to the reading.

Each reading is followed by questions. These questions are designed to help you test your comprehension, learn from the writer, and strengthen your critical thinking skills.

Step 5 *Summarize*

In the **summarize** step, mark main points in the reading and make a list of important points. These notes will improve your class discussion performance because you'll already have thought carefully about the main points in the reading.

Use the Reading Process

In this section, you'll apply what you have just learned. As with all Reading Assignments in this book, you'll move step by step through the *reading process*.

Reading Assignment— *"from Martha Martin's Diary"*

Preview Read the title and author's name. Read the introductory material that is in smaller print.

Anticipate What do you think this diary will be about? Make a few guesses here about specific things that you think might come up in the diary.

For the *anticipate* step to be helpful, your guesses need to be specific. For example, if you think she'll write about surviving alone, list some items needed for basic human survival.

_____

_____

_____

_____

Read Read the diary quickly. Mark unknown words, but don't look up any meanings in the dictionary yet. *Note:* In the first three paragraphs, Martin begins to tell us about her encounter with a sea otter. In paragraph 4, she starts again at the beginning of her story, and explains in more detail what happened with the sea otter.

from Martha Martin's Diary

Notes

By Martha Martin

Martha Martin is the **pseudonym** of the wife of an Alaskan gold **prospector**. Sometime during the 1920s, she kept a diary of her remarkable, self-sufficient survival during a winter **marooned** in an Alaskan camp. Alone and pregnant, she had been injured by an avalanche that separated her from her husband. She **improvised** a splint for her broken arm and a cast for her broken leg and, when help did not arrive, prepared for the birth of her child. Later, in 1952, she was encouraged to submit the diary for publication. In it she **emerges** as the female Robinson Crusoe,* proud of her self-sufficiency and her relationship with a harsh natural world.

A **pseudonym** is a fake name.

A **prospector** is a person looking for gold or other minerals.

Marooned is to be alone with no immediate way of getting to "civilization."

Improvised means made with supplies that were available.

Emerges means to come into view.

[The four dots that follow many of the sentences here tell you that the author's sentences went on to say more. This is a shortened (or abridged) version of her actual diary.]

1   I killed a sea otter today. I actually did kill a sea otter. I killed him with the ax, dragged him home, and skinned him. I took his liver out, and ate part of it. I'm going to eat the rest of it, and his heart, too. His liver was quite large, bigger than a deer's, and it had more lobes to it. It was very good liver, and I enjoyed it.

2   Most of today was devoted to the sea otter; getting the hide off was a real task. It's a lovely skin, the softest, silkiest, thickest fur I have ever seen. I am going to make a robe for my baby out of the beautiful fur. My darling child may be born in a lowly cabin, but she shall be wrapped in one of the earth's most costly furs.

3   It was such a splendid piece of luck. Lucky in more ways than one. The otter might have killed me, although I have never heard of such a thing.

4   This morning I went to the woods to gather a load of limbs. As I was coming home with them, I saw the tide was nearly out, and I thought I'd walk over to the bar and take a look at the boat. [. . .] I was going along, swinging the ax in my left hand, managing the crutch with the right hand, [. . .] not thinking of anything in particular, when right beside me I heard a bark. It was like a dog bark; not a bow-wow bark, more of a yip. I looked around and saw a huge creature **reared up** on its **haunches**. I saw its white teeth.

Reared up means rose up.

Haunches means rear legs.

5   Without thinking, I swung the ax at the side of its head, saw it hit, felt the jar in my arm, heard the thud. As I swung the ax, I turned and tried to run. I was so terrified the thing would nab me from behind that I could hardly move. I glanced over my shoulder to see how close it was. It hadn't budged from where it dropped. . . .

*Robinson Crusoe was the male character in the fictional story *Robinson Crusoe*. In the eighteenth century, he was shipwrecked alone on an island and lived there many years by himself.

6 I got down on my knees and examined it from one end to the other. First off, I noticed the lovely fur. I took off my glove and ran my fingers through the nice, silky coat. I decided right then I would have the skin. I saw it as a baby blanket. . . .

7 It is very much against the law to kill a sea otter. Right now I don't care a rap for law. I'd like to have a picture of a game warden who could arrest me now. I am safe enough from the law, and I think I always will be. Under the circumstances I doubt if any judge would send me to jail for what I have done. . . .

8 I dragged my kill home, and was a long time doing so. I'll bet the creature weighed a hundred pounds. I worked and worked, rested, pulled, and dragged, rested some more, and by and by I reached the cabin with my prize. . . .

9 I decided to skin it exactly the way the men do a deer. I have watched them many times, but I never helped or paid much attention. I didn't know very much about skinning a furbearing animal when I went to work on that creature. How I wished I had an Indian squaw to instruct and help me. . . .

Do you know how to skin an animal? Could you figure it out and do it if you had to?

10 The head was a mess, so I just cut the skin at the neck line and let the head fur go. I chopped off the feet and threw them in the stove. After I got the legs and sides skinned, I turned the otter on his belly and worked the skin off his back down to the tail. I had more trouble with that tail than I did with all the rest of the animal, I wanted it for a neck-piece, and I tried to get the bony tail out without slitting the skin. It can't be done. . . .

11 My hands got awful cold examining the innards, rather smelly, too. I had let the fire go down, and there wasn't enough hot water for me to scrub properly. I made up the fire, washed a little, and then sat down to rest and gloat over my wonderful sea otter fur. . . .

12 I woke up in the night, and felt rested, so I got up, lit the carbide lamp, and sat here writing all about my sea otter.

13 I had planned to work on my otter skin today, but when I looked out this morning I saw Old Nick was flaunting a plume [a sign that a cold wind was coming up]. . . . I put all my energy into gathering wood and left the skin alone. . . .

14 Goodness, I have lots of work to do before I am ready for my little darling. I must get the fur finished for her. I am determined my child shall have a priceless gift. . . .

What is the main topic in this paragraph?

15 I've begun scraping off the fat from my otter skin, and it's about half done. I have learned a few things about scraping skins: they scrape better when they are stretched tight over the end of a block of wood, and the fat comes off easier when it is cold. Another thing, when a skin looks

scraped, it still has lots of fat on it. I know I'll have to go over the whole hide at least twice. . . .

16   At last I have finished scraping the otter skin. It is all very nicely done, and not one single hole did I cut in it. . . . I am going to scrub it well in lots of warm soapy water.

17   Goodness me, I have more chores than a farmer. . . .

18   Hurray! My otter skin is nailed to the door. It's the biggest thing— much bigger than I thought it was. It nearly covers the whole door. . . .

19   The wind still howls, swirls, and rages. It's awful cold, maybe ten below. All the peaks look like volcanoes with their great trailing plumes. . . . I brought in some more wood today, but I didn't stay out long. It was too cold and windy. . . .

20   While I was out in the cold, my breasts ached. They drew up and the nipples stuck out firm, and they ached. When I came in I examined them, and found they were swelling and have water in them, not milk, but clear water. Soon my child will be here, and I am not yet ready to receive her. So much to do and so little time. . . .

21   I have decided to burn the floor. I'll cut the part I have already taken up, now, and save the rest for reserve. There are seven sills, all logs ten to twelve inches through, under the floor, which is nailed to them. If I can dig around them, saw them in two, pry them out, and cut them into blocks, they'll make a lot of fine wood. They are yellow cedar, and so is the puncheon. . . .

22   The otter skin is a disappointment. It's as hard as a board, and I'm just sick about it. I might make it into a Robinson Crusoe umbrella, but it can never become an infant's robe in its present stiff state. I remember reading or hearing that the Eskimoes chew skins to make them soft. It would take a lot of chewing to make this big skin soft. I just can't chew it, and I won't even try.

23   The fur is lovely, and it smells clean. I put my face in it, and it's the softest thing I've ever touched. I do wish the skin wasn't so stiff. There must be some way I can fix it. Baby must have one present.

24   If we were home she would have many gifts—a ring, a silver cup with her name on it, a necklace, a silver spoon, a baby book, dresses with lace and ribbons, fine soft knitted things. Even in this northland she would have gifts if anyone knew we were here. . . .

25   I believe I have found a way to soften the otter skin. I doubled over a corner of it, and it didn't break as I thought it might, so I folded it some more. No breaks. I kept on folding and creasing it, and now it is no longer board-like; but it's still a very long way from being as soft as I want it to be.

26   I washed a few clothes today. I want clean things for the coming of my child. Surely she will be here soon. I am getting things ready to re-

Notes

What are the main topics in each of these paragraphs (16–19)?

Continue making a note next to each paragraph about the main topic of the paragraph.

ceive her, and I have done a lot of sewing. Tomorrow I will bathe and make myself presentable for a newborn child. . . .

27   I made a birth cloth today from one of Don's union suits. It is all wool and should serve nicely to wrap a newborn child in. . . .

28   I plan to use string raveled from a flour sack to tie the cord. I boiled a piece to make sure it is clean. . . .

29   I've worked again on the fur, and I'm pleased with the result. I used a different system—pulled it back and forth around the bunk pole. I admire the fur more and more, and I want so much to get it soft enough to use for my baby. . . .

30   The milk case is pretty well filled with baby things. Don's shaving soap is in one of the pockets. Shaving soap should be good for baby. It seems right to bathe my child in her father's shaving soap. . . .

31   Only a few more days now until I will have a child in my arms.

32   I have been working and working at the otter skin, and I am making progress. . . . A dozen times a day I pick it up, rub a part of it between my hands, brush it, hold it to my face, hold it at arm's length to admire it. . . .

33   The wind has died away. It is very much warmer, and a haze covers the sky. I went wood gathering and was delighted with my outing. I saw twenty-six deer, and I brought some boughs for the ones who will pay me a friendly call. . . . Two ravens came to eat the otter. I wonder how they knew it was there. . . . maybe they smelled it. My thrush never comes back, and I liked it so much. Those mean old jays—I really shouldn't feed them a crumb.

34   I baked bread, lots of it, far more than I need for myself. The deers are fond of bread, and I thought I'd have an extra amount on hand. Five of them came today to bum a handout, and I didn't disappoint them. I think all of them have been here several times before, but I can be sure of only one—Sammy with the mark on his throat. He is the tamest of the lot, and knows me. He even eats out of my hand. . . .

What does paragraph 35 tell us about Martin? What kind of woman is she?

35   I pounded up my cast and put it on the floor with the gravel. It was quite hard, much harder that I thought. If I had fallen, the cast would have given my arm good protection. Now that my arm is well, I haven't worn the cast for weeks. I don't use my crutch any more, either, but I'm not disposing of it yet. . . .

36   I always think of the child as a girl. What if it's a boy? Oh, it couldn't be. . . .

37   This awful deep snow and hard cold is going to kill off much of our wild life. Poor creatures, what a pity they can't all be like bears and sleep the winter through. But then, what would I do without my friendly bums to come around and ask for bread and lick their chops at me?

38   Since the baby came down to live in the lower part of my abdomen, I have been constipated, and I don't like it. I think it's the cause of my swollen ankles. I had absolutely nothing here to correct it, so I looked around to see what the wilderness might provide, and hit on the idea of eating seaweed. Certainly it can be called roughage. . . . I went along the beach and gathered a mess. . . . I picked it over well, washed it thoroughly, and ate quite a lot—ate it raw. It wasn't too awful, but I certainly don't like the stuff. It was very effective, almost more effective than I desired it to be. I was busy all day with the honey bucket. . . .

39   The otter skin is getting to be as soft as I want it to be. I have invented another way to soften it. I made a small mallet and gently pound the folded fur over a block of wood. . . .

40   The fur is finished, and it's exactly as I wished it to be. I am very proud of it. So soft and warm—such a lovely thing. I shall wrap my baby in it when she goes for her outings, and we will walk pridefully along the beach. . . .

41   Snow seals every crack, so I only burn a little wood when there is no wind, and open the door for air.

42   I have bathed and washed my head. My hair has grown about three inches and is as curly as can be.* I like short hair because it's so easy to wash and dry. I think I may keep it short and never again be bothered with hairpins. . . .

43   My body is heavy, and my movements are slow and not too definite. I am becoming clumsy and awkward. I don't like it. Maybe I should sit down and just twiddle my thumbs until Baby comes. I do hope she comes before I use up all this water and burn all my wood. . . .

44   I brought a few branches and put a bouquet of cedar and hemlock boughs on my windowsill and placed the finest of Don's ore specimens on either side of it. The window has a nice look, as though a man and a woman lived here. . . .

45   There was a little show of blood, and when I saw it I remembered my mother saying it was a sure sign that the child would be born soon. . . .

46   I have never seen a child born. I always felt inadequate to help and was too modest to want to be a spectator. I have never seen anything born—not even a cat. . . . I am no longer afraid, yet I do wish someone were with me to help take care of the child. . . .

Have you ever seen anything be born?

[Martin's child was born after two days of labor, during which she cooked, cared for herself, and wrote recollections of life with her husband to try "to order my thoughts, be calm, and not bother my head about all I don't know." Again, she

---

*Martin had treated her scalp wounds with bacon grease, but mice nibbled at the grease while she slept and she cut her hair to the roots.

Notes

found herself able to cope alone, to deliver the child, to rest, to tie the cord, cut it, and then deliver the afterbirth. And the next day she went on with her narrative.]

47   My darling little girl-child, after such a long and troublesome waiting I now have you in my arms. I am alone no more. I have my baby.

[Martin was later "rescued" by Indians—although she says she almost did not want to leave her cabin—and reunited with her husband.]

> Why do you think Martin said she almost didn't want to leave?

Reread As you reread, you may need to define terms that are unfamiliar to you. Use a dictionary and *write the definitions in the margins.*

A quick way to keep track of important information for class discussion is to *highlight* or *underline* those pieces of information.

It is also important that you *make comments in the margins* as you reread. This is your chance to respond to what you are reading. Make a note when something is interesting, confusing, similar to your own life, and so on. You can also write questions in the margins. (To get used to commenting in the margins, answer the questions already in the margins.)

Before you begin rereading and "marking up" the reading "from Martha Martin's Diary," look at how this reader responded to and marked part of the diary.

> Ooh. Yuck. I wonder if I could eat this.

1   I killed a sea otter today. I actually did kill a sea otter. I killed him with the ax, dragged him home, and skinned him. <u>I took his liver out, and ate part of it.</u> I'm going to eat the rest of it, and his heart, too. His liver was quite large, bigger than a deer's, and it had more lobes to it. It was very good liver, and I enjoyed it.

2   Most of today was devoted to the sea otter; getting the hide off was a real task. It's a lovely skin, the softest, silkiest, thickest fur I have ever seen. I am going to make a robe for my baby out of the beautiful fur. My darling child may be born in a lowly cabin, but she shall be wrapped in one of the earth's most costly furs.

3   It was such a splendid piece of luck. Lucky in more ways than one. The otter might have killed me, although I have never heard of such a thing.

> The otter story starts here again.

4   <u>This morning I went to the woods to gather a load of limbs. As I was coming home with them, I saw the tide was nearly out, and I thought I'd walk over to the bar and take a look at the boat. . . . I was going along, swinging the ax</u> in my left hand, managing the crutch with the right hand, . . . not thinking of anything in particular, when right beside me I heard a bark. It was like a dog bark; not a bow-wow bark, more of a yip. I looked around and saw a huge creature **reared up** on its **haunches.** I saw its white teeth.

> **Reared up** means rose up.
>
> **Haunches** means rear legs.

5   Without thinking, I swung the ax at the side of its head, saw it hit, felt the jar in my arm, heard the thud. As I swung the ax, I turned and tried to run. I was so terrified the thing would nab me from behind that I could hardly move. I glanced over my shoulder to see how close it was. It hadn't budged from where it dropped. . . .

6   I got down on my knees and examined it from one end to the other. First off, I noticed the lovely fur. <u>I took off my glove and ran my fingers through the nice, silky coat.</u> I decided right then I would have the skin. I saw it as a baby blanket. . . .

Notes

I think I would have been afraid to touch it.

Now, *complete the rereading step of the reading process*—reread all of Martin's diary and write down definitions, comments, and questions in the margins. Answer the questions in the margins and follow the directions you find there too.

Think Critically After rereading, answer these questions in writing to prepare for class discussion.

1. There are places in her diary when Martin seems to jump around from one topic to another. It is fine to jump around from topic to topic when you are writing in a diary or in a letter to a friend. (When writing paragraphs for college or work, writers carefully move their readers from one point to the next.) Find a place where Martin seems to jump from one topic to an unrelated topic. (Make a note in the margin next to this place or places.)
2. What types of things and events does Martin write about in her diary? Which of these things and events might show up in "public" writing like essays, books, and news articles? Which seem too personal?
3. Why do you think Martin keeps a diary?
4. Why do you think she later agreed to have it published? Why do you think she used a pseudonym? (Consider the era she lived in.)

Express Yourself

Sum Up "from Martha Martin's Diary"

Review what each paragraph of Martin's diary focuses on. Then, in writing, explain to someone who has not read "from Martha Martin's Diary" what the diary is about **and** why you think Martha Martin wrote in the diary. (Take a few minutes to plan your answer. Reread and improve your answer before turning it in.)

Notes

Connecting Chapter

Chapter 6, "Diaries and Journals," offers you the next opportunity to practice the reading process outlined in this chapter. Then, you'll find this reading process in Chapters 7 through 11 and in "The Reader" (Section VIII). By the end of the school term, this process will be familiar and natural to you. You'll find yourself using the process all the time, and you'll see that your reading enjoyment, speed, and comprehension have increased.

Using the Writing Process

Effective writers don't perform magic tricks when they write. They understand that writing is a process—an activity that requires them to move step by step. Effective writers know they will have to think, rethink, write, and rewrite.

Consider how a custom homebuilder begins a project. The builder doesn't walk out to a vacant lot with lumber and tools. The builder must plan the project and discuss ideas with subcontractors. He may have to read about the zoning requirements, and he may research what is popular among buyers. He will begin with the foundation and take the project step by step; he follows a process. He will probably have to revise his plans as he goes along.

The homebuilder doesn't worry about touching up the paint or putting in the light fixtures or the landscaping until after the structure is built. Similarly, effective writers don't worry about spelling, punctuation, and grammar until they have built their structure (or paragraph). The next section outlines the steps you should take to go from the foundation of a paragraph to the final touches.

The Writing Process

This textbook offers you the materials and guidance to practice a productive writing process. This process will help you write more effectively and will make writing easier for you. The **writing process** used in this book includes these steps:

Pre-Drafting

In this step, you'll

- Talk about the assigned topic and begin to get involved in the topic.
- Read, discuss the readings, and think critically about the readings and how they relate to the writing assignment.
- Carefully review the actual writing assignment and explore what kind of information should go into your paragraph.
- List ideas, write freely, or use one of the other idea-generation techniques discussed later in this book.

Drafting

In this step, you'll create a complete paragraph although the paragraph might be a little rough. Don't worry too much about sentence errors. Focus on ideas.

Revising

In this step, you'll change and improve the draft. You might rethink some of your ideas, add information, delete information, and move ideas around. (Reading aloud at this step can help you find areas that need improvement.)

Editing

In this step, you'll work on sentence structure, usage, punctuation, and spelling. This is the "polishing" step. (Reading your paragraph aloud may help you find errors.)

Points to Remember about the Writing Process

- *The writing process steps will not always happen in this exact order.* They may overlap, and some steps may need to be repeated. For example, if you are drafting your paragraph and think that you don't have enough good ideas to write about, you might go back to the pre-drafting step and reread your assigned readings—or go to a tutor to explore additional ideas.

- *Approaching a formal writing assignment as a series of steps will actually make your task easier.* You will be able to take your assignment one step at a time, and the writing task won't seem so overwhelming.
- *All writers have some kind of writing process.* Some processes are more effective than others and make writing easier, so it's important to refine your process until it works for you.

Use the Writing Process

This section of the chapter offers you the opportunity to practice what you have learned about the writing process. First you'll follow the steps of the reading process and read a diary entry from The Freedom Writers Diary. Then you'll be offered an Express Yourself assignment that requires you to use the writing process.

Reading Assignment—The Freedom Writers Diary

Preview Read the introductory material in brackets. Then read the first paragraph and the first sentence of each of the other paragraphs.

Anticipate What will the diary entry be about? What specific feelings and what lessons will the diary writer discuss?

_____

_____

_____

_____

Read Read the diary entry quickly, marking any unfamiliar words. Don't look up any words in the dictionary yet.

The Freedom Writers Diary

By The Freedom Writers with Erin Gruwell

[This diary entry comes from *The Freedom Writers Diary*, a collection of diary entries by students at a Long Beach, California high school. They wrote the diary entries throughout their high school years (1994–1998) in their English

Notes

classes with their teacher, Ms. Gruwell. Early in 1994, Ms. Gruwell discovered that the students were unfamiliar with the Holocaust. She also saw connections between the prejudice that led to so many deaths during the Holocaust and the prejudice that was fueling the gang wars in and around Long Beach. Ms. Gruwell decided to focus her English classes on the theme of tolerance, and her students began to learn about history, themselves, and modern society. For more diary entries from *The Freedom Writers Dairy*, go to Section VIII, "The Reader."]

Diary 17

Dear Diary,

1   In Ms. Gruwell's class today, we played the "Peanut Game." The rules of the game included one piece of paper and a description of a peanut inside and out. I wrote about the peanut and said it was small, round, and dirty. On the other side of the paper I stated that even though it looked terrible, it tasted fantastic! We categorized all of the peanuts by mentioning their different exteriors. I soon realized the "Peanut Game" was similar to the situation I had about my weight.

2   One day in junior high, I was getting off the school bus from a seat in the back. It is a seat where no one likes to sit and is always empty. I heard people shouting, "Hey, Fatso!" "You big buffalo!" A group of obnoxious girls screamed such awful comments that I, an "obese" twelve-year-old girl, will sadly remember for the rest of my life.

3   "Oh no, not again! Please not again!" I thought to myself as I stood up to get off the bus. I had tried to ignore the girls' name-calling the entire ride home. Now that we were at my stop, I knew I had to face them before getting off. In order to leave the bus I had to walk through a long crowded aisle and face the obnoxious girls. As I stood up, the girls followed. They crowded together, and approached me as if they were ready to strike at me. Why did they want to take their anger out on me? What did I do to them? All of the sudden, the girls began to kick and sock me repeatedly. I could feel the pain all over my body but felt defenseless. I did not fight back.

4   They continued to hurt me as if there was nothing more important to them than to see me in pain. The last few kicks were the hardest; all I wanted to do was to get off the bus alive. My friends were staring at me, hoping that I would do something to make the girls stop. Why? Why didn't my friends help me? Finally, after what seemed like an eternity, I was able to release myself from their torture. I got off the bus alive. Imagining that the worst had already passed, I began to walk away from the bus and the girls stuck their heads out the window and spit on me. I could not believe it! They spit on my face!

5   The feeling of their spit striking me, running down my neck, and their germs accumulating on my face, felt disgusting. I heard paper crumbling in their hands, and then they threw it at me. I began to walk faster as the bus was on its way. While I was cleaning my face with a napkin, I could still hear the girls laughing. When they waved good-bye, my nightmare was over.

6   Today in Ms. Gruwell's classroom, I realized that a peanut is still a peanut even if the shell is different. Some taste better, others look fresher, but in the end they're all peanuts. Ms. G's analogy, "Don't judge a peanut by its shell, judge it by what's inside of it," made perfect sense to me. As long as I know that I am a human being, I don't need to worry about what other people say. In the end, we all are the same!

Reread Reread the diary entry. Highlight ideas or points that you want to remember. In the margins, record your reactions and questions. Look up unfamiliar words in the dictionary.

Think Critically and Summarize

1. What do you think was the teacher's goal in playing the "Peanut Game"? What lesson was she teaching?
2. Why do you think the author uses quotations in paragraph 2? Why didn't she just say, "The girls on the bus called me names"? (You may want to use quotations when writing one of your paragraphs this school term.)
3. In paragraphs 3 and 4, the author asks questions. Mark these in the reading. What would you say to the author to answer these questions? (You may want to use questions in one of your paragraphs this school term. They are a good way of bringing up important points and of involving your reader.)
4. Explain to a reader outside of your class what this diary entry is about. Be sure to include what the author learns from the "Peanut Game."

Express Yourself

Unfair Judgments

At some time in our lives, we have all judged other people unfairly, and we have all been misjudged by others. Sometimes we judge strictly according to appearance—skin color, age, clothing, and so on. The girl

Continued

who wrote the diary entry in this chapter was discussing a time when she was unfairly judged by her weight. The "obnoxious" girls on the bus had decided that they didn't like the way the girl looked, and they judged her to be an unattractive person on the inside, someone undeserving of decent treatment. While this girl's experience may not be unheard-of—people are judged daily by their appearance—we should acknowledge that the "obnoxious" girls acted in an extreme manner. Most of our judgments (fair or unfair) do not result in violence.

Perhaps it is more common for people to make judgments according to appearances and actions. Imagine the following scene: Jill is a devoted single mother of two who does a good job juggling a full-time job, motherhood, and school. The first time that Steve sees Jill, Jill has been up all night studying for an exam. Steve sees Jill running into the grocery store to get milk for her kids' breakfasts. She is wearing pajamas and slippers. Her hair is messy, and she looks grouchy. Steve judges Jill by her appearance and by her action of buying milk at the breakfast hour and decides she is an unorganized, grumpy woman who probably neglects her children. He is judging her unfairly by her appearance and her actions.

Here is your writing assignment:
Write a paragraph in which you discuss a single instance when a person was unfairly judged just by his or her appearance or by his or her appearance and action.

Pre-Drafting

With your classmates, discuss instances when you or someone you know has been judged unfairly. You should also think about times when you may have judged someone unfairly. To get started, discuss some of these situations:

- A person was judged unfairly because of a physical handicap.
- A person was judged unfairly because of his or her skin color.
- A person was judged unfairly because of his or her action.

Your class discussion may have given you a clear idea of what you want to write about, or you may still be exploring options. Take time now to freewrite. **Freewriting** (also called **brainstorming**) is the act of writing without worrying about correctness. Write about any ideas you have that connect to the assigned topic. Don't be concerned about spelling or grammar. Write for at least 10 minutes.

This book has a subject index (p. 459). If you want to learn more about any term, concept, or technique discussed in this book (not just bold face terms), check the listings in the subject index. The subject index lists all the page numbers where the term, concept, or technique is discussed. Now, for practice, look up *brainstorming* in the subject index and find out where this technique is discussed later in the book.

Skill Spotlight

The Writing Process and Your Tutor

A tutor can help you at any stage of the writing process.

If you want help getting started on a writing assignment, *see a tutor at the pre-drafting step:*

- Discuss class readings.
- Review vocabulary in the readings.
- Discuss the writing assignment. What is it asking you?
- Brainstorm with the tutor. Make lists of ideas.

If you have a draft completed and you want to improve it, *see the tutor at the revising step.*

- Ask a tutor to read it over and describe the draft's strengths and weaknesses. (Ask the tutor to focus on the ideas in the draft and not on the grammar.)
- As an independent writer, you'll have to make the decisions about what changes you should make.

If you feel confident about the ideas in your draft and feel you now need help on the grammar, *see the tutor at the editing step.*

- Ask the tutor to read your paragraph and tell you what types of errors he or she sees.
- After finding out how to identify and fix these types of errors, check your own work and make corrections.
- Review your corrections with the tutor.

Drafting

Decide which single instance you want to focus on. Write a draft of your paragraph. Explain who the person is, why he or she was judged unfairly and who did the judging. What is this person really like?

Revising

Share your paragraph with a reader (a classmate, instructor, or tutor). Ask the reader to consider these questions:

- Is the paragraph "on topic"? That is, does the paragraph clearly answer the writing assignment?

Continued

Notes

- Does the paragraph explain why the person was judged unfairly, who did the unfair judging, and what this person is really like? Does the paragraph need more information? More details? Would a quotation or question help make the ideas clearer?
- Does any piece of information seem unnecessary? Should something be left out?

After the reader has responded to your paragraph, consider his or her suggestions. Then make your own decisions about the changes you want to make.

Editing

After you have revised and improved your paragraph, edit your paragraph. Read your paragraph aloud and look for grammar, punctuation, and spelling errors. Is there a particular error that you tend to make? Review your paragraph carefully, line by line, and make corrections.

Connecting Chapter

All Express Yourself assignments should be completed using the writing process although you may not be asked to spend as much time on those assignments as on your formal writing assignments. In this book, all formal writing assignments will include step-by-step instructions for using the writing process. Chapter 7, "Academic Paragraphs," offers you your first opportunity to put this writing process into action with a formal paragraph assignment.

Improving Your Vocabulary

Improving your vocabulary is an important step toward improving your reading and writing (and speaking) skills. If you understand most of the words you are reading, you will read faster and understand more. In addition, if you have many words to choose from as a writer (and speaker), you will be able to express your ideas more clearly and in more interesting ways.

There are many ways to improve your vocabulary. You can study word parts (roots, suffixes, and prefixes.) You can drill yourself using vocabulary improvement books. Perhaps one of the easiest ways is to read. People who read frequently are exposed to many words, and, even without consulting the dictionary much, they improve their vocabulary just through extensive exposure to words.

Expressions offers various methods to help you improve your vocabulary. You will

+ Read.
+ Use the dictionary.
+ Study the words defined in the margins.
+ Make definition and sentence cards.
+ Use newly learned words in sentence work and paragraph assignments.

Consider the Context

The first step in improving your vocabulary is to know that you don't need to look up unfamiliar words immediately when you see them. If you interrupt yourself frequently to look up words, you will read slowly and probably lose track of the main idea. Also, looking up words in a dictionary can be tedious and boring. The first time you read something, read it all the way through, just marking unfamiliar words.

As you read, highlight important terms and instructions. Record any questions you have in the margins.

Then reread the piece and try to figure out words by studying the context. **Studying the context** means that you look at the sentences that come before the unknown word and the sentences that come after. These sentences will often give you a good idea of what the word means.

Sometimes the meaning you figure out from context is even better than a dictionary definition because with context, you are considering how the word is *being used* in that particular situation. Occasionally, writers define words as they write or give obvious clues as to what a word means. Consider the introductory paragraph in "from Martha Martin's Diary" and the two words in italics.

A **pseudonym** is a fake name.

> Martha Martin is the **pseudonym** of the wife of an Alaskan gold prospector. Sometime during the 1920s, she kept a diary of her remarkable, self-sufficient survival during a winter *marooned* in an Alaskan camp. Alone and pregnant, she had been injured by an avalanche that separated her from her husband. She *improvised* a splint for her broken arm and a cast for her broken leg and, when help did not arrive, prepared for the birth of her child. Later, in 1952, she was encouraged to submit the diary for publication. In it she emerges as the female Robinson Crusoe, proud of her self-sufficiency and her relationship with a harsh natural world.

If you weren't sure what *marooned* means, you could look at the context clues. The sentence also has the term *self-sufficient*. The next sentence says she was *alone . . . separated from her husband*. These clues suggest that *marooned* has to do with being alone and stranded. Knowing the exact definition of the word may not be necessary. Simply having a general sense of its meaning in the paragraph may be enough.

If you consider what the first three sentences are telling you, the next word, *improvised,* becomes clearer. If she is alone and stranded, she cannot get help or particular supplies. This information helps you guess at the meaning of *improvised*. She must have to *make do* with the supplies she has.

Using context clues, you may want to try guessing what word could be used *instead* of the unknown word. For example, in a letter, Mother Jones (a child and labor activist who lived from 1830–1930) uses the word *espoused:*

> I have *espoused* the cause of the laboring class in general and of suffering children in particular. For what affects the child must ultimately affect the adult. It was for them that our march of principle was begun. We sought to bring the attention of the public upon these little ones, so that ultimately sentiment would be aroused and the children freed from the workshops and sent to school.

The rest of the paragraph tells you that she is concerned for children. She is working to make their lives better, to make people aware of their suffering. Therefore, you might guess that instead of saying she "*espoused* the cause of the laboring class in general and of suffering children in particular" she could have said she "*supported* the cause . . ." or she "*fought for* the cause. . . ." The word *supported* and the phrase *fought for* seem to fit well and help you to understand the meaning of *espoused*.

Consider the word *toils* in the following paragraph.

> The child of to-day is the man or woman of to-morrow, the citizen and the mother of still future citizens. I ask Mr. President, what kind of citizen will be the child who *toils* twelve hours a day, in an unsanitary atmosphere, stunted mentally and physically, and surrounded with immoral influences?

What do people do "twelve hours a day"? Often, back then, they *worked*. You might guess that the word *toils* could be replaced by the word *works*.

Learning vocabulary by studying the context requires that you pay attention to the overall meaning of the paragraph and to the specific clues that may be found within the paragraph. As you do this, you will be

- Strengthening your reading skills.
- Cutting down on the number of times you'll have to go to the dictionary (thereby speeding up your reading).
- Getting an accurate idea of how the words are actually used by writers.

However, there may be times when the context doesn't give you clues and you can't guess a replacement. You may also want to double-check your guesses. Then you need to turn to a dictionary.

Use the Dictionary

For your work in this class (and others), you should purchase a good paperback dictionary that you can carry with you. You may also want to purchase a larger dictionary to keep at home. Paperback dictionaries contain fewer definitions than larger dictionaries, so make sure that the one you use contains enough definitions (approx. 60,000 or more) and that the definitions are detailed enough to give you an accurate sense of the meaning of words and their different uses.

How to Understand a Dictionary Entry

In this paragraph from Mother Jones's letter, the word *stunted* may be unfamiliar to you.

> The child of to-day is the man or woman of to-morrow, the citizen and the mother of still future citizens. I ask Mr. President, what kind of citizen will be the child who toils twelve hours a day, in an unsanitary atmosphere, *stunted* mentally and physically, and surrounded with immoral influences?

You may be able to guess from the context clues that *stunted* has a negative meaning. (You know that children shouldn't be *stunted* mentally and physically.) However, the precise meaning of *stunted* may be unclear. If you look in the dictionary, you will not find a separate listing for *stunted*. In fact, you may not see *stunted* at all. You will need to look up the base form of the word: *stunt*. The **base form** of the word is the word with no special endings like *–ed* or *–ly*.

In the *Merriam-Webster Dictionary*, you will find two listings.

> ¹stunt \ˈstənt\ *vb* : to hinder the normal growth or progress of
> ²stunt *n* : an unusual or spectacular feat. [If the word *feat* is unfamiliar to you, you may have to look it up. *Feat* means an act notable for courage, skill, endurance, or ingenuity.]

In the first dictionary entry, you see the base form followed by letters and symbols that tell you how the word should be pronounced: \ˈstənt\. Next is the part of speech: *vb*. This means that this dictionary entry is for the word *stunt* when it is used as a verb. Then you are given the definition.

The other listing begins with the number 2 and the base form. This tells you that you are being given a second way that the word can be used. The *n* tells you this is the definition for *stunt* when it is used as a noun.

As you can see, the listings give two very different meanings for the word *stunt*. Your first task is to decide how the word is being used in the sentence. Is it being used as a verb or as a noun?

Here is the sentence again:

> I ask Mr. President, what kind of citizen will be the child who toils twelve hours a day, in an unsanitary atmosphere, *stunted* mentally and physically, and surrounded with immoral influences?

The −ed suggests that this it is being used as a verb or a verb form. While *stunted* can be a past-tense verb, in this case it is being used to describe *child*. Therefore, *stunted* is being used as a descriptive verb form. You want to pay attention to the first definition. Mother Jones is talking about a child whose mental or physical growth has been hindered or stopped. She is not talking about *a spectacular act of courage or skill.*

It is important to pay attention to how a word is used in your reading. Consider the word *espoused.*

> I have *espoused* the cause of the laboring class in general and of suffering children in particular.

You may have guessed that it means *support,* but to make sure, you might look up *espouse* in the dictionary. The 1997 paperback *Merriam-Webster Dictionary* doesn't list *espouse.* It lists *espousal* and gives this definition:

> *n* 1 : BETROTHAL also : WEDDING 2: a taking up (as of a cause) as a supporter − espouse \ vb

You know that Mother Jones is not talking about weddings and getting married. Therefore, you must look at the second definition that says *a taking up (as of a cause) as a supporter.*

The *hardback* 1999 Merriam-Webster Dictionary gives a separate listing for *espouse:*

> espouse \ *vt* espoused; espousing 1 : MARRY 2 : to take up and support as a cause : become attached to syn see ADOPT − espouser *n*

The *vt* at the beginning of this entry tells you that *espouse* is a transitive verb. That means that it is a verb that must be followed by an object (you must *espouse* something). Again, you should ignore the first definition and pay attention to the second.

Note: Toward the end of the definition for *espouse,* you will see these words: "syn see ADOPT." These words tell you that *adopt* is a *syn*onym for *espouse*. A **synonym** is a word that means the same thing. To further understand the word *espouse*, you can look up *adopt*.

Word Form and Usage

Learning definitions is an important step in improving your vocabulary. However, you must also understand *how* a new word can be used and *what other forms* of the word can be used. A dictionary can help you with meaning, word form, and word usage.

For example, with the word *espouse*, the dictionary gives you very useful information. *Espouse* can mean *to marry*. It can also mean *to support*. The dictionary also listed its other forms: *espousing, espoused, espouser*. This information will help you use the word in different situations:

- He is *espousing* the neglected animals in our city.
- I *espoused* the cause of the freedom riders.
- An *espouser* of women's rights, she fought for alimony legislation.

After all, your goal isn't to recite dictionary definitions. Your goals are to increase your vocabulary and *use* your new words to express yourself more clearly and exactly.

The dictionary can also give you hints about usage. With the word *espouse*, the dictionary says *to take up and support as a cause*. In fact, *espouse* is often followed by the words *the cause of* or the name of a specific cause, concern, or right.

- I espouse *the cause of* that radical group.
- I espouse everyone's *right* to free speech.

Vocabulary Cards

Throughout this book, you'll be using two different sets of 3 in. × 5 in. index cards to help you learn new vocabulary. The first set of cards—definition cards—will help you improve your ability to figure out word meanings by studying context and by looking in the dictionary. You'll also become more familiar with different forms of each word.

The second set of cards—sentence cards—will give you practice in actually using the words. You can use both sets of cards to quiz yourself and classmates.

Every reading in this book will be followed by a list of vocabulary words for you to make cards for. You may, of course, make more cards for other words you want to learn.

Definition Cards

Front of Card

Your Name

Chapter #

The word

The original sentence the word appeared in

The source

Back of Card

Your guess of what the word means from studying the context

The dictionary definition

The part of speech for how the word was actually used in the reading

Other forms of the word

Example:

Josie Smith

Chapter 8

Emancipation

I speak for the <u>emancipation</u> from mills and factories of the hundreds of thousands of young children who are yielding up their lives for the commercial supremacy of the nation.

(from Mother Jones letter, paragraph 1)

I think emancipation has something to do with slavery—being freed.

"The act or process of emancipating." (<u>Emancipate</u> means "to free from restraint.")

Noun

Emancipator, emancipate, emancipated, emancipating

Notes

Requirements for definition cards:

- Put your name and the chapter number on the front of each card.
- Write the vocabulary word next.
- Write the *entire* sentence that the word shows up in, and underline the vocabulary word.
- Give the source information. (In which reading and in which paragraph did the word appear?)
- On the back of the card, make a guess about what it means. If you don't have any guesses, write "I can't guess what it means."
- If a word is being used as a noun, give the noun definition from the dictionary. If it is being used as a verb, adverb, or adjective, give the corresponding definition from the dictionary.
- If the definition contains a word that is unfamiliar, define that unfamiliar word as well.
- Tell how the word is being used in the sentence on the front of the card. Is it being used as a noun? Verb? Adjective? Adverb?
- List the other forms the word can take.
- When you look for other forms of the word, look at the beginning of the dictionary definition for other endings (like –*ing*) and at the end of the definition. Write out the entire word, not just other endings. (For example, on the card for *emancipation*, write *emancipating* as another form of that word. Don't write just –*ing*.)

On page 441, you'll find Vocabulary Lists for Chapters 8 through 11 and Section VIII, "The Reader."

You can use these definition cards to quiz yourself. Keep them with you so that when you are waiting in line, riding the bus, waiting for an appointment, and so on, you can review your words. You may want to tape them to your bathroom mirror or next to the kitchen sink—somewhere that you will see them often. You can also use these cards for quizzing your classmates or study partners.

Understanding these words will help you understand your current readings and writing assignments and your future readings, for these words will show up again.

Sentence Cards   *Notes*

These cards will help you learn how to *use* your new words, and they are great for quizzing yourself and classmates.

Front of Card

> Your Name
>
> Chapter #
>
> Create a new sentence of your own, but put a blank where your vocabulary word should be. This sentence must have context clues in it. This means that the sentence must have other words in it that hint at which word is missing.

Back of Card

> Write the vocabulary word that fits in the blank.

Example: **Front of Card**

> Josie Smith
>
> Chapter 8
>
> The teenager was tired of so many rules and wished for _____ from his parents.

Back of Card

> Emancipation

Requirements for sentence cards:

- Put your name and the chapter number on the front of the card.
- On the front of the card you will write a sentence with a blank where the vocabulary word would fit.
- This sentence must have *context clues* that hint at which word would fit.
- This sentence must also be grammatically correct (and have no spelling errors).

Notes
- Use the word in the same form as you found it in the reading, and use it so that it expresses the same general meaning that it did in the original sentence. (In other words, use *espoused*—not *espousing*. Also, use *espoused* in a sentence about supporting a cause, not in a sentence about marriage. There will be other opportunities to experiment with word form and meaning.)
- On the back of the card, write the vocabulary word that fits in the blank.

Note: Creating the sentence cards can be difficult. Studying the original sentence from the reading is helpful, and you may want to try to imitate that original sentence. In addition, you may want to work with a tutor or study group on some of the sentence cards.

These sentence cards will get you started on using new words, but don't stop here! Look for opportunities to use your new vocabulary in any writing (or speaking) you do at school or work.

Make Vocabulary Cards

Read paragraphs 1 through 4 of Mother Jones's letter on page 80 in Chapter 8. (And review Chapter 5.)

Make definition and sentence cards for the following words:

- emancipation
- espoused
- toils

You may want to compare your cards to those made by your classmates to see if you have completed them correctly. You may even want to begin quizzing your classmates. (Use the examples in this chapter to make your task easier, but be sure you create original sentences for your sentence cards.)

Connecting Chapter

Beginning with Chapter 8, "Letters and E-mail," you will find vocabulary lists following each reading. After you have read a selection twice, you'll make both definition and sentence cards for each word listed. Use the cards as a study tool, and use them to quiz your classmates.

Variety in Expression

In this section of *Expressions,* each chapter focuses on a single type of expression. You'll see how writers adjust their language and the form of their writing to fit different purposes and audiences. You'll then get opportunities to write your own diaries, paragraphs, letters, autobiographical paragraphs, fairy tales, and essays.

Diaries and Journals

This chapter discusses these themes:

✦ Memories
✦ Survival

📓 ***Journal Assignment***

Engaging in the Themes of Chapter 6

Write a journal entry in which you explore what the artist is expressing through his painting. What is the artist telling you about this moment of survival? How does the painting make you feel? What would you say to the artist if you could respond directly to him?

• Remember, Journal Assignments are opportunities for you to express your thoughts freely. Don't worry about grammar and punctuation. (See Chapter 1, p. 3, for more information.)

Writing is usually a form of public communication. We write ideas down and expect others to read and perhaps respond. However, sometimes people write without intending to communicate to others. Diaries and journals are examples of such private expressions.

In this chapter, you'll explore the power of private writing—why, how, and when people use diaries and journals to express themselves. You'll read excerpts from a young girl's diary. Then you'll keep your own journal for a few days.

Connecting Chapter

In this chapter, you will study diaries and journals. Study Chapter 3, "Using the Reading Process," in preparation for completing the reading assignments in this chapter and the following chapters.

Diaries and Journals

Diaries, from the Latin root meaning "daily," were used by the Greeks (beginning in perhaps 400 BC) to record weather conditions, seasons, harvesting times, astrological notes, and other practical pieces of information. Later the Romans began to include more private information concerning politics and people's private lives. Then, for a period, there is no historical proof that people kept diaries. Perhaps during the Middle Ages people didn't have as much personal time to keep diaries.

Then, late in the Renaissance period (1400–1600 AD), people had time to think about more than just getting through the day. Historical records show they began to write their private thoughts and observations in diaries. Later, many people—such as Samuel Pepys (1633–1703), an English politician; Virginia Woolf (1882–1941), an English writer; and Anne Frank (1929–44), a Jewish girl who hid from the Nazis—wrote diaries that have given us great insight into the politics, people, and daily routines of earlier times. Today, diaries are still popular. Many people keep diaries to record daily events, problems, ideas, feelings, and special moments.

Diaries and journals are fascinating to read because they offer us insight into other people's lives—and most humans love to peek into other people's lives. In addition, diaries can be quite enjoyable to write because they are a stress-free writing opportunity. They offer the writer great freedom of expression—he or she does not have to worry about form or correctness. The diary writer does not have to fully explain ideas and can wander back and forth (or in circles) in exploring ideas.

Reading Assignment: Diaries and Journals

In this chapter you'll read an excerpt from *The Diary of a Young Girl*, by Anne Frank. In these diary entries, Frank records her memories and her family's fight to survive during World War II. As you work through this chapter, consider how people benefit from writing diaries.

Reading Assignment—"The Diary of a Young Girl"

Preview Read the introductory information in brackets and the author's name and the title. Then skim through the entries, reading a few sentences on each page.

Notes

Anticipate What do you expect the author to write about? What would most thirteen-year-old girls write about? What is special about Anne Frank's situation?

_____

_____

_____

_____

Read Read the diary entries. Mark unknown words, but don't look up any meanings in the dictionary yet.

The Diary of a Young Girl

By Anne Frank

The Nazi **concentration camps** were prisons where most prisoners were eventually killed by being "showered" with poisonous gases.

[Anne Frank was a Jewish girl who lived in Holland during the German occupation of that country during World War II. She was thirteen years old when she began writing in her diary. Less than a month later, the Frank family was forced to go into hiding to avoid the Nazis, who would have sent them to **concentration camps.** In her diary, Frank recorded information about the time she and her family spent in hiding (almost two years). Frank wrote nearly every day. The complete diary can be found in book form in most libraries. Here, you will find a few of her most memorable entries. Pay attention to the dates so that you know when many entries have been left out.]

Sunday, 14 June, 1942

1   On Friday, June 12th, I woke up at six o'clock and no wonder; it was my birthday. But of course I was not allowed to get up at that hour, so I had to control my curiosity until a quarter to seven. Then I could bear it no longer, and went to the dining room, where I received a warm welcome from Moortje (the cat).

2   Soon after seven I went to Mummy and Daddy and then to the sitting room to undo my presents. The first to greet me was *you,* possibly the nicest of all. Then on the table there were a bunch of roses, a plant, and some peonies, and more arrived during the day.

3   I got masses of things from Mummy and Daddy, and was thoroughly spoiled by various friends. Among other things I was given *Camera Obscura,* a party game, lots of sweets, chocolates, a puzzle, a brooch, *Tales and Legends of the Netherlands* by Joseph Cohen, *Daisy's Mountain Holiday* (a terrific book), and some money. Now I can buy *The Myths of Greece and Rome*—grand!

4   Then Lies called for me and we went to school. During recess I treated everyone to sweet biscuits, and then we had to go back to our lessons.

5   Now I must stop. Bye-bye, we're going to be great pals!

Saturday, 20 June, 1942

6   I haven't written for a few days, because I wanted first of all to think about my diary. It's an odd idea for someone like me to keep a diary; not only because I have never done so before, but because it seems to me that neither I—nor for that matter anyone else—will be interested in the **unbosomings** of a thirteen-year-old schoolgirl. Still, what does that matter? I want to write, but more than that, I want to bring out all kinds of things that lie buried deep in my heart.

Unbosomings means confessions.

7   There is a saying that "paper is more patient than man"; it came back to me on one of my slightly **melancholy** days, while I sat chin in hand, feeling too bored and limp even to make up my mind whether to go out or stay at home. Yes, there is no doubt that paper is patient and as I don't intend to show this cardboard-covered notebook, bearing the proud name of "diary," to anyone, unless I find a real friend, boy or girl, probably nobody cares. And now I come to the root of the matter, the reason for my starting a diary: it is that I have no such real friend.

Melancholy means sad.

8   Let me put it more clearly, since no one will believe that a girl of thirteen feels herself quite alone in the world, nor is it so. I have darling parents and a sister of sixteen. I know about thirty people whom one might call friends—I have strings of boy friends, anxious to catch a glimpse of me and who, failing that, peep at me through mirrors in class. I have relations, aunts and uncles, who are darlings too, a good home, no—I don't seem to lack anything. But it's the same with all my friends, just fun and joking, nothing more. I can never bring myself to talk of anything outside the common round. We don't seem to be able to get any closer, that is the root of the trouble. Perhaps I lack confidence, but anyway, there it is, a stubborn fact and I don't seem to be able to do anything about it.

This is the first time that Frank explains why she keeps a diary and how she feels about writing. As you reread these diary entries, make a note in the margin every time she talks about writing in her diary and writing in general.

9   Hence, this diary. In order to enhance in my mind's eye the picture of the friend for whom I have waited so long, I don't want to set down a series of bald facts in a diary like most people do, but I want this diary itself to be my friend, and I shall call my friend Kitty. No one will grasp what I'm talking about if I begin my letters to Kitty just out of the blue, so, albeit unwillingly, I will start by sketching in brief the story of my life.

Do you ever find it difficult to share your thoughts with people in your life?

10   My father was thirty-six when he married my mother, who was then twenty-five. My sister Margot was born in 1926 in Frankfort-on-Main, I followed on June 12, 1929, and, as we are Jewish, we emigrated to Holland in 1933, where my father was appointed Managing Director of Travies N .V. This firm is in close relationship with the firm of Kolen & Co. in the same building, of which my father is a partner.

11   The rest of our family, however, felt the full impact of Hitler's anti-Jewish laws, so life was filled with anxiety. In 1938 after the **pogroms,**

A **pogrom** is the systematic killing of a group of people.

Notes

A **capitulation** is a surrender.

To distinguish them from others, all Jews were forced by the Germans to wear, prominently displayed, a **yellow six-pointed star.**

A **veranda** is a porch.

my two uncles (my mother's brothers) escaped to the U.S.A. My old grandmother came to us, she was then seventy-three. After May 1940 good times rapidly fled: first the war, then the **capitulation,** followed by the arrival of the Germans, which is when the sufferings of us Jews really began. Anti-Jewish decrees followed each other in quick succession. Jews must wear a **yellow star!** Jews must hand in their bicycles, Jews are banned from trams and are forbidden to drive. Jews are only allowed to do their shopping between three and five o' clock and then only in shops which bear the placard "Jewish shop." Jews must be indoors by eight o' clock and cannot even sit in their own gardens after that hour. Jews are forbidden to visit theaters, cinemas, and other places of entertainment. Jews may not take part in public sports. Swimming baths, tennis courts, hockey fields, and other sports grounds are all prohibited to them. Jews may not visit Christians. Jews must go to Jewish schools, and many more restrictions of a similar kind.

12   So we could not do this and were forbidden to do that. But life went on in spite of it all. Jopie used to say to me, "You're scared to do anything, because it may be forbidden." Our freedom was strictly limited. Yet things were still bearable.[. . .]

Wednesday, 8 July, 1942

Dear Kitty,

13   Years seem to have passed between Sunday and now. So much has happened, it is just as if the whole world had turned upside down. But I am still alive, Kitty, and that is the main thing, Daddy says.

14   Yes, I'm still alive, indeed, but don't ask where or how. You wouldn't understand a word, so I will begin by telling you what happened on Sunday afternoon.

15   At three o'clock (Harry had just gone, but was coming back later) someone rang the front doorbell. I was lying lazily reading a book on the **veranda** in the sunshine, so I didn't hear it. A bit later, Margot appeared at the kitchen door looking very excited. "The S.S. have sent a call-up notice for Daddy," she whispered. "Mummy has gone to see Mr. Van Daan already." (Van Daan is a friend who works with Daddy in the business.) It was a great shock to me, a call-up; everyone knows what that means. I picture concentration camps and lonely cells—should we allow him to be doomed to this? "Of course he won't go," declared Margot, while we waited together. "Mummy has gone to the Van Daans to discuss whether we should move into our hiding place tomorrow. The Van Daans are going with us, so we shall be seven in all." Silence. We couldn't talk any more, thinking about Daddy, who, little knowing

what was going on, was visiting some old people in the Joodse Invalide; waiting for Mummy, the heat and suspense, all made us very overawed and silent.

16   Suddenly the bell rang again. "That is Harry," I said. "Don't open the door." Margot held me back, but it was not necessary as we heard Mummy and Mr. Van Daan downstairs, talking to Harry, then they came in and closed the door behind them. Each time the bell went, Margot or I had to creep softly down to see if it was Daddy, not opening the door to anyone else.

17   Margot and I were sent out of the room. Van Daan wanted to talk to Mummy alone. When we were alone together in our bedroom, Margot told me that the call-up was not for Daddy, but for her. I was more frightened than ever and began to cry. Margot is sixteen; would they really take girls of that age away alone? But thank goodness she won't go, Mummy said so herself; that must be what Daddy meant when he talked about us going into hiding.

18   Into hiding—where would we go, in a town or the country, in a house or a cottage, when, how, where . . . ?

19   These were questions I was not allowed to ask, but I couldn't get them out of my mind. Margot and I began to pack some of our most vital belongings into a school satchel. The first thing I put in was this diary, then hair curlers, handkerchiefs, schoolbooks, a comb, old letters; I put in the craziest things with the idea that we were going into hiding. But I'm not sorry, memories mean more to me than dresses.

20   At five o'clock Daddy finally arrived, and we phoned Mr. Koophuis to ask if he could come around in the evening. Van Daan went and fetched Miep. Miep has been in the business with Daddy since 1933 and has become a close friend, likewise her brand-new husband, Henk. Miep came and took some shoes, dresses, coats, underwear, and stockings away in her bag, promising to return in the evening. Then silence fell on the house; not one of us felt like eating anything, it was still hot and everything was very strange. We let our large upstairs room to a certain Mr. Goudsmit, a divorced man in his thirties, who appeared to have nothing to do on this particular evening; we simply could not get rid of him without being rude; he hung about until ten o'clock. At eleven o'clock Miep and Henk Van Santen arrived. Once again, shoes, stockings, books, and underclothes disappeared into Miep's bag and Henk's deep pockets, and at eleven-thirty they too disappeared. I was dog-tired and although I knew that it would be my last night in my own bed, I fell asleep immediately and didn't wake up until Mummy called me at five-thirty the next morning. Luckily it was not so hot as Sunday; warm rain fell steadily all day. We put on heaps of clothes as if we were going to

Notes

the North Pole, the sole reason being to take clothes with us. No Jew in our situation would have dreamed of going out with a suitcase full of clothing. I had on two vests, three pairs of pants, a dress, on top of that a skirt, jacket, summer coat, two pairs of stockings, lace-up shoes, woolly cap, scarf, and still more; I was nearly stifled before we started, but no one inquired about that.

21 Margot filled her satchel with schoolbooks, fetched her bicycle, and rode off behind Miep into the unknown, as far as I was concerned. You see I still didn't know where our secret hiding place was to be. At seven-thirty the door closed behind us. Moortje, my little cat, was the only creature to whom I said farewell. She would have a good home with the neighbors. This was all written in a letter addressed to Mr. Goudsmit.

22 There was one pound of meat in the kitchen for the cat, breakfast things lying on the table, stripped beds, all giving the impression that we had left helter-skelter. But we didn't care about impressions, we only wanted to get away, only escape and arrive safely, nothing else. Continued tomorrow.

Yours, Anne

If you would like to learn more about Frank's hiding place and her life in hiding, turn to Section VIII, "The Reader," for more excerpts.

Reread Reread the diary entries. As you read, try to use context clues to figure out the meanings of unfamiliar words. Look up the meaning of any words that remain unclear. Use the margins to mark important and interesting points. Answer the questions in the margins and record any additional questions or comments in the margins.

 Get Involved!

Rent the movie *The Diary of Anne Frank,* directed by George Stevens. This 1959 film offers a moving look at what it was like for this family to hide from the Nazis. You'll also see how Frank's diary was important to her, her father, and all of us.

Think Critically and Summarize

1. Based on the diary entries you have read, describe in writing what the diary is about. Assume that the person you are writing to has no knowledge of Anne Frank.

2. Written over half a century ago, this diary gives us examples of how life then was different from life today. What is different about Frank's life—as compared to the life of a thirteen-year-old today?

3. Of course, some things in life don't seem to change from year to year. What do you see in Frank's diary that suggests she experienced some of the same things that young people experience today?

4. As you reread the diary entries, you marked the places where Frank discusses writing. In your own words, why did Frank keep a diary?

5. How would you describe Frank? What kind of girl was she?

Express Yourself
Changes

In her entry dated Wednesday, July 8, 1942, Frank begins to describe her family's escape. Her life is changed forever as they go into hiding. Write a paragraph in which you describe a significant change in your life. For example, you could write about moving to a new city or state, getting married, starting college, or living on your own.

Journal Assignment

Diaries/Journals

Write a journal entry. Here are some options:

1. Make up a story about going into hiding. Explain why you are going into hiding. Explain where you will go and what you will do to survive. Describe what your troubles and successes might be and how you will react to different situations.
2. Some people would say that a journal is like a time capsule. Write about what you would put in a time capsule that is to be launched into space for aliens to find. What items would give aliens important information about you and your society? What might you explain in a letter or note?
3. Journals can help a writer remember the details about people, places, and events. Write about an event from your past that you'd like to remember in detail. Explain why this event is important to you.
4. Write on a topic of your choice.

Writing Assignment: Keep Your Own Journal

Part One

Keep your own journal for the next 4–8 days. Here are the requirements:

- Spend 10–30 minutes writing each day. To truly experience the benefits of writing a journal, you must write at least every other day. (Don't write all entries on the last day.)

Notes

- Be honest in what you say in your journal. Write about the things you do during the day, your interactions with people, your thoughts and ideas. (Your journal entries don't have to be "exciting." They should reflect normal days.)

Your instructor will check to see that you have completed the journal, but he or she won't read it, so express yourself freely.

Part Two: My Journal Experience

After you have written your last diary entry, write a response called "My Journal Experience," in which you describe your experience as a journal writer.

Did you enjoy keeping a journal? Why or why not?

- What might be the benefits to you or other people in keeping a journal?
- What can people learn through writing a journal?
- How might a journal increase a person's enjoyment of life?
- Besides learning and enjoyment, why else might someone keep a journal? Can you think of any professional reasons to keep a journal?

When answering these questions, discuss your reaction to keeping a journal. Also think about other people you know and which of them you think might benefit from keeping a journal.

Get Involved!
Go online and do a search using the term *diaries*. Visit a few sites and report back to your class. What kinds of diaries can you find online? (Create a list to show the variety.) Which one interested you most? Why?

Additional Readings

(See Section VIII, "The Reader.")
The Diary of a Young Girl (more excerpts) by Anne Frank. This diary records a young girl's experiences while she and her family hid from the Nazis during World War II.
The Freedom Writers Diary (excerpts). These diary entries are by students at a high school in Long Beach, California (1994–98).

Sentence Basics

The chapters listed here are designed specifically to coordinate with topics in Chapter 6.

Chapter 12: Verbs, Part One
Chapter 13: Verbs, Part Two

Academic Paragraphs

Battle

Waking early
again.
He lifts his weight
from our repose.

I have dreamt
a lion
amidst
snakes.
Crimson
forked
carefully posed.

Sitting
Shoulders hunched,
Roar repressed,
He gazes into the glass.

He pulls on two pairs of socks
To make
His dead father's shoes
last.

—Christine Burroughs

This chapter discusses these themes:

✦ Feelings
✦ Memories
✦ Goals
✦ Creative forms of expression

 Journal Assignment

Engaging in the Themes of Chapter 7
Write a journal entry in which you explore the meaning behind this poem by Burroughs. What ideas and feelings is she expressing? What memories might she be recalling? What do you think of poetry as a form of expression?

Writing effective paragraphs is one key to succeeding in college. Instructors will ask you to write paragraphs to demonstrate that you have learned the required material. They'll also ask you to write paragraphs so that you may share your unique perspective on an issue. In fact, writing paragraphs in college gives you the opportunity to do many things. You can

- Learn and demonstrate what you learn.
- Express your ideas.
- Strengthen your reading, writing, and critical thinking skills.
- Prepare yourself for writing letters, memos, and reports at work.

Connecting Chapter
In this chapter, you will study the form of the academic paragraph and then write one (or more) of your own. Study Chapter 4, "Using the Writing Process," in preparation for completing the writing assignments in this chapter and the following chapters.

Notes

The Academic Paragraph

Paragraphs that you write in college and paragraphs that you read in your textbooks may be different from the paragraphs you see in diaries, letters, novels, magazines, and newspapers. For example, a paragraph in a newspaper may be short—containing a single quote or a sentence or two.

Academic paragraphs are longer and more formal. Your *purpose* in writing an academic paragraph should be to state and fully explain a specific idea to an academic audience. When thinking about your purpose in writing, ask yourself, "Why am I writing this?" "What do I want my audience to know, believe, or learn?" If you can explain your purpose clearly—in writing or out loud—you'll communicate more clearly in your paragraph. You can also think about purpose when you are reading; ask yourself, "Why did the writer write this?" "What did he or she want me to know?"

Writers can use academic paragraphs to argue, describe, analyze, compare and contrast, and so on. But *the purpose of a single paragraph is generally narrow and specific*. The paragraph must focus on one idea, one purpose. (Academic essays, as Chapter 11 explains, have a broader scope.)

The *audience* of an academic paragraph includes your instructor, your classmates, and perhaps other instructors and students. These people expect you to use standard American English (no slang) and standard paragraph form. This means that your paragraph should begin with a focused main point. Your audience also expects you to develop your idea with interesting support in an organized fashion.

Pieces of the Academic Paragraph

Academic paragraphs have some specific requirements. The academic paragraph begins with a **topic sentence,** a sentence that expresses your main point. Though there is no hard-and-fast rule about length, the topic sentence is generally followed by 5–10 sentences that explain and develop your main point. These 5–10 sentences are called the **body** of the paragraph.

Often, but not always, an academic paragraph ends with a **wrap-up sentence** that reminds the reader of what the main point is.

Here is an academic paragraph written by a student.

| | Notes |

| **Student Sample** | |

My Own Writing Goal

By Lucky Le

My most important writing goal this semester is to learn to achieve sentence clarity on my own without a red pen mark. I constantly have grammar, subject-verb agreement, and fragment mistakes. I cannot correct my own mistakes. I have tried a method of correcting over and over again till my eyes turn blurry, but I still fail. For example, in my tenth grade English class, I had to write a response assignment before class session ended. In the last couple of minutes of class, I corrected my sentence clarity. The grade to the assignment was a C-. I was disappointed in myself. I thought I had the skill or knowledge I learned from my teacher. I have also tried taking the response assignment home for a couple of days without a glance. I kept my mind fresh before rereading the assignment again. I edited to the best of my ability. Unfortunately, the assignment had no grade so I was stuck with a C-. This semester I am determined to correct one sentence at a time. I will underline my verb twice, subject once, and cross out prepositional phrases. This will be more time consuming but will greatly improve my sentence clarity. Once I master this new method, I will smile with a red mark of "EXCELLENT." ■

— Topic Sentence

— Body

— Wrap-up Sentence

The Five Qualities of Effective Writing

To help you understand more completely what your instructor and other people in your audience are expecting when you write paragraphs, remember these five qualities of effective academic writing:

- Interesting and thoughtful
- Focused
- Organized
- Developed
- Clearly written

The terms **interesting and thoughtful** are easy to understand, but students often worry about making their writing interesting and thoughtful. Here are some suggestions.

- *Be honest in your writing.* Use appropriate words you are comfortable with, and say what you believe—not what you think others

You should highlight the first sentence in each bulleted item here to help you remember the main points.

Notes

want you to say. If you think your ideas are radically different from your classmates' ideas or your instructor's ideas, talk to your instructor and classmates.

- *Read about your topic.* Writers get interesting information from reading. Of course, you must tell your reader when you borrow information from another source.
- *Discuss your readings and ideas with classmates, a tutor, and your instructor.* Everyone learns from exchanging ideas. Think critically. Ask, "Why?"
- *Freewrite on the topic.* That means write down all of your ideas. Write and don't worry about grammar and spelling. A good freewrite is long. It'll have good ideas and some not-so-good ideas. That's okay. Later you can go back and pick out only the interesting ideas. The key here is not settling on the first idea that jumps into your head. Often the first idea is the most obvious and the least interesting.

Highlight the topic sentence here and in the following paragraphs, so that you can easily find the main points later.

The term **focused** means that you clearly present one main idea, and you stick to that idea. When you talk, you may wander off your initial topic. When you write an academic paragraph, however, you must stick to your main idea and leave out everything that doesn't connect to that main idea.

In a paragraph, your main idea will be stated in the *topic sentence,* which is the first sentence in the paragraph. All other sentences in the paragraph must connect directly to the topic sentence. To attain this kind of focus, writers follow a process that allows them to do pre-drafting work (reading, discussing, freewriting), and they write more than one draft. This process helps writers clarify their ideas.

The term **organized** means that the ideas in the paragraph are presented in a logical order. When you speak, you can jump around and go forward and backward. However, a final draft of an academic paragraph shouldn't jump around. To create organized paragraphs, writers carefully do their pre-drafting work because this helps them sort through their many ideas and organize them. They also revise their drafts.

In addition, writers often use **transitions**—words or phrases that help the reader move smoothly from one idea to the next. For example, suppose a writer wants to explain two similar reasons for keeping a diary. The writer may present the first reason and then say, "in addition" as he or she begins to explain the other reason. The words *in addition* tell the reader that a similar supporting idea is coming. There are many different transition words, which you'll study in future chapters.

The term **developed** means that the main idea is fully explained and supported. Writers come up with ideas for developing their points during their pre-drafting phase and while drafting their essays. For example, a writer might look back at his or her brainstorm, class discussion notes, or readings and find information that helps explain a particular idea. Writers also use comparisons, specific examples, and quotes to help support points in a paragraph.

The key idea to remember here is that readers want a lot of information when they are reading. This is another case in which writing and speaking are very different. When you are speaking to a friend, he or she can ask you questions if you don't give enough information. But when you are writing, your audience can't do this. As a result, writers must provide enough information to be sure that their ideas are understood. In addition, a well-developed paragraph will have details and information that add interest to the writing.

The term **clearly written** refers to the sentences in paragraphs. Sentences should be clear and varied. That means writers must edit their sentences, eliminating grammar and punctuation errors, and writers must think about how they shape their sentences. Readers want some short sentences and some long sentences.

You may have begun this course thinking that 99% of your work would be on sentences. However, before you work on the sentences in your paragraphs, you must make sure that you have written a paragraph that is interesting, focused, developed, and organized. Why fix sentences in a boring, confusing paragraph? Sentence work (editing) comes last in the writing process.

A Model Paragraph

Here is an example of a good academic paragraph written by a student. The topic sentence is highlighted.

Student Sample

From "How Not to Pop Your Top"

By Gloria Ayala-Partida

If you have problems with your temper, like I do, an easy way to keep track of the things that upset you most often would be to write in a diary each day. Even writing in it only when you are angry can be beneficial. For instance, when I'm at work and someone makes me mad,
Continued

The topic sentence is followed by an explanation.

Notes

The body. Details (like the mocha) add interest.

The wrap-up sentence sums up the main point.

instead of lashing out at them, I write down, in detail, exactly what happened. It is important to use as many details as possible in your writings, like who the person was that made you mad, what they did, and what time they did it. Even something as simple as whether or not you had your morning mocha can be an important detail. After about a month or so you may want to refer back to your diary to look for patterns. Maybe you are grouchiest before lunch. Either way, you'll find you are better able to handle the anger, and sometimes avoid it all together, if you know which people and situations push your buttons. ■

In this paragraph, Ayala-Partida clearly expresses to her audience how she uses a diary. She has achieved her purpose by using the writing process and keeping in mind the requirements and qualities of an effective paragraph.

Specifically, Ayala-Partida's paragraph stays focused on the topic sentence. All of the information and examples clearly connect to the main idea, and the ideas seem to flow from one to the next. The explanations and details in the body make this a well-developed paragraph. Finally, Ayala-Partida finished her paragraph with an effective wrap-up sentence, and then she worked hard to polish her sentences and make them clear and varied.

Reading Assignments: Academic Paragraphs

In the next section, you are presented with two academic paragraphs. Read them as models of good academic writing, and watch for these themes: *memories*, *feelings*, and *goals*.

Reading Assignment—"Why I Write Poetry"

Preview Read the title and author's name. Think about what the paragraph will focus on and what qualities of good writing you expect to see in this paragraph.

Anticipate Write down what you think the paragraph will be about. Make specific guesses.

Read Read the paragraph.

Why I Write Poetry

By Christine Burroughs

I write poetry to capture images and memories. I see and experience things in my everyday life that I don't want to forget, and poetry lets me hold those moments still. For example, a few years ago, my husband's father died. My father-in-law owned a lumber business, and my husband was learning the business so that one day he could own and run the company himself. I woke one morning soon after my father-in-law's sudden death, and with the fogginess of early morning moments, I saw my husband getting ready to go into the office. He would have to battle investors to prevent a corporate take-over and to maintain his father's good reputation. My mother-in-law had given my husband some of his dad's shoes and clothing. That morning, my husband was putting on two pairs of socks to make a pair of his father's shoes fit. I couldn't get the image out of my mind. I wrote a poem about my husband that day. I didn't want that image to slip away from me.

Reread Reread the paragraph. In the margin, write down your responses to what Burroughs is saying. Mark places where you think the paragraph has the qualities of effective academic writing.

Think Critically Answer these questions in writing on another sheet of paper to prepare for your class discussion:

1. What are the parts of an academic paragraph?
2. Highlight Burroughs's topic sentence. Does she have a wrap-up sentence? If so, mark it.
3. What type of support does Burroughs use to develop her idea? Does she use statistics? Research? Personal experience? Many examples or just one? Would a different type of support have worked better? Explain.
4. What part of the paragraph seems strongest to you? Why?
5. On page 57, you were asked to interpret Burroughs's poem. Did anything in this paragraph surprise you? In your earlier interpretation,

Notes

did you identify any of the feelings or ideas that she expresses in her paragraph?

Sentence Style

Study this sentence from the paragraph by Burroughs:

> I see and experience things in my everyday life that I don't want to forget, and poetry lets me hold those moments still.

Compare that sentence to this one:

> There are things in my everyday life that I don't want to forget, and poetry is helpful for remembering those moments.

Both of these sentences communicate basically the same idea, but the first one is clearer and more interesting for these reasons:

- It is often better to start a sentence with a strong, clear subject like *I.* Be careful of starting sentences with *there.*
- Action verbs like *see* and *experience* are more interesting and expressive than a verb like *are. Hold* is more vivid than *is.*

Your Turn Create a sentence of your own (or use one from your journal) in which you use *I* and an interesting verb. (Avoid beginning with *there,* and don't use *is, am, are, was,* or *were.*) (For a review of subjects and active verbs, see Chapters 12 through 14.)

Reading Assignment—"Writing Well is a Step to My Goal"

Preview Read the title, the author's name, and the topic sentence.

Anticipate List some guesses here of specific things you think the writer might mention in his paragraph.

_____

_____

_____

_____

Read Read the paragraph quickly.

Writing Well Is a Step to My Goal

anonymous

I am going to improve my writing skills because I want to be a police detective and must pass a writing test. Currently, I write reports of crime scenes I am called to, and my supervisor has said that my reports are sometimes confusing. He says that I won't have much chance of becoming a detective if I don't learn how to give facts more clearly. Some of my reports have been missing important information, and some have a lot of grammatical mistakes. Therefore, the skills I'm going to focus on this term are giving enough information and writing clear sentences. I'm sure I'll be able to pass the writing test if I work hard.

Reread Reread the paragraph, and respond in the margin to what this writer is saying. Underline the topic sentence. Can you relate to his or her situation? Explain in the margin.

Think Critically Respond in writing to these questions:

1. This paragraph was written in college. Write down what you think the assignment question might have been.
2. Why do you think the author wanted to remain anonymous?
3. Writers need to be specific when developing ideas. Where is this writer specific? Where do you think he or she should have been more specific?
4. Is there a wrap-up sentence?

Sentence Style

Study this sentence:

I am going to improve my writing skills because I want to be a police detective and must pass a writing test.

In this sentence, the writer has used a strong voice. He says "I am going to," not "I'll try" or "I might." He also uses *because* to explain an effect and a cause. Without *because*, he might have written two sentences that don't explain his goal and his reasons as clearly: "I am going to improve my writing skills. I want to be a police detective and must pass a writing test."

Your Turn Write a sentence that has a strong voice and that uses *because*. (For a review of the subordinator *because*, go to pages 228–229, and 293–295.)

Notes

Express Yourself
What Have You Learned about Academic Paragraphs?

In writing, explain to a student who has not yet taken a college writing course what he or she should know about academic paragraphs. It's a good idea to review the information in this chapter, but when you write your response, be sure to use your own words.

Suggestions: Remember your audience. Stay focused on what this audience needs to know. Plan your answer and then revise and edit as necessary.

Journal Assignment
How's It Going?

Discuss in writing how your writing class and other classes are going so far. Are you having any difficulties? Have there been any surprises? Which classes are you enjoying most, and why?

Paragraph Assignment: One of Your Writing Goals

You will now have the opportunity to express yourself in an academic paragraph. This section of the chapter takes you through all stages of the writing process, focusing special attention on the pre-drafting stage.

The Writing Process for This Paragraph

Here is the assignment you are preparing for:

Review this chapter, and then write a paragraph in which you tell your instructor and your classmates what one of your most important writing goals will be this semester.

Here are some good topics for this paragraph:

- *Staying focused*
- *Organizing ideas*
- *Finding interesting ideas*
- *Using the writing process*

There are many other possible topics. Review the beginning of this chapter, and familiarize yourself with the terms you might need to use in your paragraph.

Pre-Drafting

To write effectively, you must take time to complete the pre-drafting step of the writing process. During this step, you'll make sure that you understand the topic and the specific assignment. Also, you'll explore your own responses to the assignment. You'll find out what you think and develop interesting things to say on the topic.

If a writer skips the pre-drafting step of the writing process, he or she may mistakenly write on the wrong topic. He or she may also have trouble finding enough interesting things to say. Spending time on the pre-drafting step will help the rest of the writing process go more smoothly.

First, you must *read, think critically, and discuss the topic.* You have already completed this part of the pre-drafting step when you read this chapter, answered the critical thinking questions, and completed the response assignment.

Now, go back and review this chapter.

- Reread sections that seem important to you. Pay particular attention to any sections that are unclear.
- Look at the comments you wrote in the margins, the sections you highlighted, and the boldface terms.
- Write more notes as you need to.
- Look again at your lecture notes and the answers you wrote to the critical thinking questions.

The next step in pre-drafting is to *explore the writing assignment.* Now, in your own words and without looking at the assignment, tell a classmate what your assignment is asking you to write about.

What do you think the key words are in the writing assignment? Underline the key words. Here is the writing assignment again.

Review this chapter, and then write a paragraph in which you tell your instructor and classmates what one of your most important writing goals will be this semester.

Here are some good topics for this paragraph:

- *Staying focused*
- *Organizing ideas*
- *Finding interesting ideas*

There are many other possible topics.

 Get Involved!

Review the table of contents of this book and find sections that you think will be the most important for you and your classmates as you work toward your writing goals. Share what you find with your class.

Notes   One of the words you should underline in the writing assignment is *one*.

In a small group or as a whole class, list things that you might want to discuss in your paragraph.

- What do you want to tell your instructor and classmates?
- Are there areas of writing that frustrate you?
- What good and bad experiences have you had in the past?
- What do these experiences show about your skills?
- What role will writing play in your future?

Don't try to narrow your topic yet.

Moving from the blank page to the draft can be a little scary at times. All writers have had the experience of staring at a blank page while waiting for a complete, interesting paragraph to come to mind. This, of course, doesn't work. After exploring the assignment, discussing and making notes, don't try to jump directly to a draft. Take an intermediate step.

There are several strategies for getting your ideas on paper. This book introduces you to different methods, one at a time. For this assignment, try the clustering method. To begin, write your general topic in the middle of a page and draw a circle around it. Then write related, more specific points around the first circle. Circle those ideas, and keep branching out and getting more and more specific. Look at the cluster on p.69 that a student wrote on your current topic.

Skill Spotlight

Brainstorming, Clustering . . . Keep the Ideas Coming

Some students have trouble writing for very long when they first try brainstorming or clustering. They may run out of ideas or forget what they want to say because they keep stopping to correct spelling and grammar. Or they try to write down only great ideas. It is really hard to write if you think everything you write must be great. Let yourself write things that might not be great. You don't have to—and should not—use everything you have written in your cluster as part of your final draft. If you find it difficult to brainstorm or cluster for 15 minutes, these techniques might help.

- Reread your own cluster whenever you run out of things to say. Often, rereading your own ideas helps you get going again.   *Continued*

- Reread parts of the chapter or your lecture notes to find more ideas to write about.
- Reread the writing assignment to help you stay focused.
- Think about examples and specifics that might fit with the topic.
- Keep track of how much time you spend creating a cluster of ideas for this assignment. Set a goal that with each writing assignment this school term, you'll cluster for 1–2 minutes longer.
- Read your classmates' clusters to get an idea of what other people write when they cluster.

Notes

Brainstorming

Drafting

Look now at your cluster, and highlight the ideas that you want to put in your paragraph. What will your main point be? What main idea do you want to express?

Notes

At this point, it is important to narrow your topic. Choose *only one* of your important writing goals to discuss in this paragraph. Paragraph assignments are narrow, and it is important that you have a clear, narrow main point in your topic sentence. Experiment with different topic sentences until you create one that clearly expresses your main point. You may want to turn the writing assignment into a question:

What is one of your most important writing goals this semester?

When you have created a topic sentence that answers the question, begin to draft your paragraph. Again, don't interrupt yourself too often. Certainly don't think about spelling, grammar, or punctuation while you are trying to get your ideas down.

When you're developing your paragraph, consider these questions:

- Why is this goal important to you? Think critically about why you have chosen this goal over others.
- How do you know you need improvement in this area?
- Will it be difficult for you to achieve this goal? Why or why not?
- Do you have an example of something you have written that shows you need to work on this area?
- Do you have an example of something someone else wrote that shows strong writing skills? Do any of the writers in this chapter write in ways that you would like to?
- What specific actions will you take to achieve this goal? Will you seek assistance? Where? From whom? When? Why?

Reread your draft, and ask yourself where you might be more specific or where you might add an example. If you want to borrow an example or an explanation from this chapter, be sure that you put those ideas in quotation marks to show that you borrowed them.

You may want to write more than one draft.

Revising

Share your draft with classmates, your instructor, or a tutor, and get some responses from this audience. What does your audience think about the following?

- Is the paragraph focused on the assignment?
- Is the topic sentence strong?

Computer Note
If you don't already know how, learn to type! Revising is much easier on a computer, and the student who uses the computer typically produces a stronger piece of writing. See if your computer lab has typing tutorials on the computers.

- Does it respond directly to the assignment?
- Is it narrow enough?
- Does the body of the paragraph stay focused on the main point that is announced in the topic sentence?
  - Are the explanations clear?
  - Are there enough examples?
- Are the ideas organized?
  - Do the sentences flow in a logical order?
- Is there a wrap-up sentence? Does a wrap-up sentence seem necessary?

Consider the responses you get, and then make your own decisions as a writer. What do you think needs to be improved? Think about "The Five Qualities of Effective Writing" (pp. 59–61).

Student Sample

One Student's Writing Goal

Here is part of one student's draft and her revised version.

Draft

My most important writing goal for this semester is learning to develop the body of a paragraph by focusing on the main point. I want the body of the paragraph to contain interesting, thoughtful and supportive ideas that is organized and well developed. Sometimes, when writing, I often deviate from the topic of the paragraph which leads me into the arena of unrelated subject matter. The body of the paragraph loses its zeal and become limp and boring. For example, I wrote a paper about President Roosevelt's contributions to America. A broad subject, but I tried to focus mainly on his American contributions but wandered in the direction of his contributions to other countries as well.

A well-developed paragraph body evokes attention from the audience, by that, causing, a stimulating response . . .

The body of a paragraph is like the meat and potatoes, the heart of the meal that brings everything together. I lack these ingredients. When writing a paragraph, the ideas should transition so smoothly that the audience does not recognize the transitory stage. . . .

I believe as I continue to work hard and practice writing, I will learn to produce writing assignments that are eloquently written and carefully organized.   *Continued*

Notes

Once I can master creating a visual thought producing paragraph that will captivate the audience, even for a moment, then I have succeeded in reaching my writing goal for this semester.

Revision

My most important writing goal for this semester is learning to focus on the main point or topic sentence. Sometimes, when I am writing, I often deviate from the topic of the paragraph which leads me into the arena of unrelated subject matter. The body of the paragraph loses its zeal and becomes limp and boring. For example, I wrote a paper about President Roosevelt's American contributions but wandered in the direction of his contributions to other countries as well. I believe to be successful, I must continue to practice writing and concentrate on the main point. In the end, I will have learned to produce writing assignments that are completely focused on the topic and eloquently written. Once I have mastered this task, I will also succeed in writing paragraphs that will captivate the audience, if only for a moment.

—Judy Hudson

Think Critically

1. Hudson's draft had five paragraphs. Because the assignment asked for a single, focused paragraph, Hudson had to make some changes and create just one paragraph. Highlight the parts of the draft that also show up in the final, revised version.
2. Explain what Hudson decided to do when she revised.
3. What do you particularly like about Hudson's paragraph?
4. What can you learn from studying Hudson's draft and revision? ■

Editing

Review your paragraph and check your spelling.

Study the verbs and subjects in your paragraph.

If you are struggling with spelling, look up *spelling* in the subject index which begins on p.000. Turn to the page number listed next to *spelling* for help with your spelling.

- Are irregular verbs in the correct form? (See Chapter 13, pp. 191–193.)
- Can you combine any sentences by having more than one verb in a sentence? (See Chapter 13, pp. 195–196.)
- Make sure that each sentence has a subject. (See Chapter 14, pp. 199–207.)
- Could you get rid of any repetition in your paragraph if you created a sentence with two subjects? (See Chapter 14, p. 204.)

- Should you revise a sentence and use an *–ing* word as a subject for variety? (See Chapter 14, pp. 201–202.)
- Do you have any *there* sentences? Revise them so that they have clearer subjects. (See Chapter 14, pp. 205–206.)
- Check your verbs to make sure that you are being consistent with your tenses. (See Chapter 15, pp. 210–212.)
- Check your subjects and verbs to make sure they agree in number. (See Chapter 15, pp. 212–220.)
- Use what you learned from the "Sentence Style" sections in this chapter (pp. 64 and 65).
- Read your paragraph aloud, and correct any errors you find.
- Make sure that your final draft follows the format rules your instructor has set. (Does your instructor want a title? Should the paragraph be typed and double-spaced?)

Paragraph Assignment: One Way You Express Yourself

In this chapter, you have seen some ways that people express themselves. Christine Burroughs uses poetry to record memories and feelings and a paragraph to explain her poetry. Lucky Le and the anonymous student expressed their ideas in academic paragraphs, and Gloria Ayala-Partida expresses her feelings in her diary and communicates her suggestions in a paragraph.

With this assignment, you will explore the different ways that *you* express yourself or record memories.

Here is the assignment you are preparing for:

Write a paragraph in which you discuss one way you express your feelings or ideas. Explain when and why that method is effective for you. (You may focus on the present or the future.)

The Writing Process for This Paragraph

Pre-Drafting

With your classmates, discuss the many ways that humans express themselves. Create charts similar to the one that follows. You'll be making generalizations and guesses.

Clothing	What we are expressing with our clothes and what we are revealing about ourselves
Suits	The desire to conform, to fit in. Wealth. Status. Our conservative beliefs. Our commitment to a company and its reputation. And?
Tie-dyed T-shirts	
Baggy pants	

Notes

Do other charts for some of these topics:

- Voice (singing, giving speeches, slang)
- Home decorating
- Makeup, body piercing, and tattoos
- Cars
- Gardens
- Writing (poems, songs, stories, essays)
- Art (painting, sculpting, photography, and so on)
- Dancing
- Other hobbies or methods of expression

Consider your goals of expression in your future. Do you hope to be a professional song writer someday?

Here is your writing assignment again:

Write a paragraph in which you discuss one way you express your feelings or ideas. Explain when and why that method is effective for you. (You may focus on the present or the future.)

Underline the key terms in the writing assignment. Explain in your own words what your assignment is. What type of information will you include in the paragraph?

Reread the writing assignment. Focusing on that assignment, freewrite for at least 15 minutes. You may want to experiment by writing about two or three different methods of expression. For each method of expression, answer these questions as you freewrite:

- What is one way you express yourself?
- What does it reveal about you?
- What are you telling other people when you use this form of expression?
- What interests, values, or morals are you revealing?
- What strengths or weaknesses are you revealing?
- With whom do you use this form of expression? Why?
- Where do you use this form of expression? Why?
- When do you use this form of expression?
- How often do you use this form of expression?
- Why is this form of expression useful to you? Why is it powerful?

Drafting

Write your draft, keeping your audience in mind.

- Is your method of expressing yourself one that is very common?
- Will you need to explain this method to your audience?
- You can make the method interesting to your reader by giving specific details and analyzing its power and usefulness.
- Will your audience understand why you choose this method?

Be sure to use your freewriting notes and explain precisely when, how, and why you use this method. Begin your paragraph with a strong topic sentence that announces your main point.

Revising

Share your draft with a reader. Ask your reader to consider these questions:

- Does the paragraph respond directly to this assignment?
- Does the paragraph begin with a clear topic sentence?
- Does the paragraph include specific, detailed examples? Does the paragraph explain when the writer uses this method of expression and why? Will readers want more information?
- Can any information be added that will make the reasons for using this type of expression clearer?

Editing

Review your paragraph and check your spelling.
    Study the verbs and subjects in your paragraph.

Notes

- Are irregular verbs in the correct form? (See Chapter 13, pp. 191–193.)
- Can you combine any sentences by having more than one verb in a sentence? (See Chapter 13, pp. 195–196.)
- Make sure that each sentence has a subject. (See Chapter 14, pp. 199–207.)
- Could you get rid of any repetition in your paragraph if you created a sentence with two subjects? (See Chapter 14, p. 204.)
- Should you revise a sentence and use an *–ing* word as a subject for variety? (See Chapter 14, pp. 201–202.)
- Do you have any *there* sentences? Revise them so that they have clearer subjects. (See Chapter 14, pp. 205–206.)
- Check your verbs to make sure that you are being consistent with your tenses. (See Chapter 15, pp. 210–212.)
- Check your subjects and verbs to make sure they agree in number. (See Chapter 15, pp. 212–220.)
- Use what you learned from the "Sentence Style" sections in this chapter (pp. 64 and 65).
- Read your paragraph aloud, and correct any errors you find.
- Make sure that your final draft follows the format rules your instructor has set. (Does your instructor want a title? Should the paragraph be typed and double-spaced?)

Additional Readings

(See Section VIII: The Reader.)
"Don't Want to Be a Dummy Writer," by Calvin Mak. This student paragraph responds to the Paragraph Assignment: One of Your Writing Goals.
"Singing My Heart Out," by Cecilia Miles. This student paragraph responds to the Paragraph Assignment: One Way You Express Yourself.

Sentence Basics

The chapters listed here are designed specifically to coordinate with the topics and "Sentence Style" sections in Chapter 7.

Chapter 13: Verbs, Part Two
Chapter 14: Subjects
Chapter 15: Understanding, Correcting, and Avoiding Verb Errors

8

Letters and E-mail

This chapter discusses these themes:

✦ Social change
✦ Personal change

Letters are perhaps one of the most common types of writing we do. From childhood through adulthood we write notes, letters, and now e-mail. Letters and e-mail provide an inexpensive, convenient way for us to communicate when we cannot be with our audience. But as you'll explore in this chapter, saving money and convenience are not the only advantages to expressing ourselves through letters and e-mail.

Connecting Chapter

In this chapter, you'll look at how effective letters and e-mail are written. You'll also begin to formally study the vocabulary in your readings. Read Chapter 5, "Improving Your Vocabulary," in preparation for completing the vocabulary work in this chapter and the following chapters.

Letters and E-mail

Letter writing is a unique type of communication because the style of letters varies widely. Most diaries tend to be written in a casual, personal style. Most academic paragraphs are formal and have specific requirements. But letters can vary from the casual note to a best friend to the formal business letter.

The *purpose* and the *audience* of a letter determine its style. This is very similar to speech. We have many different ways of expressing ourselves with speech. Think about a situation in which you might need a loan. If you were to ask your best friend, you would use casual language and perhaps slang. If you were to ask your grandmother, your language would probably change a bit. If you were to speak to a bank loan officer, your language would become even more formal.

Letters are similar. Your purpose for writing and your audience will determine how you write. Even the form of your letter will change. A personal letter has no form requirements. You can put the date on the letter if you wish, and you can address the person you are writing to in many different ways ("Dear Sue," "Hey girl!" and so on). A business letter, however, requires formal, polite language, and it has a few requirements for form. Most modern business letters will follow this format:

[sender's address and date written]
1121 Hurley Ave.
Elk Grove, CA 95758
January 4, 2001

[receiver's name, title, business, and address]
Ms. Fiona Berry
Hugs and Kisses Child Care Center
78 Pond Lane
Darien, IL 60561

Dear Ms. Berry:

Here the writer composes paragraphs that each focus on one point at a time. A business letter requires that the writer go through much of the same process that you go through when

Continued

Notes

writing paragraphs and essays for college: think about and plan your writing; focus and organize your thoughts; draft, revise, and edit.

Sincerely,

Charles Applegate [the sender's name]

As you read the letter and e-mail in this chapter, consider each author's purpose. Who was the audience for each writer? Look at the form of the letter and the vocabulary used. Being aware of purpose, audience, and style will make you a stronger reader and writer.

Reading Assignments: Letters and E-mail

In this section, you'll find one letter and one e-mail. The first letter was written approximately 100 years ago to the first Roosevelt to be president (Theodore Roosevelt). The second reading selection is a news column that reprints a series of e-mails between a college student and Nike, the sporting goods manufacturer.

Reading Assignment—"Mother Jones to President Theodore Roosevelt"

Preview Read the introductory paragraph, and note the date of the letter. Then read the first paragraph of Jones's letter.

Anticipate What *specific* things do you think Jones might write about in her letter?

_____

_____

_____

_____

Read Read the letter quickly. Mark unknown words, but don't look up any meanings in the dictionary yet.

Notes

Mother Jones to President Theodore Roosevelt

A passionate spokesperson for the rights of workers and anti-child labor laws, Mary Harris "Mother" Jones fought doggedly to bring attention to these issues through letters, speeches, marches, and other forms of social protest throughout the country—"[I have] no abiding place," she once said, "but wherever a fight is going on against wrong, I am always there." In the following letter, Jones implores President Theodore Roosevelt, who was visiting Oyster Bay, New York, at the time, to sponsor federal laws that would end child labor practices in America.

NEW YORK, July 30th, 1903

The Hon. Theodore Roosevelt, President U.S.A.

Your Excellency:

1   Twice before I have written to you <u>requesting an audience that I might lay my mission before you and have your advice on a matter</u> which bears upon the welfare of the whole nation. I speak for the emancipation from mills and factories of the hundreds thousands of young children who are yielding up their lives for the commercial supremacy of the nation. Failing to receive a reply to either of the letters; I yesterday went to Oyster Bay, taking with me three of these children that they might plead to you personally.

2   Secretary Barnes informed us that before we might hope for an interview, we must first lay the whole matter before you in a letter. He assured me of its delivery to you personally, and also that it would receive your attention.

3   I have espoused the cause of the laboring class in general and of suffering children in particular. For what affects the child must ultimately affect the adult. It was for them that our march of principle was begun. We sought to bring the attention of the public upon these little ones, so that ultimately sentiment would be aroused and the children freed from the workshops and sent to school. I know of no question of to-day that demands greater attention from those who have at heart the **perpetuation** of the Republic.

4   The child of to-day is the man or woman of to-morrow, the citizen and the mother of still future citizens. I ask Mr. President, what kind of citizen will be the child who toils twelve hours a day, in an unsanitary atmosphere, stunted mentally and physically, and surrounded with immoral influences? Denied education, he cannot assume the true duties of citizenship, and enfeebled physically and mentally, he falls a ready victim to the <u>perverting influences which the present economic conditions have created.</u>

5   I grant you, Mr. President, that there are State laws which should regulate these matters, but results have proven that they are inadequate. In my little band are three boys, the oldest 11 years old, who

Instead of this underlined part, why doesn't she just say, "asking to see you so we can talk"?

Perpetuation means the act of making something continue on forever.

What bad influences are created by poor economic conditions? List possibilities here.

have worked in mills a year or more without interferences from the authorities. All efforts to bring about reform have failed.

6   I have been moved to this crusade, Mr. President, because of actual experiences in the mills. I have seen little children without the first rudiments of education and no prospect of acquiring any. I have seen other children with hands, fingers and other parts of their tiny bodies mutilated because of their childish ignorance of machinery. I feel that no nation can be truly great while such conditions exist without attempted remedy.

7   It is to be hoped that our crusade will stir up a general sentiment in behalf of enslaved childhood, and secure enforcement of present laws.

8   But that is not sufficient.

9   As this is not alone the question of the separate States, but of the whole Republic, we come to you as the chief representative of the nation.

10   I believe that Federal laws should be passed governing this evil and including a penalty for violation. Surely, Mr. President, if this is practicable—and I believe that you will agree that it is—you can advise me of the necessary steps to pursue.

11   I have with me three boys who have walked a hundred miles serving as living proof of what I say. You can see and talk with them, Mr. President, if you are interested. If you decide to see these children, I will bring them before you at any time you may set. Secretary Barnes has assured me of an early reply, and this should be sent care of the Ashland Hotel, New York City.

Very respectfully yours,

MOTHER JONES

The president's secretary, B. F. Barnes, responded by saying that the president was not unsympathetic to her cause, and that an anti-child labor law was passed under his administration when he was governor of New York, but there was nothing the president could do on a federal level. (Jones vehemently disagreed and went on to campaign against Roosevelt in 1904.)

Reread   Reread the letter. As you read, try to use context clues to figure out the meanings of unknown words. Look up the meanings of any words that remain unclear. Mark important and interesting points. In addition to responding to the questions printed in the margins, record your own questions and reactions to the reading in the margins.

Vocabulary cards: Make definition cards and sentence cards for the words listed here.

- *emancipation*, paragraph 1
- *espoused*, paragraph 3

Notes

Highlight or underline the main points in paragraphs 6–10. Use your own words and phrases in the margins to note what the main points are.

 Computer Note

When you are working on a computer, the word processing program you use will probably have a dictionary you can use. Check the Tools menu. You can also use an online dictionary. Try this one: www.m-w.com/dictionary.htm

Notes

- *toils,* paragraph 4
- *stunted,* paragraph 4
- *vehemently,* paragraph immediately following the letter

Think Critically In preparation for your class discussion, be sure that you mark the text as suggested earlier. Also answer these questions in writing:

1. What is Mother Jones's purpose for writing this letter?
2. How would you describe the style of her writing? (formal? casual?) Find some words or a sentence that clearly show her style.
3. Does her style fit with her purpose and audience? Explain.
4. Mother Jones says that working children will not become good citizens. List here some of the things a person has to do to be a good citizen in the United States. What skills must a person have? Why won't working children have these skills?
5. What do you know about the current child labor situation in the United States and other countries?

Summarize Make a list of Jones's main points.

Sentence Style

Study this sentence:

> I grant you, Mr. President, that there are State Laws which should regulate these matters, <u>but</u> results have proven that they are inadequate.

In this sentence, Jones used *but* (a coordinating conjunction) to join two complete sentences that have opposite meanings:

> I grant you, Mr. President, that there are State Laws which should regulate these matters.
> Results have proven that they are inadequate.

A reader might be surprised to see these two sentences next to each other. The *but* helps prepare the reader to read one idea that is the opposite of the other.

Your Turn Write two sentences that express opposite ideas. Then write them again and join them as one sentence by using *but* in the middle as the coordinating conjunction. *Note:* When you join the sentences, don't delete any words. Keep the subject and verb for each sen-

Get Involved!

Go to the Internet and do a search for "child labor." Take notes, and record website addresses. Share your findings with your classmates.

tence. (See Chapters 16 and 23 for more information about coordinating conjunctions.)

Notes

Express Yourself

What Are Your Concerns about Child Labor?

Thinking about Mother Jones's letter and your class discussion, what are your greatest concerns about 15- to 17-year-olds working in the United States? Are there certain situations when children 15 to 17 years old should be allowed to work? What rules do you support? (Consider things like days of the week, hours, types of duties, and so on.)

Reading Assignment—"Nike: 'Sweatshop' Order Not Funny"

Preview This is a newspaper column with e-mails in it. Read the title, author's name, and introductory information in paragraphs 1–4.

Anticipate What topics and issues do you expect to read about in this newspaper column and e-mails?

_____

_____

_____

Read Read the column quickly. Mark unknown words, but don't look up any meanings in the dictionary yet.

Nike: "Sweatshop" Order Not Funny

By Diana Griego Erwin

Sacramento Bee
February 20, 2001

[Nike has been criticized for employing children at very low wages in other countries. Doing so allows Nike to keep manufacturing costs low and profits high. See http://nikebiz.com/labor/ for Nike's response.]

1   Freedom. Individuality. Innovation. It's a dog-eat-dog world on the edge of hip. Just ask Nike.

2   Or take in an e-mail exchange between the global corporation and a brainy, smart-aleck college student originally from Oakland. That would be Jonah Peretti, an MIT graduate student who ordered shoes through

Notes

"Nike iD," a program that lets customers personalize products with a word or phrase of their choice stitched under the Nike Swoosh.

3 Having vaguely followed news about labor actions against Nike, Peretti, 27, ordered shoes with the word "sweatshop" added. Nike was not amused.

```
File Edit View Message Tools Window Help
```

4 From: Personalize, NIKE iD

5 To: Jonah Peretti

6 Subject: RE: Your NIKE iD order.

7 Your NIKE iD order was canceled for one or more of the following reasons:
1) Your Personal iD contains another party's trade-mark or other intellectual property.
2) Your Personal iD contains the name of an athlete or team we do not have the legal right to use.
3) Your Personal iD was left blank. Did you not want any personalization?
4) Your Personal iD contains profanity or inappropri-ate slang, and besides, your mother would slap us.

8 If you wish to reorder your NIKE iD product with a new personalization please visit us again at www.nike.com.

9 Thank you, NIKE iD

```
File Edit View Message Tools Window Help
```

10 From: Jonah H. Peretti

11 To: Personalize, NIKE iD

12 Greetings,

13 My order was canceled, but my personal NIKE iD does not violate any of the **criteria** outlined in your message. The Personal iD on my custom ZOOM XC USA running shoes was the word "sweatshop." Sweatshop is not: 1) another's [sic] party's trademark, 2) the name of an athlete, 3) blank, or 4) a profanity. I choose the iD because I wanted to remember the toil and labor of the children (who) made my shoes. Could you please ship them immediately?

14 Jonah Peretti

Criteria means requirements or descriptions.

Notes

File Edit View Message Tools Window Help

15   From: Personalize, NIKE iD.
16   To: Jonah H. Peretti

17   Dear NIKE iD Customer,
18   Your NIKE iD order was canceled because the iD you have chosen contains . . . "inappropriate slang." If you wish to reorder your NIKE iD product with a new personalization, please visit us again at nike.com.
19   Thank you, NIKE iD

File Edit View Message Tools Window Help

20   From: Jonah H. Peretti
21   To: Personalize, NIKE iD

22   Dear NIKE iD,
23   Thank you for your quick response to my inquiry about my custom ZOOM XC USA running shoes. Although I commend you for your prompt customer service, I disagree with the claim that my personal iD was inappropriate slang. After consulting Webster's Dictionary, I discovered that "sweatshop" is, in fact, standard English and not slang. The word means: "A shop or factory in which workers are employed for long hours at low wages and under unhealthy conditions," and its origin dates from 1892. So my personal iD does meet the criteria detailed in your first e-mail.
24   Your Web site advertises that the NIKE iD program is "about freedom to choose and freedom to express who you are." . . . The site also says that "If you want it done right . . . build it yourself." . . . My personal iD was offered as a small token of appreciation for the sweatshop workers **poised** to help me realize my vision. I hope that you will value my freedom of expression and reconsider your decision to reject my order.

Poised means ready and patiently waiting.

25   Thank you, Jonah Peretti.

26   Nike didn't reconsider. (Nike's response to sweatshop allegations online at nikebiz.com/labor/ is **voluminous** and interesting.) Needing to get back to his master's thesis, Peretti finally changed the wording on his order, adding one small request. "Could you please

Voluminous means large or lengthy.

Notes

Irreverence means a lack of respect or seriousness.

send me a color snapshot of the 10-year-old Vietnamese girl who makes my shoes?"

27   Nike doesn't have the corner on the market for **irreverence,** that's for sure.

Reread Reread the newspaper column. As you read, use context clues to figure out the meanings of unknown words. Look up the meanings of any words that remain unclear. Mark interesting points.

Vocabulary cards: Make definition cards and sentence cards for the words listed here.

- *commend*, paragraph 23
- *prompt*, paragraph 23
- *allegations*, paragraph 26

Think Critically In preparation for class discussion, answer these questions in writing on another sheet of paper:

1. Why did Peretti ask Nike to put *sweatshop* on his shoes?
2. Why did Peretti continue to ask for *sweatshop* on his shoes after Nike e-mailed him and told him they wouldn't do it? (There may be a number of reasons.)
3. Do you think Nike has a good reason for denying Peretti's request? Explain.
4. What are the signs that Nike is "irreverent"? What are the signs that Peretti is "irreverent"?
5. In which sentences does Peretti address Nike formally and respectfully?

Sentence Style

Study this sentence:

Although I commend you for your prompt customer service, I disagree with the claim that my personal iD was inappropriate slang.

In this sentence, Peretti respectfully compliments Nike on their service and then immediately emphasizes his disagreement with Nike about the use of *sweatshop*.

Peretti uses *although* to join these opposite ideas and emphasize his position. When you use one of the subordinators *although, even though,* or *though,* you will be able to discuss opposite ideas in a single sentence. Whatever idea is introduced by the subordinator will be less important. In this case, Peretti's compliment sounds less important than his disagreement.

If Peretti had wanted to emphasize his compliment, he would have written the sentence in one of these two ways:

> I commend you for your prompt customer service although I disagree with the claim that my personal iD was inappropriate slang.

> Although I disagree with the claim that my personal iD was inappropriate slang, I commend you for your prompt customer service.

Your Turn Join two of the following sentences using one of these subordinators *although, though, even though.*

- I see Peretti's point.
- I agree with Nike's position.

  Or

- I see Nike's position.
- I agree with Peretti's point.

Compare the meaning of your sentence with the sentences your classmates create. (Where you place the subordinator will change the meaning of the sentence.) (See Chapters 16 and 24 for more information about subordinators.)

Express Yourself

Dish Out Some Praise or Some Criticism

We all run into problems with products or services. For example, you might buy an item that broke easily or shrank. Or perhaps an employee at a store didn't treat you appropriately. Sometimes, however, we find a product or an employee at a store that makes our day.

Write a paragraph in which you describe the types of things or people that really bother you.

Or

Write a paragraph in which you describe the types of things or people that really make your day.

Suggestion: Explore different ideas and brainstorm. Then create a strong topic sentence that explains *the types* of things that either bug you or make your day. Then offer your reader interesting, specific examples in the body of your paragraph.

Notes

> ### *Journal Assignment*
>
> **Letters**
>
> Write a personal letter to a friend or family member. You may discuss anything you like.

Paragraph Assignment: One Reason to Express Ideas in a Letter

In this section, you will use your reading, writing, and critical thinking skills as you complete a paragraph and analyze why one writer wrote a letter. You will follow all the steps of the writing process, giving special attention to your topic sentence.

Here is the assignment you are preparing for:

In a paragraph, explain to a college reader outside of your classroom why Mother Jones wrote her letter or *why Jonah Peretti wrote his e-mail.*

Another option: with your instructor's permission, read a letter or e-mail from Section VIII, "The Reader," and explain to a college reader outside of your classroom why the author of that letter or e-mail wrote.

The Writing Process for This Paragraph

Pre-Drafting

Review your work in this chapter. Look at the readings again, and review your notes, answers, responses, and journals. You may want to make more notes in the margins or on your work as you do this reviewing.

One way to familiarize yourself with the writing assignment is to turn it into a question. Because you have a letter and an e-mail you could write about, write a question for each letter or e-mail. Begin your question with, "Why did Mother Jones . . . ?" Then write a question for Peretti.

You may already know which letter or e-mail you want to write about. However, take time to explore each one to be sure you have made a good choice.

Under each question you have written, make a list of ideas and facts you might use when answering the question. Use the readings and your notes to help you complete this work.

If you have the opportunity, exchange your lists with other classmates so that you can see what ideas they came up with. Add ideas to your lists.

Review your lists. Which list seems most promising? Most interesting? Choose one letter or e-mail to focus on, and write a single sentence that answers the question you wrote for that letter. Then write freely. Don't let anyone or anything interrupt you. Write for at least 15 minutes, letting your thoughts flow freely. Don't censor yourself. That is, don't criticize your ideas, spelling, or sentence structure. You are simply getting some ideas on paper—and some won't ever show up in your paragraph.

If you have trouble writing, imagine that you are writing to an audience that has never read this particular letter or e-mail. Imagine that your audience is asking you these questions:

- Who is this writer?
- What did this writer say in his or her letter (or e-mail)?
- What can I or anyone else learn from this letter (or e-mail)?
- When did the author write this letter (or e-mail)?
- How does the letter (or e-mail) make the audience feel?
- Why did he or she write this letter (or e-mail)?
- Why should I or anyone else be interested in this letter (or e-mail)?

Reread the letter or e-mail as you need to.

Drafting

Look at the one-sentence answer you wrote to the question about the letter. Will this make a good topic sentence? Do you need to improve it now?

A strong topic sentence will have the correct scope. This means it will not be too broad or too narrow. Consider these topic sentences.

Too broad:

Mother Jones wrote to President Roosevelt to express some concerns. The words *some concerns* are too general. The reader needs more specific information. How could you make this topic sentence more interesting and more informative?

Too narrow:

Mother Jones wrote a letter to President Roosevelt to tell him about the three children she brought to him. This topic sentence focuses

Notes

Computer Note

If you can type well, consider freewriting on the computer. You will be able to get many ideas on paper (or screen) fast.

Notes

on just a part of Mother Jones's actions and concerns. What is her bigger concern? How could you make this topic sentence slightly broader in scope—and more accurate?

Here's another topic sentence that is too narrow:

Jonah Peretti wrote his letter to be funny.

Peretti didn't write his letter just to be funny. What would be a better topic sentence for a paragraph about Peretti?

When you are writing your own paragraph, you might choose to draft your whole paragraph before deciding if your topic sentence is as strong as you want it to be. Sometimes writers have to go forward with their writing and then go back and change things like topic sentences when there appears to be a problem. If you can, improve your topic sentence now so that it is appropriately narrow and offers important details.

Look at your lists and freewriting, and underline or highlight the ideas you want to put in your draft. Do they need to be presented in a more organized fashion?

Write a draft of your paragraph. Make further improvements to your topic sentence if necessary. This draft will not be perfect, but it will have a topic sentence and body sentences that help explain and support the topic sentence.

Reread your draft, and ask yourself if your audience will believe your topic sentence. Do you need to add any information about who the writer is?

You may want to write more than one draft.

Skill Spotlight

Explaining Clearly (The Reason Was Because)

Sometimes writers mistakenly use the phrase "the reason is (or was) because." The word *because* is not necessary here, and writers should avoid adding unnecessary words. For example, the following topic sentence needs to be reworded:

> The reason Peretti wrote was because he wanted to express his concerns about cheap foreign labor.

This topic sentence can be reworded a number of ways:

- The reason Peretti wrote was he wanted to express his concerns about cheap foreign labor.
- The reason Peretti wrote was to express his concerns about cheap foreign labor.

Continued

- Peretti wrote to express his concerns about cheap foreign labor.
- Writing gave Peretti the opportunity to express concerns about child labor.

Which sentence do you like most?

Notes

Class Activity—Revising a Topic Sentence

Choosing from the four topic sentences in this Skill Spotlight, revise the sentence you like best, by including an explanation that the paragraph will focus on a *letter*. Also add information that tells (or suggests) *when* the letter was written and *to whom* it was written.

Revising

Share your draft. Show it to your classmates, your instructor, or a tutor and get some responses from this audience.

Does the topic sentence respond directly to the assignment?
- Does it focus on just Jones's letter or on just Peretti's e-mail?
- Does it explain why the writer wrote?

Is the topic sentence developed and supported?
- Will the audience understand who wrote the letter or e-mail and why?
- Does the paragraph mention what you or the audience might learn from the letter or e-mail? Should the paragraph mention this?

What advice did you get? Review "The Five Qualities of Effective Writing" (Chapter 7, pp. 59–61), review your Evaluation Chart (p. 453), and consider what your instructor said about your previous paragraphs. Revise, making your own choices about what you should change and improve.

Editing

First consider the types of errors you've been making in your writing assignments. Refer to your chart for tracking sentence errors (p.452). Look for errors that you tend to make.

Review your paragraph and look at the spelling and punctuation. Read your paragraph aloud, and correct any errors you find.

Look at the sentence structure in your paragraph. (See Chapter 16.)

- How many of your sentences are short? How many are long?
- Have you expressed complex ideas by joining independent clauses with coordinators or semicolons? Have you used any transition words with semicolons?

Computer Note

Many word processing programs include a grammar check feature. If you use that feature, you should keep in mind that the grammar check is wrong sometimes. Devoting time to your sentence exercises and learning grammar and punctuation rules are your best bets.

Notes

- Have you used any subordinators?

  Can you use prepositional or participial phrases to add information to your sentences? (See Chapter 17.)

- Check for fragments. (See Chapter 18.)
- Check sentences that begin with *-ing* words.
- Check sentences that have *because* or other subordinators in them.
- Can you use any of your vocabulary words in your paragraph?
- Does your paragraph follow the format requirements given by your instructor? Does your instructor expect you to turn in your brainstorm or draft with your final version?

Multiparagraph Assignment: Analyzing the Other Side

In this section of the chapter, you'll write one paragraph and analyze the actions of the people to whom the letter or e-mail was addressed, and then you'll write another paragraph in which you explain your reaction to the "other side." You'll follow all the steps of the writing process. Here is the assignment you are preparing for:

In a paragraph, explain to a college reader outside of your classroom

- *Why Theodore Roosevelt did not give Jones what she wanted*

  Or

- *Why Nike did not fill Peretti's original order*

Then, in another paragraph, explain your reaction to the other side. Do you support the position of Roosevelt or Nike? Why? Or do you disagree with the position? Why?

The Writing Process for These Paragraphs

Pre-Drafting

Review your work in this chapter. Look at the readings again, and review your notes, answers, responses, and journals. You may want to make more notes in the margins or on your work as you do this reviewing.

To get the ideas flowing, create a chart like the one that follows and list some ideas under each question. (If possible, do this work with a classmate.)

What was Theodore Roosevelt's (and B. F. Barnes's) response to Mother Jones?
What reasons might he have had for responding this way? List any ideas that seem reasonable.
Do you agree with this response? Why or why not?
What was Nike's response to Peretti's order?
What reasons might Nike have had for responding this way? List any ideas that seem reasonable.
Do you agree with this response? Why or why not?

Which response are you most interested in? Choose one person to focus on. Reread the assignment, and then write freely for 15 minutes. Remember:

Notes

- Don't let anyone or anything interrupt you.
- Let your thoughts flow freely.
- Don't criticize your ideas, spelling, or sentence structure.
- Reread the letter or e-mail as you need to.

Drafting

Experiment with topic sentences until you find two (one for each paragraph) that clearly and directly respond to the assignment.

Your first paragraph must accurately explain the position of Roosevelt or Nike. Study the letter or e-mail and any additional information that comes before and after the letter or e-mail. Using your own words, give an accurate, complete explanation of the position.

Notes

You may also include some guesses about why Roosevelt or Nike acted as they did, but these must be reasonable guesses based on the information that you have. For example, Roosevelt's response might lead you to guess that child labor wasn't a major concern of his. However, it would not be reasonable to guess that Roosevelt disliked children. You have no proof to back that up. Be careful of trying to cover too much in your paragraph. Choose your best point and develop it well.

Note: It is okay in your paragraph to admit you are making a guess. You can use words like *perhaps* and *maybe* to let your reader know that you are making a guess.

In your second paragraph, explain your own reaction. As you draft this paragraph, refer to the notes on your chart. It is okay to both agree and disagree. Make sure that your topic sentence explains your reaction accurately.

Revising

Share your draft. Show it to your classmates, your instructor, or a tutor and get some response from this audience.

For the first paragraph:

- Does the topic sentence accurately explain what comes in the body of the paragraph?
- Is the body of the paragraph well developed?
- Would quotes help support the topic sentence?
- If the body has quotes in it, are they explained?
- If the writer has made some guesses, do they seem reasonable?
- Has the writer used words like *perhaps* or *maybe* to show that he or she is making some guesses?

For the second paragraph:

- Does the topic sentence clearly explain what comes in the body of the paragraph?
- Is the body well developed?
- Do any points need further explanation?
- Do the points seem reasonable?

What advice did you get? Review "The Five Qualities of Effective Writing" (Chapter 7, pp. 59–61) and your Evaluation Chart (p. 453) and consider what your instructor said about previous paragraphs. Revise your draft.

Editing

First consider the types of errors you've been making in your writing assignments. Refer to your chart for tracking sentence errors (p. 452). Look for errors that you tend to make.

Review your paragraph and look at the spelling and punctuation. Read your paragraph aloud, and correct any errors you find.

Look at the sentence structure in your paragraph. (See Chapter 16.)

- How many of your sentences are short? How many are long?
- Have you expressed complex ideas by joining independent clauses with coordinators or semicolons? Have you used any transition words with semicolons?
- Have you used any subordinators?
- Can you use prepositional or participial phrases to add information to your sentences? (See Chapter 17.)
- Check for fragments. (See Chapter 18.)
- Check sentences that begin with *–ing* words.
- Check sentences that have *because* or other subordinators in them.
- Can you use any of your vocabulary words in your paragraph?
- Does your paragraph follow the format requirements given by your instructor? Does your instructor expect you to turn in your brainstorm or draft with your final version?

Multiparagraph Assignment: Write a Public Letter

In this section, you will use your reading, writing, and critical thinking skills as you write a two-paragraph business letter.

The Writing Process for This Letter

Here is the assignment you are preparing for:

In a business letter, explain a problem you are having and express your idea for fixing the problem.

Write to one of these people:

Senator Michael Barns

Mr. Frederick Silva, *Manager of the Skyway Apartments*

Ms. Susan Donovan, *Supervisor at Belltone Phone Company*

Mrs. Vivica Seals, *Principal of Old Oak Elementary School*

 Get Involved!

Find out who your government representatives are. Go to the library or the Internet and find the names and addresses for any of the following people: city council members, assembly members, senators, or representatives. Share this information with your classmates. Someone may want to write to a government representative.

Notes

Or you can substitute real names.

(If you have a current business problem, see your instructor and maybe you can write a letter addressing that problem. Or perhaps you'd like to write to one of your government representatives or the editor of your local newspaper and express your thoughts on a current issue.)

You will need to decide for yourself what the problem is. Then you will need to figure out what solution you are aiming for. Your letter should explain the problem in one paragraph and the solution in another paragraph.

Pre-Drafting

While this chapter has helped you engage in the topic of letters, it has not focused on problems you might have with your landlord, phone company, or child's school. Discuss with your classmates some problems a person might have with each of these people or organizations. Create a list of problems (create a chart like the one that follows). Be creative and make notes.

Landlord	Phone Company	School	Other

Review the section of the chapter that deals with business letters—their form, style, and audience (pp. 78–79). What will your letter look and sound like? Specifically, how will your business letter be different from a personal letter? What kind of language and form will help you say and get what you want?

Here is your assignment again:

In a business letter, explain a problem you are having and express your idea for fixing the problem.

Write to one of these people:

Senator Michael Barnes

Mr. Frederick Silva, Manager of the Skyway Apartments

Ms. Susan Donovan, Supervisor at Belltone Phone Company

Mrs. Vivica Seals, Principal of Old Oak Elementary School

Or you can substitute real names.

(If you have a current business problem, see your instructor and maybe you can write a letter addressing that problem. Or perhaps you'd

like to write to one of your government representatives or the editor of your local newspaper and express your thoughts on a current issue.)

You will need to decide for yourself what the problem is. Then you will need to figure out what solution you are aiming for. Your letter should explain the problem in one paragraph and the solution in another paragraph.

Underline what you think are the key words in this assignment. Explain in your own words to a classmate, friend, or tutor what you must cover in your business letter. What specific information should you include? What will you leave out?

Choose the person you want to write to. Freewrite for about 10 minutes on what the problem might be. Freewriting, remember, is when you write one long paragraph—or maybe a series of paragraphs—that focuses on your assignment, but you write freely. This means you don't stop to think about grammar, spelling, or even how good each idea is. The goal is simply to get ideas on paper. Let your thoughts flow freely.

Write about different problems. When you run out of ideas, go back to each problem and write possible details about the problem. For example, if one of your problems is that you want screens on your windows, list details about that problem: *mosquitos are coming in. My kids are covered with red polka dots because of all the bites. A squirrel jumped from the tree next door onto my bed while I was sleeping* . . . and so on.

Then freewrite for about 10 minutes on what the solution might be. You may want to propose more than one solution, so explore the possibilities. For example, maybe you want the manager to install new screens. Or maybe you could install them yourself and charge the manager for your time and materials. Or . . . ?

Drafting

You are writing two paragraphs for this letter. The first paragraph should begin with a topic sentence that clearly states what the problem is.

Example of a topic sentence that does *not* yet state the problem: I am writing to you about my phone bill.

Example of a stronger topic sentence that states the problem clearly: I am writing to you because I have been overcharged for my phone service for the last three months.

The body of this first paragraph should give details of the problem.

The second paragraph should begin with a topic sentence that clearly states your solution (or solutions) to the problem. Then the body of the

Notes

paragraph will explain your solution in detail. You can even figure out the exact costs or time involved. Perhaps more than one person needs to be involved in the solution. Perhaps the solution has a number of steps.

Write a draft of the entire letter, using the correct business letter format and offering two solid paragraphs. Be prepared to share your paragraph and change and improve it.

Revising

Share your draft. Show it to your classmates, your instructor, or a tutor and get some responses from this audience.

- Is the draft in business letter form?
- Are there two paragraphs, one focusing on the problem and the other focusing on the solution?
- Do they each begin with a clear, focused topic sentence?
- Does each paragraph include enough detail and information? Underline the details that help add interest to the letter.
- Is the vocabulary appropriate for a business letter? Underline any vocabulary that seems particularly effective.

What advice did you get? Review "The Five Qualities of Effective Writing" (Chapter 7, pp. 59–61) and your Evaluation Chart (p. 453) and consider what your instructor said about previous paragraphs. Revise your draft.

Student Sample

A Business Letter

Read the following business letter.

```
                                    Elizabeth Villars
                                    1120 Arch Way
                                    Elk Pine, CA 95758

Ms. Donovan
Belltone Phone Company
7 Pond Lane
Elk Pine, CA 95758

Dear Ms. Donovan,

    I am writing to you about a mistake in my past two
phone bills. Two months ago I received a two hundred
```
Continued

and fifty dollar phone bill with long distance charges that were not mine. I was concerned about my bill so I called your 24-hour customer service number, which by the way kept me on hold for 20 minutes. When I finally got put through to someone, a young lady named Kristy helped me. I told her my problem, and when we were finished discussing it, she told me that it was a company error, and that she was sorry for any trouble it might have caused. She also told me that she was going to send me a $50.00 check for being such an understanding customer with your company. I was very pleased with her service. Then the following month I received a bill of three hundred dollars which included the bill of two hundred-fifty from the previous month, late charges, and my present phone bill.

All I ask is for this problem to be fixed. You can look into my records, and you will see that I have been a good customer to your company. I also ask for this to be fixed as soon as possible, or I will no longer be needing your long distance service. I expect to hear from someone soon.

Your Customer,

Elizabeth Villars   ■

Apply the revision questions to this letter. (Make notes or do this orally with classmates.)

- Is the letter in business letter form?
- Are there two paragraphs, one focusing on the problem and the other focusing on the solution?
- Do they each begin with a clear, focused topic sentence?
- Does each paragraph include enough detail and information? Underline the details that help add interest to the letter.
- Is the vocabulary appropriate for a business letter? Underline any vocabulary that seems particularly effective.

What can you learn from Villars's letter?

Editing

First consider the types of errors you've been making in your writing assignments. Refer to your chart for tracking sentence errors (p. 452). Look for errors that you tend to make.

Notes

- Review your paragraph, and look at the spelling and punctuation.
- Read your paragraph aloud and correct any errors you find.
- Look at the sentence structure in your paragraph (See Chapter 16.)
- How many of your sentences are short? How many are long?
- Have you expressed complex ideas by joining independent clauses with coordinators or semicolons? Have you used any or transition words with semicolons?
- Have you used any subordinators?
- Can you use prepositional or participial phrases to add information to your sentences? (See Chapter 17.)
- Check for fragments. (See Chapter 18.)
- Check sentences that begin with –*ing* words.
- Check sentences that have *because* or other subordinators in them.
- Can you use any of your vocabulary words in your paragraph?
- Does your paragraph follow the format requirements given by your instructor? Does your instructor expect you to turn in your brainstorm or draft with your final version?

Additional Readings

(See Section VIII, "The Reader.")

"Out of Silence," by Anne LeClaire. In this letter, Anne LeClaire writes to her mother to express her complex feelings about her mother and communication in their family.

Now You Know (e-mails from an AOL website). These e-mails were sent to an AOL website after the writers saw the movie *Saving Private Ryan*. (These e-mails were published as a book called *Now You Know*. The introduction to that book is also included.)

Sentence Basics

The chapters listed here are designed specifically to coordinate with the themes and the "Sentence Style" sections in Chapter 8.

Chapter 16: Clauses
Chapter 17: Phrases
Chapter 18: Understanding, Correcting, and Avoiding Fragments

Autobiographies

> 📝 **Journal Assignment**
>
> **Engaging in the Themes of Chapter 9**
>
> This chapter focuses on autobiographies and authors telling their own stories. The sculpture on this page is a "self-portrait." What story do you think the artist is telling us? Which of the themes might connect to this sculpture?

A popular *genre*—or type—of writing is the autobiography. With the autobiography, the writer can tell his or her own life story—recalling, highlighting, and analyzing events and people who are important to him or her. (*Note:* The prefix *auto* means "self," *bio* means "life," and *graph* means "to write." An "autobiography" is the written story of the writer's own life.)

A writer of an autobiography, like the writer of a novel, must rely on **narration**—the act of telling a story. Sometimes academic paragraphs and essays also call for narration. This personal information can bring great interest to academic writing and help readers understand ideas. This chapter introduces you to autobiographies and to using narration as a writing tool in your formal writing assignments in college.

This chapter discusses these themes:

- ✦ Childhood memories
- ✦ Lessons learned
- ✦ Skills discovered

Autobiographies

It probably won't surprise you that autobiographies date back to ancient times. People love to tell their own stories, and we love to get inside the minds and lives of others.

Historians point to the inscriptions on Egyptian tombs as signs of biography. The people who made the inscriptions were telling the life story of the person entombed there. The inscriptions serve as a record of great events and actions. Today, you can go to a bookstore and find a large biography and autobiography section.

Are we just nosy? Or is there greater value in autobiographies?

Consider the following quotation from *The Autobiography of Malcolm X*:

> I learned early that crying out in protest could accomplish things. My older brothers and sister had started to school when, sometimes, they would come in and ask for a buttered biscuit or something and my mother, impatiently, would tell them no. But I would cry out and make a fuss until I got what I wanted. I remember well how my mother asked me why I couldn't be a nice boy like Wilfred; but I would think to myself that Wilfred, for being so nice and quiet, often stayed hungry. So early in life, I had learned that if you want something, you had better make some noise.

Here Malcolm X is sharing a lesson he learned in his childhood. You might also say that he is offering his own advice to the reader: Speak up for what you want!

An autobiography can also help us understand how people have overcome great obstacles and succeeded. Such an autobiography can give a reader inspiration and guidance.

In addition, autobiographies can help us understand historical events—how and why people acted as they did—and perhaps we can learn lessons from these historical events. Can you think of other ways that autobiographies can be valuable? (Use the margin to record your ideas.)

Get Involved!

Read *The Autobiography of Malcolm X*. It's a fascinating story about a man who transforms his anger into a powerful tool for human rights.

As you read pages 102–105, highlight or underline boldface terms, italicized terms, and main points. (Pay special attention to topic sentences.) Also write your own questions and comments in the margins.

Narrating

Novelists narrate. They tell stories that didn't actually happen. A person who writes an autobiography is also telling a story—although it is a true story (we assume).

Narration can also be a tool for the college writer. You may be asked to write a fictional story in college and use your narration skills, but it is even more likely that an instructor will ask for your opinion on something and say that you may use personal experience to explain your point.

This may mean that you simply offer a short example from your life. Or you may choose to tell a story (long or short) to explain your idea or opinion. This is when you will be narrating. This section gives you some pointers on how to use narration when writing in college.

Copyright © 2003 by Addison Wesley Longman, Inc.

Notes

Make a Point

When you want to *develop* (support or prove) an idea in a piece of academic writing, you can use examples, statistics, comparisons, quotes, and narration. The greatest challenge when narrating is to not get so wrapped up in your story that you forget to make your point.

Most college instructors will want you to clearly state your main point. Consequently, the assignments in this text ask you to follow the writing process—explore ideas, find a main point, create a topic sentence (a main point), and then begin your narration.

Present Interesting Details

Narration is fun to write and to read because people love stories. (Most forms of entertainment—books, television shows, songs—are forms of storytelling.) We want to hear what other people have done, to see the similarities and differences between us.

The key to making a narrative interesting is offering interesting details. Consider these sentences:

> I am young, and I want to go with my dad to the fair. The car is small, so not everyone can go. I know I look pretty and ask to go.

Now consider the following excerpt from a paragraph in Alice Walker's autobiographical essay, "Beauty: When the Other Dancer Is the Self." (The full essay appears later in this chapter.)

> I am two and a half years old. I want to go everywhere my daddy goes. I am excited at the prospect of riding in a car. Someone has told me fairs are fun. That there is room in the car for only three of us doesn't faze me at all. Whirling happily in my starchy frock, showing off my biscuit-polished patent-leather shoes and lavender socks, tossing my head in a way that makes my ribbons bounce, I stand, hands on hips, before my father. "Take me, Daddy," I say with assurance; "I'm the prettiest!"

The second paragraph is clearly more interesting and more fun to read. The writer captures our attention with the details. Instead of saying "young," Walker says "two and a half years old." Being specific is important. Readers need help forming pictures in their minds. "Two and a half years old" makes the picture much clearer than simply "young."

Instead of saying "I know I look pretty," Walker says, "Whirling happily in my starchy frock, showing off my biscuit-polished patent-leather shoes and lavender socks, tossing my head in a way that makes my ribbons bounce. . . ." Walker has given us a moving picture of herself—"whirling happily"—and the details of her clothing help us to understand precisely what she looks like. We also get the sense that the little girl is aware, in a childishly vain way, of all the details of her own appearance.

Notice too that Walker uses dialog when it is useful: "'Take me, Daddy,' I say with assurance; 'I'm the prettiest!'" This little bit of dialog tells us a lot about Walker's self-confidence at this young age.

Consider this selection, also from Walker's autobiographical essay:

> I am eight years old and a tomboy. I have a cowboy hat, cowboy boots, checkered shirt and pants, all red. My playmates are my brothers, two and four years older than I. Their colors are black and green, the only difference in the way we are dressed. On Saturday nights we all go to the picture show, even my mother; Westerns are her favorite kind of movie. Back home, "on the ranch," we pretend, we are Tom Mix, Hopalong Cassidy; Lash LaRue (we've even named one of our dogs Lash LaRue); we chase each other for hours rustling cattle, being outlaws, delivering damsels from distress. Then my parents decide to buy my brothers guns. . . .

Underline or highlight the details in the first four sentences that help paint a clear picture for the reader. Notice how Walker doesn't just mention movies but actually names the movie stars she and her family like.

Shape Your Information

When using narration in your college assignments, you need to start with a main point—that your narration will explain—and you need to shape the information you present. You do not want to simply list all events and details. The reader might not know what point you are making with these events and details.

You can shape information by carefully choosing what details to use, what to leave out, and by commenting on your own information. Look again at Walker's paragraph about playing cowboys and Indians, and pay special attention to the second half.

I am eight years old and a tomboy. I have a cowboy hat, cowboy boots, checkered shirt and pants, all red. My playmates are my brothers, two and four years older than I. Their colors are black and green, the only difference in the way we are dressed. On Saturday nights we all go to the picture show, even my mother; Westerns are her favorite kind of movie. Back home, "on the ranch," we pretend, we are Tom Mix, Hopalong Cassidy; Lash LaRue (we've even named one of our dogs Lash LaRue); we chase each other for hours rustling cattle, being outlaws, delivering damsels from distress. Then my parents decide to buy my brothers guns. These are not "real" guns. They shoot "BBs," copper pellets my brothers say will kill birds. Because I am a girl, I do not get a gun. Instantly I'm relegated to the position of Indian. Now there appears a great distance between us. They shoot and shoot at everything with their new guns. I try to keep up with my bow and arrows.

Notice how Walker pauses in her story to explain why she doesn't get a gun. Then she explains the effect of not getting a gun: "I'm relegated to the position of Indian. Now there appears a great distance between us." Then she returns to her narrative, continuing to explain how their playtime has changed. Can you tell how she feels about not getting a gun? What words hint at how she feels? What point is she making here? (Use the margin to record your ideas.)

In choosing what to describe in detail and in choosing specific adjectives, writers shape their story and tell us how they feel.

Points to Remember about Narration

- *Follow the writing process.* Explore the assignment, brainstorm for ideas, and decide what your main point will be. Put that main idea in your topic sentence.
- *Offer your reader interesting details.* You can describe people (age, clothing, expressions, mannerisms, appearance) and places (appearance, smell, mood). Use your five senses—taste, touch, sight, hearing, smell—when looking for details.
- *Shape your information.* Think carefully about which details belong and which don't. Comment on your own information by adding explanation or using particular adjectives or adverbs.

Reading Assignment: An Autobiographical Essay

In this section, you will read an autobiographical essay written by the African American writer Alice Walker, author of many stories and novels including *The Color Purple*. The essay included here focuses on her

Notes

life as an African American woman growing up in the United States through the 1950s and 1980s.

As you read this selection, think about these themes: childhood memories and lessons learned. Why are these memories important to the writer? How do these moments affect the rest of her life? What lessons did she learn?

Reading Assignment— *"Beauty: When the Other Dancer Is the Self"*

Preview Read the title, the author's name, and the first seven paragraphs of this autobiographical essay.

Anticipate Walker is telling us about her life in this essay. What issues or ideas does she seem to be emphasizing in the title and the first seven paragraphs? What do you think she might say in the rest of her autobiographical essay?

_____

_____

_____

_____

Read Read the essay quickly. Mark unknown words, but don't look up any meanings in the dictionary yet.

Beauty: When the Other Dancer Is the Self

By Alice Walker

1   It is a bright summer day in 1947. My father, a fat, funny man with beautiful eyes and a subversive wit, is trying to decide which of his eight children he will take with him to the county fair. My mother, of course, will not go. She is knocked out from getting most of us ready: I hold my neck stiff against the pressure of her knuckles as she hastily completes the braiding and then beribboning of my hair.

2   My father is the driver for the rich old white lady up the road. Her name is Miss Mey. She owns all the land for miles around, as well as the house in which we live. All I remember about her is that she once

offered to pay my mother thirty-five cents for cleaning her house, raking up piles of her magnolia leaves, and washing her family's clothes, and that my mother—she of no money, eight children, and a chronic earache—refused it. But I do not think of this in 1947. I am two and a half years old. I want to go everywhere my daddy goes. I am excited at the prospect of riding in a car. Someone has told me fairs are fun. That there is room in the car for only three of us doesn't faze me at all. Whirling happily in my starchy frock, showing off my biscuit-polished patent-leather shoes and lavender socks, tossing my head in a way that makes my ribbons bounce, I stand, hands on hips, before my father. "Take me, Daddy," I say with assurance; "I'm the prettiest!"

3   Later, it does not surprise me to find myself in Miss Mey's shiny black car, sharing the back seat with the other lucky ones. Does not surprise me that I thoroughly enjoy the fair. At home that night I tell the unlucky ones all I can remember about the merry-go-round, the man who eats live chickens, and the teddy bears, until they say: that's enough, baby Alice. Shut up now, and go to sleep.

4   It is Easter Sunday, 1950. I am dressed in a green, flocked, scalloped-hem dress (handmade by my adoring sister, Ruth) that has its own smooth satin petticoat and tiny hot-pink roses tucked into each scallop. My shoes, new T-strap patent leather, again highly biscuit-polished. I am six years old and have learned one of the longest Easter speeches to be heard that day, totally unlike the speech I said when I was two: "Easter lilies/pure and white/blossom in/the morning light." When I rise to give my speech I do so on a great wave of love and pride and expectation. People in the church stop rustling their new crinolines. They seem to hold their breath. I can tell they admire my dress, but it is my spirit, bordering on sassiness (womanishness), they secretly applaud.

5   "That girl's a little *mess*," they whisper to each other, pleased.

6   Naturally I say my speech without stammer or pause, unlike those who stutter, stammer, or, worst *of* all, forget. This is before the word "beautiful" exists in people's vocabulary, but "Oh, isn't she the *cutest* thing"' frequently floats my way. "And got so much sense! " they gratefully add . . . for which thoughtful addition I thank them to this day.

7   *It was great fun being cute. But then, one day, it ended.*

8   I am eight years old and a tomboy. I have a cowboy hat, cowboy boots, checkered shirt and pants, all red. My playmates are my brothers, two and four years older than I. Their colors are black and green, the only difference in the way we are dressed. On Saturday nights we all go

Notes

to the picture show, even my mother; Westerns are her favorite kind of movie. Back home, "on the ranch," we pretend, we are Tom Mix, Hopalong Cassidy; Lash LaRue (we've even named one of our dogs Lash LaRue); we chase each other for hours rustling cattle, being outlaws, delivering damsels from distress. Then my parents decide to buy my brothers guns. These are not "real" guns. They shoot "BBs," copper pellets my brothers say will kill birds. Because I am a girl, I do not get a gun. Instantly I'm relegated to the position of Indian. Now there appears a great distance between us. They shoot and shoot at everything with their new guns. I try to keep up with my bow and arrows.

9   One day while I am standing on top of our makeshift "garage"—pieces of tin nailed across some poles—holding my bow and arrow and looking out toward the fields, I feel an incredible blow in my right eye. I look down just in time to see my brother lower his gun.

10   Both brothers rush to my side. My eye stings, and I cover it with my hand. "If you tell," they say, "we will get a whipping. You don't want that to happen, do you?" I do not. "Here is a piece of wire," says the older brother, picking it up from tile roof; "say you stepped on one end of it and the other flew up and hit you." The pain is beginning to start. "Yes," I say. "Yes, I will say that is what happened." If I do not say this is what happened, I know my brothers will find ways to make me wish I had. But now I will say anything that gets me to my mother.

11   Confronted by our parents we stick to the lie agreed upon. They place me on a bench on the porch and I close my left eye while they examine the right. There is a tree growing from underneath the porch that climbs past the railing to the roof. It is the last thing my right eye sees. I watch as its trunk, its branches, and then its leaves are blotted out by the rising blood.

12   I am in shock. First there is intense fever, which my father tries to break using lily leaves bound around my head. Then there are chills: my mother tries to get me to eat soup. Eventually, I do not know how, my parents learn what has happened. A week after the "accident" they take me to see a doctor. "Why did you wait so long to come?" he asks, looking into my eye and shaking his head. "Eyes are sympathetic," he says. "If one is blind, the other will likely become blind too."

Why does Walker put quotation marks around "accident"?

13   This comment of the doctor's terrifies me. But it is really how I look that bothers me most. Where the BB pellet struck there is a glob of whitish scar tissue, a hideous cataract, on my eye. Now when I stare at people—a favorite pastime, up to now—they will stare back. Not at the "cute" little girl, but at her scar. For six years I do not stare at anyone, because I do not raise my head.

14 Years later, in the throes of a mid-life crisis, I ask my mother and sister whether I changed after the "accident." "No," they say, puzzled. "What do you mean?"

15 *What do I mean?*

16 I am eight, and, for the first time, doing poorly in school, where I have been something of a whiz since I was four. We have just moved to the place where the "accident" occurred. We do not know any of the people around us because this is a different county. The only time I see the friends I knew is when we go back to our old church. The new school is the former state penitentiary. It is a large stone building, cold and drafty; crammed to overflowing with boisterous, ill-disciplined children. On the third floor there is a huge circular imprint of some partition that has been torn out.

In paragraphs 16–19, what point is Walker making while narrating?

17 "What used to be here?" I ask a sullen girl next to me on our way past it to lunch.

18 "The electric chair," says she.

19 At night I have nightmares about the electric chair, and about all the people reputedly "fried" in it. I am afraid of the school, where all the students seem to be budding criminals.

20 "What's the matter with your eye" they ask, critically.

21 When I don't answer (I cannot decide whether it was an "accident" or not), they shove me, insist on a fight.

22 My brother, the one who created the story about the wire, comes to my rescue. But then brags so much about "protecting" me, I become sick.

Why does she become sick?

23 After months of torture at the school, my parents decide to send me back to our old community, to my old school. I live with my grandparents and the teacher they board. But there is no room for Phoebe, my cat. By the time my grandparents decide there is room, and I ask for my cat, she cannot be found. Miss Yarborough, the boarding teacher, takes me under her wing, and begins to teach me to play the piano. But soon she marries an African—"prince," she says—and is whisked away to his continent.

24 At my old school there is at least one teacher who loves me. She is the teacher who "knew me before I was born" and bought my first baby clothes. It is she who makes life bearable. It is her presence that finally helps me turn on the one child at the school who continually calls me "one-eyed bitch." One day I simply grab him by his coat and beat him until I am satisfied. It is my teacher who tells me my mother is ill.

25 My mother is lying in bed in the middle of the day, something I have never seen. She is in too much pain to speak. She has an abscess in her ear. I stand looking down on her, knowing that if she dies I cannot live.

Notes

Notes

She is being treated with warm oils and hot bricks held against her cheek. Finally a doctor comes. But I must go back to my grandparent's house. The weeks pass but I am hardly aware of it. All I know is that my mother might die, my father is not so jolly, my brothers still have their guns, and I am the one sent away from home.

26   "You did not change," they say.

27   *Did I imagine the anguish of never looking up?*

28   I am twelve. When relatives come to visit I hide in my room. My cousin Brenda, just my age, whose father works in the post office and whose mother is a nurse, comes to find me. "Hello," she says. And then she asks, looking at my recent school picture, which I did not want taken, and on which the "glob," as I think of it, is clearly visible, "You still can't see out of that eye?"

29   "No," I say, and flop back on the bed over my book.

30   That night, as I do almost every night, I abuse my eye. I rant and rave at it, in front of the mirror. I plead with it to clear up before morning. I tell it I hate and despise it. I do not pray for sight. I pray for beauty.

31   "You did not change," they say.

32   I am fourteen and baby-sitting for my brother Bill, who lives in Boston. He is my favorite brother and there is a strong bond between us. Understanding my feelings of shame and ugliness he and his wife take me to a local hospital, where the "glob" is removed by a doctor named O. Henry. There is still a small bluish crater where the scar tissue was, but the ugly white stuff is gone. Almost immediately I become a different person from the girl who does not raise her head. Or so I think. Now that I've raised my head I win the boyfriend of my dreams. Now that I've raised my head I have plenty of friends. Now that I've raised my head classwork comes from my lips as faultlessly as Easter speeches did, and I leave high school as valedictorian, most popular student, and *queen,* hardly believing my luck. Ironically, the girl who was voted most beautiful in our class (and was) was later shot twice through the chest by a male companion, using a "real" gun, while she was pregnant. But that's another story in itself. Or is it?

33   "You did not change," they say.

Why does Walker repeat this sentence "You did not change"? (See paragraphs 26 and 31 too.)

34   It is now thirty years since the "accident." A beautiful journalist comes to visit and to interview me. She is going to write a cover story for her magazine that focuses on my latest book. "Decide how you want to look on the cover," she says. "Glamorous, or whatever."

35   Never mind "glamorous," it is the "whatever" that I hear. Suddenly all I can think of is whether I will get enough sleep the night before the photography session: if I don't, my eye will be tired and wander, as blind eyes will.

36   At night in bed with my lover I think up reasons why I should not appear on the cover of a magazine. "My meanest critics will say I've sold out," I say. "My family will now realize I write scandalous books."

37   "But what's the real reason you don't want to do this?" he asks.

38   "Because in all probability," I say in a rush, "my eye won't be straight."

39   "It will be straight enough," he says. Then, "Besides, I thought you'd made your peace with that."

40   And I suddenly remember that I have.

41   *I remember:*

42   I am talking to my brother Jimmy, asking if he remembers anything unusual about the day I was shot. He does not know I consider that day the last time my father, with his sweet home remedy of cool lily leaves, chose me, and that I suffered and raged inside because of this. "Well," he says, "all I remember is standing by the side of the highway with Daddy, trying to flag down a car. A white man stopped, but when Daddy said he needed somebody to take his little girl to the doctor, he drove off."

43   *I remember:*

44   I am in the desert for the first time. I fall totally in love with it. I am so overwhelmed by its beauty, I confront for the first time, consciously the meaning of the doctor's words years ago: "Eyes are sympathetic. If one is blind, the other will likely become blind too." I realize I have dashed about the world madly, looking at this, looking at that, storing up images against the fading of the light. *But I might have missed seeing the desert!* The shock of that possibility—and gratitude for over twenty-five years of sight—sends me literally to my knees. Poem after poem comes—which is perhaps how poets pray.

On Sight

I am so thankful I have seen
The Desert
And the creatures in the desert
And the desert itself.

The desert has its own moon
Which I have seen
With my own eye.

There is no flag on it.

Trees of the desert have arms
All of which are always up
That is because the moon is up
The sun is up

Notes

Also the sky
The stars
Clouds
None with flags.

If there *were* flags, I doubt
the trees would point.
Would you?

45   *But mostly I remember this:*

46   I am twenty-seven, and my baby daughter is almost three. Since her birth I have worried about her discovery that her mother's eyes are different from other people's. Will she be embarrassed? I think. What will she say? Every day she watches a television program called "Big Blue Marble." It begins with a picture of the earth as it appears from the moon. It is bluish, a little battered-looking, but full of light, with whitish clouds swirling around it. Every time I see it I weep with love, as if it is a picture of Grandma's house. One day when I am putting Rebecca down for her nap, she suddenly focuses on my eye. Something inside me cringes, gets ready to try to protect myself. All children are cruel about physical differences, I know from experience, and that they don't always mean to be is another matter. I assume Rebecca will be the same.

47   But no-o-o-o. She studies my face intently as we stand, her inside and me outside her crib. She even holds my face maternally between her dimpled little hands. Then, looking every bit as serious and lawyer-like as her father, she says, as if it may just possibly have slipped my attention: "Mommy, there's a *world* in your eye." (As in, "Don't be alarmed, or do anything crazy.") And then, gently, but with great interest: "Mommy, where did you *get* that world in your eye?"

48   For the most part, the pain left then. (So what, if my brothers grew up to buy even more powerful pellet guns for their sons and to carry real guns themselves. So what, if a young "Morehouse man" once nearly fell off the steps of Trevor Arnett Library because he thought my eyes were blue.) Crying and laughing I ran to the bathroom; while Rebecca mumbled and sang herself off to sleep. Yes indeed, I realized, looking into the mirror. There was a world in my eye. And I saw that it was possible to love it: that in fact, for all it had taught me of shame and anger and inner vision, I *did* love it. Even to see it drifting out of orbit in boredom, or rolling up out of fatigue, not to mention floating back at attention in excitement (bearing witness, a friend has called it), deeply suitable to my personality, and even characteristic of me.

49   That night I dream I'm dancing to Stevie Wonder's song "Always" (the name of the song is really "As," but I hear it as "Always"). As I

dance, whirling and joyous, happier than I've ever been in my life, another bright-faced dancer joins me. We dance and kiss each other and hold each other through the night. The other dancer has obviously come through all right, as I have done. She is beautiful, whole and free. And she is also me.

Reread Reread the essay. As you read, use context clues to figure out the meanings of unknown words. Look up the meanings of any words that remain unclear. Mark important and interesting points. In addition to responding to the questions already in the margins, record your own questions about and responses to the reading in the margins. Also, mark the places where the issue of *guns* comes up.

Vocabulary cards: Make definition cards and sentence cards for the words listed here.

- *chronic*, paragraph 2
- *relegated*, paragraph 8
- *confronted*, paragraph 11
- *boisterous*, paragraph 16

Think Critically In preparation for class discussion, answer these questions on a separate piece of paper:

1. List some adjectives that would describe Alice Walker's personality before the accident. Then list adjectives that would describe her personality when her eye had the ugly scar tissue on it.
2. Walker writes in the present tense. Why is that? What is the effect of using the present tense? (Rewrite a sentence or two and put them in the past tense. How is the essay different in the past tense?)
3. How many times are guns mentioned in the essay? How does Walker feel about guns?
4. Beauty is important to Walker as a child. Why? What does beauty give her?
5. How did Walker's injury to her eye improve her life? Can you point to a place in the text where she acknowledges what she gained from being hurt?
6. What lessons did Walker learn as a child?
7. How important is beauty in our society? Give examples to support your statement.

Notes

8. People find beauty in many different things. When is beauty important to you? (For example, does your house, car, garden, city, or
spouse have to be beautiful?)

Summarize Mark the important events and people in the essay. In your
own words, explain what the most important events are in the essay,
and what messages Walker is sending with her narrative autobiographical essay. What does she want her readers to learn?

Sentence Style

Study these sentences:

> The new school is the former state penitentiary. It is a large stone building,
> cold and drafty; crammed to overflowing with boisterous, ill-disciplined chil-
> dren. (paragraph 16)

In the second sentence, Walker uses some of her five senses to help her
describe the school. Which of her five senses does she use? (Sight,
touch, smell, taste, hearing?) Explain.

Your Turn Write a sentence describing a school you once attended. Using your five senses, offer your reader adjectives that will paint a picture. (See Chapter 22 for more about adjectives.)

Express Yourself

When Does a Person Care Too Much about Beauty?

Often when people are creating beauty in their world, they are expressing their artistic interests and skills. (A beautifully set table can be one
person's artistic expression. Building a bookcase can be another person's
artistic expression.) However, you might argue that some people are too
attached to the beauty of things. Explain a situation when a person may
be too interested in beauty.
    Use the writing process: pre-drafting, drafting, revising, editing.

Journal Assignment

Write a Piece of Your Autobiography

Imagine that you are writing a section of your autobiography. This sec-
tion will focus on your education. What have been the best times?
What have been the worst? When did learning excite you? When has it
Continued

bored you? (Be specific.) Do certain teachers stick out in your mind? Did you learn any lessons about life that you would want to pass on to your readers?

Paragraph Assignment: An Autobiographical Paragraph, Options 1 and 2

In her autobiography, Walker used narration to tell the story of her life. She also shared some lessons about life that she learned as she grew up. In this section, you will have the opportunity to express yourself through narration.

You have two options. Prepare for *one* of these assignments:

Option #1: In a paragraph, tell your instructor and classmates a story about a lesson you learned as a child.

Option #2: In a paragraph, tell your instructor and classmates a story about how you discovered what you are good at or not good at.

The Writing Process for This Paragraph

Pre-Drafting

Review Walker's essay, your notes, and critical thinking questions. Then, with your classmates, discuss these questions:

- What lessons did Walker write about?
- Who were the people involved in these lessons?
- Do you have any similar experiences that you might want to write about?

Before choosing Option 1 or 2, explore ideas. Individually, write responses to the following questions (on another sheet of paper):

- When did you first learn about the value of honesty? Who was involved in this lesson?
- When did you learn about perseverance? What difficult task did you face? Why was it difficult? Who was involved?
- When did you learn about self-defense? Why did you need self-defense? Who was involved?
- When did you learn about studying? What did you learn? Who was involved?

- When did you learn about losing? What did you lose? Who was involved?
- When did you learn about winning? What did you win? What did you learn? Who was involved?
- What other lessons have you learned? Who were the people involved in those lessons?

Write in response to these questions that connect to the second option (on a separate piece of paper):

- What sport are you good at? How old were you when you began playing this sport? What has been difficult about learning to play this sport well? Who has helped you?
- What type of artistic activity are you good at—painting, writing, singing, drawing, woodworking, cooking, or something else? When did you discover your strength? Who was involved? What obstacles have you faced in becoming good at this activity?
- What type of mental activity are you good at—playing chess, programming computers, or perhaps figuring out mathematical equations? When did you discover your strength? Who was involved? What obstacles have you faced in becoming good at this activity?
- What other activities are you good at—caring for children, caring for animals, selling products, teaching, or something else? When did you discover your strength? Who was involved? What obstacles have you faced in becoming good at this activity?
- What are you not good at? Think about some of the same activities mentioned earlier (sports, arts, activities). When did you discover this? Who was involved? How did this discovery make you feel?

Share your thoughts and experiences with your classmates. A comment from one of your classmates might remind you of an interesting memory or lesson of your own. Take notes as you share ideas.

Here is your writing assignment again:

Option #1: In a paragraph, tell your instructor and classmates a story about a lesson you learned as a child.

Option #2: In a paragraph, tell your instructor and classmates a story about how you discovered what you are good at or not good at.

In each option, underline the important terms. Change each option into a question.

Think about what you learned about using narration in academic writing (see pages 102–105). What will you need to do in your paragraph?

Choose one lesson or experience to write about, and write freely for 15 minutes. (If you are unsure which topic you want to write on, freewrite for 15 minutes on more than one topic.) Try to recall details. Use your five senses as you write about the place and people involved (smell, touch, taste, sight, hearing). You may want to do some of your freewriting in a chart like this.

A Chart of Details—for one experience				
What did you see?	What did you hear?	What did you taste?	What did you smell?	What did you feel? (refers to your sense of touch)

Drafting

Look at your freewriting. Highlight or underline the parts you like the most.

Review the writing assignment question you made earlier, and write a topic sentence answering that question. You may need to write a few sentences until you find one that says what you want.

Begin drafting your paragraph. First concentrate on getting down the basic facts of your story. Plan on going back to add detail and explanation.

Before going back to add detail and explanation, read the following Skill Spotlight to get ideas about how to add interesting information to your paragraph.

Computer Note
It is helpful to compose your draft on a computer. Then it is easier to go back and add information later.

Notes

Skill Spotlight

Making Your Writing Interesting with Detail

When you are narrating, it is particularly important to supply details that will paint a picture in your reader's mind. Here are some ways that you can create an interesting, vivid picture.

- Use brand names, pet names, and proper names. (note the highlighted words):

    Her name is Miss Mey. (Walker, paragraph 2)

    I want to go everywhere my daddy goes. (Walker, paragraph 2)

    Every day she watches a television program called "Big Blue Marble." (Walker, paragraph 46)

    So, I asked Pop what he thought.

- Mention texture, appearance, type, and color of objects:

    Whirling happily in my starchy frock, showing off my biscuit-polished patent-leather shoes and lavender socks . . ." (Walker, paragraph 2)

- Describe sounds, smells, tastes, and age:

    People in church stop rustling their new crinolines. (Walker, paragraph 4)

    the musty basement in the depression-era home

    the bitter tea

- Describe proportions and temperatures:

    It is a large stone building, cold and drafty . . . (Walker, paragraph 16)

    She is being treated with warm oils and hot bricks held against her cheek. (Walker, paragraph 25)

- Use dialogue when appropriate. Dialogue can help your reader feel part of the event or learn something about the speaker:

    "Take me, Daddy," I say with assurance; "I'm the prettiest." (Walker, paragraph 2)

    I am so overwhelmed by its beauty, I confront for the first time, consciously the meaning of the doctor's words years ago: "Eyes are sympathetic. If one is blind, the other will likely become blind too." (Walker, paragraph, 44)

- Use adjectives to describe people:

    boisterous, ill-disciplined children (Walker, paragraph 16)

    Then, looking every bit as serious and lawyerlike as her father, she says, as if it may just possibly have slipped my attention. . . . (Walker, paragraph 47)

Continued

- Use active verbs and adverbs to describe action, movement and gestures:
  One day I simply grab him by his coat and beat him until I am sat-isfied. (Walker, paragraph 24)

  I rant and rave at it. I plead with it to clear up before morning. (Walker, paragraph 30)

  For practice, revise the following sentences using the previous ad-vice on adding detail. See how many different kinds of detail you can add. (This is a fun activity to do with a group of classmates.)

1. My aunt was a schoolteacher.
2. The house was in town.
3. I went home.
4. The kitchen was busy.
5. I lived on this street.
6. He said I was wrong.

Now go back to your autobiographical paragraph, and use what you have learned about adding details and explanation. Work on mak-ing your paragraph vivid, clear, and interesting.

Revising

Share your draft with a classmate, tutor, or your instructor. Consider these questions:

- Does the paragraph begin with a topic sentence that responds di-rectly to one of the writing assignment options? Which option?
- Is the topic sentence supported by narration?
- Do all of the sentences in the paragraph relate to the topic sentence and the story being told? Should anything be left out?
- Underline any parts of the paragraph that could be described in greater detail. What would the reader like to know about these items?

For practice, what would you say about this draft?

When I was young, I learned a hard lesson about listening to authority. My family and I were camping near the ocean, and I was impatient for my mom to take me to the beach. She always took a long time to get ready. Like, if we were going to the grocery store, she could take an hour just making a list and making herself "presentable." Anyway, I kept nagging her to get ready faster. She finally got irritated with me and told me to go sit on the bench at the be-ginning of the beach trail and wait for her. Well, I sat on that bench for a little

Notes

while before deciding that I could get down to the beach on my own. Walking down the path, I again got impatient and decided to take a short cut. There were signs everywhere warning people to stay on the path, but I went through the fence to take a more direct path down to the beach. Within moments, I was sliding down the cliff. I tried to grab a bush, but it just broke off in my hand. I tried to dig my fingers into the side of the cliff, but it was too hard. I kept sliding down, and I began to fear that the cliff would drop off suddenly and that I would be sent flying down on top of the rocks I had seen placed along the bottom. Fortunately, there was a flat area before the drop and I stopped sliding. I decided then that perhaps listening to mom and paying attention to danger signs might be a good idea in the future.

After getting a reader's response to your paragraph, make your own decisions about what changes you should make. Revise your paragraph.

Editing

Read your paragraph aloud, and see if you find any editing errors. What errors do you tend to make when writing? (Look at your chart for tracking sentence errors. See p. 452.) Read your paragraph, looking specifically for those errors. Then consider these questions:

- Have you created any run-ons when you use transitions? (See Chapter 19.)
- Have you created any run-ons when ideas seem closely related? (See Chapter 19.)
- Have you created any comma splices when you used transitions? (See Chapter 20.)
- Have you created any comma splices when ideas seem closely related? (See Chapter 20.)
- Review your paragraph and check to see if you have used pronouns correctly. (See Chapter 21.)
- Do you have clear antecedents?
- Do your nouns and pronouns agree in number?
- Can you use synonyms to make your writing clearer or more interesting?
- Have you avoided sexist language?
- Can you add some adjectives and adverbs to make your paragraph more lively? (See Chapter 22.)
- Check the spelling of any words you are uncertain about.
- Can you use any of your vocabulary words in your paragraph?

Computer Note

If you are using a computer, you can use the spell-check feature. However, keep in mind that if you type in the wrong word—but spell it correctly—the computer probably won't catch your error. (For example, if you type in *their,* when you should have typed *there,* the computer may not correct your error.)

Paragraph Assignment: An Autobiography You Would Like to Read

In this assignment you will do a little research as you consider what autobiography you would like to read in the future.

Here is the assignment you are preparing for:

Write a paragraph in which you explain to your instructor and classmates why you would like to read a specific person's autobiography.

The Writing Process for This Paragraph

Pre-Drafting

Review Walker's autobiographical essay, your notes, journals, responses, summaries, and critical thinking questions. What interesting things happened to Walker? What might you or other people learn from reading her complete autobiography?

With your classmates, discuss some interesting people you would like to know more about. Consider these questions:

- Who would you like to learn more about?
- What has this person done or experienced that would be interesting to read about?
- What might you learn from reading his or her autobiography?

On your own, find out more about two or three people who could write (or did write) interesting autobiographies. Do some or all of the following:

- Look in an encyclopedia to find some interesting, famous people.
- Read the front and back covers and skim through autobiographies that you see in the library.
- Talk to a friend, neighbor, or family member who has had an interesting life.
- Read the excerpts from Donald Trump's autobiography in Section VIII, "The Reader."

With each person or autobiography you investigate, write down answers to these questions:

- What interesting things has this person done? Make a list.
- What might you learn from this person's autobiography?

 Computer Note

The Internet is a great source of information. If you're new to the Internet, your school librarian can help you get started. Do a search on the Internet by typing in the names of 2–3 people you are interested in.

Get Involved!

Go to a bookstore and browse through the autobiography section. Who has written autobiographies? Study a few book covers. Read the information on the back. What books have an appealing appearance? Make notes and share your findings with your class.

Notes

Share your research with your classmates.

Here again is the writing assignment you are preparing for:

Write a paragraph in which you explain to your instructor and class-mates why you would like to read a specific person's autobiography.

Underline the key words in this assignment. For each person you are interested in, rewrite the writing assignment and make it a question using a person's name.

For each person you are interested in, write freely for 15 minutes. What specific events do you want to learn about, and why? What lessons might you learn? How might this information affect your life?

Drafting

Review your notes and freewriting, and underline or highlight some of the most important or interesting ideas. Experiment with topic sentences until you find one that responds clearly and directly to the writing assignment. Then write a draft of your paragraph.

As you are writing, keep your audience in mind. Assume that your audience has never been very interested in the person that you have se-lected, or perhaps your audience has never even heard of this person. You will need to offer some compelling reasons for reading this per-son's life story. Consider these questions:

- Why does this person interest you?
- When did you first learn about this person?
- When did this person live?
- Where did this person live and work?
- What did this person do that makes his or her life worth reading about?
- Who encouraged your interest in this person?
- Who does this person remind you of?
- How might this autobiography affect your life?

You may want to give some specific examples of interesting points that would be (or are) covered in that person's autobiography.

 Skill Spotlight

Developing Your Ideas

A well-developed paragraph goes beyond being clear. A well-developed paragraph is interesting because the author has offered examples, de-tails, comparisons, and other pieces of information.   *Continued*

One key is to keep your reader in mind. Your reader is curious and interested and wants information from you—not just the bare bones. When you are drafting and revising, consider these suggestions for developing your ideas:

- Offer comparisons. Compare your idea, person, or item to another idea, person, or item the reader can relate to.
- Offer statistics or research with explanation. If your topic calls for evidence, find statistics or facts in a reliable source. Be sure to explain in your own words what these facts mean and how they relate to your point.
- Offer detailed examples. (See the Skill Spotlight on pp. 118–119.)
- Offer thoughtful explanations. Consider these questions—Why? When? Where? Who? How? (See the "Drafting" section on p. 122.)
- Offer personal experience. Give a short example from your life or a longer one that calls for narration.
- Offer quotes with explanation. Choose a respected source to quote, and explain how the quote supports your point.

Of course, you wouldn't use all these types of support in a single paragraph. Choose the type of support that best fits your main point.

Revising

Share your draft with a reader. Consider these questions:

- Is the topic sentence clear? Does it respond to the assignment?
- Is there enough explanation offered to support the topic sentence?
- Are there any examples suggesting that this person had an interesting life, or that the reader would enjoy or benefit from reading the autobiography?
- Are there helpful adjectives or adverbs that make the paragraph come alive?
- Consider the advice you get from your reader. Revise your draft.

Editing

Read your paragraph aloud, and see if you find any editing errors. What errors do you tend to make when writing? Look at your chart for tracking sentence errors. (See p. 452.) Read your paragraph, looking specifically for those errors. Then consider these questions:

- Have you created any run-ons when you use transitions? (See Chapter 19.)

Notes

- Have you created any run-ons when ideas seem closely related? (See Chapter 19.)
- Have you created any comma splices when you used transitions? (See Chapter 20.)
- Have you created any comma splices when ideas seem closely related? (See Chapter 20.)
- Review your paragraph, and check to see if you have used pronouns correctly. (See Chapter 21.)
  - Do you have clear antecedents?
  - Do your nouns and pronouns agree in number?
  - Can you use synonyms to make your writing clearer or more interesting?
  - Have you avoided sexist language?
- Can you add some adjectives and adverbs to make your paragraph more lively? (See Chapter 22.)

Check the spelling of any words you are uncertain about.
Can you use any of your vocabulary words in your paragraph?

Additional Readings

See Section VIII, "The Reader."
The Art of the Deal, "Chapter 3: Growing Up," by Donald J. Trump with Tony Schwartz. Donald Trump, the real estate developer and multimillionaire, discusses how he got started in his career in this chapter of his autobiography.

Sentence Basics and Creating Expressive Sentences

The chapters listed here are designed specifically to coordinate with the themes and the "Sentence Style" section in Chapter 9.

Chapter 19: Run-ons
Chapter 20: Comma Splices
Chapter 21: Pronouns
Chapter 22: Adjectives and Adverbs

Fairy Tales

THE QUIGMANS

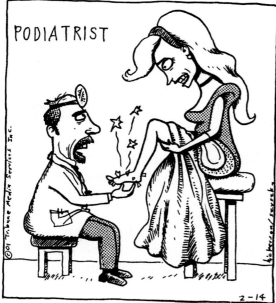

"So let me get this straight …
You KNEW it was a glass slipper?"

This chapter discusses these themes:

✦ Morals
✦ Values
✦ Lessons

> ### Journal Assignment
>
> **Engaging in the Themes of Chapter 10**
>
> Part One: Write a journal entry in which you answer the following questions and analyze the cartoon on this page. What has happened to Cinderella? How is she feeling? How do you think the doctor sees Cinderella's situation? Do you agree with the doctor? Why or why not?
>
> Part Two: Discuss cartoons and humor. What do you think about cartoons as a form of written expression? Why do people create cartoons? What do you think about humor as a method of expression? When do you use humor? With whom do you most often use humor?

Fairy tales are often thought of as stories for children. However, as you will see in this chapter, fairy tales are sometimes told to larger audiences—children and adults. They are a form of entertainment and a method of passing on information, values, and morals.

In this chapter you'll find two different versions of "Cinderella," and you'll be introduced to the skill of analyzing. After reading the narrative tales, you will analyze parts of each tale to find important similarities and differences. Then you may be asked to write your own Cinderella tale and analyze your own work. *Analyzing* is an important skill that you will use often in academic writing.

Fairy Tales

As children (and adults), we have been exposed to fairy tales. American children are often told the tales of "Rumplestiltskin," "The Princess and the Pea," and "Hansel and Gretel," to name a few. In the margin, make some notes in response to these questions: What fairy tales do you remember reading or hearing as a child? Who were some of your favorite characters? Who were some of the worst villains? Which was your favorite tale? Which was your least favorite tale?

Elements of Magic and Storylines

As you may remember, a key element in fairy tales is the magic. Characters may have special powers, or fairies or godmothers may step in and use magic. In the margin, list some examples of magic in fairy tales.

Some of the older versions of popular fairy tales reveal things like **pagan** superstitions. For example, you will notice in the Grimm version of "Cinderella" in this book that things often happen in threes. This may be a connection back to pagan beliefs that supernatural events always happened in threes.

It is also interesting to note that fairy tales from many countries share some of the same storylines: princesses who must prove themselves, children who must struggle against evil stepparents or guardians, godmothers or angels or fairies who step in to help the good children. Do you know of any fairy tales from another culture that are similar to the tales that are popular in America? (Make notes in the margin.)

Here **pagan** is an adjective referring to superstitions related to a faith system in which people believed in many gods.

Entertaining and Teaching

Fairy tales are clearly meant to entertain, and the audience for this entertainment used to be quite broad. Many years ago before books were commonplace, when people relied on oral storytelling, these tales were probably told to adults and children at the same time. Later, German scholars Jacob Ludwig Carl Grimm (1785–1863) and Wilhelm Carl Grimm (1786–1859) interviewed peasants to learn their folktales and then wrote the tales down. You may find signs in the Grimm version of "Cinderella" that the tale was meant for an audience of many ages.

Another purpose of fairy tales, as with many stories, is to teach morals and lessons. You may have noticed that mothers often die early in fairy tales. Sometimes the mother is gone before the tale starts. Do fairy tale writers hate mothers? No. Possibly mothers are removed from the tale so that the children are more vulnerable and must then face evil and difficult challenges from which their mothers might have shielded them. Without mothers, the children in the tale must learn the lessons and morals that the story focuses on. Keep in mind, too, that people used to have much shorter life expectancies. Dying when your children were young was not uncommon.

By studying the lessons taught in fairy tales, we can learn much about a society and time period. What lessons were important to the people who told and listened to the tales? What did that society think made a person "bad"? What made a person "good"? You can find such information when you analyze fairy tales.

Analyzing

To **analyze** something is to break it down into smaller parts and study it. When an advertising firm gets a new client, the firm must analyze the product and the market. What does the product do? What does it not do? What is unique about it? Who will be interested? What are these people like? How much money can they spend to buy the product? What kind of music, colors, and designs will attract these buyers? This analysis helps the advertiser create an advertising campaign that is suitable for the product.

College writing also requires you to analyze things. For example, your history professor may ask you to write a report explaining what caused the U.S. Civil War. Many factors may have contributed to the war. You would have to break your answer into parts, discussing and explaining one factor at a time. By analyzing the parts, you would be able to present a clearer picture of this important historical period.

In this chapter, you'll exercise your analytical skills as you analyze two different versions of "Cinderella." You'll be looking at *how* the writers express themselves and at *what* messages and moral lessons they are expressing.

Study the Pieces

Whether you are analyzing a manufacturing process or a piece of literature, you will have to break the subject into smaller parts. With the Cinderella stories in this chapter, you may want to analyze the characters.

Notes

As you read pages 127 to 130, highlight or underline the boldface terms and the italicized words and phrases. Pay close attention to topic sentences, and mark important points. Record your questions and responses in the margins.

- Who are the major characters?
- Are they good, bad, or both? Why?
- What do they do?
- What do they not do?
- What is important to each of them? What values do they have?
- Besides labeling them as *good* and *bad,* what other adjectives can you use to describe them?

You may also need to break down the storyline.

- What happens first? What happens second? And so on.
- What is the major problem in the story?
- How is it solved?
- What lessons are being taught?
- What important morals and values are represented in the story?
- What do these lessons, morals, and values say about the writer, about the audience, and about the time period?

Another step in analyzing written works is to study the language used.

- What kind of vocabulary does the writer use?
- Is it formal, casual, old-fashioned, or modern?
- Is it colorful? Factual?
- Does the writer use slang?

Find specific words, phrases, and sentences that support your description of the style. Then, think about what the style tells you about the audience.

- Was this tale intended for a modern audience? Or was this story originally told many years ago?
- What are the ages and interests of this audience?
- What is the writer assuming about the audience?

Compare

Often, you can get a better understanding of a subject by comparing it to something similar. For example, if you support Suzanne Eason as a candidate for mayor of your city, you might help a friend see your point of view by explaining how Eason is similar to a political figure you both like and how she is different from a political figure neither of you like.

Similarities and differences can tell us many things about two (or more) items. The fairy tales in this chapter are similar in many ways. You will want to find these similarities and think about what similar messages each tale sends. The tales are also different in important ways. The contrasts (differences) will help you identify how the audiences are different for each tale. The contrasts will also reveal how values and morals vary among different groups of people.

Discuss

Discussing your interpretations and evidence will help you build a complete, well-rounded analysis. If a subject is complex enough to require analysis, chances are you will not see and understand all aspects of the subject on your own. Other people can help you broaden your understanding of the subject.

As you work through this chapter, your classmates and instructor may see things in the tales that you missed. Or they may interpret things differently. It is important to share ideas and respect different interpretations. You may find that you change your interpretation, or you may need to acknowledge in your paragraph that not everyone will immediately agree with you.

Write Your Analysis

A good analysis offers conclusions and evidence. Some topics will allow for more than one possible conclusion. For example, if you were to analyze the effects of spanking children, you would find different opinions and studies. Not everyone would agree with a single analysis and conclusion. Instead, your goal would be to present a logical, thoughtful analysis of the subject. You would do this by researching, discussing, and thinking carefully. After presenting your point of view, you would need to offer reasonable, trustworthy, specific evidence.

In this chapter, you and your classmates may not interpret all aspects of each tale the same way. That is okay. Your responsibility is to offer a reasonable, thoughtful analysis *supported by evidence*. You

Notes   will find your evidence in the words, phrases, and sentences in the tales themselves. The "Skill Spotlight" in this chapter will guide you in finding evidence.

Points to Remember about Analyzing

- *When you analyze a subject, you must break it down into smaller pieces.*
- *You may want to compare your subject to similar subjects.* Look for significant similarities and differences.
- *Discuss your ideas, conclusions, and evidence with other people.* Other people may see things differently and help you to deepen and broaden your interpretation.
- *When writing your analysis, support your conclusions with specific evidence.*

Reading Assignments: Fairy Tales

This section offers you two different versions of the fairy tale "Cinderella." You will begin with an old folktale version, and then you'll find a modern version. First, though, warm up your reading muscles by discussing these questions with your classmates. If you are unfamiliar with the tale, listen as your classmates recall some of the details they remember. Take notes—in the margin or on a separate piece of paper.

- Who are the characters in "Cinderella?"
- What happens in the story?
- What lessons are being taught?

Reading Assignment—"Cinderella," by The Brothers Grimm

Preview   Read the authors' names, the title, and the first paragraph.

Anticipate   From reading the first paragraph, what can you say about the style and language of the story? Will this style and language be difficult for you? How, if at all, will you adjust your reading strategies? Will you have to read slower? Will you read aloud? Is *rereading* this story more important than usual?

Notes

_____

_____

_____

_____

Read Read the story. Mark unknown words, but don't look up any meanings in the dictionary yet.

Cinderella

By The Brothers Grimm

1   Once upon a time the wife of a certain rich man fell very ill, and as she felt her end drawing **nigh** she called her only daughter to her bedside, and said, "My dear child, be **pious** and good, and then the good God will always protect you, and I will look down upon you from heaven and think of you." Soon afterwards she closed her eyes and died. Every day the maiden went to her mother's grave and wept over it, and she continued to be good and pious; but when the winter came, the snow made a white covering over the grave, and in the spring-time, when the sun had withdrawn this covering, the father took to himself another wife.

Nigh means near.

Pious means following the teachings of religion—being virtuous.

2   The wife brought home with her two daughters, who were beautiful and fair in the face, but treacherous and wicked at heart. Then an unfortunate era began in the poor step-child's life. "Shall the stupid goose sit in the parlour with us?" said the two daughters. "They who would eat bread must earn it; out with the kitchenmaid!" So they took off her fine clothes, and put upon her an old grey cloak, and gave her wooden shoes for her feet. "See how the once proud princess is decked out now," said they, and they led her mockingly into the kitchen. Then she was obliged to work hard from morning to night, and to go out early to fetch water, to make the fire, and cook and scour. The sisters treated her besides with every possible insult, derided her, and shook the peas and beans into the ashes, so that she had to pick them out again. At night, when she was tired, she had no bed to lie on, but was forced to sit in the ashes on the hearth; and because she looked dirty through this, they named her CINDERELLA.

3   One day it happened that the father wanted to go to the fair, so he asked his two daughters what he should bring them. "Some beautiful dresses," said one; "Pearls and precious stones," replied the other, "But

A **bough** is a branch of a tree.

Notes

you, Cinderella," said he, "what will you have?" "The first **bough,** father, that knocks against your hat on your way homewards, break it off for me," she replied. So he bought the fine dresses, and the pearls and precious stones, for his two step-daughters; and on his return, as he rode through a green thicket, a hazel-bough touched his hat, which he broke off and took with him. As soon as he got home, he gave his step-daughters what they had wished for, and to Cinderella he gave the hazel-branch. She thanked him very much, and going to her mother's grave she planted the branch on it, and wept so long that her tears fell and watered it, so that it grew and became a beautiful tree. Thrice a day Cinderella went beneath it to weep and pray; and each time a little white Bird flew on the tree, and if she wished aloud, then the little Bird threw down to her whatever she wished for.

4   After a time it fell out that the King appointed a festival, which was to last three days, and to which all the beautiful maidens in the country were invited, from whom his son was to choose a bride. When the two step-daughters heard that they might also appear, they were very glad, and calling Cinderella, they said, "Comb our hair, brush our shoes, and fasten our buckles, for we are going to the festival at the King's palace." Cinderella obeyed, crying, because she wished to go with them to the dance; so she asked her stepmother whether she would allow her.

5   "You, Cinderella!" said she; "you are covered with dust and dirt—will you go to the festival? You have no clothes or shoes, and how can you dance?" But, as she urged her request, the mother said at last, "I have now shaken into the ashes a tubful of beans; if you have picked them up again in two hours, you shall go."

6   Then the maiden left the room, and went out at the back-door into the garden, and called out, "You tame pigeons, and doves, and all you birds of heaven, come and help me to gather the good beans into the tub, and the bad ones you may eat." Presently, in at the kitchen-window came two white pigeons, and after them the doves, and soon all the birds under heaven flew chirping in down upon the ashes. They then began, pick, pick, pick, and gathered all the good seeds into the tub; and scarcely an hour had passed when all was completed, and the birds flew away again. Then the maiden took the tub to the stepmother, rejoicing at the thought that she might now go to the festival; but the stepmother said, "No Cinderella, you have no clothes, and cannot dance; you will only be laughed at." As she began to cry, the stepmother said, "If you can pick up quite clean two tubs of beans which I throw amongst the ashes in one hour, you shall accompany them;" and she thought to herself, "She will never manage it." As soon as the two tubs had been shot into the ashes, Cinderella went out at the back door into the garden, and called out as before, "You tame pigeons, and

doves, and all you birds under heaven, come and help me to gather the good ones into the tubs, and the bad ones you may eat." Presently, in at the kitchen-window came two white pigeons, and soon after them the doves, and soon all the birds under heaven flew chirping in down upon the ashes. They then began, pick, pick, pick, and gathered all the seeds into the tub; and scarcely had half-an-hour passed before all was picked up, and off they flew again. The maiden now took the tubs to the step-mother, rejoicing at the thought that she could go to the festival. But the mother said, "It does not help you a bit; you cannot go with us, for you have no clothes, and cannot dance; we should be ashamed of you." Thereupon she turned her back upon the maiden, and hastened away with her two proud daughters.

7   As there was no one at home, Cinderella went to her mother's grave, under the hazel-tree, and said,—

"Rustle and shake yourself, dear tree,
And silver and gold throw down to me."

8   Then the Bird threw down a dress of gold and silver, and silken slippers ornamented with silver. These Cinderella put on in great haste, and then she went to the ball. Her sisters and stepmother did not know her at all and took her for some foreign princess as she looked so beautiful in her golden dress; for of Cinderella they thought not but that she was sitting at home picking the beans out of the ashes. Presently the Prince came up to her, and, taking her by the hand, led her to the dance. He would not dance with anyone else, and even would not let go her hand; so that when anyone else asked her to dance, he said, "She is my partner." They danced till evening, when she wished to go home; but the Prince said, "I will go with you, and see you safe," for he wanted to see to whom the maiden belonged. She flew away from him, however, and sprang into the pigeon-house; so the Prince waited till the father came, whom he told that the strange maiden had run into the pigeon-house. Then, the stepmother thought, "Could it be Cinderella?" And they brought an axe wherewith the Prince might cut open the door, but no one was found within. And when they came into the house, there lay Cinderella in her dirty clothes among the ashes, and an oil-lamp was burning in the chimney; for she had jumped quickly out on the other side of the pigeon-house, and had run to the hazel-tree, where she had taken off her fine clothes, and laid them on the grave, and the Bird had taken them again, and afterwards she had put on her little grey cloak, and seated herself among the ashes in the kitchen.

9   The next day, when the festival was renewed, and her stepmother and her sisters had set out again, Cinderella went to the hazel-tree and sang as before:—

"Rustle and shake yourself, dear tree,
And silver and gold throw down to me."

10   Then the Bird threw down a much more splendid dress than the former, and when the maiden appeared at the ball everyone was astonished at her beauty. The Prince, however, who had waited till she came, took her hand, and would dance with no one else; and if others came and asked, he replied as before, "She is my partner." As soon as evening came she wished to depart, and the Prince followed her, wanting to see into whose house she went; but she sprang away from him, and ran into the garden behind the house. Therein stood a fine large tree, on which hung the most beautiful pears, and the boughs rustled as though a squirrel was among them; but the Prince could not see whence the noise proceeded. He waited, however, till the father came, and told him, "The strange maiden has escaped from me, and I think she has climbed up into this tree." The father thought to himself, "Can it be Cinderella?" and taking an axe he chopped down the tree, but there was no one on it. When they went into the kitchen, there lay Cinderella among the ashes, as before, for she had sprung down on the other side of the tree, and, having taken her beautiful clothes again to the Bird upon the hazel-tree, she had put on once more her old grey cloak.

11   The third day, when her stepmother and her sisters had set out, Cinderella went again to her mother's grave, and said,—

"Rustle and shake yourself, dear tree,
And silver and gold throw down to me."

12   Then the Bird threw down to her a dress which was more splendid and glittering than she had ever had before, and the slippers were of pure gold. When she arrived at the ball they knew not what to say for wonderment, and the Prince danced with her alone as at first, and replied to everyone who asked her hand, "She is my partner." As soon as evening came she wished to go, and as the Prince followed her she ran away so quickly that he could not overtake her. But he had contrived a stratagem, and spread the whole way with pitch, so that it happened as the maiden ran that her left slipper came off. The Prince took it up, and saw it was small and graceful, and of pure gold; so the following morning he went with it to the father, and said, "My bride shall be no other than she whose foot this golden slipper fits." The two sisters were glad of this, for they had beautiful feet, and the elder went with it to her chamber to try it on, while her mother stood by. She could not, however, get her great toe into it, and the shoe was much too small; but the mother, reaching a knife, said, "Cut off your toe, for if you are queen, you need not go any longer on foot." The maiden cut it off, and squeezed her foot into the shoe, and,

concealing the pain she felt, went down to the Prince. Then he placed her as his bride upon his horse, and rode off; and as they passed by the grave, there sat two little doves upon the hazel-tree, singing,—

Copyright © 2003 by Addison Wesley Longman, Inc.

Notes

"Backwards peep, backwards peep,
    There's blood upon the shoe;
The shoe's too small, and she behind
    Is not the bride for you."

13   Then the Prince looked behind, and saw the blood flowing; so he turned his horse back, and took the false bride home again, saying she was not the right one. Then the other sister must needs fit on the shoe, so she went to the chamber and got her toes nicely into the shoe, but the heel was too large. The mother, reaching a knife, said, "Cut a piece off your heel, for when you become queen you need not go any longer on foot." She cut a piece off her heel, squeezed her foot into the shoe, and, concealing the pain she felt, went down to the Prince. Then he put her upon his horse as his bride, and rode off; and as they passed the hazel-tree, there sat two little doves, who sang,—

"Backwards peep, backwards peep,
    There's blood upon the shoe;
The shoe's too small, and she behind
    Is not the bride for you."

14   Then he looked behind, and saw the blood trickling from her shoe, and that the stocking was dyed quite red; so he turned his horse back, and took the false bride home again, saying, "Neither is this one the right maiden; have you no other daughter?" "No," replied the father, "except little Cinderella, daughter of my deceased wife, who cannot possibly be the bride." The Prince asked that she might be fetched; but the stepmother said, "Oh, no! she is much too dirty; I dare not let her be seen." But the Prince would have his way; so Cinderella was called, and she, first washing her hands and face, went in and curtseyed to the Prince, who gave her the golden shoe. Cinderella sat down on a stool, and taking off her heavy wooden shoes, put on the slipper, which fitted her to a shade; and as she stood up, the Prince looked in her face, and recognising the beautiful maiden with whom he had danced, exclaimed, "This is my true bride." The stepmother and the two sisters were amazed and white with rage, but the Prince took Cinderella upon his horse, and rode away; and as they came up to the hazel-tree the two little white doves sang,—

"Backwards peep, backwards peep,
    There's no blood on the shoe;

Notes

It fits so nice, and she behind
    Is the true bride for you."

15 And as they finished they flew down and lighted upon Cinderella's shoulders, and there they remained; and the wedding was celebrated with great festivities, and the two sisters were smitten with blindness as a punishment for their wickedness.

Reread Reread the story. As you read, use context clues and the dictionary to learn meanings of new words. Mark important and interesting parts of the story. Record your questions and responses to the story in the margins. Make a special note in the margin to mark places where things happen three times.

Vocabulary cards: Make definition cards and sentence cards for the words listed here.

- *treacherous*, paragraph 2
- *derided*, paragraph 2

Think Critically In preparation for class discussion, answer these questions on a separate piece of paper:

Get Involved!
Rent Disney's 1950 version of *Cinderella* and report to your class about the similarities and differences you see between Disney's version and the Brothers Grimm version. Be sure to take notes as you watch the film.
OR
Rent Rodgers and Hammerstein's *Cinderella*, 1997 (starring Brandy and Whitney Houston). Then report to your class about the similarities and differences. Be sure to take notes as you watch the film.

1. What does Cinderella's dying mother tell Cinderella? Use your own words.
2. When Cinderella's father goes to the fair, what do the stepsisters ask him to bring them? What does Cinderella ask for? Why does she ask for this? What does her gift represent to her? What does her request tell us about Cinderella?
3. How would you describe the stepsisters? What kind of people are they? What evidence do you have to support your description?
4. Why do you think the pigeons, doves, and other birds help Cinderella pick beans out of the ashes?
5. In this story, Cinderella does not have a fairy godmother who suddenly appears. In paragraph 3, we learn about a bird that lives in the hazel tree. This bird is there whenever Cinderella needs it. Yet, Cinderella doesn't ask this bird for anything until the ball. What does this tell you about Cinderella? What kind of person is she?
6. What happens to the stepsisters at the end of this story? What do you think about this?
7. What do you know about the father? What do you think about him?

8. What lessons are being taught in this story?

Summarize Make a list of the main events in this story.

Sentence Style

Study these sentences:

> Once upon a time the wife of a certain rich man fell very ill, and as she felt her end drawing nigh she called her only daughter to her bedside, and said, "My dear child, be pious and good, and then the good God will always protect you, and I will look down upon you from heaven and think of you." Soon afterwards she closed her eyes and died. Every day *the maiden* went to her mother's grave and wept over it, and she continued to be good and pious; but when the winter came, the snow made a white covering over the grave, and in the spring-time, when the sun had withdrawn this covering, the father took to himself another wife.
>
> The wife brought home with her two daughters, who were beautiful and fair in the face, but treacherous and wicked at heart. Then an unfortunate era began in the *poor step-child's* life.

In the first two sentences the pronoun *she* is used to refer to the mother. In the third sentence, the writer could have used *she* instead of *the maiden*, but that might have been confusing. The reader might wonder if the *she* was still referring to the mother.

Instead of using *she*, the writer used a synonym *the maiden*. A synonym is a word that is very similar in meaning to another word. In the second sentence of the second paragraph, the writer uses *the poor step-child's* to refer to Cinderella (the maiden). This phrase is also a synonym. Use synonyms in your writing when a pronoun might cause confusion and when you want to add a little variety to your writing. Repeating "Cinderella" over and over could be boring.

Your Turn Write some synonyms for *Cinderella's stepmother*. (See Chapter 21 for more on synonyms and pronouns.)

Express Yourself

Who Was the Audience for the Grimm Tale?

Review the Grimm's "Cinderella," your critical thinking responses, and your class discussion notes. Who was the intended audience for this tale? What evidence do you have? What did the people of this time value and believe in? What evidence do you have?

Reminder: Plan, draft, revise, and edit your response.

Reading Assignment—"The Truth about Cinderella and Her Evil Stepsisters"

Preview Read the first three paragraphs.

Anticipate From reading the first three paragraphs, what do you know about the style and language of this version of "Cinderella"? How, if at all, will you adjust your reading strategies?

_____

_____

_____

_____

Read Read the story. Mark unknown words, but don't look up any meanings in the dictionary yet.

The Truth about Cinderella and Her Evil Stepsisters

By Bill Harbaugh

1   Once upon a time there was a beautiful young girl named Cinderella. She lived in a lovely house with her father, a famous fashion designer, and her mother, who taught her how to play the harp, arrange flowers, and keep a spotless house.

2   When Cinderella was still quite young her mother died, in a tragic fire caused when a careless butler carried a flaming dessert too close to the lace curtains. Cinderella's father remarried, and when he went on a long business trip, she was sent to live at her new stepmother's house in the country.

3   Even though her indulgent stepmother gave her the nicest bedroom in the house, and her generous stepsisters offered to share all their toys with her, Cinderella was not at all happy with country life. The furniture was very old and out of style, and, to be blunt, the toys were rather shabby. (Picture of C in her elaborate **French provincial**

French provincial refers to a style of architecture and furniture similar to the French styles popular in the 17th and 18th centuries. It is formal and fancy.

bedroom, with balcony, writing in her diary. "They've put me in a horrid little garret. It's dark and drafty, and these horrid little birds are always flying in the windows.")

4   Not only that, but her new stepsisters were quite uncouth. They constantly tramped through the house in their muddy riding boots, and they had no idea which fork to use when at dinner, despite Cinderella's patient explanations. Time and time again Cinderella would complain to her stepmother about their lack of manners, only to be told, "Well Cinderella, girls will be girls you know. Really, it's just a little dirt. I don't mind if the house looks lived in. Perhaps *you* should try playing outside someday."

5   The stepsisters desperately wanted Cinderella to join in their games, but she thought they looked so very dangerous. Besides, she was afraid she might get sweaty. So, she spent most of her time doing her best to keep the house looking prim and proper. It was quite a chore.

6   One day, when Cinderella was scrubbing the remains of her younger stepsister's chemistry experiment off the parlor ceiling, she heard a knock at the door. It was the Prince's herald, bringing an invitation for the whole family to attend the annual Ball.

7   "Oh no," said the older stepsister when she heard the news, "not another boring party! Mom, can't we skip this one and go on a camping trip?"

8   "Hmm," said her mother, "I think we did that last year. The Prince will think we're trying to avoid him. Really, he's such a nice boy."

9   "I know," said the younger stepsister. "Let's tell him we've all come down with the bubonic plague!"

10   "Oh, that's perfect," said their Mother. "Find me a pen and I'll write a note."

11   Suddenly, the three of them heard a piercing shriek. Naturally, it was Cinderella.

12   "*Aargh!* What is wrong with you people? I've been living out here in the *sticks* for 6 months with absolutely *nothing* to do. No shopping malls, lousy TV reception, just nothing. You don't even have cable! Then finally I get a chance to buy some new clothes, go to a fancy ball, and dance with a real *Prince.* And you three *hicks* want to tell everyone that I've got a *fatal disease!*" She threw down her mop and stormed up the stairs to her room.

13   "Goodness," said the Mother. "Perhaps we're being a little selfish here. I suppose it wouldn't be that hard to go, just for an hour or two."

Notes

14   "I guess," said the stepsisters, "but just for the food. As soon as they run out of sweets, we're leaving."

15   Cinderella was very happy to hear the news.

16   "If only I'd managed to rescue my collection of original designer gowns from the fire. I don't have a thing to wear."

17   "Don't worry," said the stepsisters. "We're very good at making things. We'll help you make a dress. You can use the silk from our hot air balloon."

18   "It's not a very becoming shade," said Cinderella, "but I suppose it will have to do."

Aghast means shocked or horrified.

19   The stepsisters stared at her, **aghast.** "OK, that's it Cinderella!" they said. "We've been trying our best to be nice to you, seeing as how your Mother died and everything, but we are really fed up with your persnickety behavior. You can just make the dress by yourself. Honestly!"

20   Cinderella didn't know what to do. She had never had to make anything. Before, she would just drive her BMW to the mall and charge whatever she wanted to her parents' credit card. She cried herself to sleep, thinking of how unfair life could be.

21   Later that night, as Cinderella slept, a sparkly mist drifted in through the balcony doors. It was Cinderella's Fairy Godmother. She gazed down at the sleeping child.

22   "How sad," she thought, "to see my precious Cinderella treated like a commoner. I must help her." So, next to Cinderella's silver hairbrush, the godmother left a magic gold credit card, and a note. (Picture of sparkly mist leaving through balcony doors, with note in very elegant script: "Dear Cinderella: I'm so sorry to see you living in such dismal poverty. Use this magic credit card to buy whatever you want for the Ball. Just remember, however, that at the last stroke of midnight the magic will end and whatever you have bought will turn to rags.")

23   When Cinderella awoke and saw her Fairy Godmother's gift, her heart was filled with joy. She rushed to the phone and ordered a limo to take her to the mall. There she bought a gorgeous gown, dancing slippers, had her hair permed and, of course, a complete makeover.

24   Meanwhile, her stepsisters had begun to feel guilty about what they had said to Cinderella. They told their mother what they had done.

25   She said, "Now girls, Cinderella is a few years older than you, after all. I seem to recall reading that girls her age get very concerned about their appearance for some reason. Maybe you shouldn't take it so personally."

26   "She's really not so bad, sometimes," said one stepsister.

27   "Yes," said the other. "It's not her fault her parents were so overprotective and never let her use power tools or sewing machines."

28   So to make up they decided to make a beautiful gown for her after all. The younger stepsister gathered wild plants and made a dye in a becoming shade of aubergine, while the older one starting cutting up the silk from their balloon. In no time at all they made a stunning party dress, and proudly spread it out on Cinderella's bed for her to see.

29   As the day wore on without a sign of Cinderella, the family began to worry more and more. Finally, the hour of the Ball arrived. They had no idea where Cinderella had gone, and the stepsisters feared that their harsh words had caused her to run away. But, since they had agreed to attend the ball, in the end they drove off to the Palace. (Picture of them driving off in VW van with canoe on top.)

30   Cinderella finally arrived at the Ball after the mall closed. With her makeup on neither the stepsisters or their mother recognized the radiant young beauty who strode confidently into the ballroom. The awestruck Prince would dance only with Cinderella. (Picture of the family, staring openmouthed at Cinderella dancing with the Prince.)

31   "Wow, you sure can dance. I've never met a girl like you before," the Prince said. "You're not from around here, are you?"

32   Cinderella smiled, trying to think of something clever to say in reply. But before she could, the clock began to strike 12 midnight. Remembering her Fairy Godmother's warning, Cinderella turned from the Prince and began to run from the palace, losing a slipper as she fled. The Prince picked up the slipper. He stood staring after her, trying to think if he had done anything rude or stupid. You could never be sure with girls, he thought to himself.

33   By the time Cinderella got to her limo, it had turned into a mountain bike. She pedaled madly home and rushed up to her room, crying in disappointment.

34   There on her bed was the gown that her stepsisters had cut up their balloon to make. (Picture of ruined balloon outside.)

35   Cinderella stared at it. She thought of all the things her new family had given her, and how ungrateful she had been. Then and there she decided to do her best to be more fun.

36   The only thing left from the mall was the single bejeweled slipper. For some reason it and it alone was unchanged by the ending of the Fairy Godmother's spell. The next morning, Cinderella pedaled off to the mall. She had decided to return the jewel-encrusted slipper and use

Notes

the money to buy something nice for her stepsisters, like maybe a telescope, or a new snake for their herpetarium.

37   Meanwhile, the Prince had become quite obsessive about Cinderella. He had decided that he could not rest until he had found the beautiful girl from the Ball. He took the slipper she had dropped to every shoe store in the mall, asking the clerks if they could remember who had bought it. No one could. (Picture of Prince, in royal costume, asking dorky looking shoe salesman.)

38   Finally, as he entered the last store, he saw Cinderella standing at the counter, returning the matching slipper. Even in her bike riding clothes he recognized her instantly. (Picture of Cinderella in bike shorts, helmet, gloves, etc.)

39   The Prince dropped to his knee and kissed the surprised Cinderella's hand.

40   "Cinderella, may I have your hand in Marriage?" he asked. She gazed deep down into his adoring eyes.

41   "Are you kidding?" she replied. "We've only been on one date. Sure, you're a great dancer, but we barely talked and anyway the music was so loud I couldn't hear a word you said. I don't even know if you like cats, or if you care about the environment, or what kind of books you read. This doesn't seem a little sudden to you?"

42   It's true that the Prince was a little awkward around girls, but he was a quick thinker, and not the sort to give up easily. He jumped to his feet. "Well, will you walk down to the bookstore with me then?" he asked. "I've been wanting to buy a book on the significance of cats in early Egyptian religion, and then we could get a cappuccino and I could tell you all about my new plan to increase the Kingdom's recycling rate by 15%."

43   "Sure," said Cinderella. "Now that sounds fun. And I'll tell you what *really* happened at the Ball. You won't believe the story!" She put the money from the slipper in her backpack and the two of them strolled off together.

Reread Reread this story. As you reread, use context clues to figure out the meanings of unfamiliar words. Look up the meanings of any words that remain unclear. Mark important or interesting moments in the story. In the margins, record your questions about and your reactions to the story.

Vocabulary cards: Make definition cards and sentence cards for the words listed here.

- *indulgent*, paragraph 3

Get Involved!

Rent *Ever After,* starring Drew Barrymore and Angelica Huston (directed by Andy Tennant, 1998) and report to your class on the similarities and differences between *Ever After* and the other Cinderella stories you are familiar with. (Be sure to make notes as you watch the film.)

• *blunt*, paragraph 3

Think Critically and Summarize In preparation for class discussion, answer these questions on a separate piece of paper:

1. Make a list of the important events in this story. (You are creating a plot line when you do this.)
2. What is Cinderella like in this story? Give adjectives that you think fit her, and give evidence from the story (with paragraph numbers). Think about what she enjoys and what she values.
3. What are the stepsisters like in this story? Give adjectives that you think fit them, and give evidence from the story (with paragraph numbers). Think about what they enjoy and what they value.
4. What is the stepmother like in this story? Give adjectives that you think fit her, and give evidence from the story (with paragraph numbers).
5. What are the most interesting and most important differences between this version and the earlier two versions of Cinderella?
6. Choose two of the most interesting or most important differences, and explain what they reveal about the writer or the audience.
7. What was your favorite part of the story, and why?

Sentence Style

Study this sentence:

> When Cinderella awoke and saw her Fairy Godmother's gift, her heart was filled with joy.

Circle the comma in this sentence. That comma separates the dependent clause from the independent clause. It is the word *when* that makes the first clause dependent. Write the clauses as separate, complete sentences by leaving out the *when*.

Using a subordinator like *when* to create a dependent clause that can attach itself to an independent clause is an effective way to explain the relationship between two ideas. In this case, the *when* explains that first one event happened and then the other event happened. Connecting your ideas in this way will help your reader see the connections that you see. Your writing will be less choppy, and your ideas will be clearer.

Notes

Your Turn Write a sentence that has a dependent clause that begins with *when*, followed by an independent clause. (See Chapter 24 for a review of subordinators.)

Express Yourself

What Was Cinderella's Childhood Like?

In the first two paragraphs of this fairy tale, Harbaugh manages to give us a lot of information about Cinderella and her early upbringing. Study the first two paragraphs carefully. Then explain in a paragraph what you learned about Cinderella and her early upbringing.

   Reminder: Plan, draft, revise, and edit your response.

Journal

Fairy Tales

Reflect on the fairy tales you have read in this class or that were read to you as a child. What did you learn from these tales? Were all of the lessons positive? What fairy tales would you like children to read? Do you know of any fairy tales that they should avoid? Explain.

Paragraph Assignment: Analyzing Differences

While reading the Grimm version and the Harbaugh version of "Cinderella," you noted many similarities and differences. Some of the differences between the tales help you to better understand the audience of each tale and their values. In this writing assignment you'll analyze those important differences.

   Here is the writing assignment you are preparing for. Your instructor may have you complete both options or only one.

   Option 1: How can you tell the Grimm version and the Harbaugh version were written for audiences of two different time periods?

   Option 2: Audiences of different time periods will often want different values emphasized. Compare the Grimm version and the Harbaugh version and show how each tale emphasizes different values.

The Writing Process for This Paragraph

Pre-Drafting

When you completed the readings and the critical thinking questions and shared those responses, you read, discussed, and thought critically. Now review your margin and class notes and your critical thinking responses.

With your classmates, create a chart like the one that follows.

	The Grimm version	The Harbaugh version
Differences in vocabulary		
Differences in the activities the characters perform		
Name and describe the bad characters. What do they do? What do they say? What is important to them?		
Name and describe the good characters. What do they do? What do they say? What is important to them?		

Here is your writing assignment again:

Option 1: How can you tell the Grimm version and the Harbaugh version were written for audiences of two different time periods?

Option 2: Audiences of different time periods will often want different values emphasized. Compare the Grimm version and the Harbaugh version and show how each tale emphasizes different values.

Notes

Highlight or underline the important words in the option you have chosen to focus on. Talk to a classmate, friend, or tutor and explain in your own words what you must write about. Try to explain without looking at the assignment.

Review the "Analyzing" section in this chapter (pp. 127–130). What kind of information will you need to include in your paragraph?

Reread the option you are focusing on and freewrite for 15 minutes. You may want to consider these questions:

- What *significant* differences are you most interested in?
- What does each of these significant differences tell you about the audience?

After you are done freewriting, reread and highlight the parts of your freewriting that you like most. You might use these parts in your draft.

Drafting

Write a draft of your paragraph. With this assignment, your topic sentence will restate the assignment. For example, if you are writing on Option 1, your topic sentence will say something like this:

> The Grimm version and the Harbaugh version were clearly written for audiences of two different time periods.

You can adjust this topic sentence many different ways. For example, you might want to start the sentences with "I have found evidence that . . ." Or you might want to start with a descriptive phrase. For example, you might say "After studying the tales closely . . ." Experiment with topic sentences until you create one you are comfortable with.

After stating the main point in your topic sentence, you will need to support it. Writers support their ideas in many ways. They use examples (from readings and personal experience), statistics, comparisons, definitions, quotations, and so on.

With this assignment, you will need to refer back to the readings to find pieces of evidence to support your main point. For example, with Option 1 perhaps a writer wants to say that the vocabulary and the characters' actions prove that the tales were written for audiences of different time periods.

- First the writer states his main point in the topic sentence. Then he might write the following sentences:

Computer Note

Remember to save your work on a disk about every 15 minutes. You don't want to lose any of your work because of a power shortage or because you give the computer the wrong command! Also, print a hard copy occasionally. Disks can malfunction.

For example, in the Grimm version, the stepsisters call Cinderella a "stupid goose" and a "kitchenmaid." They also "shook the peas and beans into the ashes, so that she had to pick them out again." These mean names and strange chores show that the Grimm tale was written many years ago when women were either ladies who could sit around or maids who had to do difficult work all the time. On the other hand, the stepsisters in the modern version . . .

Notes

- Notice that the writer first gives proof and then explains the proof and what he can guess about the audience of each tale.

Notice how the writer uses the phrase *for example* to tell the reader that evidence is coming, and the writer uses *on the other hand* to tell the reader that an opposite idea is coming. *For example* and *on the other hand* work as transitions—words or phrases that help the reader move smoothly from one idea to the next. In this case, the transition words help the writer introduce evidence.

Consider another scenario. Imagine that a writer working with Option 2 wants to show how the two audiences have different values.

- The writer would state his main point in the topic sentence, and then he might write the following sentences:

    For example, the Brothers Grimm say that Cinderella's mom wants her to be "pious." The mother believes that "the good God will always protect you." These sentences suggest that religion was very important to the Grimm audience. However, Harbaugh describes the good characters in his tale as athletic girls who like to. . . .

- Then the writer has to finish explaining what these differences are, what they mean, and what he can guess about the audience of Harbaugh's tale.

Notice the transition words in that example: *for example* and *however*. These transition words help the writer introduce evidence. *For example* and *however* may also work well in your paragraph. (For more on *transitions*, see Chapter 25.)

Revising

Share your draft with a classmate, tutor, or your instructor.

Notes

Consider these questions:

- Does the paragraph begin with a topic sentence that tells the reader what single difference the writer will focus on, and in which two tales? Does the topic sentence tell the reader why this difference is important?
- Is there specific evidence from the tales to support the main idea?
- Does the writer then discuss the evidence and explain why the difference is important?
- Consider the advice you get from your reader and review your Evaluation Chart (p. 453).

Revise your paragraph.

Editing

Read your paragraph aloud to see if you can identify any editing errors. What errors do you tend to make when writing? (Review your sentence error chart; see p. 452.) Read your paragraph, looking specifically for those errors. Then consider these options for revising and shaping some of your sentences:

- Have you used spell check or a dictionary to check all questionable spellings? If you have created your own spelling list, refer to that list also.
- Have you used coordinators and subordinators when appropriate? (See Chapters 23 and 24 for a review.)
- Have you used transitions when appropriate? (See Chapter 25 for more on transitions.)
- Can you use any of your vocabulary words in your paragraph?

Story Assignment: Your Modern Version

While reading and analyzing the different versions of "Cinderella," you saw how writers made choices and changed the stories to fit their audiences and interests. You will now have a chance to be the storyteller and make your own choices about how "Cinderella" should be told.

Here is the writing assignment you are preparing for:

Write your own modern version of Cinderella that reflects your choices about audience, characters, events, lessons, and style.

Note: One of the Cinderella stories you read was humorous, but your story does not need to be funny.

The Writing Process for This Story

Pre-Drafting

Discuss your options with your classmates. Use these questions to guide your discussion:

- What different audiences might you write the story for? Think about age, race, geographical location, interests, economic group, and so on.
- What did you like in the other versions of Cinderella? (Maybe you will keep or imitate these parts.)
- What didn't you like in the other versions of Cinderella?
- What lessons would your audience respond to?
- What kinds of detail can you put in your story to attract your audience?

Review the readings in this chapter, and make a list of all major characters. Then make a list of all major events in the stories.

Discuss with your classmates what characters and events you might delete, add, or change. Why would you make these deletions, additions, or changes?

Here is your writing assignment again:

Write your own modern *version of "Cinderella" that reflects your choices about audience, characters, events, lessons, and style.*

Underline the important words in the writing prompt. Talk to a classmate, friend, or tutor and explain in your own words what you must write about. Try not to look at the assignment when you explain.

Plan your storyline. Write for 15 minutes, sketching out your entire story from beginning to end. You won't be including details. You may not even write in complete sentences. In a sense you are making an outline or summary of your own story. You may want to read "Cindy Ellie" in Section VIII to see how others have interpreted and written fairy tales.

Drafting

Using your "outline," draft your story. Add the characters' names and describe the characters when necessary. Describe where the scenes take place. Use dialog when appropriate. Have fun with the draft. Don't try to make the first draft perfect. Think about interesting details to include. (You may want to review the Skill Spotlight on pages 118–119 in Chapter 9 about narration and detail.) Of course, you will also want to think about the lesson you want to teach in your story.

Notes

An Original Cinderella Tale

Read the following tale.

The Tale of Cindi Spirelli

By Theresa Michelini

Once upon a time there lived a teenage girl name Cindi Spirelli. Cindi was 16 years old, and she was a junior in high school. Cindi loved school and she was extremely smart. She was a very shy girl with absolutely no friends. Although Cindi would love to have friends, she was quite content with her schoolwork and spending time with her family. Cindi lived on a small ranch with her father, mother, and her three small sisters Megan 5, Marissa 4, Makaila 2. Every day when Cindi came home from school she would do her homework, and then she would help her mother around the ranch; they had livestock and an enormous garden. Cindi's father worked two jobs and went to school part-time. Although they were a poor family they were committed to helping each other as well as others in any possible way. Cindi loved her family very much, and they filled her with much happiness. Then without warning tragedy struck! Cindi's mother was diagnosed with terminal cancer. Cindi's life as she knew it would be changed forever.

Think Critically

1. Where do you think Michelini went from here? Do you think the father remarries? Does he have to? Will he be a distant, uninvolved father, or will he be different from most fathers in Cinderella tales?
2. What details did Michelini include to help her tale come alive?
3. What problems and topics do you think will come up in this story? What hints do you see that tell you where the tale is going? ■

Revising

Share your story with a classmate, tutor, or your instructor. Consider these questions:

- Is the story modern? What evidence is there that this is a modern tale?
- Can you tell who the audience is for this story? How? Point to details that help you identify the audience. Could the writer include more details?

- What lesson is the writer teaching? Are there any confusing parts in the storyline or lesson?
- What do you like most about the story?

After getting a reader's response to your story, make your own decisions about what changes you should make. If you think you need to further develop a scene, you might want to create a five-senses chart to help you think of details you should include. Your chart would look like this:

What do you see?	What do you hear?	What do you taste?	What do you smell?	What do you feel? (sense of touch)

Revise your story.

Editing

Read your paragraph aloud to see if you can identify any editing errors. What errors do you tend to make when writing? (Review your sentence error chart. See p. 452.) Read your paragraph, looking specifically for those errors. Then consider these options for revising and shaping some of your sentences:

- Have you used spell check or a dictionary to check all questionable spellings? If you have created your own spelling list, refer to that list also.
- Have you used coordinators and subordinators when appropriate? (See Chapters 23 and 24 for a review.)
- Have you used transitions when appropriate? (See Chapter 25 for a review.)
- Can you use any of your vocabulary words in your paragraph?

Computer Note

When you are revising and editing, you may want to find a synonym rather than using a word over and over. (Synonyms can also add important information to your writing.) Your word processing program probably has a thesaurus built in. Highlight the word you want a synonym for, and then go to the Tools menu and see if you can click on a thesaurus.

Notes

Multiparagraph Assignment: Choices You Made

To complete this paragraph assignment, you must first complete the previous one that asks you to write your own Cinderella tale.

As you wrote your own Cinderella tale, you made important choices about the storyline, characters, lessons, and style. In this assignment, you will explain two of the choices you made when you wrote your Cinderella tale.

Here is the assignment you are preparing for:

In two paragraphs, analyze two aspects of your Cinderella story. You may analyze any of the following:

- *The style of your story*
- *The lesson of your story*
- *A character in your story*
- *An event in your story*

Also, tell your reader what your analysis reveals about your audience.

The Writing Process for This Assignment

Pre-Drafting

Working with one classmate or a small group of classmates, discuss briefly the types of things you might cover in your paragraph.

With the same group of classmates, read each other's stories. Discuss the most interesting changes each author made. How would the readers describe the audience for each story?

Here is your writing assignment again:

In two paragraphs, analyze two aspects of your Cinderella story. You may analyze any of the following:

- *The style of your story*
- *The lesson of your story*
- *A character in your story*
- *An event in your story*

Also, tell your reader what your analysis reveals about your audience.

Highlight or underline the important words in this writing assignment. Talk to a classmate, friend, or tutor and explain in your own words what you must write about. Try not to look at the assignment when you explain.

Freewrite for 20 minutes. Review your story and the assignment as you need to. Use this time as an opportunity to explore your different options in writing.

When you have finished freewriting, highlight the parts of your freewriting that you like most. What parts of your Cinderella story will you focus on in your paragraph—the style, a lesson, a character, or an event?

Drafting

Referring to your freewriting, write a draft of your paragraph. Create a topic sentence for each paragraph that tells your reader what aspect of your Cinderella story you will focus on and why. Find pieces of evidence from your story that you can use to support your topic sentence.

Skill Spotlight

Supplying and Explaining Evidence

Your assignments in college will often require you to state a main point that is supported by information or *evidence*.

Here are some common types of evidence:

- Information from the reading you are analyzing
- A quotation from the reading you are analyzing
- A quotation from research you have done
- Statistical information
- Results from studies
- Information from your own observations
- Information you got from films or interviews

If you get your evidence from a source that your instructor and classmates are not familiar with, be sure that the source is one that they will respect and have faith in. Remember to name your source.

After you have given your evidence, explain what it means. Explain why it is significant. Do not expect your reader to draw the same conclusions that you do.

Here's an example of a writer supplying evidence from a Cinderella story she wrote earlier. This writer uses information from her

Continued

Notes

story (followed by explanation) and a quote from her story (followed by explanation).

> The father in my Cinderella story is a really good father. For example, the father in my story encourages his daughter and his girlfriend to get to know one another before he and his girlfriend get married. This is important because he is showing that he cares about Cinderella and is considering how this marriage will affect her and her life. He is also there to raise Cinderella. He doesn't just "disappear" like the fathers in all of the other versions. He says to Cinderella: "Blended families are difficult, Cindy, but we're going to have regular family meetings so that we can deal with our problems." This is a father that recognizes his responsibility as a parent. He doesn't just hand over all the parenting duties to his wife. He doesn't disappear on long trips or allow his wife to mistreat his daughter.

Revising

Share your draft with a reader. Consider these questions:

- Are the topic sentences clear? Do they respond to the assignment?
- Is there enough evidence to support the topic sentences?
- Do the paragraphs explain the significance behind your choices?
- Consider the advice you get from your reader.
- Review your Evaluation Chart (p. 453) and consider what your instructor said about previous writing assignments.

Revise, making your own choices about what you should change and improve.

Editing

Read your paragraph aloud to see if you can identify any editing errors. What errors do you tend to make when writing? (Review your sentence error chart; see p. 452.) Read your paragraph, looking specifically for those errors. Then consider these options for revising and shaping some of your sentences:

- Have you used spell check or a dictionary to check all questionable spellings? If you have created your own spelling list, refer to that list also.
- Have you used coordinators and subordinators when appropriate? (See Chapters 23 and 24 for a review.)
- Have you used transitions when appropriate? (See Chapter 25 for a review.)
- Can you use any of your vocabulary words in your paragraph?

Additional Reading

(See Section VIII; "The Reader.")
"Cindy Ellie: A Modern Fairy Tale," by Mary Carter Smith. This modern
African American tale takes a different approach to the story of Cinderella.

Expressive Sentences

The chapters listed here are designed specifically to coordinate with the
themes and the "Sentence Style" section in Chapter 10.

Chapter 23: Coordinators
Chapter 24: Subordinators
Chapter 25: Transitions

Essays: An Introduction

11

This chapter discusses this theme:

✦ Dreams

☞ *Journal Assignment*

Engaging in the Theme of Chapter 11

Write a journal in which you explore what the artist is expressing through his photograph. How might the photograph connect to the theme of this chapter? What dreams do you have for your life? For your community?

Essays are multiparagraph pieces of writing that focus on and develop a single, complex main point. Essays have a perfect structure for analytical college writing because you can use them to analyze the parts of a complex topic piece by piece in paragraphs.

In this chapter, you'll study the parts of the academic essay. Then you'll read a student essay and write an essay of your own.

Essay Form

Essays—like letters, news articles, autobiographies, stories, and other types of writing—can be written in many different styles. Essay writers will adjust the structure and vocabulary of their essays to fit their purposes and audiences. This section gives you an overview of how most *academic* essays are set up.

Here is a visual overview of essay form:

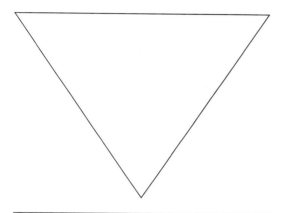

Introduction Paragraph
Begins with mention of a broad topic. Ends with a *specific* main point called the *thesis*.

Topic Sentence begins paragraph—supports one part of the thesis.
(Offer support for topic sentence: examples, comparisons, personal experience, quotations, and so on.)

Body Paragraph
Develops one supporting point.

Transition and topic sentence that supports another part of the thesis.
(Offer support for topic sentence: examples, comparisons, personal experience, quotations, and so on.)

Body Paragraph
There can be any number of body paragraphs.

Conclusion Paragraph
This paragraph draws the essay to an end.

Notes

As you read this chapter, remember to highlight important points and terms. Record your questions and comments in the margin.

Message, Purpose, and Audience

Writers must always think first about *what* they want to say and *why*. They must also think about *who* the intended audience is. The message, purpose, and audience will affect how writers put ideas down on paper.

An essay, for example, can be written to argue a point, to explain a process, or to define a complex term. Sometimes a writer will want to accomplish two or more of these goals in a single essay. For example, a writer may want to *explain* the history of racism in the United States and then *argue* that more must be done to end racism.

When the writer has a clear sense of what the message and purpose are, the writer will have a better idea of what the structure of the essay must be.

During this thinking and planning process, the writer also considers to whom he or she is writing. Addressing state legislators is different from addressing parents at a preschool or teenagers in high school. The writer must think ahead about the audience he or she wants to reach.

Introduction and Thesis

The **introduction** of an essay is usually the first paragraph or two. (The introduction to a *book* would be longer, perhaps a whole chapter.) The *function* of the introduction is to warm up the reader and get the reader focused on the main point.

Imagine that your reader has just finished reading a magazine article on how to lower cholesterol. Then the reader picks up your essay on ending racism in the United States. Your introduction needs to help the reader shift her attention from the subject of cholesterol to the topic of equality. Your introduction, in an academic essay, will probably express your main point in the last sentence of the introduction. This sentence is called the *thesis statement*.

A **thesis statement,** then, is the sentence or two at the end of your introduction that expresses the focused main point of your essay. Your *topic* may be *ending racism,* but that is a *broad* topic. Your thesis statement must explain what you want to say about this topic. Here are some possible thesis statements that connect to the broad topic of *ending racism:*

- Teaching kids in school about other cultures will help end racism.
- Martin Luther King Jr.'s "I Have a Dream" speech affected my path in life.

- Modern music is a powerful weapon against racism in America.

There are many different directions a writer could take with a broad topic like *ending racism.*

To review, the introduction of an essay usually begins by focusing the reader on a broad topic. There are many ways to begin. Here are a few:

- Offer an interesting, thought-provoking quotation or question.
- Paint a scene for the reader to consider.
- Explain the history behind the main topic.
- Explain how you became personally interested in the topic.
- Define important terms that relate to your topic.

Then the writer gradually gets more and more specific in the introduction, until he has explained a focused, complex main point in the thesis statement.

Besides expressing the message and purpose of the essay, the introduction should also give clues as to who is in the audience. The tone and vocabulary should be tailored to fit the intended audience.

Body Paragraphs

The paragraphs that come after the introduction are called body paragraphs. The function of each **body paragraph** is to develop a single point that supports the thesis.

A body paragraph usually begins with a *topic sentence* that announces the main point of the paragraph. This main point should clearly and directly connect to the thesis. Often a writer uses a transition word in the topic sentence that helps the reader see how paragraphs connect to one another and to the thesis. The paragraphs should be presented in a logical order.

Within the paragraph, the writer offers explanations, details, quotes, comparisons, and so on. These pieces of information develop the idea and add interest to the piece of writing.

Conclusion

The last paragraph in an essay is usually the **conclusion paragraph.** The function of the conclusion paragraph is to draw the essay to an end. If the essay has been long and complex, the writer might choose to summarize all of the supporting points in the essay. However, summarizing

Notes

isn't necessary with shorter essays—and summarizing can seem repetitive and boring if used in short essays.

In concluding a short essay (one with fewer than 10 paragraphs), think about how you started the essay. Is there a definition, quote, or scene in your introduction that you would like to return to?

Also consider these ideas:

- Is there a new quote or scene that would help bring together the ideas you expressed in your essay?
- Would it be helpful to explain how your main point may affect your everyday life or the lives of your readers?
- Should you say anything about the future of this topic?
- Is there something you or your reader should do about the main topic?
- How does this topic connect to larger groups of people—your neighborhood, city, state, or country?

Qualities of Effective Essays

The same qualities that make a paragraph effective also apply to essays. In Chapter 7, you learned about the five qualities of effective writing. Here is a brief review of those qualities and how they apply to essays.

Interesting and Thoughtful

An effective essay is the product of careful thinking and planning. The writer doesn't have to express a "new" idea, but the writer must give his unique perspective. As the writer reads, discusses, brainstorms, and drafts, he will find information and ideas to mention in the essay. The writer can offer personal experiences, quotations, analyses, and so on that draw the reader in and help explain the main point.

Focused

The focused essay expresses a clear main point in a thesis statement. Occasionally, you will see effective essays that only hint at the main point, or that give the main point at the end of the essay. However, usually writers offer their main point in a thesis statement at the end of the introduction. A focused essay then sticks to the main point expressed in the thesis. Through revision, the writer will cut out all pieces of information that don't directly support the main point.

Each body paragraph addresses one part of the main point. The topic sentences in each paragraph are crucial tools that help the reader not only to stay focused on the main point but also to see connections between paragraphs.

Developed

An effective essay is well developed. The writer offers a significant amount of support—quotations with analysis, explanations, specific examples, comparisons, and so on. The writer may do research, draw from assigned readings, or offer personal experience as part of the support.

Organized

The body paragraphs in an effective essay are organized in a logical pattern. There are many different organizational patterns. The writer must think about which pattern works best with his ideas and then stick to that pattern. Here are some common organization patterns a writer may use:

- Least important points first, most important points last
- Most obvious points first, least obvious points last
- Ideas in the order that they happened

Ideas *within* paragraphs must also be organized. The writer must make sure that ideas flow. Transition words can often help a writer show how ideas connect.

Clearly Written

Sentences within the essay must be clearly written. The writer needs to read his work aloud and carefully proofread to avoid typing, spelling, and grammar problems. The writer must also look at sentence structure and vary the length and complexity of sentences, so that the writing does not become repetitive or boring. Complex sentences also help the writer express complex ideas.

Points to Remember about Essays

- *The first paragraph (or two) in an essay is the introduction paragraph.* It announces the general topic and gradually brings the reader to the complex, main point of the essay.

Notes

- *The main point of the entire essay is expressed in a sentence called the thesis statement.* The thesis statement appears at the end of the introduction.
- *The body paragraphs of an essay each focus on one point that supports the thesis.* These paragraphs may contain different kinds of support—examples, explanations, quotations, statistics, comparisons, and so on.
- *The conclusion paragraph draws the essay to an end.* It may express what the writer learned from writing the essay and what the writer hopes the reader will learn.
- *The five qualities of effective writing apply to both essays and individual paragraphs:*
  - Interesting and thoughtful
  - Focused
  - Developed
  - Organized
  - Clearly written

Variety in Essays

Readers have certain expectations when they read essays. But you will find that as you read and write more essays, there is some variety in the way they are structured. Usually, writers present a clear thesis statement right where you expect it—at the end of the introductory paragraph. Sometimes, however, writers only hint at their thesis in the introduction. Or maybe a writer will pose a specific question early, and the answer that comes later is actually the thesis.

Just keep in mind that an essay must be focused around a single, complex point. Also remember that most college instructors will expect you to offer a thesis statement at the end of the introduction and topic sentences at the beginning of each body paragraph.

Even within this formal academic structure, there is room for creativity. As suggested earlier, your introduction and conclusion are good places to paint a scene for your reader or offer an interesting quotation (from a song, a poem, or another reading). You can also use interesting detail, adjectives, adverbs, and embedded phrases to add compelling information to your essay.

One of the surest ways to make your essay unique and interesting is to keep your audience in mind and use your own clear voice. As you write, picture your audience listening to you. Use your voice to reach them. That doesn't mean you should use casual speech. It does mean that you should use words you are comfortable with, and that you should use information from your own life to help you explain your ideas.

As you read the essay that follows, you will want to pay attention to how the writer uses formal essay structure to help her express her ideas. Also watch for ways that the writer makes her essay unique and interesting.

Reading Assignment: An Essay

In the student essay that follows, Ivana Kim explores the topic of dreams and expectations. As you read, think about the different kinds of dreams people have and the actions they will take to make these dreams come true.

Reading Assignment—"Dreams as Conscious Visions"

Preview Because this is an academic essay (from a freshman composition class) you can preview easily by reading the title, author's name, introduction (and thesis statement), and the topic sentences for each body paragraph. Read these parts now.

Anticipate In your own words, what is the general topic of the essay? What does the writer want to accomplish in writing about this topic? What does she want you to learn from the essay?

_____

_____

_____

_____

Read Read the essay. Mark unknown words.

Notes

Dreams as Conscious Visions

By Ivana Kim

Note that Kim begins her introduction by explaining how the broad topic of dreams came up in her life.

1 One day during Freshman English as we were discussing the idea of keeping dream journals, I said to myself, "How can I keep a dream journal? I don't remember any of my dreams. I'm not even sure if I do dream." However, I soon realized that I do indeed dream and that there are certain dreams I never forget. These are not dreams I have while I am sleeping; they are visions I create in my conscious mind, visions of what I want for my future. I believe our most important dreams are those we have when fully conscious. "Dream" in this sense of the word, does not merely refer to images that appear to us in our sleep; it is something more specific. Our conscious dreams are expressions of our most meaningful desires, desires that are more significant to our futures than those hidden ones which psychologists such as Freud and Jung believe are expressed in our **nocturnal** dreams. We can act on our waking **aspirations** because we can understand the desires which are embodied in them; these wishes are concrete. Our conscious hopes do not need to be interpreted. Instead of leaving us mystified with only a vague idea of their messages, these dreams guide us and clearly point out the direction of our lives. Conscious dreams are hopeful visions of what we want to be, what we want to happen, what we want to do. Such dreams are not altogether realistic, but they help us set and achieve the goals that enable us to find fulfillment in life.

Nocturnal means nighttime.
Aspirations are hopes and goals.

Highlight the thesis and the topic sentences when you reread.

2 When Martin Luther King, Jr. said, "I have a dream," he was referring to this visionary type of dream. He wanted the United States to become a nation in which people would be judged "not by the color of their skin but by the content of their character." His greatest desire was to obtain freedom and justice for all. His dream was not completely realistic; it is not possible to erase prejudice totally from the minds of all citizens. However, this vision of an ideal America motivated King's actions, driving him to set smaller more realistic goals as a means of nearing the ideal. His dream was not a fleeting image which occurred in the darkness of night; it was a source of permanent inspiration. He said, "I *have* a dream. . . . I have a dream *today."* He didn't say, "I had a dream last night." King's words exemplify the meaning of the word "dream" as a conscious, idealistic, long-lived hope which gives direction to a person's life. Additionally, King's dream was not simply a personal dream; it sparked an enthusiasm that was contagious. His dream was shared by all of those involved in the civil rights movement, strengthening them to endure pain and hardship in order to move closer to the fulfillment of

What would be your dream for your country today?

their vision. Thus, a dream is not necessarily limited to an individual; many people can believe in the same dream.

3   Those who live in America share a common hope: the American Dream, which is a conscious vision of opportunity and success. The same idealistic belief that anything is possible through hard work motivates the average American, although specific ideas of success may differ among individuals. One person's dream might consist of finding a secure job, marrying an attractive person, buying a comfortable suburban house and a nice car, and having two children. Another person might long to live in a log cabin in the woods and open an outdoors school in order to teach people about nature. The common link between the two visions is both people's belief that they can attain what they dream if only they strive hard enough and take advantage of the opportunities America offers. Neither of these dreams includes realities such as paying taxes and bills, changing diapers, facing harsh weather and wild animals, or dealing with all the paperwork and problems of starting a school. Such mundane details are unnecessary in dreams. Dreams should *not* be totally realistic. When they become burdened with reality they are no longer inspirational and cease to be dreams. Our conscious dreams represent ideal situations consciously constructed and sustained to embody personal values and priorities, and therefore inspire us to work and to achieve.

4   We also have dreams that are purely personal. They do not have to be common to millions of people, like the American Dream, or to be so profound that they involve the entire nation, like King's. Every individual has a personal dream which gives meaning and direction to his or her life. I dream about becoming a doctor, of being called "Dr. Kim," doing rounds in a hospital, having the knowledge and skill to relieve pain and cure illness, feeling the emotional satisfaction that comes from such work. Although many others may share the same dream, I believe my vision is unique because it involves my own values and reasons for wanting to become a doctor and because I solely am sustaining it. I could choose to abandon this dream at any time, but I don't. It is my creation. As I continue to keep it before me, it influences the courses I select, the activities in which I choose to participate, the amount of time I study, and my general attitude toward academics. The dream I have for my career is one of my most important sources of motivation. I do not dream of the many years of study, sleepless nights, and other details of reality; I dream of the rewards and fulfillment in attaining something I so strongly desire. Thus, my personal dream is an image of my highest aspirations, which I sustain in my conscious mind to guide and inspire my choices and actions.

Notes

What is your personal dream?

Notes

⁵   The word "dream" then, as defined through the preceding examples, means a vision of our hopes and desires which we purposefully retain in our minds to help direct our lives but which is not completely buried in reality. This definition gives dreams much more significance than one in which dreams are simply pictures we see in our sleep. To quote Walt Disney, "A dream is a wish your heart makes." A conscious dream is a wish somewhere in between a fantasy and a goal. Such aspirations are not as imaginary and unattainable as fantasies, but they are loftier and more idealistic than practical goals. They are the wishes of our conscious mind and heart which make us reach higher and grow.

Reread   Reread the essay. As you reread, use context clues and the dictionary to learn meanings of new words. *Mark the thesis and the topic sentences.* Also, in the margins, label the different types of support Kim uses—quotes, examples, details, and comparisons. Finally, record your reactions and questions in the margins.

Vocabulary cards: Make definition cards and sentence cards for the words listed here.

- *fleeting*, paragraph 2
- *contagious*, paragraph 2
- *mundane*, paragraph 3

Think Critically

1. What is Kim's purpose in writing? Explain her thesis in your own words. Then, in your own words, explain the main point in each of her body paragraphs.
2. Kim does a good job of using quotations for support. The quotations connect well to the topic, and they do not take over the essay. If you haven't already, mark the places where she uses quotations.
3. Kim also uses detailed examples well. If you haven't already, mark places where she uses interesting examples to make her essay stronger and more interesting.
4. According to Kim, why should people have conscious dreams?
5. How does Kim explain the differences between a fantasy, a plan (or goal), and a dream?

Summarize   In just a few sentences, explain to someone who has not read this essay what it is about.

_____

_____

_____

_____

Sentence Style

Study these sentences:

> One person's dream might consist of <u>finding</u> a secure job, <u>marrying</u> an attractive person, <u>buying</u> a comfortable suburban house and a nice car, and <u>having</u> two children. Another person might long to <u>live</u> in a log cabin in the woods and <u>open</u> an outdoors school in order to teach people about nature.

Kim has made her verb forms *parallel.* **Parallel** means having similar form. When Kim lists items, they all have similar forms. For example, all of the following words end in *–ing:*

finding

marrying

buying

having

The following words are in the infinitive form. That is, they are verb forms with *to* in front. The *to* appears only once in the sentence, but it is actually working with both words.

(to) live

(to) open

This parallelism makes Kim's sentences easy to read. In the following sentence, underline the parallel verb forms:

> Neither of these dreams includes realities such as paying taxes and bills, changing diapers, facing harsh weather and wild animals, or dealing with all the paperwork and problems of starting a school.

Your Turn Write a sentence in which you list three verb forms that are parallel in form. (For more on parallelism, see Chapter 26.)

Notes

Express Yourself

Explain the Traditional American Dream

America is known as the "land of opportunity," where people can fulfill dreams. Today, people might point to the homeless or minority groups and say that they don't have the opportunities necessary for achieving the American dream.

In a paragraph, define the traditional American dream. In your paragraph, mention who can achieve this dream and how. Stick with old-fashioned, traditional beliefs.

Additional Paragraph Assignment: In a paragraph, explain who may not be able to achieve the American dream in our modern society. Also explain why.

Journal Assignment

Ask Others about Their Dreams

This journal has two parts:

First create a definition of the traditional American dream. Write down your own thoughts. Then seek out additional definitions from other people or books, and write down what you find out. You may want to ask a history instructor on campus. Or you might ask a librarian for help finding a definition.

Second, interview family and friends to find out what their American dream is. Write down what you find out.

Essay Assignment: Your Dream

You often hear people refer to "the American dream." In this assignment, you'll explain what the traditional American dream is (or was). You will also have the chance to personalize this dream by discussing your own modern dream for your life.

Here is the assignment you are preparing for:

In an essay, explain the traditional American dream; then describe your dream for your life.

When you describe the traditional American dream, you can create one definition that fits any time period between 1776 and 1950.

The Writing Process for This Essay

Pre-Drafting

With your classmates, discuss the traditional American dream. What do most people see in this dream? Keep in mind that the idea of the American dream has been around since the beginning of this country, when the founders celebrated the idea that "all men are created equal" and stated that all Americans have certain "inalienable rights to freedom and the pursuit of happiness." What did the first Americans want? How would they reach these goals? (You may want to refer to your journal about the American dream.) What did people want in the 1950s? Who could reach these goals? How would people reach these goals?

Mother Jones (pp. 80–81) and Ivana Kim (pp. 164–166) discuss the dreams people have. You may want to reread what these authors wrote as you think critically about what people dream. How would Mother Jones have described her American dream?

What do people want today? How do they plan on reaching their goals? You may want to refer to your journal about the American dream. With your classmates, discuss each person's individual dream for their life. How will each of you reach these dreams? What steps must you take? Think about your education and the personal sacrifices you may have to make.

Here again is the writing assignment:

In an essay, explain the traditional American dream; then describe your dream for your life.

When you describe the traditional American dream, you can create one definition that fits any time period between 1776 and 1950. Underline the important terms in this assignment. Then explain to someone else what you must write about.

Write freely for at least 15 minutes. What images and ideas do you think came to the minds of people in the past when they spoke of the American dream? Has this dream changed for you? How? Why? Review your readings and class discussion notes for more ideas to write about.

When you are done with your freewriting, review it. Highlight the parts that seem most promising.

Experiment with thesis statements until you find one that clearly expresses your idea. Make sure that this thesis statement directly responds

Notes

to the writing prompt. You may want to change the writing prompt into a question when testing your thesis statement.

Then think about what your supporting points should be. Create a topic sentence for each paragraph. Your thesis and these topic sentences will function as your rough outline. If you have the opportunity, share this outline with a classmate or your instructor.

On a separate piece of paper, create a space for your introduction, each body paragraph, and your conclusion. In each space, make notes about what might go in each paragraph. Review your readings, class notes, and freewriting for ideas.

Drafting

In this essay, you may want to use your introduction to explain the traditional American dream. Your thesis should then state that you will explain your own American dream in the rest of the essay.

Another option is to use questions or quotes in the introduction to warm up the reader to the topic of the American dream. Perhaps you will want to briefly mention some different kinds of American dreams. Your thesis could then state that you will explain these dreams and your own American dream in the body of the essay.

A third option for your introduction is to discuss dreams in general and then end with a thesis that focuses directly on the writing assignment.

There are actually many options for how to approach this topic. You may want to experiment with more than one before committing yourself to a specific approach.

Student Sample

An Introduction

Read this introduction from a student essay.

My Personal American Dream

By Francis Vessigault

Many people in the world, and especially those in the United States focus their dreams and goals in having lots of money, an expensive car, a comfortable house and a well paid job in order to satisfy themselves or sometimes gain popularity. As for mortal life, my dreams and goals are similar to many ambitious people. I do not wish to

Continued

become a millionaire because I know that money is not always the source of happiness. I would like to gain a well paid job in order to support myself and one day my future family but I also want a stable, meaningful marriage.

Think Critically

1. How did Vessigault begin his introduction? What did he focus on in the first sentence?
2. Highlight his thesis statement.
3. What will his body paragraphs be about?
4. Do you see a place where he could have used the transition "however"?   ∎

Skill Spotlight

Essay Introduction Strategies

Writing introductions can be challenging. Some writers like to get a strong, clear introduction and thesis completed before moving on to the body of the essay.

Other writers create a thesis statement and then just write a sketch of the introduction. After (or while) drafting the body of their essays, they come back to the introduction to complete it.

Here are some strategies to consider for your introduction:

- Begin with an interesting, thought-provoking quotation or question.
  - You may want to use a quote from a history textbook or an Internet site. Or maybe you have a quotation from another source—a poem, song, or essay.
  - Another option is to begin by asking your reader some questions that will lead to your area of interest. If you use a quote or questions, be sure that they directly relate to your topic.
- Paint a scene for the reader to consider.
  Describe a scene in such a way that your readers will feel they are there with you. If you're writing about graduating from college, help your reader to see the crowds of people and feel the excitement as you stand in your gown and cap.
- Explain the history behind the main topic.
  Are there facts from a news article, Internet site, or other resources that you can use to help the reader become interested in your topic?
- Explain how you became personally interested in the topic.

Continued

Notes

Notes

See Ivana Kim's introduction on page 164 to see an example of this kind of introduction.

• Define important terms that relate to your topic.
For example, if you are writing about your dream to preserve the rain forests, you might want to define scientific terms.

The body paragraphs, remember, must begin with topic sentences. Use each body paragraph to explain (analyze) a different part of your main point. Depending on your thesis, you may discuss a different American dream in each paragraph. Or, you might explain different parts of your own dream in each paragraph. There are many different approaches you could take to support your thesis.

Student Sample

A Body Paragraph

The following is the first body paragraph in a student essay. Read the paragraph and then the topic sentence for the second body paragraph (from Lucky Le's "Good-bye American Dream").

In order to become a doctor, I must realize the reality. First, I need to transfer to a UC college. Once I transfer, I won't be working anymore. I want to fully concentrate on my major and pass all the classes. I won't have time for friends, T.V., nor the beautiful weather. Then I have about ten years of school. It will be stressful but a great challenge for me. Finally, I have to realize that I will be in a huge debt. So no matter how life will challenge me, I have to finish my major to pay every single cent back.

When I become a doctor, I promise myself that I will be involved with my patients. . . .

Think Critically

1. What do you think Le's thesis might be for this essay?
2. Highlight the topic sentence in Le's first body paragraph.
3. How does Le support the topic sentence in her first body paragraph?
4. What kind of support do you think she put in her second body paragraph? ■

Once you have a draft completed, transfer everything to note cards. Each note card should represent one paragraph. This will help you see each paragraph as a separate piece. Check to see that each paragraph has a topic sentence and that each paragraph directly supports the thesis. Does any card seem underdeveloped? Revise as necessary. Then, by moving the cards around, you can experiment with the order in which you'll present the paragraphs.

A well-organized essay presents its major points in a logical order. Readers have an easier time understanding what you have to say if your ideas are organized in a way that makes sense to them. To help readers understand your organizational pattern, you will want to use transition words.

Transitions are words that build bridges between ideas. They act as glue in your paragraphs and essays. Depending on the topic and the organizational pattern you use, you will use different transitions. For example, if you are organizing your ideas in a *chronological pattern*—organizing items by time—then you might want to use some of these transitions:

- first
- second
- third
- then
- next
- after that
- following this step

If you are presenting ideas from opposing sides, you may want to use these transitions that help writers introduce opposite ideas:

- on the other hand
- however
- on the contrary
- yet
- but

If you are presenting information that leads to other information, you may want to use words like these:

- first
- therefore

Notes

- consequently
- since
- because

Transitions can be used within a body paragraph to help ideas flow from one sentence to the next. They can also be used in topic sentences to help the reader move from one paragraph to the next.

Here is a review of how to punctuate correctly using transition words. *But* and *yet* can work with a comma and join sentences:

- I would have preferred to go to school, *but* I have had to work to support my family.

Since and *because* can join sentences—sometimes with a comma and sometimes without—depending on their placement.

- I will attain my dream *because* I am determined.
- *Because* I am determined, I will attain my dream.

Words like *however, therefore,* and *consequently* don't join sentences. They can introduce a sentence or work with a semicolon.

- My parents' dream was to own their own farm and raise cattle. However, my dream is to live in New York and work with under-privileged schoolchildren.
- My parents' dream was to own their own farm and raise cattle; however, my dream is to live in New York and work with under-privileged schoolchildren.

Here are sentences that might be topic sentences for three different body paragraphs in an essay.

- *First,* I will finish my schooling.
- *Second,* I will volunteer at the local schools while I'm still in college.
- *Finally,* I will get a job in a school where the kids really need me.

(See Chapter 25 for more information on transitions.)

Review pages 159–160 to find ideas on how you might wrap up your essay in your conclusion paragraph.

Revising
Share your draft with a reader, and consider these questions:

- Does the writer appear to understand the assignment?
- Where is the thesis? Highlight it.
- Does the thesis directly respond to the writing assignment?
- Does the introduction warm up the reader to the general topic without giving away too much detail? Does anything need to be added to or removed from the introduction?
- Do the body paragraphs begin with topic sentences?
- Do the topic sentences clearly connect to the idea expressed in the thesis?
- Do the body paragraphs contain enough information and support so that the ideas in the essay are clear and interesting?
- Are the body paragraphs and the sentences within the paragraphs logically organized? Does the writer need to add any transition words to make the organizational pattern clearer?
- Does the conclusion give the reader the sense that the essay is finished?
- Consider the advice you get from your reader.
- Review your Evaluation Chart (p. 453) and consider what your instructor said about previous writing assignments.

Revise, making your own choices about what you should change and improve.

Editing
Read your essay aloud again. Consider the following questions:

- Do you have a pair or series in any of your sentences? Have you made the pair or series parallel in structure? (See Chapter 26 for a review of parallelism.)
- Can you make your sentences more expressive by beginning some of them with an *–ing* phrase? (See Chapter 27 for a review of *–ing* phrases.)
- Can you use some of your vocabulary words in your essay?

Additional Reading
(See Section VIII; "The Reader.")
"My Vision," by Ayanna Williams. This student essay responds to the Essay Assignment: Dreams. The writer explains her personal American dream.

Notes

🖥 **Computer Note**
If you have decided to move some of your paragraphs around, or even if you are just moving a sentence or two, you should use the Cut and Paste tools on your computer. Highlight the section you want to move. Cut it (look for the scissors icon). Then put your cursor where you want the cut portion to appear and click on Paste (often looks like a clipboard.)

🖥 **Computer Note**
First "save" your essay. Tell the computer to leave 4 blank lines between every line of typed words. You can do this by going to Format and Paragraph and adjusting line spacing. (You may need to click on Line Spacing, then Multiple, and then type in "4.") This will allow you to carefully study each line and look for editing errors. Print this version of your essay. Mark corrections with a pen, and then go back to the saved version of your essay to make your corrections.

Notes

Expressive Sentences

The chapters listed here are designed specifically to coordinate with the theme and "Sentence Style" sections in Chapter 11.

Chapter 26: Parallelism

Chapter 27: Beginning Sentences with *–ing* Phrases

Sentence Basics and Avoiding Sentence Errors

In this section, you are introduced to basic sentence terms and to the most serious sentence errors.

Some exercises in these chapters ask you to underline, circle, or fill in a blank.

Other exercises will require you to write out complete sentences or paragraphs. Often you'll create original sentences.

The most important work in this section takes place when you apply your new knowledge to the paragraphs you are writing for class.

Your goals in these chapters are to become comfortable with key terms and to learn to correct and avoid the most important sentence errors during the editing stage of your writing process. In other words, this section helps you to polish your professional image.

12

Verbs, Part One

Knowing *many* technical sentence terms won't necessarily make you a better writer. But you do need to be comfortable with a *few* terms so that you can talk about your sentences and understand them better. This chapter focuses on one important term: *verb*.

Chapter 12 covers the following topics:

✦ A complete sentence
  • Verbs
  • Subjects
✦ Identifying verbs
  • Action verbs
  • Linking verbs
  • Helping verbs + –*ing* words
✦ Identifying non-verbs
  • Infinitives
  • Prepositional phrases

Notes

Computer Note

If you wanted to check that a sentence is complete, you could use grammar check to review your sentence. Highlight the sentence, go to Tools on the menu bar, and click on Spelling and Grammar. (Your word processing program may automatically underline errors.) Grammar check can be helpful, but sometimes it says you've made an error when you haven't, and sometimes it says you haven't made an error when you have. So don't rely on grammar check too much! Check your own work.

A Complete Sentence

Except on rare occasions, writers need to use complete sentences. Incomplete sentences can be unclear and will make the reader think that the writer has not done a careful job.

A **complete sentence** has a subject and a verb and expresses a complete idea.

A **subject** is the person, thing, or idea that is performing an action or that is being described.

A **verb** expresses action or links the subject of the sentence to other information in the sentence.

Here are some examples of complete sentences:

• I enjoyed the article about cloning.
  The subject is *I*.
  The verb is *enjoyed*.
  This sentence expresses a complete thought.

• What do you think about cloning?

The subject is *you.*

The verb is *do think.*

This sentence expresses a complete thought (a question).

- Sam is crazy!

  The subject is *Sam.*

  The verb is *is.*

  This sentence expresses a complete thought.

Identifying Verbs

This chapter covers one important component of a complete sentence—the verb. In fact, you'll study three kinds of verbs: *action verbs, linking verbs,* and *helping verbs* (with present participles).

Action Verbs

Verbs that express action are called **action verbs.** They make sentences interesting and lively.

Here are some sentences using action verbs. Verbs are underlined twice.

She <u>reads</u> one novel a week.

He <u>talked</u> to his father about his reading.

The grandmother <u>writes</u> in her journal.

Practice #1   *Enrolling in College (action verbs)*

Underline the action verbs twice.

Example: The student chases his essay down the windy street.

- The student <u>chases</u> his essay down the windy street.

1. The woman walks shyly up to the college registration counter.
2. She enrolls in college.
3. She studies diligently every day.
4. She reads many books in her spare time.
5. After four years, she emerges as a confident, educated woman.

Notes

> **Practice #2** *The Diary (action verbs)*
> Underline the action verbs twice.
>
> 1. I argued with my older sister.
> 2. I decided to write in my diary.
> 3. I searched for my diary.
> 4. About twenty minutes later, I found it in my younger sister's room.
> 5. Then I argued with my younger sister.

Linking Verbs

Linking verbs are verbs that do not express action. Instead, they act as an "equals sign" between the subject and other information in the sentence. These verbs are especially important when the writer needs to *describe* the subject.

Here are some sentences using linking verbs. Verbs are underlined twice.

He <u>is</u> from Japan.
The child <u>looks</u> worried.
Being in school <u>feels</u> strange.

Here are some examples of other linking verbs.

All forms of "to be"	Words associated with our five senses	Others
is am are was were	look sound smell feel taste	appear prove seem remain become grow turn

Note: When a verb is acting as a linking verb, it will be followed by descriptive information.

- Example of a linking verb: The food *tastes* delicious.
- Example of an action verb: The man *tastes* the food.

Practice #3   *Martha Martin (linking verbs)*
Underline the linking verbs twice.

Example: The diary is interesting.

- The diary <u>is</u> interesting.

1. Martha Martin was a strong woman.
2. She felt lonely.
3. She was serious about surviving.
4. The seaweed tasted salty and slimy.
5. She is my hero.

Helping Verbs and –ing Words

Words ending in *–ing* are verbs when they have a helping verb working with them. **Helping verbs** are verbs that work with another word to create a verb. Another name for the *–ing* words is **present participle**. Here are some examples of helping verbs used with present participles.

We <u>are running</u> to catch the bus. (The word *are* is the helping verb and *running* is the present participle. Together they make one complete verb.)
She <u>is listening</u> to her favorite CD.
Timothy <u>was fishing</u> with his uncle.

Here are some other helping verbs and present participles.

Helping Verbs	Present Participles
will be	looking
	talking
	researching
am	writing
is	thinking
are	discussing
was	exploring
were	arguing
	working
	helping

Notes

Practice #4 *Paragraph Skills (helpers + present participles)*
In the following sentences, underline the verbs twice.

Example: I am taking an English class.

- I <u>am taking</u> an English class.

1. I am improving my paragraph skills.
2. Many history instructors are giving short-answer tests.
3. These exams are testing my paragraph skills and my knowledge of history.
4. Some employers were asking people to write during interviews.
5. Most of these employers were looking for good paragraph skills.

Practice #5 *Tutoring (helpers + present participles)*
In the following sentences, underline the verbs twice.

1. I was discussing my writing topic with my friend.
2. My friend was confusing me.
3. Later, the tutor was reviewing the assignment.
4. She was asking me some helpful questions.
5. I am planning to go to the tutor right away next time.

Identifying Non-Verbs

When you are trying to identify the verb in your sentences, sometimes it is helpful to cross out the words that you know cannot be verbs. This section discusses *infinitives* and *prepositional phrases* because these words cannot be verbs.

Infinitives

Infinitives are phrases that include *to* + the base form of a verb. The *base form* is the verb with no special endings like *–ed* or *–ing*. Infinitives cannot act as verbs.

Here are some examples of infinitives:

Susan hates <u>to walk</u>.

Sam loves <u>to sing</u>.

I want <u>to laugh</u>.

Practice #6   *The Spaniard (infinitives)*
Cross out infinitives.

Example: I need to get to the office.

- I need ~~to get~~ to the office.

1. The young man from Spain wanted to attend school in the United States.
2. He was afraid to start college in America.
3. However, he is determined to learn English.
4. His goals are to earn a bachelor's degree in science and to earn a teaching credential.
5. He is eager to begin.

Practice #7   *Frank's Diary (infinitives)*
- Cross out infinitives.
- Underline the verbs twice.

Example: Jim wants to ride his motorcycle.

- Jim <u>wants</u> ~~to ride~~ his motorcycle.

1. Sara likes to read biographies.
2. Today she decides to try to read Anne Frank's diary.
3. Frank likes to study.
4. Frank uses writing to express ideas, hopes, and fears.
5. Sara is eager to discuss the diary with her classmates.

Prepositional Phrases

A **preposition** is a word that suggests position, location, direction, condition, or time. A **prepositional phrase** is made up of a preposition and an object. Prepositional phrases are important tools for writers because they can be used in sentences to add information that will make the sentences more interesting and detailed. However, it is important to note that *the verb is never in the prepositional phrase.*

Here are some prepositional phrases. (The *prepositions* are highlighted. The words that follow each preposition are called *objects.*)

Notes

in the box
on the street
under the house
over the hill
to the right
for a moment
at the end
by William Shakespeare
to her
without any help

If you are having difficulty identifying the verb in a sentence, cross out the prepositional phrases. This will eliminate some of the possibilities.

Practice #8 *Grandfather's Diary (prepositional phrases)*
Cross out prepositional phrases. Each sentence will have one prepositional phrase.

Example: I went up to the attic.

• I went up ~~to the attic.~~

1. I look through my grandfather's diary.
2. His descriptions of his childhood home are vivid.
3. I read the best parts to my brother.
4. For a moment, I hear grandfather's guitar in my head.
5. His letters to my grandmother are beautiful.

Practice #9 *Internet Diaries (prepositional phrases)*
• Cross out prepositional phrases. All sentences have at least one prepositional phrase. Some sentences have more than one.
• Cross out infinitives. Not all sentence have an infinitive. Some have more than one.
• Underline verbs twice.

Example: In the shadows of the attic, I found the felon's diary.

• ~~In the shadows~~ ~~of the attic,~~ I <u>found</u> the felon's diary.

Continued

1. I decided to get on the Internet to look for modern diaries.
2. I went to one strange site.
3. At this site, people made their diaries public.
4. They would share their most intimate thoughts with the whole world!
5. Feeling like a snoop, I read through a couple of entries.

Review Exercise A   *The Interview*

Underline the verbs twice. Make sure that any *–ing* words (present participles) you underline have helpers working with them. Also, don't underline infinitives or prepositions because they are never verbs.

Writing a paragraph for this interview in the anthropology department is scary. Harry is wishing that he could use a pseudonym. He is thinking about hiding his identity. Harry is angry with himself for not reviewing his notes. It is difficult to improvise in this situation. Yesterday he was relaxing while prospecting for gold. Now, he is trying to answer questions about the first creatures to sit on their haunches to eat.

Review Exercise B   *Reading to Improve Writing*

- Cross out all infinitives.
- Cross out all prepositional phrases.
- Underline all verbs twice.
- Be careful. Don't underline an *–ing* (present participle) word unless it has a helper in front of it.
- *Note:* The words *like* and *without* can work as prepositions.

Reading is a fun way to improve your writing skills. Reading teaches you new vocabulary words like *pseudonym* and *sporadic*. You learn about writing techniques too. By looking carefully, you will see how to focus, develop, organize. Reading well-written sentences is also a good way to improve your own sentence structure—without even thinking about it!

Notes

Review Exercise C   *Carla*
- Cross out all infinitives.
- Cross out prepositional phrases in the following paragraph.
- Underline all verbs twice.
- Put an *A* over action verbs.
- Put an *L* over linking verbs.
- Put an *H* over helping verbs.
- Be careful. Don't underline an *–ing* word (present participle) unless it has a helper in front of it.
- *Note:* The word *like* can work as a preposition.

    Carla is starting college in two weeks. She wants to do well. She sees a counselor for guidance. The counselor helps her to set up her schedule. Then the counselor shows Carla, a mother of two, the daycare center. The daycare center is great. It looks like a friendly, happy place. Next, Carla goes to the tutoring center. She sets up a regular time to see a writing tutor. Carla is well prepared for her trek through college.

Create Your Own Sentences

Review Exercise D   *Writing Process*
The following are groups of words that need to be shaped into complete sentences. The problem with each one is that the verb is missing or incomplete.

- On a separate sheet of paper, revise each group of words, creating complete sentences.
- Then underline verbs twice.

Example: Thinking about the topic.

- I <u>am thinking</u> about the topic.
  OR
- Thinking about the topic <u>made</u> me tired.   *Continued*

There are many ways to create a sentence out of each group of words. You and your classmates won't necessarily come up with the same solutions.

1. Working out at the gym.
2. Watching television on Friday night.
3. To pay for my retirement.
4. To buy the latest Nike tennis shoes.
5. Singing in the shower.

Review Exercise E   *Original Sentences*
Do this work on another sheet of paper.

1. Write a sentence that has an action verb. Underline the verb twice.
2. Write a sentence that has a linking verb. Underline the verb twice.
3. Write a sentence that has a helper and a present participle working together as the verb. Underline the verb twice.
4. Write a sentence that has an infinitive in it. When checking for verbs, cross out the infinitive. Underline the verb twice.
5. Write a sentence that has a prepositional phrase in it. Cross out the prepositional phrase. Underline the verb twice.

Apply Your Knowledge

Select a piece of your writing. Using your knowledge of verbs, make improvements in that piece of writing.

- Make sure all sentences have a verb. When checking for verbs, cross out infinitives and prepositions to eliminate words that cannot be verbs.
- Use action verbs whenever possible to make your writing more lively.

Verbs, Part Two

This chapter continues the discussion of verbs. You will look closely at the following topics:

✦ Verb tense

✦ Regular and irregular verbs
✦ The multiword verb
✦ Multiple verbs

Notes

Verb Tense

Verb tense tells us what time the action (or the linking) takes place. One method for figuring out if a word is a verb is to check and see if it can change tense. *Only verbs can change tense.*

The three simple tenses are *present, future,* and *past.*

Present tense	Future tense	Past tense
walk	will walk	walked
talk	will talk	talked
study	will study	studied
explain	will explain	explained

If you change the tense of a sentence, the verb must change form. Here are some different tenses for the verb *walk:*

I <u>walk</u> to work. (present tense)

I <u>will walk</u> to work. (future tense)

I <u>walked</u> to work. (past tense)

If you are uncertain which word is the verb, change the tense of the sentence and see which word changes. Here is an example of changing the tense of a sentence:

In the tutoring lab, the instructor explains how to use the spell check program. (present tense)

[Yesterday] in the tutoring lab, the instructor *explained* how to use the spell check program. (past tense)

[Tomorrow] in the tutoring lab, the instructor *will explain* how to use the spell check program. (future tense)

Notes

The only word that changes is *explains* (*explained; will explain*). *Explains* is the verb in the first sentence.

When a helping verb and an *–ing* word (present participle) are working together as a verb and the tense of the sentence changes, only the helping verb changes tense.

Today, I <u>am writing</u> my English paragraph.

Yesterday, I <u>was writing</u> my English paragraph.

Tomorrow, I <u>will be writing</u> my English paragraph.

Practice #1   *The Reading Process (verb tense)*
- On another sheet of paper, rewrite these present-tense sentences and use the past tense.
- Then underline the verbs twice.

Example: I learn about the reading process.

- I <u>learned</u> about the reading process.

1. The student uses the reading process.
2. She follows the preview and anticipation instructions.
3. Rereading really helps her.
4. The students discuss the critical thinking questions.
5. A classmate summarizes the main points of the essay.

Practice #2   *Class Discussion (verb tense)*
- On another sheet of paper, rewrite these past-tense sentences and use the present tense.
- Then underline the verbs twice.

Example: They argued all day long.

- They <u>argue</u> all day long.

1. They discussed the article.

Continued

Notes

2. Jim and Steve interpreted the article in different ways.

3. The whole class learned a lot from both Jim and Steve.

4. They each had good ideas.

5. The class was ready to move on to the next article.

Practice Review *Writing Process (verb tense)*
• On another sheet of paper, rewrite the following present-tense paragraph and use the future tense.
• Then underline all verbs twice.

Prewriting is an important step in the writing process. By discussing the topic with classmates, I get good ideas to write about. In addition, I read about the topic. Of course, understanding the topic is crucial. I want to stay on the assigned topic. My favorite step is brainstorming. I write freely, and sometimes I surprise myself with some great ideas.

Practice Review *Vocabulary (verb tense)*
• On a separate piece of paper, rewrite the following future-tense paragraph and use the past tense.
• Then underline all verbs twice.

I will study my vocabulary words, and I will use them in my reports. Specifically, I will learn these terms: *tundra, wrench, bleak, galumphing, garrulous, lassitudinal, equine,* and *muse.* I will write interesting sentences like these:

Lost in the tundra, Ranger Stevens will feel bleak.

He will be my galumphing, garrulous coworker no longer.
I will wrench words out of his mouth.
He will yearn for the lassitudinal atmosphere of a tropical island.
Finally living in a warm climate, he will sit in his chair, and he will muse about my equine face.

Regular and Irregular Verbs

You may have noticed in the "Practice Review" exercises that not all past-tense verbs have –*ed* on the end. Those verbs are *irregular*. **Regular verbs** are verbs that change form in a regular pattern. **Irregular verbs** don't seem to follow any particular rules when they change tense.

The following lists give you examples of regular and irregular verbs. Because irregular verbs don't follow the rules, you have to memorize how each irregular verb changes form.

When you are unsure about the form of a word, look in the dictionary. The first form listed in the dictionary is the *base* form (present tense). Then you'll see the *past-tense* form and the *have* form, which is also called the **past participle** form. The *have* or *past participle* form is the form of the word you would use if "have" were to come before the verb form. Some dictionaries then list the –*ing* form (*present participle* form) and the –*s* form.

Here is a list of some regular verbs.

Base form	Past tense	Have form (past participle)
walk	walked	walked
discuss	discussed	discussed
look	looked	looked
investigate	investigated	investigated
improvise	improvised	improvised

Here are some irregular verbs.

Base form	Past tense	Have form (past participle)
awake	awoke	awakened
be	was	been
become	became	become
begin	began	begun
buy	bought	bought
choose	chose	chosen
cut	cut	cut
draw	drew	drawn
eat	ate	eaten

Notes

feel	felt	felt
get	got	got, gotten
hear	heard	heard
know	knew	known
put	put	put
see	saw	seen
throw	threw	thrown
write	wrote	written

Practice #3   *Drugs and Alcohol (regular verbs)*
Write sentences changing the regular verb that is underlined to the *past-tense* form and the *have form.*

Example: Using a present tense verb: We <u>play</u> video games.

- Using a past-tense verb: We <u>played</u> video games.
- Using a have-form verb: We <u>have played</u> video games.

1. Using a present-tense verb: The teacher <u>assigns</u> a research paper.
   a. Using a *past-tense* verb:
   b. Using a *have-form* verb:

2. Using a present-tense verb: They <u>look</u> for information about legalizing drugs.
   a. Using a *past-tense* verb:
   b. Using a *have-form* verb:

3. Using a present-tense verb: I <u>argue</u> for raising the legal age for drinking.
   a. Using a *past-tense* verb:
   b. Using a *have-form* verb:

Computer Note

If you wrote this sentence on the computer—"I writed about my experience,"—the computer would probably underline the word *writed.* The computer might also underline the whole sentence. Unfortunately, spell check and grammar check programs are rarely correct in identifying verb form errors. Instead of telling you to use the word *wrote,* the computer might tell you to use *writes* or *writer.* It might also tell you that you have a fragment. This is when you need a dictionary by your side.

Practice #4   *Writing (irregular verbs)*
Write sentences changing the irregular verb that is underlined to the *past-tense* form and the *have-form.*

Example: Using a present-tense verb: I <u>choose</u> a topic.
- Using a past-tense verb: I <u>chose</u> a topic.

Continued

- Using a have-form verb: I <u>have chosen</u> a topic.

1. Using a present-tense verb: They <u>become</u> confident writers.
   a. Using a *past-tense* verb:
   b. Using a *have-form* verb:

2. Using a present-tense verb: He <u>writes</u> a complex book about the fall of Rome and the rise of Christianity.
   a. Using a *past-tense* verb:
   b. Using a *have-form* verb:

3. Using a present-tense verb: I <u>begin</u> my paragraph by discussing the topic with my study group.
   a. Using a *past-tense* verb:
   b. Using a *have-form* verb:

Practice Review   *The Attack*

A student was asked to write a paragraph using only present-tense action verbs.

- First, underline all verbs twice.
- If a verb isn't an action verb, change the sentence as necessary so that it has an action verb.
- Also make sure that all verbs are in the present tense. (For this exercise, don't use helping verbs with *–ing* words.)
- Write the new paragraph on a separate piece of paper.

   Jamie trembled with fear. She heard the dog catching up to her. The dog's growl was frightening. She finally saw the gate. In a moment, she was leaping over the gate. The Chihuahua was disappointed.

The Multiword Verb

As you have seen with present participles and the future tense, some verbs are made up of more than one word. A **multiword verb** is a verb made up of more than one word.

   Here are sentences using multiword verbs:

Ms. Dalloway <u>is reading</u> research from the Internet. (a helper verb + a present participle)

Notes

Mr. Rankin <u>will go</u> to the library for his research. (future tense)

You will see other verbs that are made of three or more words, as in these examples:

She <u>should have looked</u> in my reference books.

He <u>has been working</u> too hard.

By this time tomorrow, I <u>will have been studying</u> for twenty hours straight.

He <u>should</u> not <u>have missed</u> class. (The word *not* interrupts the verb. It isn't really part of the verb.)

Practice #5 *Helping Out (multiword verbs)*
Underline verbs twice. Some of the verbs are single words.

Example: You should have asked the owner.

• You <u>should have asked</u> the owner.

1. He helped his brother.
2. He didn't help his brother.
3. He should have helped his brother by discussing the topic.
4. His brother would have done better on the assignment.

Practice #6 *Research (multiword verbs)*
Underline verbs twice. Some of the verbs are single words.

1. I read a newspaper article on our topic.
2. You could have read a magazine article on our topic.
3. The instructor should have warned me about the *National Enquirer.*
4. She didn't respect my research source.
5. I will go to the library next time instead of the grocery store.

Practice Review *Howard's Diary*
Underline verbs twice. Some of the verbs are single words. Others are multiword verbs.

Conceited means self-important or stuck-up.

(Howard, a **conceited** young man, looks at his college roommates. He opens his diary. He begins to write.)

Continued

I should have been born to a royal family. This university is not good enough for me. I have known for some time about my greatness. I should be working with private, brilliant tutors. My roommates, like most people, should be marooned on a desert island. They would huddle together on their haunches wondering what to do. They would not know how to improvise. They would live like savages.

Multiple Verbs

To avoid unnecessary repetition, writers often create sentences that have more than one verb. These two sentences wouldn't sound good together in a paragraph because they repeat information unnecessarily:

As a zoologist, I write in my diary. As a zoologist, I record my observations.

Here is a more interesting sentence, with two verbs and no repetition:

As a zoologist, I <u>write</u> in my diary and <u>record</u> my observations.

These sentences also sound repetitious, so you wouldn't want them in your paragraph:

Stefano misses his parents. Stefano sends them e-mail frequently.

Here is a more interesting sentence, with two verbs and no repetition:

Stefano <u>misses</u> his parents and <u>sends</u> them e-mail frequently.

Practice #7   *Dad's Diary (two or more verbs)*
Underline the verbs twice. You'll find at least two verbs in each sentence. Two sentences have three verbs.

Example: I yelled at her and hung up the phone.

• I <u>yelled</u> at her and <u>hung</u> up the phone.

1. I found my father's diary and read it.
2. The diary revealed my father's quiet love for his family and reminded me of many happy times.
3. After sharing my plans with my family, I researched my father's family, found old photos, and began to write his biography.

Continued

Notes

4. I worked hard for two years and produced an excellent biography.

5. I earned a million dollars, traveled to my father's childhood home in Italy, and met many relatives.

Practice #8 *The Day Care Worker (two or more verbs)*
Underline the verbs twice. You'll find more than one verb in each sentence.

1. At the end of the day, I sit at my desk, think about each child at my day care center, and make notes about each child.
2. Sometimes I think of new activities or go to the Internet to find new activities.
3. The kids like new activities and ask for new stories.
4. My work diary reminds me of each child's interests and works as a progress chart.
5. Looking back on old entries, I see kids growing and hear kids laughing.

Review Exercise A *The Observation Assignment*
In this exercise, you will use all you have learned about verbs. Here are some key points to remember:

• Words ending in *–ing* are verbs when they have a helper verb working with them.
• Some verbs are made up of three or more words. (Example: I should have been here sooner.)
• Some sentences have more than one verb.

Underline all verbs twice in the following paragraph.

For the first few days of my observation assignment, I studied the habits of my roommate Howard. Howard is a quiet guy, and he likes to write in his diary. During the last week, he watched me and my other roommates, and then immediately he wrote in his diary. So, basically, I was observing him, and he was observing us. Probably, he is taking notes about how to be more like us. During the week, Howard didn't do much else. He doesn't have any hobbies. He doesn't seem to have any friends. Perhaps he is feeling insecure about being the new guy in the apartment. I should have tried to include him in some of our activities and discussions. Next week I will.

Create Your Own Sentences

Review Exercise B   *Action!*
- Write a paragraph of at least five sentences using only action verbs. (Hint: Write a paragraph about an event or scene that involves a lot of action. Good topics would include a basketball game, a family picnic, and so on.)
- Use only present-tense verbs.
- Underline all verbs twice.

Note: You may find it easier to first write your paragraph without thinking too much about the verbs. Then you can go back and revise, making sure all the verbs are action verbs.

Review Exercise C   *The Past*
- Rewrite your paragraph from Exercise B and change all verbs to the past tense.
- Underline all verbs twice.

Review Exercise D   *Roommates*
- On another sheet of paper, combine each pair (or group) of sentences to make a single sentence that has more than one verb.
- Then underline the verbs twice.

Example:
With my tutor, I <u>discuss</u> the topic.
I <u>talk</u> about the specific assignment.
I <u>review</u> my draft.

Continued

Copyright © 2003 by Addison Wesley Longman, Inc.

Notes

Computer Note
If you are looking for an interesting action verb, you might use the "thesaurus" in your word processing program. For example, to find a more interesting word than *run,* type *run,* highlight it, and go to Tools on the menu bar. Look for the Language option, and then click on Thesaurus. The computer will list words like *sprint, jog,* and *scurry.*

Notes

- *One sentence:* With my tutor, I <u>discuss</u> the topic, <u>talk</u> about the specific assignment, and <u>review</u> my draft.

1. On Saturday, we divided up the household chores.
   We promised to stick to the new plan.
2. My roommate does all of the cooking.
   My roommate cleans the bathroom.
3. I water the garden.
   I dust and vacuum.
4. My cat guards the house.
   My cat eats the mice.
   My cat leaves hair and other presents for us to clean up.
5. I take my laundry to my mom.
   I beg for money.

Review Exercise E   *Original Sentences*
- Do this work on another sheet of paper.
- When you are done creating your sentences, underline all verbs twice.

1. Create a sentence with a helper and an *–ing* (present participle) word working together as the verb.
2. Create a sentence that has two verbs, each made of an *–ing* word (present participle) and a helper verb.
3. Create a sentence that has *one* verb made of at least three words. (Example: I <u>should have gone</u> to church.)
4. Create a sentence that uses three verbs.

Apply Your Knowledge

Select a piece of writing you completed before studying this chapter. Using your knowledge of verbs, make improvements in that piece of writing.

- Make sure all sentences have a verb.
- Change linking verbs to action verbs when possible.
- Correct errors in verb form.
- Create sentences with more than one verb when appropriate.

Subjects

This chapter will help you become familiar with the term *subject*. Specifically, you'll cover the following topics.

✦ Identifying subjects
  • Subjects are nouns or pronouns
  • Using *–ing* words as subjects

• Subjects and prepositional phrases
• Multiple subjects
• Implied subjects
• Subjects in *there* sentences
• Subjects and verbs in another position

Identifying Subjects

Notes

A *subject* is the person or thing performing an action, or it is the item being connected to other information in the sentence. To find the subject in a sentence, first find the verb. Then ask "who or what?" before the verb.

Here are two examples:

• Susan <u>wants</u> to improve her vocabulary.
    The verb is <u>wants</u>. Who or what <u>wants</u>?

    The answer is *Susan. Susan* must be the subject.

• The student <u>is learning</u> to study the context of vocabulary words.
    The verb is <u>is learning</u>. Who or what <u>is learning</u>?
    The answer is *the student. Student* must be the subject.

You can also ask the *who or what* question before the entire predicate. The **predicate** is the verb and everything that comes after the verb. Here is an example:

• Yesterday, my instructor <u>helped</u> me guess the meaning of some words.
    The predicate is <u>helped me guess the meaning of some words</u>.
    Who or what <u>helped me guess the meaning of some words</u>?
    The answer is *my instructor. My instructor* must be the subject.

Notes

Practice #1 *Writing a Paragraph (identifying subjects)*
• Underline the verbs twice.
• Underline the subjects once.

Example: The teacher announced the new writing topic.
• The <u>teacher</u> <u>announced</u> the new writing topic.

1. She asked us to freewrite.
2. Following her directions, I tried to write quickly.
3. I wanted to stop to check my punctuation and spelling.
4. The teacher advised us to keep writing fast.
5. I filled three pages while freewriting.
6. I am writing a paragraph for class.
7. Sometimes I enjoy writing.
8. She worries about her spelling.
9. In his paragraph, Lee is arguing for lower tuition.
10. Phong asks the instructor a question.

Subjects Are Nouns or Pronouns

When you were underlining subjects in Practice #1, you were underlining either nouns or pronouns. **Nouns** name people, place, things, or ideas: *brother, mountain, car, truth, Joe.* **Pronouns** are words that can stand in the place of nouns: *I, he, she, it.*

The following sentences show how nouns and pronouns act as subjects:

My favorite <u>movie</u> <u>is</u> *The Sixth Sense.* (The subject *movie* is a noun.)
<u>It</u> <u>scared</u> me. (The subject *it* is a pronoun.)

Practice #2 *Movies (nouns and pronouns as subjects)*
• Underline verbs twice.
• Underline subjects once.
• Put a *P* over subjects that are pronouns.
• Put an *N* over subjects that are nouns.

Continued

Example: I owe money at the video store.

    P

- I <u>owe</u> money at the video store.

1. I love movies.

2. My brother wants to be an actor.

3. He would like to direct films.

4. Steven Spielberg is one of my idols.

5. I also like Ang Lee's work.

Using –ing Words as Subjects

Words ending with *–ing* can be verbs when they are used with helper verbs. At other times, they can be nouns. Sometimes these nouns can be subjects.

Here are some examples of *–ing* words working as nouns (*but not* as subjects). *–ing* words working as nouns are called **gerunds.**

I love learning.

She enjoys writing.

Mr. Garrett went into teaching.

In the following examples, *–ing* words are used in different ways.

<u>Learning</u> different forms of each word <u>is</u> important to me. (*Learning* is a noun and subject.)

<u>He</u> <u>is looking</u> for definitions in the dictionary. (*Looking* is part of the verb.)

<u>Using</u> words correctly <u>is</u> critical. (*Using* is a noun and the subject.)

Practice #3   *Counseling Children (identifying subjects and verbs)*

- Underline verbs twice.
- Then underline subjects once. Don't underline a noun unless it is working as the subject.

Continued

Notes

Example: Earning a lot of money is not important to me.
- <u>Earning</u> a lot of money <u>is</u> not important to me.

1. My goal is to work with abused kids.
2. Counseling children is rewarding.
3. Last summer, I discovered this goal while volunteering at the local children's home.
4. I need good communication skills for this job.
5. Speaking well is important to me.

Practice Review   *Sheila the Singer*
- Underline verbs twice.
- Then underline subjects once. Don't underline a noun unless it is working as the subject.

Example: Everyone should have a goal.

- <u>Everyone</u> <u>should have</u> a goal.

1. Sheila's goal was to be a professional singer.
2. Singing is her passion.
3. Performing feels natural to her.
4. The odd hours, though, are difficult with a family.
5. In this class, she wants to improve her vocabulary.
6. Writing requires a good vocabulary.

Subjects and Prepositional Phrases

You will not find your subject (or your verb) in a prepositional phrase. (Remember that a prepositional phrase consists of a preposition and its object.)

Here are some prepositional phrases:

in the letter
to her
at the end
of the week

In the following sentences, the prepositional phrases are crossed out, verbs are underlined twice, and subjects are underlined once.

~~In the letter~~, <u>she</u> <u>expressed</u> her feelings vehemently.

<u>I</u> <u>wrote</u> a note ~~to her~~ ~~at the end~~ ~~of the week~~.

Practice #4   *Expressions (prepositional phrases)*
- Cross out the prepositional phrases.

Example: I wrote a poem to my sister.

- I wrote a poem ~~to my sister~~.

1. I express myself through my art.
2. Martin Luther King communicated well by giving speeches.
3. In a difficult situation, Cynthia uses humor to express herself.
4. My sister makes a statement about her beliefs by plastering her car with bumper stickers.
5. Poetry is my favorite form of expression.

Practice #5   *Brienna Decorates (subjects, verbs, prepositional phrases)*
- Cross out the prepositional phrases.
- Underline verbs twice.
- Then underline subjects once.

Example: I ask her for advice.

- <u>I</u> <u>ask</u> her ~~for advice~~.

1. Brienna expresses her ideas through home decorating.
2. After looking at many carpet samples, she chooses the most expensive.
3. She will put Italian tile in the kitchen.
4. She picks out wood shutters and blinds at the interior-decorating store.
5. She also selects three paintings by a local artist.

Multiple Subjects

Some sentences have more than one subject. Here are a few examples:

<u>Tattoos</u> and <u>body piercings</u> are a form of self-expression.

My <u>sister-in-law</u> and her <u>brother</u> express their artistic talents by painting murals.

<u>Decorating</u> the house and <u>growing</u> a beautiful garden can be forms of self-expression.

Practice #6 *Language (multiple subjects)*

- Underline verbs twice.
- Then underline subjects once. Cross out the prepositional phrases in sentences 3 through 7.

Example: Steven and Mike thought about skipping English class.

- <u>Steven</u> and <u>Mike</u> <u>thought</u> ~~about skipping English class~~.

1. Writing well and speaking effectively can give you power.
2. Spelling and using new words accurately are important skills.
3. Jones, Fredericks, and Wemple wrote paragraphs as part of the interview process.
4. My sociology teacher and my psychology teacher have essay questions on their exams.
5. Spencer and Brooke chose the same topics for their paragraphs.
6. The instructor, the students, and the dean were eager to read the review of the play.
7. James and I knew the importance of the written review of the play.

Implied Subjects

Some sentences don't appear to have subjects. These are called *command sentences,* and the subject for each sentence is an implied *you.* Here are two examples:

Write a letter to the senator.
Tell him about my concern.

(*You*) write a letter to the senator.

(*You*) tell him about my concern.

Notes

Practice #7   *Getting Started (implied subjects)*

- Underline the verb twice.
- Underline the subject once. If the subject is an implied *you*, write "you" at the beginning of the sentence. (Four of the sentences have implied subjects.)

Example: Hand me your paper.

- (*You*) <u>Hand</u> me your paper.

1. Discuss this topic with me.
2. Give me some new ideas.
3. I need to get a draft done.
4. Tell me your opinion.
5. Ask your friends to join us.

Subjects in There Sentences

At first, it may be difficult to find the subject in a sentence that begins with *there*. *There* is not the subject. First find the verb. Cross out prepositional phrases. Then the subject will be clearer.

Here are two examples:

~~There~~ <u>is</u> a problem ~~with your plan~~. *A problem* must be the subject.

~~There~~ <u>are</u> many reasons to write ~~to your father~~. *Many reasons* is the subject.

Practice #8   *The State Fair (subjects in* there *sentences)*

- Cross out prepositional phrases.
- Underline verbs twice.
- Underline subjects once.

Example: There is an article about the state fair in today's paper.

- There <u>is</u> <u>an article</u> ~~about the state fair~~ ~~in today's paper.~~

Continued

Notes

1. There are thousands of people at the state fair.
2. There are rides and horse races for everyone to enjoy.
3. There is a large farm animal exhibit toward the back of the fairgrounds.
4. There are quilts in the exhibit hall.
5. There is a fun house for kids.

Practice Review   *Vocabulary (implied subjects and subjects in* there *sentences)*

- Cross out prepositional phrases.
- Underline verbs twice.
- Underlines subjects once. If the sentence is a command sentence and the subject is an implied *you,* write *you* at the beginning of the sentence.

Example: Take notes for me in history class.

- (*You*) <u>Take</u> notes ~~for me in history class~~.

1. There are strategies for improving vocabulary.
2. Read for pleasure.
3. Pay attention to context.
4. Use the dictionary on my desk.
5. Quiz yourself and your classmates after class.
6. There is a list of words in the back of the book.
7. Learn to use other forms of each word.

Subjects and Verbs in Another Position

Most of the sentences you have worked with so far have been written with this pattern:

Subject + verb.

It is most common for the subject to come first and then all parts of the verb. However, with questions, parts of the verb will be separated, and the subject will not come first.

Here are some examples:

<u>Will</u> this <u>topic sentence</u> <u><u>make</u></u> sense?

<u>Have</u> I <u>given</u> enough support?

<u>Do</u> I <u>need</u> a wrap-up sentence?

To clearly see the verb, you can change the questions into statements.

This <u>topic sentence</u> <u><u>will make</u></u> sense.

I <u>have given</u> enough support.

I <u>do need</u> a wrap-up sentence.

Computer Note

If you do your sentence work on a computer and you want to do a double underline, try going to Format on your menu and then to Font. You may find Underline Style. Click on that, find the double underline, click on it, and then click OK.

Practice #9   *How Do I Begin? (finding subjects and verbs)*

• On a separate piece of paper, change the following questions into statements.

• Then underline the verbs twice.

• Underline subjects once.

Example: When will we go to the lecture?

• <u>We</u> <u>will go</u> to the lecture. (Note that *when* is deleted.)

Example: Have you seen the tutor?

• <u>You</u> <u>have seen</u> the tutor.

1. How should I begin this assignment? (Delete *how*.)
2. Do I need to reread the readings?
3. Will the tutor discuss the topic with me?
4. Should I write a longer brainstorm?
5. How do you like my draft? (Delete *how*.)

Practice #10   *The Movie (finding subjects and verbs)*

• Underline the verbs twice.

• Underline the subjects once.

1. Would you like to see the Anne Frank movie?
2. Have you seen it before?
3. Will your brother go with us?
4. Can he pay for the popcorn?
5. Whom does he want to invite?

Notes

Computer Note
If you want to cross out a word when typing, go to Format, Font, and Strikethrough.

Create Your Own Sentences

Review Exercise A
- On another piece of paper, create the sentences described in 1–6.
- Cross out prepositional phrases.
- Underline verbs twice.
- Underline subjects once.
- Use new vocabulary words in at least two sentences. Underline the vocabulary words.

1. Create a sentence that uses *parachuting* as the subject.
2. Create a sentence that has these two subjects: *jogging* and *swimming*.
3. Create a sentence that has a prepositional phrase. Circle the prepositional phrase.
4. Create a sentence with two subjects.
5. Create a sentence with an implied subject.
6. Create a question.

Review Exercise B
The subject in a sentence that begins with *there* can be unclear. When you are writing, it is generally a good idea to avoid writing *there* sentences because readers appreciate reading sentences with clear subjects and verbs.

- *Part One:* In the following numbered sentences, underline the verbs twice and the subjects once. You may want to cross out prepositional phrases.
- *Part Two:* Then, on a separate piece of paper, rewrite each sentence so that they no longer begin with *there*. Although you will need to change these sentences, try not to completely change the meaning of the sentence.

Examples:

- There <u>are</u> <u>two approaches</u> ~~to writing~~ this letter.

Continued

- (rewritten) I see two approaches to writing this letter.
- There <u>is</u> <u>one audience</u> ~~for this letter~~.
- (rewritten) He wrote this letter to one audience.

Hint: When you rewrite these sentences, try starting with a noun or pronoun as the subject.

1. There are pain and honesty in this poem.
2. There can be beauty in silence.
3. There is pain in Fred's song.
4. There is not just one way to interpret this painting.
5. There is a lesson to be learned here.

Apply Your Knowledge

Review one of your paragraphs.

- Make sure that each sentence has a subject.
- Could you get rid of any repetition in your paragraph if you created a sentence with two subjects?
- Should you revise a sentence and use an *–ing* word as a subject for variety?
- Do you have any *there* sentences? Revise them so that they have clearer subjects.

Understanding, Correcting, and Avoiding Verb Errors

In this chapter, you'll learn to identify, correct, and avoid two kinds of verb errors:

✦ Unnecessary shifts in tense
✦ Subject-verb agreement errors

- Third person singular, present tense
- Indefinite pronouns
- Phrases that confuse things
- The *there* sentence

Notes

Unnecessary Shifts in Verb Tense

Your readers expect you to be consistent with your verb tenses. (Remember, verb tense tells us what time the action or linking takes place. In Chapter 13, you studied the present, past, and future tenses.) Shifting between verb tenses is like jumping around in time. Readers find this confusing.

    Here is an example of incorrect verb tense:

> Women <u>had</u> few professional choices in the 1920s. They <u>work</u> as nurses and teachers.

Computer Note
Grammar check will probably not notice unnecessary shifts in tense. None of the incorrect sentences on this page were caught by grammar check.

The first verb, *had,* is in the past tense, which seems appropriate since the writer is looking back in history. The second verb, *work,* is in the present tense. This is confusing. Is the writer now talking about modern society?

    Here is an example of correct verb tense:

> Women <u>had</u> few professional choices in the 1920s. They <u>worked</u> as nurses and teachers.

Now both verbs are in the past tense, and the idea in the sentence is clearer.

    Here is another incorrect example:

> I <u>work</u> as a biologist. (present tense)

I <u>earned</u> a decent salary. (past tense)

Notes

Here is a correct example:

I <u>work</u> as a biologist. (present tense)

I <u>earn</u> a decent salary. (present tense)

Occasionally, you may need to shift tense within a paragraph or even a single sentence:

If I <u>lose</u> my job, I <u>will have</u> to borrow money.

In this case, the first verb is in the present tense, and the second verb is in the future tense. However, this shift makes sense because the writer is thinking about losing a job now and what will happen in the future.

The general rule, however, is to consistently use the same tense throughout a piece of writing.

Practice #1   *Different Methods of Expression (verb tense errors)*
- Underline the verbs twice.
- Find the verb tense errors.
- On a separate piece of paper, correct the sentences so that the verbs in each pair of sentences are in the same tense.

Example: The girl protests against fur coats. She cared about animals.
- The girl <u>protests</u> against fur coats. She <u>cared</u> about animals. (The first verb is in the present tense and the second verb is in the past tense.)
- The girl <u>protests</u> against fur coats. She <u>cares</u> about animals. (Both verbs are now in the present tense. It would have been okay to change both to past tense.)

1. Her mother takes a sculpting class. The instructor was talented.
2. They make beautiful rugs. The rugs told stories of the past.
3. A mother sews clothes for her children. She expressed her artistic skill and her love for the children.
4. She makes intricate jewelry. The pieces represented her love of animals.
5. The girl shaves off all of her hair. She made a statement about her independence.

Continued

Notes

6. I wear suits to work. My suits helped me project a professional, successful, conservative image.
7. My grandfather was part of a sit-in during the Civil Rights Movement. His action is his way of expressing his beliefs about segregation in restaurants.
8. I like to decorate my home for each holiday. I expressed my joy of life this way.
9. Susan writes in her diary. Sometimes she copied a new, favorite poem into the diary.
10. In my youth, I wore tye-dye shirts to work. The shirts express my liberal attitudes.

Practice #2 *My Paragraph (verb tense)*
Read the following paragraph and decide what tense it should be in.

- Then rewrite the paragraph on a separate piece of paper.
- Underline the verbs twice.
- Change the tense of any verbs that are not in the correct tense.

My last paragraph was pretty good. I used the writing process finally! I read the assigned readings. Then I turn to the back of the book and read a student paragraph. That helped me. I see what to do in my own paragraph. I discuss the topic with my tutor. She had some good ideas. I wrote a draft. The next day, I revise the paragraph. I want to make the topic sentence clearer. I also need to cut a couple of sentences. They really didn't fit.

Subject-Verb Agreement Errors

Subjects and verbs must agree in number. If you have a single subject, you must have a single verb. If you have a plural subject, you must have a plural verb. (**Plural** means more than one. Example: *they* and *we* are both plural.)

Notice how the verb *think* changes in these two sentences.

While having coffee, <u>he</u> <u>thinks</u> about the assignment.
While having coffee, <u>they</u> <u>think</u> about the assignment.

Notice how the verb *enjoy* changes in these two sentences.

He <u>enjoys</u> camping near the ocean.

They <u>enjoy</u> camping near the ocean.

Sometimes when people speak, they ignore this rule, or they may be using another dialect that does not follow this rule. However, academic writing, as you know, is different from casual speech. In academic writing, subjects and verbs must agree in number.

Third Person Singular, Present Tense

The most common time for people to make a subject-verb agreement error is when they are using third-person singular, present tense.

Here are some examples:

He <u>work</u> in the safety department. (incorrect)

He <u>works</u> in the safety department. (correct)

She <u>call</u> the supervisor. (incorrect)

She <u>calls</u> the supervisor. (correct)

	Singular	Plural
First Person (the person speaking)	I work kiss write	we work kiss write
Second Person (the person or people being spoken to)	you work kiss write	you work kiss write
Third Person (the person or people being spoken about)	**he, she, it** **(Or any word that can be used instead of *he, she,* or *it*. Examples: Mr. Smith, the policewoman, the flower)** **works** **kisses** **writes**	they work kiss write

Notes

The rule to remember: When you use *he, she, it* (or another third-person singular subject) in the present tense, put an *–s* or *–es* on the verb.

Practice #3   *Autobiographies* (subject-verb agreement)

• On a separate piece of paper, rewrite these sentences in the third-person singular. Your subject in each sentence will be *he, she, it,* or other words that can be used instead of *he, she,* or *it*.

• Use the present tense.
• Underline the verbs.

Example: I buy a book about writing. (first-person singular)

• He <u>buys</u> a book about writing. (third-person singular)

1. Writing my autobiography, I confront my past. (*Hint:* Remember to change *my* so that the sentence will make sense.)
2. I write every day for two hours.
3. While talking, they remember details of their childhood.
4. I ask to use a tape recorder during the interview.
5. They leave out embarrassing information.

Look at the verbs in the table on the next page and how they change form. (There are present-tense *and* past-tense verbs listed there.)

Practice #4   *The Paragraph* (subject-verb agreement)

• On a separate piece of paper, rewrite these sentences in the third-person singular. Your subject in each sentence will be *he, she, it* or other words that can be used instead of *he, she,* or *it*.

• Do not change the tense of the sentence.
• Underline the verbs twice.

Example: I love writing. (first-person singular)

• Mr. Jones <u>loves</u> writing. (third-person singular)

Example: They ask a question. (third-person plural)

• She <u>asks</u> a question. (third-person singular)

1. I do the typing.
2. I am interested in your paragraph.

Continued

3. They were anxious to read the paragraph.

4. They do the proofreading.

5. I was finished at last.

	Singular		Plural	
First Person (the person speaking)	I	do am was	we	do are were
Second Person (the person or people being spoken to)	you	do are were	you	do are were
Third Person (the person or people being spoken about)	**he, she, it** **(Or any word that can be used instead of *he, she,* or *it.* Examples: Mr. Smith, the policewoman, the flower)** **does** **is** **was**		**they**	do are were

Practice Review   *The First Day* (subject-verb agreement)

On a separate piece of paper, rewrite the paragraph, correcting subject-verb agreement errors. Use the present tense.

• Then underline the verbs twice.

Example: The door open.

• The door <u>opens</u>.

    The man enter the room. He is nervous. This is his first English class at this college. The book seem like a good one. The assignments is interesting. The students stares at him. He want to say something

Continued

Notes

> smart. He worries about not answering the questions right. Finally, he introduce himself: "Hi! I'm Mr. O'Dell, your English instructor."

Indefinite Pronouns

An **indefinite pronoun** is a pronoun that does not name a specific person or thing: *anyone, anybody, everyone, nobody,* and so on. Writers often make mistakes with subject-verb agreement when using indefinite pronouns. Look at these examples:

<u>Everyone</u> buy a souvenir. (incorrect)
<u>Everyone</u> buys a souvenir. (correct)

The rule to remember: Generally, indefinite pronouns are considered singular and require singular verbs.

Here are some other indefinite pronouns:

any	everybody	no one
anybody	everyone	someone
anyone	nobody	something
anything	nothing	somebody

When indefinite pronouns are used as subjects they will have verbs that end in *–s* or *–es* (just like the third-person singular pronouns *he, she,* and *it*).

<u>Everybody</u> <u>reads</u> *The Autobiography of Miss Jane Pittman.*
<u>Somebody</u> <u>takes</u> notes.

Practice #5   *School Topics (indefinite pronouns)*
In the following sentences, the subjects are indefinite pronouns.

- Underline the subjects once.
- Underline the verbs twice.
- On another sheet of paper, rewrite these sentences, correcting the subject-verb agreement errors. Use *only* the present tense.

1. Nobody want to miss class.
2. Nothing scare me like an in-class exam.
3. Everybody need a computer.
4. Somebody sneak into the library after hours.
5. Someone write "interesting" on my paragraph.

Practice Review

On a separate piece of paper, write three sentences using indefinite pronouns as the subjects.

- Use singular verbs and the present tense.
- Underline verbs twice and the indefinite pronouns once.

Example: <u>Somebody</u> <u>teaches</u> that class every semester.

Phrases That Confuse Things

If a subject and verb are separated by a long phrase, it can be easy to make a subject-verb agreement error. Here is an example:

The customer in the back corner of the department waiting by the fountains want to exchange the lamp. (incorrect)

The customer in the back corner of the department waiting by the fountains wants to exchange the lamp. (correct) (*Customer* is the subject and *wants* is the verb.)

Remember, you won't find your subject or verb in a prepositional phrase, so you can cross out the prepositional phrase and see your subject more clearly. You can then make sure that the subject and verb agree:

The customer ~~in the back corner~~ ~~of the department~~ waiting ~~by the fountains~~ wants to exchange the lamp. (*Customer* is the subject and *wants* is the verb.)

Here's another example of a subject-verb agreement error:
Some of the actors in the play wants to quit. (incorrect)

Here is the sentence with the subject and verb in agreement:
Some ~~of the actors~~ ~~in the play~~ want to quit. (correct)

Remember that –*ing* words are not verbs unless they have a helper in front of them. Sometimes descriptive –*ing* phrases can cause some confusion with subject-verb agreement. You may want to cross out descriptive –*ing* phrases to help you see the subject and verb more clearly.

The instructors teaching the afternoon class is demanding. (incorrect)
The <u>instructors</u> ~~teaching the afternoon class~~ <u>are</u> demanding. (correct)

Notes

Practice #6   *The Tutoring Lab (subject-verb agreement)*

There are subject-verb agreement errors in these sentences.

- Cross out the prepositional and descriptive *–ing* phrases.
- Underline the verbs twice and the subjects once.
- On a separate piece of paper, rewrite these sentences (including the prepositional and *–ing* phrases) so that there are no subject-verb agreement errors.
- Use the present tense.

1. The students in the lab works all afternoon.
2. The tutors working all day long wants a break.
3. All of the students is grateful.
4. The computers and printers on the back table is working.
5. The student pacing the floor worry about his paragraph.
6. The tutors working tirelessly is learning a lot about teaching.

Computer Note

Grammar check will find some subject-verb agreement errors, but may miss others. In Practice #6, the computer said that only items 2, 3, 4, and 6 had errors when actually all of the sentences have errors. Don't rely on grammar check to find all of your errors!

Practice Review   *Thinking by the Pool (subject-verb agreement)*

There are subject-verb agreement errors in these sentences.

- Cross out the prepositional and descriptive *–ing* phrases.
- Underline the verbs twice and the subjects once.
- On a separate piece of paper, rewrite the sentences so that they no longer have subject-verb agreement errors.
- Use the present tense.

1. After getting a new assignment, I likes to relax by the pool and to meditate on the task.
2. The other people sitting by the pool looks at me.
3. No one on this sunny day expect me to focus on school.
4. The grouchy man wearing sunglasses ask me questions.
5. Unexpectedly, the grouchy man with the PhD in sociology give me some good ideas.

The There *Sentence*

Sentences that begin with *there* don't have a clear subject, so subject-verb agreement errors are easy to make. Remember, *there* will not be the subject.

Here is an example of a *there* sentence with a subject-verb agreement error:

There <u>is</u> two important people in my past.

Here the subject-verb agreement error has been corrected:

There <u>are</u> two important people in my past.

With *there* sentences, the subject will come later in the sentence. Find the subject and make sure that your subject and verb agree in number. You may also want to revise the sentence and get rid of the *there* since *there* sentences generally aren't effective:

There <u>are</u> seven <u>people</u> in my family.

My large <u>family</u> <u>consists</u> of seven people.

Practice #7   *Home Discipline* (there *sentences*)
These sentences have subject-verb agreement errors.

- Underline the verbs twice.
- Underline the subjects once.
- On a separate piece of paper, rewrite the sentences so that there are no subject-verb agreement errors.

Example: There are a rule against staying on the phone for more than 30 minutes.

- There <u>are</u> a <u>rule</u> against staying on the phone for more than 30 minutes.
- There <u>is</u> a rule against staying on the phone for more than 30 minutes.

1. There is five important rules in my house.
2. There are no excuse for breaking the rules.
3. There is quick punishments for bad behavior.
4. There is chore lists on the refrigerator.
5. There are a good reason for the lists.

Practice Review
There are subject-verb agreement errors in the following sentences.

- Underline verbs twice.

Continued

Notes

- Underline subjects once.
- Then rewrite the sentences so that they have no subject-verb agreement errors *and* so that they do not begin with *there*. You may add information to the sentences as you revise. Use the present tense.

Example: There is two people at the table.

- There <u>is</u> two <u>people</u> at the table.
- Two people sit at the table.

1. There is three autobiographies on the list.
2. There is two reasons to write your book.
3. There are time for research.

Review Exercise A

- In the following sentences, underline verbs twice and subjects once.
- Find the sentences with subject-verb agreement errors.
- Rewrite only the sentences with subject-verb agreement errors. Rewrite them two different ways:
  - Correct the subject-verb agreement error and keep the *there* structure.
  - Correct the subject-verb agreement error and revise the sentence so that it no longer begins with *there*.

Example: There <u>is</u> many good <u>writers</u> in this class.

- There are many good writers in this class.
- Many good writers attend class with me.

1. There is two autobiographies that I want you to read.
2. There is one by a cancer survivor, and there is one by an Olympic athlete.
3. There is many lessons that you can learn from these books.
4. There is lessons about perseverance and faith that you'll enjoy.
5. There are also some very funny and heart-warming moments.

Create Your Own Sentences

Review Exercise B

On another piece of paper, create the sentences described in the following list. In each of your sentences,

- Underline verbs twice.
- Underline subjects once.

1. Create a sentence that uses a third-person singular noun or pronoun as the subject. Use the present tense.
2. Create a sentence that has an indefinite pronoun as the subject. Use the present tense.
3. Create a sentence that begins with these words: *The crocodile swimming quickly toward the swimmers*. Use the present tense.
4. Create a sentence that begins with *there*. Use the present tense.
5. Revise your sentence in exercise 4 so that it does not begin with *there*. Use the present tense.

Avoiding Verb Errors

If you tend to make verb tense or subject-verb agreement errors, you should check all your verbs at the editing stage of your writing process. You may want to place a piece of paper over your paragraph and reveal one sentence at a time. Find the verb in each sentence, see if it is in the right tense, and see if it agrees in number with the subject. With time and practice, you will find that you make fewer verb errors.

Clauses

Good writing will have short sentences and long sentences. Too many short sentences will bore your reader and make your writing seem too simple. Too many long sentences will tire your reader and make your writing seem too difficult. Aim for a mixture of short and long. For short sentences, use a simple independent clause.

For longer sentences, use one of the following:

✦ An independent clause joined to another independent clause.

✦ An independent clause joined to a dependent clause.

✦ An independent clause joined to a phrase.

This chapter covers the following topics:

✦ The independent clause
  • Using coordinating conjunctions
  • Using semicolons and transition words
✦ The dependent (or subordinated) clause
✦ Who, that, and which clauses

Notes

The Independent Clause

A **clause** is a group of words with a subject and a verb. There are two kinds of clauses—independent and dependent. The **independent clause** can stand on its own and is the same thing as a complete sentence. (Remember, a *complete sentence* is a group of words with a subject and verb that expresses a complete idea.)

Here are some independent clauses. The verb is underlined twice. The subject is underlined once.

Mother Jones led a children's rights movement.

He believed in Jones's fight.

He was a young, frightened teenager.

A simple independent clause can be very useful. If you have provided enough information and support, a simple sentence like "She was a hero" can make your point clearly and dramatically.

Using Coordinating Conjunctions

To add variety to your writing and to help show the relationships between your ideas, you may want to join two independent clauses and make one longer sentence. A **coordinating conjunction** is a word that can join independent clauses. These words are also called *coordinators*.

There are seven coordinating conjunctions, which you will study here briefly. You will get more practice with these coordinators in Chapter 23. You can remember them by the word **FANBOYS:**

For   And   Nor   But   Or   Yet   So

When you want to join two independent clauses with a coordinating conjunction, you need to choose one of the FANBOYS that accurately expresses the relationship between the ideas you are joining.

For expresses a relationship of *effect-cause*. The idea in the first sentence is the effect. The idea in the second sentence is the cause.

- He spoke at the meeting, *for* he had good ideas and a powerful speaking voice.

And expresses a relationship of *addition*. The idea in the first sentence is added to the idea in the second sentence.

- We were moved by his speech, *and* we signed up to help.

Nor expresses a relationship of *negative addition*. The idea in the first sentence is negative, and it is added to a negative idea in the second sentence. In the following example, notice that the subject and verb in the second independent clause are not in their usual order.

- Frank did not want to join the group, *nor* did he want to explain.

But expresses a relationship of *opposites*. The idea in the first sentence is the opposite of the idea in the second sentence.

- I wanted to help, *but* I just didn't have any time.

Or expresses a relationship of *alternatives*. The idea in the first sentence is one option. The idea in the second sentence is another option.

- I think parents should write letters protesting violence on television, *or* they should boycott products advertised during violent programs.

Yet expresses a relationship of *opposition*. The idea in the first sentence is the opposite of the idea in the second sentence.

Notes

- His negative policies have caused great harm to the environment, *yet* people keep voting him into power.

    So expresses a relationship of *cause-effect*. The idea in the first sentence causes the idea in the second sentence.

- She knew her audience was young and looking to be entertained, *so* she chose to speak using slang.

    When you join independent clauses with a coordinating conjunction, you need to put a comma after the first independent clause:

- I met the first speaker, and I thought he was very interesting.

    Look back at the examples for each of the FANBOYS, and underline the comma in each.

Practice #1   *Too Much Media (using coordinators)*

Join the independent clauses with the coordinator provided. Don't forget to put your comma in. Write your new sentences on a separate piece of paper.

Example: Use *so* to join these sentences.

She believed her son was consuming too much television.
She began to limit his viewing time to one hour a day.

- She believed her son was consuming too much television, *so* she began to limit his viewing time to one hour a day.

    1. Use *for* to join these sentences.
       The father moved the computer from his daughter's bedroom to the living room.
       He was worried about her being on the Internet without supervision.
    2. Use *and* to join these sentences.
       The preschool teacher felt that television was a negative influence.
       She wished that parents would not put television sets in their children's bedrooms.
    3. Use *nor* to join these sentences. Remember to change the order of the *it* and *did*. And leave out the second *not* because the *nor* suggests *not*.
       Their home did not contain a single television set.
       It did not contain a computer.

Continued

4. Use *but* to join these sentences.

   I like to spend time on the Internet.

   My mom wants me to do the math software program.

5. Use *or* to join these sentences.

   My sister checks her e-mail.

   She goes shopping on the Internet.

6. Use *yet* to join these sentences.

   He thinks his parents are too strict.

   He does admit that young kids need some Internet supervision.

7. Use *so* to join these sentences.

   I've learned to do research on the Internet.

   My parents are more supportive of my computer time now.

Practice #2   *E-mail (using coordinators)*

On a separate piece of paper, join the following independent clauses using carefully chosen coordinators. Remember to put a comma after the first independent clause. Don't use the same coordinator twice.

1. I e-mail my grandmother once a week.

   She writes to me about once a month.

2. I think e-mail is great.

   She believes a handwritten note is more personal.

3. None of her other grandchildren ever write to her.

   She doesn't criticize me for e-mailing her.

4. Peretti's e-mail gave me some good ideas for my paragraph.

   I think I'll need some more information on the topic.

5. I'll start by asking my grandmother about her experiences work-ing in the clothing factory as a child.

   Maybe I'll first go to the Internet for information.

Practice #3   *Boycotting (using coordinators)*

On a separate piece of paper, join the following independent clauses using carefully chosen coordinators. Remember to put a comma after the first independent clause. Don't use the same coordinator twice.

Continued

Notes

1. My husband is very interested in children's rights.
   I am too.
2. He won't buy products that are manufactured by children.
   I have trouble staying away from some of those products because I really like them.
3. I point out that sometimes children need to work in other countries.
   They need to help support their families.
4. They need the work.
   The family won't have enough to eat.
5. My husband sees my point.
   He still won't buy any products made by children.

Using Semicolons and Transition Words

Another way to join independent clauses is to use a semicolon. A semicolon is as strong as a period. Use a semicolon when the ideas in each independent clause are closely related.

- I read the article again and again; I was preparing to summarize it.
- I called the police; I was tired of all the noise next door.

You can also use a transition word with a semicolon. Transition words like *however, therefore,* and *then* cannot join independent clauses with a comma like coordinators do, but you can use them with semicolons.

- I was preparing to summarize the article; therefore, I read it again and again.
- He listened to my speech with an open mind; however, he simply didn't agree.
- Jessica reviewed her notes from speech class; then, she began to practice her speech.

Practice #4 *Work (using semicolons)*
On a separate piece of paper, create the sentences described.

Example: Join these sentences with a semicolon. *Continued*

We need to review our files on each employee.

The boss wants to reward the best employees.

- We need to review our files on each employee; the boss wants to reward the best employees.

1. Join these sentences with a semicolon.

   He has been fully committed to our company.

   I want to commend him.

2. Join these sentences with a semicolon.

   He toils in the factory for fourteen hours a day.

   He is seeking his emancipation from this job.

3. Join these sentences with a semicolon and the transition word *therefore*.

   I completely disagreed with her position.

   I vehemently argued against hiring her.

4. Join these sentences with a semicolon and the transition word *however*.

   The board listened to my argument.

   The president persuaded everyone to hire her.

5. Join these sentences with a semicolon and the transition word *then*.

   I left the room.

   I went looking for another job.

6. Join these sentences with a semicolon and one of these transition words: *therefore, however, then*.

   Companies have a right to make money.

   They shouldn't be forced to say anything that would hurt profits.

7. Join these two sentences with a semicolon and one of these transition words: *therefore, however, then*.

   He supported the rights of the working children in his speech.

   He joined the march around the city.

Practice Review   *The Readings (joining independent clauses)*

On a separate piece of paper, complete the following work.

Continued

Notes

1. In paragraph 5 of Mother Jones's letter (p. 80) find a sentence that contains two independent clauses joined by a coordinator.

2. In paragraph 13 of Jonah Peretti's e-mail (p. 84) find a sentence that contains two independent clauses joined by a coordinator.

3. These sentences come from an e-mail in *Now You Know* (p. 421 of "The Reader"). The writer wrote them as separate sentences. Rewrite them as one sentence by joining them with a semicolon. Why does a semicolon work well here?

   Words do not reign supreme as a form of expression. We need pictures and music as well.

4. These sentences come form Anne LeClaire's letter to her mother (p. 416 of "The Reader"). The writer wrote them as two separate sentences. Rewrite them as one sentence by joining them with a semicolon and an appropriate transition word (*therefore, however,* or *then*). Compare your sentence with your classmates' sentences. How does each transition change the meaning of the new sentences?

   You taught me to be silent. I learned to write.

The Dependent (or Subordinated) Clause

The **dependent** or **subordinated clause** is a group of words with a subject and verb that cannot stand on its own. It is *not* a complete sentence. Here are some dependent clauses:

When <u>Frank</u> <u>read</u> the letter

Even though <u>I</u> <u>found</u> the wallet on my lawn

Because <u>he</u> <u>needed</u> a car

The words *when, even though,* and *because* change the independent clauses into dependent clauses. If you read the dependent clauses carefully aloud, you will hear how they sound "unfinished."

Subordinators are words that can attach to independent clauses and make them dependent (or subordinated). Here are some subordinators:

- if
- since
- while
- though
- although
- even though
- because
- when

Joined to independent clauses, dependent clauses can be very useful because they allow you to express complex ideas and the relationships between those ideas. For example, *when* allows you to tell your reader that two ideas are connected by time. In the following examples, the dependent clause is highlighted. The independent clause is left unmarked.

When Frank read the letter, he was shocked to learn that he had inherited 5 million dollars.

Even though allows you to tell your reader that one idea is the opposite of another.

Even though I found the wallet on my lawn, I knew the money didn't belong to me.

Because allows you to tell your reader that the ideas have a cause-effect relationship.

Because he needed a car, he got a second job.

Practice #5   *Protesting (dependent clauses)*
- Underline the dependent clause.
- Circle the independent clause.
- Highlight commas. *Note:* When the dependent clause comes first, it is followed by a comma. When the dependent clause comes second, no comma is necessary.

Example: When he saw how the animals were being treated, he decided he had to get involved.

- When he saw how the animals were being treated, he decided he had to get involved.

1. If you want to change society, you have to participate by voting and speaking up.
2. When you participate in a sit-in, you run the risk of being arrested.
3. I wrote a letter of protest to my senator because I wanted to change things for women in Afghanistan.
4. Although I didn't march in the protest, I did send a check.
5. I volunteered at the affirmative action picnic since I feel racial diversity at our college campus is important.

Notes

Practice #6 *Letters and Landlords (subjects and verbs in the clauses)*
- Circle the independent clause in each sentence.
- Underline the subject and verb in the independent clause. Underline verbs twice. Underline subjects once.
- Underline the subject and verb in the dependent clause. Underline verbs twice. Underline subjects once.

Example: Since I couldn't reach him by phone, I called my landlord.

- Since I couldn't reach him by phone, (I went to my landlord's house.)

1. If you write a letter to your landlord, you will have a record of your complaints.
2. My landlord responded promptly to my letter even though he had ignored my phone calls again and again.
3. While it may take time to write a letter, you will probably find a letter to be worth every minute.

Practice #7 *The Field Trips (using subordinators)*
On a separate piece of paper, join the sentences with the subordinator provided. Don't forget to use commas when necessary.

Example:
  You will get a raise.
  (if) You complete this extra training.

- You will get a raise if you complete this extra training.

1. I was surprised.
   (when) My daughter came home from school in tears.
2. The school cancelled all field trips.
   (because) Someone vandalized the auditorium.
3. (since) Not all of the students were guilty.
   My daughter felt it was not fair to cancel the field trips.
4. (even though) She wasn't sure she would be taken seriously.
   She decided to write a letter of protest.
5. She asked other students to write too.
   (if) They wanted to get their field trips.

Practice #8   *The Baseball (using subordinators)*

Join the sentences with an appropriate subordinator. Use commas when necessary.

Example:

　Mr. Fazio is always yelling at everyone.

　My kids are afraid of him.

- Because Mr. Fazio is always yelling at everyone, my kids are afraid of him.

　1. I was gone on my vacation.

　　Someone threw a baseball through the front window of my house.

　2. I called my landlord.

　　I believed he should pay for the window.

　3. He believed that my renter's insurance should cover the damage.

　　He agreed to send a repairperson over right away.

　4. My landlord is a great guy.

　　He won't let me have a dog in the house.

Who, That, and Which Clauses

The words *who*, *that*, and *which* can create dependent clauses that can be joined to independent clauses. In the examples that follow, the independent clause is unmarked. The *who/that/which* dependent clause is highlighted.

　I think that I should pay attention to the news more.

　Reading that news article, I learned that King was also concerned about poverty.

　He believed that wealth wasn't distributed fairly in the United States.

　James is the man who should lead the committee.

　The president wanted to know who wrote the letter of protest.

　I worked for the organization which Smith had founded.

Note: When *who* introduces a clause, *who* is the subject. *Which* and *that* sometimes act as subjects. In the following examples, verbs are underlined twice and subjects are underlined once:

Notes

I <u>wanted</u> to know <u>who</u> <u>was speaking</u> at the march.

<u>Frank</u> <u>decided</u> to speak <u>which</u> <u>was</u> a good idea.

Practice #9   *Martin Luther King Jr. (who/that/which clauses)*
- Underline the *who/that/which* clause and circle the independent clause.
- Use *S* and *V* to identify the subjects and verbs in the *who/that/which* clause.
- Use *S* and *V* to identify the subjects and verbs in the independent clause.

Note: One sentence has two *who/that/which* clauses.

Example:

I enjoy reading about heroes who work hard to make our nation a better place.

- (I enjoy reading about heroes) <u>who work hard to make our nation a better place</u>.

1. Some people don't realize that Martin Luther King Jr. was a radical.

2. He was a soldier who was not violent.

3. The article said that he was beginning the Poor People's Campaign which I didn't know about.

4. Martin Luther King Jr. was a powerful, articulate speaker which is one reason that he was so successful.

5. I think that young people need to learn to speak effectively.

Practice Review   *Mother Jones's Letter*
- Read paragraphs 2, 5, 6, and 7 of Mother Jones's letter (pp. 80–81). Copy any sentences that have a dependent clause or a *who/that/which* clause.
- Underline the dependent clauses and the *who/that/which* clauses.

Create Your Own Sentences

Review Exercise A

On a separate piece of paper, create original sentences that fit the descriptions given.

- Your sentences must be on the same topic as your current reading or writing assignment.
- Use new vocabulary words in at least two of your sentences. Underline your new vocabulary words.

1. Create one sentence for each coordinating conjunction (see page 223). You'll be creating seven different sentences.
2. Create one sentence using a semicolon.
3. Create one sentence using a semicolon and one of these words: *therefore, however,* or *then.*

Computer Note

If your word processing program underlines errors you have made, right-click on the underlined word. The program will explain the suspected error. The program also underlines people's names that it does not recognize even though you may have spelled the name correctly. Double-check spelling of all underlined words.

Review Exercise B

- Write five original sentences that have a dependent clause.
- Underline the dependent clause. The sentences must connect in topic to your current reading or writing assignment.
- Use new vocabulary words in at least two of your sentences.

Review Exercise C

- Write five original sentences that have a *who/that/which* clause.
- Underline the *who/that/which* clause. The sentences must connect in topic to your current reading or writing assignment.
- Use new vocabulary words in at least two of your sentences.

Apply Your Knowledge

Review one of the paragraphs you have written, and look at the sentence structure.

Notes

- How many of your sentences are short? How many are long?
- Have you expressed complex ideas by joining independent clauses with coordinators, semicolons, or transition words with semicolons?
- Have you used any subordinators?

Rewrite the paragraph, improving the variety in your sentence structure. Here are the coordinators, subordinators, and transition words you can choose from.

Coordinators	Subordinators	Transition Words
for	if	therefore
and	since	however
nor	while	then
but	though	
or	although	
yet	even though	
so	because	
	when	
	who	
	that	
	which	

17

Phrases

In this chapter, you'll learn how phrases can help you write more sophisticated sentences.

The following topics are covered:

✦ Understanding phrases—in general
✦ Prepositional phrases
✦ Participial phrases

Understanding Phrases—In General

Notes

A **phrase** is a group of words that is missing a subject, a verb, or both. Phrases are very useful because they allow writers to insert critical pieces of information into sentences. Phrases are one key to writing longer, more sophisticated, more expressive sentences.

Here are some examples of phrases—groups of words missing one or more sentence ingredients:

consuming six hours

of television a day

in his schoolwork

startled by the researcher's report

in street dialect

at the youth center

These phrases can become part of nicely shaped, sophisticated sentences that will add variety and interest to a paragraph. Look at these examples (phrases are highlighted):

Consuming six hours of television a day, the child fell behind in his schoolwork.

Startled by the researcher's report, the committee decided to make a press release.

He spoke in street dialect at the youth center.

Prepositional Phrases

Prepositional phrases are groups of words made up of a preposition and its object. A *preposition* is a word that suggests position, location, direction, condition, or time. An *object* is the noun that follows the preposition. Sometimes a prepositional phrase also includes descriptive information (between the preposition and the object.) In the following examples, the preposition is highlighted:

at the rally

in his eloquent, thoughtful speech (note that *eloquent* and *thoughtful* describe the object)

after much practice (*much* describes the object)

Notice that there is neither a subject nor a verb in prepositional phrases.

Prepositional phrases add information to sentences and often help the writer avoid unnecessary repetition. Here is an example of unnecessary repetition:

I read an article. The article was in *Time* magazine. The article was about biodiversity and extinction.

Here is a better sentence that uses prepositional phrases (prepositional phrases are highlighted):

I read an article in *Time* magazine about biodiversity and extinction.

Practice #1 *Biodiversity (finding prepositional phrases)*
Highlight the prepositional phrases in the following sentences. Note how the prepositional phrases add information to each sentence. Sentences may have more than one prepositional phrase.

Example: I picked up a magazine at the grocery store.

• I picked up a magazine at the grocery store.

1. I read Richard Leakey's article in *Time*.
2. I am worried about the extinction of so many species.
3. Leakey says that we should focus on poorer countries.
4. The majority of our biodiversity is in those poorer countries.
5. His suggestion of a global fund is an interesting idea.
6. I will write a letter to my congressman.

Computer Note
Time is in italics because it is the name of a magazine. Titles of magazines, newspapers, and books are underlined when you are writing by hand. These titles are italicized when you type.

Practice #2   *Fitting In (finding prepositional phrases)*

Highlight the prepositional phrases in the following sentences. Note how the prepositional phrases add information to each sentence. Sentences may have more than one prepositional phrase.

1. My daughter was expelled from her private elementary school.
2. The principal and the teacher said they don't have room for kids who don't like to sit still.
3. My daughter has trouble with sitting and reading for long periods of time.
4. I thought the school was supposed to be a nontraditional school that offered many types of learning activities.
5. I know some kids learn by doing projects and activities.
6. I wrote a letter of complaint to the board of directors.

Practice #3   *Jonah Peretti's E-mail*

Read paragraph 23 of Jonah Peretti's e-mail on p. 85.

- Copy the entire paragraph on a separate piece of paper.
- Underline all prepositional phrases.

Practice #4   *Reasons to Write Letters*

Add the prepositional phrases to each sentence to make a longer, more complex sentence.

Example:

Many are a waste of time.
of the programs
on television

- Many of the programs on television are a waste of time.

1. Some is not suitable.
   of the music
   on the radio
   for kids or teenagers

Continued

Notes

2. The afternoon disc jockey often talks.
   on my favorite station
   about topics that aren't appropriate
   for my kids
3. Should I read the lyrics my son listens to?
   for every song
4. I am going to write a letter.
   to the owner
   of my favorite radio station
5. My sister warned me.
   in a recent e-mail
   about kids getting into trouble on the Internet
6. I decided to restrict his Internet use.
   After looking (*Hint:* Begin the sentence with this phrase.)
   over my son's shoulder
7. My cousin leaves his dog outside every day.
   on a cement porch
   with no shade or water
8. The poor dog is suffering.
   from dehydration
9. I have spoken.
   with my cousin
   about treating the dog better
10. My cousin, unfortunately, ignores all.
    of my concerns
11. I am going to write an anonymous letter asking.
    after one more try
    to the SPCA
    for prompt attention
    to this terrible situation.

Participial Phrases

A **participial phrase** consists of a present or past participle and the words attached to that participle.

Present participles end in *–ing*. Here are some examples of present participles:

laughing

running

concerning

hunting

Here are some present participial *phrases:*

laughing in the hallway

running quickly

concerning the welfare of animals

hunting wild coyotes

Past participles usually end in *–ed,* but sometimes they have an irregular form:

confused

written (irregular)

discussed

chosen (irregular)

Here are some past participial phrases:

confused by the many technical terms (Note that participial phrases can include prepositional phrases.)

written clearly

discussed in class

chosen by the students

In this chapter, you'll focus on participial phrases that describe nouns. (Chapter 12 explains how present participles can be used as verbs, and Chapter 14 explains how they can be used as subjects.) Participial phrases can add interesting information to sentences and often help the writer express ideas with fewer sentences.

Notes

Here are some sentences that repeat information unnecessarily:

The woman is laughing in the hallway. The woman is making too much noise.

The child is running quickly. The child trips and falls.

Larry was confused by the many technical terms. Larry was frustrated.

The paragraph was written clearly. The paragraph was persuasive.

These sentences are more interesting and have less repetition.

Laughing in the hallway, the woman is making too much noise.

Running quickly, the child trips and falls.

Confused by the many technical terms, Larry was frustrated.

The clearly written paragraph was persuasive.

Though participial phrases can be used in several positions in sentences, in this chapter, you'll focus on participial phrases that begin sentences.

In the following examples, the participial phrases describe a noun that immediately follows. The participial phrase is highlighted. The noun is circled.

Hunting endangered species, (the poachers) deserved to go to jail.

Writing an essay, (the student) expressed her feelings about the role of media in modern society.

Speaking clearly, (Charlene) explained her theory.

Practice #5   *Writing Letters (find participial phrases)*

• Highlight the participial phrases that are describing nouns.

• Circle the nouns each phrase describes.

You may find prepositional phrases within the participial phrases.

Example: Hoping to start a romance, Jess wrote to an old friend.

• Hoping to start a romance, (Jess) wrote to an old friend.

1. Needing some extra money, Sara wrote to her parents.

2. Startled by the results of his experiment, the scientist e-mailed his colleague and asked for his opinion.

Continued

3. Explaining his concerns in a passionate letter, he showed that he was a wonderful writer.

4. Rallied by the inspirational speech, the students decided to write a letter of protest to the president of the college.

5. Seeking the truth, the girl wrote to her grandmother and begged for more information.

Practice Review   *Mother Jones*

Study paragraphs 1 and 4 of Mother Jones's letter (p. 80).

- On another piece of paper, copy down all sentences that begin with a participial phrase describing a noun.
- Highlight the phrase and circle the noun that the phrase describes.
- Discuss these sentences with your classmates.

Practice Review   *Writing and the Workforce (using participial phrases)*

On a separate piece of paper, write new sentences that include the participial phrases given. *Hint:* Place the participial phrases at the beginning of the new sentences.

Example:

The day care provider stopped showing so many videos.
Reflecting on the reports about media

- Reflecting on the reports about media, the day care provider stopped showing so many videos.

1. James did not project a professional image in his cover letter.
   Using slang

2. The man called his old college and complained.
   Discouraged by the cover letters

3. The curriculum committee decided to require more essays in all classes.
   Hoping to help students improve their writing skills

Continued

Notes

4. Some students were unhappy with the new writing requirements. Feeling uncertain about their writing skills
5. Sam signed up for a writing tutor. Determined to have the skills necessary for the work world

Create Your Own Sentences

Review Exercise A *Treasure (using participial phrases)*
- On a separate piece of paper, complete each sentence.
- Be sure that the part you add begins with a noun that the participial phrase can describe.

Example: Thinking about her aunt,

- Thinking about her aunt, <u>Trina</u> decided to write a letter to her.

1. Finding the small chest in the forest
2. Scuba diving off the coast of Mexico
3. Buying forty lottery tickets a week
4. Hearing about his neighbor's imheritance
5. Watching the dog bury its bone

Review Exercise B *Adding Description (using participial phrases)*
Make the following sentences more interesting by adding a participial phrase to the beginning of each sentence. Write your new sentences on a separate piece of paper.

Example: I checked my e-mail.

- Hoping to hear from my best friend, I checked my e-mail.

1. I ran all the way home.
2. Sara fired Jim.
3. I borrowed the book.
4. Mr. Field cancelled the trip.
5. Susan wrote a letter to the judge.

Review Exercise C   *Using Prepositional Phrases*

Create five original sentences that have prepositional phrases in them. (Review p. 236)

- The sentences must connect to the topics of your current reading and writing assignments.
- Highlight the prepositional phrases.
- Use new vocabulary words in at least two of your sentences. Circle your new vocabulary words.

Example: I asked my instructor to help me with an important letter.

Review Exercise D   *Using Participial Phrases*

- Create five sentences that each begin with a participial phrase.
- The sentences should connect to the topics of your current reading or writing assignments.
- Highlight the participial phrases.
- Use new vocabulary words in at least two of your sentences. Circle the vocabulary words.

(*Hint:* This is the sentence pattern to follow: Participial phrase, noun + verb + completing information.)

Apply Your Knowledge

Review the paragraphs you have written, and look at the sentence structure. Can you use prepositional or participial phrases to add information to your sentences? Rewrite a paragraph, improving the variety in your sentence structure.

Understanding, Correcting, and Avoiding Fragments

Readers expect most sentences to be complete and clear. Incomplete sentences can damage both the clarity of your message and your professional image.

This chapter covers the following topics:

✦ Understanding fragments
  • Missing words
  • Dependent clauses
✦ Correcting fragments
✦ Avoiding fragments

Notes

Understanding Fragments

A **fragment** is an incomplete sentence. It may be a phrase—a group of words missing a subject, or a verb, or both. Or it may be a dependent clause—a group of words with a subject and verb that cannot stand on its own. Here are some examples of fragments and complete sentences:

Computer Note
Grammar check did not catch the two fragments written here. Remember that grammar check cannot find all of your errors.

Idea in the topic sentence. (fragment; no subject or verb)

I express my main idea in the topic sentence. (complete sentence)

If she cut out a lot of the ideas that don't connect to her topic sentence. (fragment; dependent clause that cannot stand on its own)

If she cut out a lot of ideas that don't connect to her topic sentence, her paragraph would be stronger. (complete sentence)

Practice #1 *Narrating (find the fragments)*
Place an F next to each sentence that is actually a fragment.
Put a C next to complete sentences.

Example: If I want to tell a story.

• If I want to tell a story. F

1. When I narrate.
2. Making a point is important in this narrative paragraph.

Continued

3. Because I included some interesting details.
4. I will shape the information.
5. By leaving out some details and adding some comments.
6. If I look back at the readings.
7. Although I tried to be honest.
8. I enjoy sharing my work with my classmates.
9. Grading my narrative.
10. When I get home, I'll take a nap.

Notes

 Computer Note
Grammar check didn't find these fragments. Here again, you will do better work than grammar check.

Correcting Fragments

There are a number of ways to correct fragments. If you have a fragment that is missing a subject, or a verb, or both, you can add the missing element. Here are some examples of how to correct fragments by adding missing elements:

Writing her letter. (incorrect)

There is no subject or verb here.

Writing her letter gave LeClaire the chance to express her feelings about silence. (correct)

A verb with a *completer* has been added. A **completer** is the word or phrase that completes the idea. *Writing* has become the subject, and *gave* is the verb for that subject.

or

LeClaire enjoyed writing her letter. (correct)

A subject and verb have been added. *LeClaire* is the subject; *enjoyed* is the verb, and *writing her letter* is the completer.

Practice #2

On another piece of paper, correct these fragments by adding the missing elements. There are a few different ways to correct each fragment, so you and your classmates may come up with different answers. Write down the solutions you like best.

Example: Worried about expressing my thoughts well.   *Continued*

Computer Note
You must make some choices when you are correcting fragments. Know what your options are. The computer can't make these decisions for you.

Notes

- I was worried about expressing my thoughts well.

or

- Worried about expressing my thoughts well, I practiced by talking to the mirror.

Part 1 *Expressing Thoughts in Letters* (correcting fragments)
1. Wanting to express her feelings.
2. Fearful of how her mother might react.
3. A determined girl.
4. A new desire to speak up.
5. Wrote a clear letter.

Part 2: *Child Labor* (correcting fragments)
1. Needing a way to get the president's attention.
2. Worried about the welfare of the children.
3. The state laws about child labor.
4. Continue today.
5. The media's attention to this topic.

If you have a fragment that is really a dependent (or subordinated) clause, you can

- Get rid of the subordinator. A *subordinator* is a word that attaches to an independent clause and changes it into a dependent clause. (See the list that follows.)

or

- Finish the sentence by adding an independent clause before or after the fragment.

Here is a fragment and two ways of correcting the fragment.

When she agreed to have the letter published. (fragment)
She agreed to have the letter published. (Corrected fragment; the subordinator is deleted.)

I was surprised when she agreed to have the letter published. (Corrected fragment; an independent clause is added, so the idea is now complete.)

Notes

Here is a list of subordinators that can be used to create dependent clauses:

- if
- since
- while
- though

- although
- even though
- because
- when

Practice #3
Correct each of these fragments in two different ways.

- Get rid of the subordinator.
- Keep the subordinator and complete the idea. (You can add information before or after the subordinated clause.)

Write your new sentences on a separate piece of paper. You'll be writing 10 new sentences.

Example: If you are concerned about the animals at the shelter.

- You are concerned about the animals at the shelter.
- You should contact the police if you are concerned about the animals at the shelter.

Part 1 *The Cats* (correcting fragments)
1. When I saw the cats' cages.
2. Although the police sergeant was not really an animal lover.
3. Because the shelter's manager was on vacation.
4. If my sister had heard about the inhumanity of that shelter.
5. Since the law is clear on such offenses.

Part 2 *Injuries on the Job* (correcting fragments)
1. When the boys got injured.
2. Because they wanted to keep their jobs.
3. If they had received medical attention.

Continued

Notes

4. Since their families need the extra money.

5. Although child labor laws are more closely observed now.

Review Exercise A   *Warren's Letter (finding and correcting fragments)*
Rewrite the following paragraph, correcting all of the fragment sentences. You can add words and combine phrases and clauses as necessary. *Hint:* You should find five fragments.

When I read Warren's letter. I was reminded that bad luck can change your life. For instance, when Warren was young, he was a gifted artist. Creative and insightful. People loved his work. Teachers paid attention to him, and he did well in school. Later, because of the accident. He gave up his art. Didn't pick up a brush for years. People stopped paying attention to him. Because he had decided his artistic life was over. He didn't have much hope then.

Review Exercise B   *Beauty (finding and correcting fragments)*
Rewrite the following paragraph, correcting all of the fragment sentences. You can add words and combine phrases and clauses as necessary. *Hint:* You should find three fragments.

Modern culture celebrates beauty. When I look at the magazines in the grocery store. I see perfect people. I know I don't look like any of those people. I have stopped looking at those magazines. Reminders that I am a long way from being perfect. Of course, if I had my own makeup artist, hair stylist, and special lighting. I might look almost as good.

Review Exercise C   *LeClaire's Mom (finding and correcting fragments)*
Rewrite the following paragraph, correcting all of the fragment sentences. You can add words and combine phrases and clauses as necessary.

I am intrigued by Anne LeClaire's mother. Is she really a bad person? Or is she simply trying to raise her family the best way she

Continued

knows how? Maybe if she had been raised differently herself. She would have been more comfortable with communicating. She wanted to make Anne strong. Because she didn't want her to be hurt later in life. Although some might say that she was controlling and mean-spirited. I think she might have been a protective mom. Who wanted only the best for Anne.

Avoiding Fragments

If you see that you are writing fragments in your paragraphs, look to see if there is a pattern.

- Do you create a fragment when you begin a sentence with an *–ing* word?
- Do you end up with a fragment when you use *because* or other sub-ordinators?
- Don't stop using *–ing* words or subordinators. Just begin watching out for them, and make sure that you complete your sentences.

When you reach the editing stage of your writing process, review your paragraph sentence by sentence, keeping an eye out for *–ing* words or subordinators that might create fragments.

It is important that you be able to find and fix your own fragments, but if you need help at first, ask a tutor to check for fragments. Find out how many you have—but not where they are. Then find and fix them on your own. Check your work with your tutor.

19

Understanding, Correcting, and Avoiding Run-ons

To keep your message clear and to maintain a professional image, you must demonstrate in your writing that you understand where sentences begin and where they end.

This chapter covers the following topics:
✦ Understanding run-ons
✦ Correcting run-ons
✦ Avoiding run-on sentences

Notes

Understanding Run-ons

A **run-on sentence** is really two sentences that run together with no punctuation between. A run-on sentence is sometimes called a **fused sentence.**

A writer may accidentally create a run-on when ideas in two sentences are closely related. In this situation, the writer may make the mistake of presenting two sentences as one. Here are some examples of run-ons:

I see why she said my paragraph seems too lengthy it is three pages long. (The first sentence ends after the word *lengthy.*)

The tutor will tell me how many run-ons I have then I'll find them and fix them. (The first sentence ends after the word *have.*)

> **Practice #1** *Doris and Alice (finding the run-ons)*
>
> Identify which of the following sentences are actually run-ons. When you find a run-on, put an R next to the sentences and mark where one sentence ends and the other begins. Mark correct sentences with a C.
>
> Example: I read the book/it was required reading.
>
> • I read the book it was required reading. R
>
> 1. Doris was an "old" six-year-old she enjoyed doing adult chores.
> 2. She had a lot of confidence she went right out and sold magazines.
>
> *Continued*

Copyright © 2003 by Addison Wesley Longman, Inc.

3. I can just picture this little girl pounding on the neighbors' doors.

4. That image was funny to me I think the author wanted me to laugh at it.

5. I think that Russell admired his tough little sister.

6. Alice Walker has fond memories of her childhood she was her father's favorite.

7. She was confident because of her beauty.

8. Her brothers didn't want to get into trouble they asked her to lie.

9. Walker's mother became ill she had a chronic earache.

10. Walker has strong feelings about guns they keep coming up in her essay.

Notes

Computer Note
Grammar check didn't find any run-ons here. You'll find some though.

Correcting Run-ons

Consider this run-on:

The author said being a girl is a defect he was simply expressing the view of society at that time.

There are four ways to correct run-on sentences.

1. Put a period after the first sentence and capitalize the first letter of the second sentence.

The author said being a girl is a defect. He was simply expressing the view of society at that time.

2. Separate the two sentences with a semicolon. A semicolon is just as strong as a period.

The author said being a girl is a defect; he was simply expressing the view of society at that time.

3. Join the two sentences with a comma and a coordinating conjunction. (The seven coordinating conjunctions are *for, and, nor, but, or, yet, so.*)

The author said being a girl is a defect, but he was simply expressing the view of society at that time.

4. Add a subordinator and change one of the complete sentences to a subordinated clause. (Some subordinators include *if, when, because, although, since.* If the new subordinated clause comes first, put a comma after it.)

Notes

When the author said being a girl is a defect, he was simply expressing the view of society at that time.

> ## Practice #2
>
> Correct each run-on two different ways. (See methods listed on p. 251.) Write your new sentences on a separate piece of paper.
>
> Example: Frieda didn't know much about Alice Walker's life she had only read *The Color Purple.*
>   a. Correct this run-on using method 2.
>   b. Correct this run-on using method 4.
>
> - (a) Frieda didn't know much about Alice Walker's life; she had only read *The Color Purple.*
> - (b) Frieda didn't know much about Alice Walker's life since she had only read *The Color Purple.*
>
> ### Part 1 *Walker and Guns* (correcting run-ons)
>   1. Alice Walker didn't want to look up she was embarrassed about the way her eye looked.
>   a. Correct this run-on using method 1.
>   b. Correct this run-on using method 3.
>
>   2. After the accident, she doesn't do as well in school she has lost her confidence.
>   a. Correct this run-on using method 2.
>   b. Correct this run-on using method 4.
>
>   3. I wasn't allowed to play with guns as a child my cousins had many guns.
>   a. Correct this run-on using method 1.
>   b. Correct this run-on using method 3.
>
> ### Part 2 *Aptitudes* (correcting run-ons)
>   1. Russell did not have the aptitude for selling magazines he didn't have that kind of confidence.
>   a. Correct this run-on using method 1.
>   b. Correct this run-on using method 3.
>
>   2. Doris would have made a great salesperson she had plenty of gumption.
>
> *Continued*

a. Correct this run-on using method 2.

b. Correct this run-on using method 4.

3. I discovered what I wanted to do I read a book about working for the Peace Corps.

   a. Correct this run-on using method 2.

   b. Correct this run-on using method 4.

Using Transitions to Correct Run-ons

A *transition* is a word or phrase that creates a meaningful bridge between ideas and sentences. Transitions can be very useful when correcting run-ons. Here are some transitions:

however

consequently

therefore

then

Here is an example of how to fix a run-on with a transition:

I was looking for an inspirational story Malcolm X's autobiography was perfect. (run-on)

I was looking for an inspirational story; consequently, Malcolm X's autobiography was perfect. (correct)

When using transitions, keep in mind that they are different from coordinating conjunctions or subordinators that can join sentences with commas. Transitions do not join sentences. You must keep the two sentences separate or use a semicolon. Notice that a comma follows the transition. Here are more examples of how to use transitions:

I enjoyed Walker's autobiography. *However,* I enjoyed Malcolm X's more.

I enjoyed Walker's autobiography; *however,* I enjoyed Malcolm X's more.

My father died shortly before I was born. *Consequently,* I had to rely on his personal letters and diary when I needed information for my autobiography.

Notes

My father died shortly before I was born; *consequently,* I had to rely on his personal letters and diary when I needed information for my autobiography.

Practice #3 *Good Autobiographies (fixing run-ons)*

The following are run-on sentences. Rewrite them using transitions. (Use semicolons in some sentences. Use periods to separate other sentences.)

Example: Use the transition *therefore.*
I am interested in World War II I read Winston Churchill's memoirs.

- I am interested in World War II; therefore, I read Winston Churchill's memoirs.

1. Use the transition *then.*
   I finished Malcolm X's autobiography I loaned it to my sister.
2. Use the transition *consequently.*
   Malcolm X's story was honest and interesting I couldn't put it down.
3. Use the transition *therefore.*
   My mother is interested in African American history I gave her *The Autobiography of Miss Jane Pittman.*
4. Use the transition *however.*
   I have read many books on how to become a real estate developer I haven't read Donald Trump's autobiography.

Practice #4 *Reading (fixing run-on sentences)*

The following are run-on sentences. Correct each sentence using a carefully chosen transition from this list:

- however
- consequently
- therefore
- then

Use semicolons in some sentences. Use periods to separate other sentences.

Continued

1. I love old movies I read Katherine Hepburn's autobiography.
2. My cousin is interested in flying I bought him *Into the Night*.
3. I love to read autobiographies I don't really like novels.
4. He reads a book a week he wants to discuss each one with me.

Review Exercise A   *Narrating*

Rewrite the following paragraph, correcting all of the run-on sentences. Use three of the four methods for correcting run-ons. You may also use transitions. *Hint:* There are three run-ons.

When I use narration to develop an idea, I have to remember a number of things. For example, first I need to remember to make a point I can't get too caught up in my story. I can do this by following the writing process brainstorming and creating a topic sentence must come first. Then I will need to offer interesting details in my story. I can use adjectives, adverbs, and active verbs to help me do this. My goal is to paint a picture in my reader's mind then they will get my point and enjoy reading.

Review Exercise B   *My Sixth-Grade Teacher*

Rewrite the following paragraph, correcting all of the run-on sentences. Use a variety of methods for correcting run-ons. You may also use transitions.

One person I will always remember is my sixth-grade teacher because she treated all of her students like her own kids. We were a small class there were less than twenty of us. We would stay after school in our classroom it was really a portable building. We had no air conditioning, but we didn't mind the heat. My teacher would sit quietly grading homework, glancing up occasionally with a slight smile on her face she would watch us as we danced to the latest pop songs. I'm sure our dancing and our childish attempts at flirting were pretty comical however she never made us feel silly. She gave us a safe place to learn social skills.

Avoiding Run-ons

If run-ons are showing up regularly in your paragraphs, look to see if there is a pattern.

- Do you create a run-on when you use transitions?
- Do you create a run-on when ideas seem closely related?

When you reach the editing stage of your writing process, review your paragraph sentence by sentence, keeping an eye out for transitions and closely related sentences that might create run-ons. It is important that you be able to find and fix your own run-ons, but if you need help at first, ask a tutor to check for run-ons. Find out how many you have—but not where they are. Then find and fix them on your own. Check your work with your tutor.

Understanding, Correcting, and Avoiding Comma Splices

A **comma splice** is created when two sentences are incorrectly joined with a comma. A comma splice can confuse your readers, making them wonder where a sentence begins and where a sentence ends.

This chapter covers the following topics:

✦ Understanding comma splices
✦ Correcting comma splices
✦ Avoiding comma splices

Understanding Comma Splices

Notes

A writer may create a comma splice when the ideas in two sentences are closely related and the writer feels the need to pause. The writer might then insert a comma between the two sentences. However, a comma cannot do the job of a period.

If you separate complete sentences with a comma, you'll have an error called a comma splice. Here are some examples of comma splices:

I want to write a paragraph about my grandfather, he taught me about charity. (The first sentence ends where the comma is.)

I need to continue writing my brainstorm, I still have so many different ideas about my grandfather and his lessons. (The first sentence ends where the comma is.)

You may have heard that every time you "hear" a pause in your writing you should use a comma. This is *not* a good rule to follow. There are specific reasons for using commas, and you shouldn't use a comma unless you can name a specific comma rule (see Chapter 29). Where you hear a pause and where your reader hears a pause may be quite different, and scattering commas on your paper will cause confusion.

Computer Note
Grammar check found two comma splices here, but you'll find more!

Practice #1 *Lessons and Discoveries (finding the comma splices)*
Identify which of the following sentences have comma splices. When you find a comma splice, put *Cs* next to the sentence, put a period where the comma is, and begin the second sentence with a capital letter. If the sentence is correct, put a *C* next to the sentence.

Example: I learned about cooking from my grandfather he was a professional chef.

- I learned about cooking from my grandfather. He was a professional chef. *Cs*

1. I learned about manners from my aunt, she had seen how badly my sister behaved in public.
2. She taught me that manners would help me make friends, do well in school, and get good jobs.
3. I learned about being kind to animals one day when I was six years old, I played a trick on my neighbor's dog and hurt the poor animal.
4. When I was eight years old, I learned a painful lesson about empathy.
5. I learned about mourning a death when I was fifteen years old, people mourn in different ways.
6. As a Girl Scout selling cookies, I realized that I wasn't a good salesperson, I am too shy.
7. I used to help my grandmother in her garden, I discovered I wanted to get into landscaping.
8. Even though I really like kids, I learned that I don't have the patience to be an elementary school teacher.
9. Because I argued with him all the time, my father suggested that I become an attorney.
10. When I was in high school, I discovered I was a talented wrestler, so I'm trying to get a wrestling scholarship.

Correcting Comma Splices

Consider this comma splice:
- My neighbor's autobiography would be interesting to read, he was a career infantry soldier in the United States army.

There are four ways to correct comma splice errors. Notice that these are the same methods you can use to correct run-ons.

1. Put a period after the first sentence and capitalize the first letter of the second sentence.

   My neighbor's autobiography would be interesting to read. He was a career infantry soldier in the United States army.

2. Separate the two sentences with a semicolon. A semicolon is just as strong as a period.

   My neighbor's autobiography would be interesting to read; he was a career infantry soldier in the United States army.

3. Join the two sentences with a comma and a coordinating conjunction. The seven coordinating conjunctions are *for, and, nor, but, or, yet, so.*

   My neighbor's autobiography would be interesting to read, for he was a career infantry soldier in the United States army.

4. Add a subordinator and change one of the complete sentences to a subordinated clause. (Some subordinators include *if, when, because, although, since.*) If the new subordinated clause comes first, put a comma after it.

   My neighbor's autobiography would be interesting to read since he was a career infantry soldier in the United States army.

Practice #2   *Autobiographies (correcting comma splices)*
Correct each comma splice two different ways. Write your new sentences on a separate piece of paper.

Example: I searched the shelves at the book store, I needed to bring an autobiography to class on Monday.

  a. Correct this comma splice using method 2.
  b. Correct this comma splice using method 4.

- (a) I searched the shelves at the bookstore; I needed to bring an autobiography to class on Monday.
- (b) I searched the shelves at the bookstore because I needed to bring an autobiography to class on Monday.

1. I would like to read Oprah Winfrey's autobiography, I admire her intelligence and charitable actions.

Continued

Notes

   a. Correct this comma splice using method 1.
   b. Correct this comma splice using method 3.

2. My sister could write an interesting autobiography, she has worked in an Alaskan fishery and as a New York cab driver.

   a. Correct this comma splice using method 2.
   b. Correct this comma splice using method 4.

3. One day I will write my autobiography, I am a very interesting person.

   a. Correct this comma splice using method 1.
   b. Correct this comma splice using method 3.

4. I spent a lot of time in the bookstore, there were many interesting autobiographies on the shelves.

   a. Correct this comma splice using method 2.
   b. Correct this comma splice using method 4.

5. My brother only reads books about war, I only read books about famous people.

   a. Correct this comma splice using method 1.
   b. Correct this comma splice using method 3.

6. Eric wanted to get a few facts on Malcolm X, he looked in the encyclopedia.

   a. Correct this comma splice using method 2.
   b. Correct this comma splice using method 4.

Using Transitions to Correct Comma Splices

Methods 1 and 2 for correcting comma splices require you to use a period or a semicolon to separate complete sentences. Occasionally, you may want to use a transition with these methods. (You cannot use these transitions with just a comma to join complete sentences.)

   Here are some transitions:

however
consequently
therefore
then

These sentences show how to use a transition to correct a comma splice:

It was a harsh lesson, I needed to learn it. (comma splice)

It was a harsh lesson; *however,* I needed to learn it.

It was a harsh lesson. H*owever,* I needed to learn it.

Here is another example. Note that the transition is followed by a comma.

Einstein was bored in school, he didn't do very well. (comma splice)

Einstein was bored in school; *therefore,* he didn't do very well.

Einstein was bored in school. *Therefore,* he didn't do very well.

Practice #3   *My Autobiography (using transitions to correct comma splices)*

The following sentences have comma splice errors. On a separate piece of paper, rewrite them using transitions. Use semicolons in some sentences. Use periods to separate other sentences.

Example: Use the transition *therefore.*

I wanted to explain my "roots," I did some research into my family's history.

- I wanted to explain my "roots;" therefore, I did some research into my family's history.

1. Use the transition *consequently.*

   My grandfather had no life insurance, my grandmother and father had to get jobs.

2. Use the transition *then.*

   My grandmother looked at the unfinished painting, she got out her brushes and went to work on it.

3. Use the transition *however.*

   Many years ago, I began to write my autobiography, I could tell I wasn't being objective.

4. Use the transition *therefore.*

   I'm older and wiser now, I think I can write an honest, interesting autobiography.

Notes

Practice #4 *The Hairdresser's Life (using transitions to correct comma splices)*

The following sentences have comma splice errors. On a separate piece of paper, rewrite them using transitions. Choose transitions from this list:

- however
- consequently
- therefore
- then

Use semicolons in some sentences. Use periods to separate other sentences.

Example: I probably shouldn't admit this, I love gossip.

- I probably shouldn't admit this; however, I love gossip.

1. My aunt was a hairdresser for 30 years, she knows many interesting people.
2. I think she should write her autobiography, she thinks her life isn't "special" enough.
3. I told her to write it for the family, her children would have a record of her life.
4. She respects people's privacy, she doesn't feel she should write about her clients.

Review Exercise A *Walker and I (correcting comma splices)*

Rewrite the following paragraph, correcting all of the comma splice errors. Underline all the changes you make. Use a variety of methods for correcting comma splices. You may also use transitions. *Hint:* There are four comma splices.

I found Alice Walker's essay interesting, I could relate to many of her experiences. I wasn't injured as a child, I did have to wear a back brace because of scoliosis. Wearing the brace made me feel embarrassed about my appearance, it also prevented me from participating in regular play at recess, not to mention sports. Finally, when I was older and got to stop wearing the brace, I felt like a new person, I was no longer different. I stood up straight and looked people in the eye.

Review Exercise B   *My Father and I (correcting comma splices)*
Rewrite the following paragraph, correcting all of the comma splice errors. Underline all the changes you make. Use a variety of methods for correcting comma splices. You may also use transitions.

"Chapter Two" from Russell Baker's autobiography reminded me of my struggle with my father. My father wanted me to be an architect, he thought that was the perfect job. I think, really, that was what he wanted to be, but he never got to go to college. I hated the first drafting class I took, I didn't have the aptitude for being an architect. I loved my first plant biology class. Without telling my father, I switched my major in college from architecture to botany, I knew I would enjoy studying and working with plants. I was right.

Avoiding Comma Splices

If comma splices are showing up regularly in your paragraphs, look to see if there is a pattern.

- Do you create a comma splice when you use transitions?
- Do you create a comma splice when ideas seem closely related?

When you reach the editing stage of your writing process, review your paragraph sentence by sentence, keeping an eye out for transitions and closely related sentences that might lead you to create comma splices. Remember, there are specific rules for using commas. Review the chart in Appendix C and the exercises in Chapter 29. It is important that you be able to find and fix your own comma splices, but if you need help at first, ask a tutor to check for comma splices. Find out how many you have—but not where they are. Then find and fix them on your own. Check your work with your tutor.

Beyond the Basics: Creating Expressive Sentences

In this section of *Expressions,* you'll find seven chapters that focus on sentence style.

Each chapter focuses on a single technique that can help you to write more interesting, more sophisticated, and more expressive sentences.

21

Pronouns

As readers and writers, we rely on pronouns.

✦ Pronouns give writers more options, so that we don't always have to use the same nouns.
✦ Pronouns help readers to see how ideas connect, and they save us from boring repetition.

This chapter covers the following topics:

✦ Identifying pronouns
✦ Antecedents
✦ Pronoun agreement and avoiding sexist language

Notes

Identifying Pronouns

A *pronoun* is a word that can be used in place of a noun. In these examples, the pronouns are underlined:

> Alice Walker wrote an autobiographical essay. <u>She</u> wrote about beauty.
> Russell Baker wrote a book-length autobiography. In one chapter, <u>he</u> explained how <u>he</u> got started in journalism.

Pronouns come in different forms: subject form, possessive form, relative/interrogative form, and indefinite form.

Subject form	I, he, she, it, they, we, you, this
Object form	me, him, her, it, them, us, you, this
Possessive form	my/mine, his, her/hers, its, their/theirs, our/ours, your/yours, this
Relative/Interrogative form	who, that, which
Indefinite form	someone, everybody, each, neither, anybody, anyone

Here are examples of the different pronoun forms:

<u>I</u> (subject form) gave <u>him</u> (object form) Malcolm X's autobiography to read.

After reading <u>her</u> (possessive) autobiography, I wanted to watch some Katherine Hepburn films.

Hepburn was a woman <u>who</u> (relative form) epitomized strength and determination.

<u>Everybody</u> (indefinite) can learn something from <u>her</u> (object form).

If we didn't use pronouns, we would be stuck repeating the person's name (or the noun) over and over. This would be not only more work, but it would be very repetitive.

Read this example aloud, and you'll notice how repetitive and awkward writing is without pronouns:

In my grandmother's autobiography, my grandmother revealed my grandmother's strength and determination. My grandmother wrote about growing up on a horse ranch and then going to UC Berkeley. My grandmother explains what it was like to go from a small town, which mostly consisted of relatives and close friends, to a city where my grandmother was unknown. After just one year of college, my grandmother got married and moved to another city. In my grandmother's book, my grandmother explains how my grandmother became active in local politics and local arts programs. My grandmother's autobiography inspires me to try new things and be brave even when I feel alone and scared.

Here is the same paragraph with pronouns. Read this aloud:

In <u>her</u> autobiography, my grandmother revealed <u>her</u> strength and determination. <u>She</u> wrote about growing up on a horse ranch and then going to UC Berkeley. <u>She</u> explains what it was like to go from a small town, which mostly consisted of relatives and close friends, to a city where <u>she</u> was unknown. After just one year of college, my grandmother got married and moved to another city. In <u>her</u> book, my grandmother explains how <u>she</u> became active in local politics and local arts programs. My grandmother's autobiography inspires me to try new things and be brave even when I feel alone and scared.

Note that "grandmother" is still used occasionally in the paragraph for variety and so that there is no confusion.

Notes

Practice #1
Underline the pronouns in the following sentences.

Example: Television and magazines give us models of beauty that are hard to live up to.

- Television and magazines give <u>us</u> models of beauty that are hard to live up to.

Part 1 *Gathering Information and Autobiographies* (identifying pronouns)
1. Joe is using a tape recorder as he thinks about his paragraph out loud.
2. Sue needed a few facts about Hitler, so she did a search on the Internet.
3. The president has a lot of secrets; therefore he doesn't want to write an autobiography.
4. Has Tiger Woods written his autobiography?
5. The students say they need more time at the library.

Part 2 *Beauty* (identifying pronouns)
1. When Alice Walker was young, she was proud of her beauty.
2. After her eye was injured, Walker felt ugly.
3. Everyone likes to feel beautiful.
4. However, your worth as a human being is determined by more than your appearance.

Antecedents

An **antecedent** is the noun a pronoun refers to. It is important for pronouns to have clear antecedents so that the reader knows to whom or what you are referring. In these examples, the antecedents are highlighted:

My grandmother began writing her autobiography when she was 92 years old.

Captain McCloud was an interesting man because he was brutally honest.

Practice #2   *Interests and Skills (find the pronouns and antecedents)*

Underline the pronouns. Draw an arrow from each pronoun to its antecedent.

Example: Doris is confident, so she should be a salesperson.

• Doris is confident, so <u>she</u> should be a salesperson.

1. Sid loves playing the guitar, and he would like to form a band.

2. At age four, Keely tries to imitate fine art; maybe she will be a professional artist when she is older.

3. Ann has always been fascinated with fashion; perhaps she will be a designer someday.

4. Brienna loves language and can win an argument with anyone, so maybe she will be an attorney or judge.

5. With her sensitivity for animals, Bethany should be a veterinarian.

Practice #3   *People Worth Reading About (finding the pronouns and antecedents)*

Underline the pronouns. Draw an arrow from each pronoun to its antecedent.

Example: The students wanted to compile a report on the ten most influential people in their town, so they divided up the tasks and began researching.

• The students wanted to compile a report on the ten most influential people in <u>their</u> town, so <u>they</u> divided up the tasks and began researching.

1. Music stars lead pretty wild lives, and my sister likes to read about their adventures.

2. Ghandi was an important figure in history; consequently, I'd like to learn more about him.

3. I wonder what Abe Lincoln would have said in his autobiography?

4. My neighbor should write his autobiography since he has been a truck driver, a California Highway patrolman, and a caterer.

5. Coach Jim used to be the mayor, and he is currently our soccer coach and a captain in the sheriff's department.

If a pronoun does not have a clear antecedent, an instructor may use the phrase "unclear pronoun reference." But, when pronouns like *I, everyone,* and *anyone* are used as subjects, an antecedent is not necessary because your reader will not be confused by these pronouns.

Here's an example of unclear pronoun reference:

Father got along really well with grandfather. In <u>his</u> autobiography, <u>he</u> explains how they enjoyed going to baseball games together.

Who wrote the autobiography? The father or the grandfather?

In this situation, the writer needs to make the antecedent clear. The writer can do this without repeating "my father." The writer can use a synonym like "my dad" instead. A word is a *synonym* to another if it means basically the same thing. Here's an example:

Father got along really well with Grandfather. In <u>my dad's</u> autobiography, he explains how they enjoyed going to baseball games together.

Here's another example of an unclear pronoun reference:

After Walker's brother shot her in the eye, her father didn't pay as much attention to her. She resented <u>him</u> for this.

Who does *him* refer to? The brother or the father? And what does *this* refer to? The shooting or the father's change in attitude? Here are two ways to express the idea in a clearer sentence:

After Walker's brother shot her in the eye, her father didn't pay as much attention to her. She resented <u>her brother</u> <u>for causing this change.</u>

or

After Walker's brother shot her in the eye, her father didn't pay as much attention to her. She resented <u>her father</u> <u>for caring so much about her beauty.</u>

Obviously, the two revisions result in very different ideas. It is up to the writer to provide clear antecedents (clear pronoun reference) so that the reader will understand the writer's point.

Be careful that pronouns refer directly to clear antecedents, and don't use *this* to refer to large, complex ideas or events:

Computer Note

The computer can help you find a synonym. Go to Tools in the menu bar and then to Language and Thesaurus. However, sometimes this doesn't work. If you type *father* and try to find a synonym this way you will be offered *priest.* A thesaurus in book form can be helpful in such cases.

Denying women the right to vote revealed many prejudices that people held. You should discuss *this* in your paper. (Incorrect—does *this* refer to denying women the right to vote? Or does *this* refer to *many prejudices? Many prejudices* names more than one thing, but *this* suggests only one thing.)

Denying women the right to vote revealed many prejudices that people held. You should discuss *some of these prejudices* in your paper. (correct)

Practice Review   *Aunt Cathy's Diary (correcting pronoun errors)*

The following paragraph has some unclear pronouns and some unnecessary repetition.

- Read the paragraph aloud.
- On a separate piece of paper, rewrite the paragraph, making the suggested substitutions.
- Read the paragraph aloud again.

Suggested substitutions:
- Replace *diaries* with the synonym *journals*.
- Replace the unclear *she* with the appropriate noun or a synonym.
- Replace *Aunt Cathy's diary and her mother's diary* with *records*.
- Replace the unclear *she* with the appropriate noun or a synonym.
- Replace *diaries* with the synonym *memoirs*.

    Collette looks at Aunt Cathy's diary and her mother's diary as she begins to write. The two <u>diaries</u> are so different. Collette wonders why <u>she</u> couldn't have been more detailed in the diary. Aunt Cathy's diary, on the other hand, mentions dates, names, colors, smells, everything! Yet, Collette is glad to have both <u>Aunt Cathy's diary and her mother's diary</u> because information in one will often fill in the gaps in the other. In addition, <u>she</u> is often a bit more honest about events than mother. The diaries will help Collette paint a clearer picture of the past as she begins her own autobiography. Aunt Cathy and her mother would be pleased to know their <u>diaries</u> are being put to good use.

Notes

Rewrite this paragraph, using pronouns and synonyms to make this paragraph clearer and less repetitive.

Hints:
- Replace some of "my mother" phrases with the pronoun *she* or the synonyms *mom* or "his 9-year-old daughter."
- Replace some uses of "my mother" with the pronoun *her*.
- Find a place where you can replace "to surf" with the more interesting adjective and synonym "a manly sport."
- Replace *surfing* with the synonym "riding waves."
- Read your new paragraph aloud to check your changes before turning in the paragraph.

   In the second chapter of my mother's autobiography, my mother goes into detail describing what it was like to learn to surf. First my mother explains that my mother's father, originally from Kansas, didn't approve of my mother hanging out with older boys and learning to surf. For almost a year, my mother had to sneak out to surf. My mother also explains that the key to surfing is really in the mind. My mother had to develop confidence in herself and lose her fears of the powerful ocean. Eventually, my mother says, my mother's father came to terms with girls surfing, and my mother's father actually expressed admiration for my mother's grace and strength as a surfer.

Pronoun Agreement and Avoiding Sexist Language

Pronouns must have clear antecedents, and the pronouns must agree in number with those antecedents. If the antecedent is singular, the pronoun must be singular. If the antecedent is plural, the pronoun must be plural. Note that *indefinite* pronouns are always singular.

Singular Pronouns	Plural Pronouns
he, she, it	we, they
my, mine, his, hers	their, theirs
someone, everybody, each	
neither, anybody, anyone	

Here are examples of correct pronoun agreement:

My sister said <u>she</u> will call back.

Sally said this cell phone is <u>hers.</u>

Someone left <u>her</u> purse in the theater.

The neighbors said <u>they</u> would be gone for a week.

My grandparents asked me to feed <u>their</u> cat.

A common mistake is to use *their* to refer to a singular antecedent, as in this example.

An FBI agent who writes <u>their</u> autobiography would have interesting stories to tell.

The antecedent "FBI agent" is singular. *Their* is plural. Writers make this mistake most often when the gender of antecedent is unknown or unimportant. The writer is unsure about using *he* or *she*. However, it isn't correct to use *their*.

Traditionally, writers have used *he* or *him* when the gender of the person is unknown. However, this can seem sexist, as in this example:

An FBI agent who writes <u>his</u> autobiography would have interesting stories to tell.

It isn't accurate to suggest that all FBI agents are men.

To make your antecedents and pronouns agree in number *and* avoid sexist language, consider these solutions.

- Change the antecedent to plural and then use the plural pronouns *they* or *their*.
- Keep the singular antecedent and use *he or she,* or *his or her.*

Here's the sentence about FBI agents again, using the solutions:

FBI agents who write <u>their</u> autobiographies would have interesting stories to tell. (Note how the verb changes from *writes* to *write,* and *autobiography* changes from the singular to plural.)

An FBI agent who writes <u>his or her</u> autobiography would have interesting stories to tell.

Occasionally, you may need a singular antecedent and pronoun to keep the meaning of your idea clear. In the following paragraph, using *he or she* or changing the antecedents and pronouns to the plural

Computer Note

Since grammar check will often miss pronoun agreement errors, double check yourself whenever you use *their*.

Notes

would actually make the paragraph less clear. In such a case, the writer has to choose either the female pronoun or the male pronoun and then stick with it.

A person who wants to write an autobiography should interview other people to see how they remember important events. The writer needs to know if <u>her</u> memory of significant moments is accurate. If the people <u>she</u> interviews remember things differently than <u>she</u> does, <u>she</u> will have to do some careful thinking and make decisions about what information to include. Perhaps <u>she</u> will want to include two or three versions to show readers how different people recall the events.

Practice #4   *Donating Money (making antecedents and pronouns agree in number)*

The following sentences have singular antecedents but plural pronouns. This is incorrect. On a separate piece of paper, rewrite these sentences and make the underlined antecedent in each sentence plural so that it fits with the plural pronoun already in the sentence.

Example: <u>A person</u> who wants to write their autobiography needs to gather information about their past.

• People who want to write their autobiographies need to gather information about their pasts. (Note that *wants, autobiography, need,* and *pasts* all had to change to fit with the new plural noun.)

1. After graduating, <u>a student</u> should donate money to their college.

2. <u>Even a person</u> with an average income can find a few dollars to give to their school. (*Hint:* The words *an* and *income* must also change to work with a plural noun.)

3. <u>A college</u> may rely heavily on donations from their students.

4. I think <u>a business</u> that expects local colleges to train future employees for their workforce should donate a lot of money. (*Hint:* The word *expects* must change to work with a plural noun.)

5. Is there <u>a famous person</u> who gives more than a million dollars of their income to charity each year? (*Hint: Is, gives,* and *income* must also change to work with a plural noun.)

Practice #5   *Life Stories (making antecedents and pronouns agree in number)*

The following sentences have singular antecedents but plural pronouns. This is incorrect. On a separate piece of paper, rewrite the following sentences and make the underlined pronoun in each sentence singular, so that it fits with the singular antecedent already in the sentence.

Example: An avid reader might spend 5 percent of <u>their</u> salary on books.

• An avid reader might spend 5 percent of his or her salary on books.

1. If a person wants to be a good narrator, <u>they</u> will analyze the events in <u>their</u> life.

2. Even a professional writer will have to revise and edit <u>their</u> work.

3. If a photographer starts young, <u>they</u> might be able to tell <u>their</u> life story through photographs.

4. A person might record important events in <u>their</u> life through song, dance, or art.

5. Does a writer have to reveal the real names of <u>their</u> sources?

Practice #6   *Write! (making antecedents and pronouns agree)*

The following sentences have antecedent-pronoun agreement errors. Rewrite sentences 1–3 so that they have plural pronouns and plural antecedents. Rewrite sentences 4–6 so that they have singular pronouns and singular antecedents.

1. A person writing an autobiography must carefully study their past.

2. A person who has trouble being honest about their lives probably shouldn't bother writing an autobiography.

3. I think a good activity at a convalescent home would be to ask a sharp-minded resident to write their autobiography.

4. Maybe the resident would have to be persuaded that their life was worth writing about.

Continued

Notes

5. Or perhaps the resident would immediately recognize that their family and friends would treasure such a record.
6. The resident might also see that reviewing their life and analyzing their motives would keep their mind active and healthy.

Create Your Own Sentences

Review Exercise C   *Original Sentences*
On a separate piece of paper, create the following sentences.

1. Create a sentence that has a clear antecedent and pronoun. Draw an arrow from the pronoun to the antecedent. Use a new vocabulary word in your sentence.

2. Write two or more synonymous phrases that mean basically the same thing as "drinking coffee."

3. Write two or more synonymous phrases that mean basically the same thing as "talking with my friends."

4. Write a sentence that shows you can use "a college graduate" as an antecedent and "his or her" as pronouns that refer to "a college graduate." Draw an arrow from the pronoun to the antecedent.

5. Write a sentence that shows you can use *children* as an antecedent and *their* as a pronoun that refers to *children*. Draw an arrow from the pronoun to the antecedent. Use a new vocabulary word in your sentence.

Apply Your Knowledge

Review one of the paragraphs you have written, and check to see if you have used pronouns correctly.

• Do you have clear antecedents?
• Do your nouns and pronouns agree in number?
• Can you use synonyms to make your writing clearer or more interesting?
• Have you avoided using sexist language?

Adjectives and Adverbs

Adjectives and adverbs can help you add interesting information to your writing. You can take a dull piece of writing and add color, smell, taste, movement, dimensions, and attitude.

This chapter covers the following topics:

◆ Identifying single adjectives
◆ Identifying adjective phrases
◆ Adding adjectives and adjective phrases to sentences
◆ Identifying adverbs
◆ Adding adverbs to sentences

Identifying Single Adjectives

An **adjective** is a word that describes a noun. A *noun* names a person, place, thing, or idea. In these examples, the adjectives are highlighted, and the arrows show which nouns they describe:

The tired parent set the child down in front of the television.
The young child watched the silly dinosaur.
The dinosaur is rich.
I am envious.

Some *–ing* and *–ed* words can work as adjectives. Remember, *–ing* words are present participles and *–ed* words are past participles. See pp. 239–240 in Chapter 17 for a review. Here are some examples using *–ing* and *–ed* words as adjectives:

The <u>singing</u> frog was teaching viewers how to count.
The <u>excited</u> boy danced as he sang along with Big Bird.

Notes

Computer Note
You can use the thesaurus on your computer to help you find interesting adjectives. Go to Tools on your menu bar. If you type in *nice,* you'll be offered *pleasant.* Press Look up again and you'll be offered *amiable, congenial,* and *affable.* You may also need to use a dictionary to be sure that you choose an adjective that best fits your message.

Practice #1
In the following sentences, highlight the adjectives. Then draw arrows to the nouns they describe.

Example: My picky husband was searching for an exciting book.

• My picky husband was searching for an exciting book. *Continued*

277

Notes

Some nouns, like *mountain climber,* are made up of two words. Other examles of compound nouns are *phone call, fig tree, German shepherd,* and *college instructor.*

Part 1 *An Interesting Book (identify adjectives)*

1. The interesting book about the courageous mountain climber captured his attention.

2. This was not like the other boring books he had read.

3. He wanted to learn to climb monstrous mountains.

4. After reading the book, the man thumbed through the thick phonebook and found a reputable teacher.

5. This would be a demanding sport.

Part 2 *A Bike Ride (identifying adjectives)*

1. The quirky kid rode his squeaky bike down the dark path that ran along the swirling river.

2. The malicious, moronic teenagers sat on the damp dirt behind an old fig tree and waited for the kid to appear.

3. However, today the kid wasn't alone.

4. Tiny—the boy's husky, protective German shepherd—ran next to the bike.

5. Tiny had a mean growl.

Identifying Adjective Phrases

In Practice #1, the adjectives are single words, and most of them come *before* the nouns they describe.

Adjectives can come in phrases (participial phrases). Adjective phrases can come before or after the nouns they describe. The adjective phrases in the following sentences are highlighted:

Flipping through the channels, the woman lying on the couch found her favorite show.

People stranded on an island were wrestling over the last bite of coconut.

Practice #2   *A College Course (identifying adjectives and adjective phrases)*

Highlight the single adjectives and the adjective phrases in these sentences. Draw arrows to the nouns they describe.

Continued

Example: Interested in a raise, I enrolled in a demanding course at the local college.

- Interested in a raise, I enrolled in a demanding course at the local college.

1. My first instructor in college had high expectations.

2. Hoping we would gain some insight about ourselves, he asked us to write our autobiographies.

3. He expected detailed, honest writing.

4. Obvious lies or missing detail could earn you a failing grade.

5. Using all of my creative energy, I wrote an autobiography dripping with colorful adjectives and adverbs.

Practice Review   *Reviewing Walker*

Review Alice Walker's essay "Beauty: When the Other Dancer Is the Self" (pp. 106–111).

1. Copy the sentence in paragraph 1 that describes Walker's father. Underline the adjectives in that sentence. In your own words, what do these adjectives tell you about her father?

2. Copy the sentence in paragraph 45 that describes how the Earth looks on the television show *Big Blue Marble*. Underline the adjectives in that sentence. In your own words, how does the Earth appear to Walker?

3. Copy the sentence in paragraph 47, in which her little girl holds Walker's face. Also copy the sentence that follows it. Underline the adjectives in those sentences. In your own words, what do the adjectives tell you about the little girl?

Adding Adjectives and Adjective Phrases to Sentences

Notice here how the following sentences say so much more when adjectives are added.

Without adjectives: The man had a life.

With adjectives: The man living in the old rail car had an adventurous and sometimes dangerous life.

Notes

Without adjectives: The student handed her narrative to the instructor.

With adjectives: The anxious student bursting through the classroom door handed her beloved, heart-wrenching narrative over to the curious instructor.

Practice #3

On a separate piece of paper, revise these sentences by adding the adjectives given.

- The noun to be described is in parentheses.
- Put the adjectives or adjective phrases close to the noun they describe.

Example:

- My classmate read the article.
  studious (classmate)
  interesting (article)
- New sentence: My studious classmate read the interesting article.

Part 1 *Writing a Summary* (adding adjectives)

1. I am learning to write summaries.
   clear and concise (summaries)
2. He wrote a summary.
   including too much detail (he) (*Hint:* Begin the sentence with this adjective phrase.)
   long (summary)
3. Joan found the main points.
   discussing the reading with her classmates (Joan) (*Hint:* Begin the sentence with this adjective phrase.)
4. I put the article away and wrote a draft.
   original (article)
   quick (draft)
5. At work I prepared a summary for my boss.
   excellent (summary)
   demanding (boss)

Continued

When completeing #5, remember the **a/an rule.** Use *a* before words that start with *a* consonant sound and *an* before words that start with a vowel sound.

Part 2 *Clinton's Autobiography* (adding adjectives)

1. I want to read Bill Clinton's autobiography.

   not-yet-published (autobiography)

2. I think he is a figure.

   fascinating (figure)

   political (figure)

3. He's not exactly a man.

   ideal (man) (*Hint:* remember the a/an rule)

   family (man)

4. And he probably could have accomplished much more if he had not made mistakes.

   foolish (mistakes)

5. However, he made many moves and will be remembered as a figure in United States history.

   savvy (moves)

   political (moves)

   significant (figure)

Practice Review   *Finding an Autobiography*

Add adjectives to the following sentences to make them more expressive. First find the noun or nouns in the sentence. Then add one or more adjectives that describe the noun.

Example: I bought a car.

• I bought a rusted, gas-guzzling, old car.

1. I needed an autobiography.
2. I went to the bookstore.
3. As I read the book I bought, I drank coffee.
4. The person in my book was a fisherman who worked off the coast of New England.
5. He led a life on the sea.

Practice Review   *A Colorful Sentence (using adjectives)*

Create an original sentence, using as many adjectives as possible. Underline all adjectives and draw arrows to the nouns they describe. Share your sentence with your classmates.

Notes

Identifying Adverbs

An **adverb** is a word that describes a verb, another adverb, or an adjective. In these examples, the adverbs are highlighted, and the arrows show which words they describe:

He watched television attentively. (The adverb describes a verb.)

The child argued vehemently for his own VCR. (The adverb describes a verb.)

I seriously doubt that we need that extremely expensive computer. (The first adverb describes a verb, and the second adjective describes an adjective.

As you may have noticed, many adverbs end in *–ly*. However, not all adverbs end in *–ly*. Here are a few examples:

He speaks well. (The adverb *well* describes the verb *speaks*.)

I ran more quickly than the others. (The first adverb *more* describes the adverb *quickly,* and the second adverb *quickly* describes the verb *ran*.)

She was most interested in the issue of poverty. (The adverb *most* describes the adjective *interested*.)

Some *–ly* words are not adverbs.

He spoke with a princely manner. (*Princely* is an adjective because it is describing the noun *manner*.)

You can tell if a word is an adverb by looking at what it is describing. Remember, an adverb will describe a verb, an adjective, or another adverb.

💻 Computer Note
Your online dictionary or thesaurus can help you find interesting adverbs. Look for words that are followed by (adv.). For example, if you type the word *fast* and look for words labeled with (adv.), you'll be offered *rapidly, hastily,* and *quickly.*

> **Practice #4**
> Highlight the adverbs in these sentences, and draw arrows to the words they describe.
>
> Example: The committee politely invited me to the meeting.
>
> • The committee politely invited me to the meeting.
>
> **Part 1** *My Presentation* (identifying adverbs)
> 1. I carefully researched my facts before making my presentation.
> 2. However, the committee still argued forcefully against my proposal.
>
> *Continued*

3. I know I spoke clearly.
4. They are stubbornly refusing to listen to reason.
5. I will quietly approach the CEO.

Part 2 *My Crime* (identifying adverbs)

1. I sadly admitted my crime.
2. My father screamed loudly.
3. My mother wept quietly.
4. My grandmother and grandfather shook their heads despairingly.
5. By now, the dye had fully soaked in, and the dog ran out of our gate to show the dogs in the neighborhood his beautifully tie-dyed fur.

Practice Review   *Reviewing Trump*

Review Donald Trump's chapter of his autobiography, *The Art of the Deal* (pp. 424–429).

1. Copy the first sentence in paragraph 5 and highlight the the adverb that begins the sentence. How would the meaning of the sentence change if the adverb were left out?

2. Copy the last three sentences in paragraph 18 and highlight the adverbs. How would the meaning of the sentence change if the adverbs were left out?

3. Copy the last sentence in paragraph 20 and highlight the first adverb. How would the meaning of the sentence change if the adverb were left out?

Adding Adverbs to Sentences

Notice how these sentences can become more expressive when adverbs are added.

Martin Luther King Jr. spoke against racism and poverty.

Martin Luther King Jr. spoke passionately against racism and poverty.

Yesterday, the speaker concluded by stating his main point and calling for change.

Yesterday, the speaker brilliantly concluded by clearly and powerfully stating his main point and calling for change.

Practice #5

On a separate piece of paper, revise these sentences by adding the adverbs given. The word to be described is in parentheses.

Example: I listened to the lecture.
attentively (listened)

- I listened attentively to the lecture.

Part 1 *A News Article (adding adverbs)*

1. The reporter researched the story about the dying woman.

   diligently (researched)
2. He discussed the controversial points of his article with his editor.
   calmly (discussed)

3. He produced a memorable article.
   slowly (produced)

4. People will read this article.
   carefully (will read) (*Hint:* Put the adverb between *will* and *read.*)

5. They will reach out to help this woman and her family.
   certainly (will reach out)

Part 2 *The Draft Workshop (adding adverbs)*

1. My peers reviewed my paragraph.
   conscientiously (reviewed)

2. They stared at one another.
   blankly (stared)

3. I thought I would cry.
   surely (would cry)

4. I looked down at the floor.
   disappointedly (looked)

Continued

5. Then they shouted, "Wow! This is a great paragraph."
   shouted (suddenly)

Practice Review   *Into the Unknown (adding adverbs)*
Add adverbs to these sentences to make them more expressive.

1. I went where no man had gone before.
2. I fought the beasts.
3. Challenging myself, I refused help from anyone.
4. At the end of each day, I slept.
5. I greeted each morning by singing.

Create Your Own Sentences

Using adjectives and adverbs in your writing will add interest and complexity to your writing. Some of your vocabulary words in this text are adjectives or participles that can be used as adjectives (see pp. 239–240 in Chapter 17 for a review of participles). Here are some examples:

stunted (Jones, p. 80, paragraph 4)
prompt (Peretti, p. 85, paragraph 23)
chronic (Walker, p. 107, paragraph 2)
relegated (Walker, p. 108, paragraph 8)
confronted (Walker, p. 108, paragraph 11)
boisterous (Walker, p. 109, paragraph 16)

Some of your other vocabulary words have adjective forms that you can find in the dictionary:

emancipation (noun) (Jones p.80, paragraph 1)
emancipating (participle that can be used as an adjective) The man emancipating the hostages is a federal agent.
toils (verb) (Jones p.80, paragraph 4)
toiling (participle that can be used as an adjective) Toiling in the hot sun, they got sunburned.
vehemently (adverb) (Jones p.81)

Notes

vehement (adjective) He was vehement in his desire to throw his television in the trash.

Some of your vocabulary words (and the words defined in the margins) in this text are adverbs:

vehemently

Some of your other vocabulary words have adjective forms that you can find in the dictionary:

prompt (adjective)
promptly (adverb) I promptly called the hospital.
chronic (adjective)
chronically (adverb) She is chronically late to work.
boisterous (adjective)
boisterously (adverb) The crowd cheered boisterously.

Review Exercise A
On a separate piece of paper, create original sentences using the following words as described. In your new sentences, label your adjectives and adverbs (as adj. or adv.) Then underline the words that the adjectives and adverbs are describing.
Example: Sporadically (adverb)

adv.
• I am so busy that I only <u>write</u> sporadically to my parents.

1. boisterous (adjective)
2. toiling (adjective)
3. vehement (adjective)
4. vehemently (adverb)
5. promptly (adverb)
6. chronically (adverb)

Apply Your Knowledge

Review one of your paragraphs and revise it, adding adjectives and adverbs where appropriate.

Coordinators

One method of making your sentences more interesting and more expressive is to join independent clauses with *coordinating conjunctions.*

This chapter covers the following topics:

+ Understanding coordinating conjunctions
+ Punctuating correctly with coordinating conjunctions
+ Using coordinating conjunctions

Understanding Coordinating Conjunctions

Notes

Coordinating conjunctions are words that can join two complete sentences to make one sentence. There are seven coordinating conjunctions (coordinators.) You can remember them by the word FANBOYS:

For And Nor But Or Yet So

When you want to join two independent clauses with one of the FANBOYS, you need to choose one of the FANBOYS that *accurately* expresses the relationship between the ideas you are joining.

For expresses a relationship of *effect-cause.* The idea in the first sentence is the effect. The idea in the second sentence is the cause.

I am pleased with the topic for my paragraph, for I feel the reader will be interested.

And expresses a relationship of *addition.* The idea in the first sentence is added to the idea in the second sentence.

I take the time to freewrite, and I carefully revise my topic sentence.

Nor expresses a relationship of *negative addition.* The idea in the first sentence is negative, and it is added to a negative idea in the second sentence. Notice that the subject and verb in the second independent clause are not in their usual order.

Notes

I don't want to bore my reader with too many details, nor do I want to rush through and leave out important information.

But expresses a relationship of opposition. The idea in the first sentence is the opposite of the idea in the second sentence.

I used to skip the predrafting stage, but now I think it's an important step.

Or expresses a relationship of *alternatives*. The idea in the first sentence is one option. The idea in the second sentence is another option.

I usually show my tutor a rough draft of my essay, or I will have my dad take a look at it.

Yet expresses a relationship of *opposition*. The idea in the first sentence is the opposite of the idea in the second sentence.

I appreciate getting advice from the tutor and my dad, yet sometimes I get discouraged when they say something isn't clear.

So expresses a relationship of *cause-effect*. The idea in the first sentence causes the idea in the second sentence.

Improving my writing skills is really important to me, so I will hang in there and seek their advice.

Punctuating Correctly with Coordinating Conjunctions

When you use a coordinating conjunction, you are combining two independent clauses and making one sentence. This combination requires that you use a comma after the first independent clause.

Here are sentences that use commas correctly with the FANBOYS:

I wanted a good meal, so I went to the diner down the street.

My husband was offended, for he considers himself a great chef.

Practice #1 *Don't Forget the Comma*
Review the seven sample sentences for the FANBOYS (pp. 287–288) and underline each comma.

Continued

Example:

- I am pleased with the topic for my paragraph, for I feel the reader will be interested.

Using Coordinating Conjunctions

Coordinating conjunctions can help you create smoother, clearer sentences. Consider these sentences:

I came to the United States. This country offered me more educational opportunities. My mother was worried about me being so far from home. She understands the importance of this move.

The first two sentences sound choppy, and the second two sentences seem to contradict each other. With coordinating conjunctions, the sentences are smoother, and the ideas are clearer.

I came to the United States, for this country offered me more educational opportunities. My mother was worried about me being so far from home, yet she understands the importance of this move.

The rest of this chapter asks you to practice using coordinating conjunctions (the FANBOYS). To get the most out of the exercises in this chapter, follow these guidelines:

- Write out complete sentences on a separate piece of paper. Don't attempt to just draw arrows or insert words.
- Join two independent clauses with one of the seven FANBOYS. Even if you see other ways to combine the sentences, stick with the FANBOYS for now.
- Make sure that you are joining two complete independent clauses. Don't delete any of the subjects.

Practice #2   *Thinking about Writing (using coordinators)*
Combine the following sentence pairs, using the coordinator in parentheses. Remember to use a comma after the first independent clause.

Example:
My employer wants me to take on more tasks. My day is already full. (but)   *Continued*

Notes

- My employer wants me to take on more tasks, but my day is already full.

1. My first step as a writer is to think about why I am writing. The second step is to think about the audience. (and)
2. I do a better job with my paragraph if I picture a specific audience. I feel more motivated to communicate clearly and powerfully. (for)
3. I don't think about my grade when I am drafting an essay. I don't think much about grammar. (nor)
4. I am a terrible speller. I love spell check on my computer. (so)
5. I have three really good main ideas for my paragraph. I know I have to pick just one. (yet)
6. I might make all the people in my Cinderella story male. Maybe I'll only change the stepmother into a stepfather. (or)
7. He explained the lesson in his fairy tale. I was still confused. (but)

Note: When completing #3, keep in mind that you have to change the order of the subject and verb in the second sentence. See the *nor* example from earlier in the chapter. Also, when combining sentences using *nor,* you must delete the negative word in the second sentence.

Practice #3   *My Message (using coordinators)*

On a separate piece of paper, join the following independent clauses using carefully chosen coordinators. Use each coordinator once, and remember to put a comma after the first independent clause.

1. I want to teach kids about looking past beauty. I'd like to say something about forgiveness.
2. The lesson in the story shouldn't be too obvious. The language shouldn't be too formal.
3. I want to make this a truly modern story. I think I will mention cell phones and the Internet.
4. I want the stepmother in my story to be nice. I think that stepmothers are picked on too much.
5. I'd like to make my story funny. I'm not sure if I can be humorous when I write.
6. I'll have my little sister read the story. Maybe I'll have my little cousin look it over.
7. My story may not be perfect. I think I did a pretty good job.

Continued

Practice Review   *Fairy Tales and Kids (using coordinators)*

On a separate piece of paper, join the following independent clauses using carefully chosen coordinators. Use each coordinator once, and remember to put a comma after the first independent clause.

1. When I first read The Brothers Grimm's "Cinderella," I thought the story was too gross. Then I saw some children's cartoons on television that were worse.
2. Children's fairy tales shouldn't have a lot of violence in them. They shouldn't be too sugary sweet.
3. The stories need to have details in them that children will find interesting. The children will not want to pay attention.
4. I haven't read any fairy tales for years. I still remember them clearly.
5. My mom used to read one fairy tale each night to me. I plan to do the same for my kids.
6. Fairy tales are good for kids. They teach kids good values and morals.
7. I have revised my draft again. It is time to begin editing.

Create Your Own Sentences

Review Exercise A   *Original Sentences with FANBOYS*
- Create seven original sentences that contain independent clauses which you have combined with one of the FANBOYS. Use each coordinator once.
- Remember to put a comma after the first independent clause.
- Use new vocabulary words in at least two of your sentences.

Review Exercise B   *Quiz Your Classmate*
- Choose one coordinator.
- Create two sentences that could be logically joined by that coordinator. Write the two sentences down, but keep the coordinator a secret.
- Repeat this procedure until you have three pairs.

Continued

Notes

- Exchange your sentence pairs with a classmate. Did he or she join the sentences correctly? It's okay if your classmate uses *yet* when you used *but* or vice versa. Remember to check his or her punctuation.

Computer Note

An advantage to writing on a computer is that you can print a fresh copy occasionally. When you are at the editing stage, print a new copy and highlight all the FANBOYS that you find. If you don't find many (or any), read your draft aloud and look for places where the idea might be clearer if sentences were joined with one of the FANBOYS.

Apply Your Knowledge

When you are drafting, don't think too much about using coordinators. Focus, instead, on your ideas. Then, as you edit your writing assignments, look for places where you can combine independent clauses with one of the FANBOYS. Reading your draft aloud will help you find places to do this.

Choose a piece of your writing now, and look to see where you might join sentences with a coordinator.

Subordinators

To express complex ideas, writers often rely on subordinators. Subordinators can express relationships of opposition, time, effect-cause, and condition.

This chapter covers the following topics:

✦ Understanding subordinators
✦ Punctuating correctly with subordinators
✦ Using subordinators

Understanding Subordinators

Notes

There are many subordinators. Here is a list of the most common subordinators.

although	even though
though	while
after	since
when	because
if	unless

In the following list, you'll find a description of the type of relationship created when you use each subordinator.

- *although, even though, though, while:* express a relationship of opposition

  Although I don't usually write stories, my fairy tale is turning out to be pretty good.

- *after, since, when, while*:* express a relationship of time

  When I first heard about the assignment, I thought I'd never be able to complete it.

- *because, since:* express an effect-cause relationship

  I decided to talk to my best friend about the assignment *because* he loves to write stories.

- *if, unless:* express a relationship of condition

  If I get a chance, I want to read my story to my best friend.

Note: While can express a relationship of opposition or time, depending on how it is used.

Punctuating Correctly with Subordinators

When a subordinator attaches to an independent clause, the clause becomes a subordinated clause that can no longer stand on its own. Here are two examples:

Independent clause: I wrote a creative story.

Add a subordinator and the clause becomes subordinated: *When* I wrote a creative story. . . . (This subordinated clause cannot stand on its own.)

Independent clause: We discussed the reading assignment.

Add a subordinator and the clause becomes subordinated: *Although* we discussed the reading assignment. . . . (This subordinated clause cannot stand on its own.)

When you join these subordinated clauses to independent clauses, you need to punctuate carefully. Remember these two rules when using subordinators:

- When you begin a sentence with a subordinated clause, put a comma after the subordinated clause:

    <u>If my car insurance goes up again,</u> I might have to get a second job!

- When the subordinated clause comes after the independent clause, you do not need a comma:

    I might have to get a second job <u>if my car insurance goes up again!</u>

Practice #1   *Using Commas*
Return to the sentences that follow the explanation of each subordinator (p. 293).

- Underline all of the subordinated clauses.
- Circle the commas you find.

Example:

- <u>*Although* I don't usually write stories,</u> my fairy tale is turning out to be pretty good.

Using Subordinators

Using subordinators will make your writing clearer and more sophisticated.

Notice how these sentences seem to contradict one another. The reader might think that the writer is confused:

> I respect my father's opinion that the United States should take military action. I believe that we should use peaceful methods for resolving the conflict.

The subordinator *although* makes the idea much clearer and shows that the writer has sophisticated thinking skills:

> *Although* I respect my father's opinion that the United States should take military action, I believe that we should use peaceful methods for resolving the conflict.

The rest of this chapter asks you to practice using subordinators. To get the most out of the exercises in this chapter, follow these guidelines:

- Write out complete sentences on a separate piece of paper. Do not just draw arrows or insert words.
- Join two independent clauses with one of the subordinators listed on p. 293. Even if you see other ways to combine the sentences, stick with the subordinators for now.
- Make sure that you are joining two complete independent clauses. Don't delete any of the subjects.

Practice #2   *My Cinderella (using subordinators)*

On a separate piece of paper, combine the following sentence pairs, using the subordinator in parentheses. Remember to punctuate correctly.

Examples: (since) I didn't really know the story of Hansel and Gretel. I asked the children's librarian to find me a copy.

- Since I didn't really know the story of Hansel and Gretel, I asked the children's librarian to find me a copy.

I appreciated the humor in his tale (although) I think my tale has a better lesson.

- I appreciated the humor in his tale although I think my tale has a better lesson.   *Continued*

Notes

1. (although) My Cinderella had average looks. She had an outstanding personality.
2. I created her this way. (because) I didn't want the focus of the story to be on beauty.
3. (since) I wanted to make people think about the roles of stepfathers. I got rid of the mean stepmother and created a good stepfather instead.
4. (if) My classmates say I have too little detail. I will go back over my story and add more.
5. (even though) I don't usually enjoy writing that much. I loved this assignment.

Practice #3   *Cinderman (using subordinators)*

- On a separate piece of paper, combine the following sentence pairs, using the subordinator in parentheses. Remember to punctuate correctly.
- With some sentences, put the subordinator at the beginning of the new sentence. With other sentences, the subordinator will have to come right before the second clause. Decide which position is best in each case.

Example: My mom will not read fairy tales to my kids. The tales have absolutely no violence. (unless)

- My mom will not read fairy tales to my kids unless the tales have absolutely no violence. (Note that *unless* wouldn't make sense if it was attached to the first clause. Be careful about where you put your subordinator.)

1. Cinderman wanted to get married. He didn't want to marry just anyone. (while)
2. He would adopt a child. He got married within the next two years. (unless)
3. He first met Princess Catherine. He didn't like her. (when)
4. He thought she was conceited and selfish. She was shy and didn't trust him. (because)

Continued

5. He fell in love with her. He got to know her better. (after)

6. Cinderman was eager to start a family. He and Catherine were only in their first year of college. (although)

7. Their parents agreed to pay for half of their tuition. They agreed to wait until after college to get married. (if)

8. They thought that their parents were being too controlling. Cinderman and Princess Catherine finally accepted the plan. (though)

9. Cinderman finishes his BA degree. He plans to get his Master's in business. (when)

10. Princess Catherine has enjoyed her business classes. She's decided that she'd rather be a high school science teacher.

Practice Review   *The Escape (using subordinators)*

- On a separate piece of paper, join the following independent clauses using carefully chosen subordinators. Don't use any subordinators twice.

- Check your punctuation. Some sentences should begin with the independent clause. Others should begin with the dependent clause.

1. The mean stepsisters left. Cinderella decided it was time to open up her secret trunk.

2. She had been saving money and making plans. She knew that her day would come.

3. She had hoped to have more money saved by now. She figured she had enough to escape.

4. She had also hidden a passport and nice clothes. She planned to leave the country and start a new life.

5. Anyone she knew saw her at the airport. She planned to tell them she was picking up lobsters her stepmother had ordered from Maine.

Create Your Own Sentences

Review Exercise A   *Original Sentences*

- Create five sentences that contain independent and dependent clauses joined by subordinators.   *Continued*

Notes

- Your sentences should connect to your current writing topic.
- Check your punctuation.
- Use new vocabulary words in at least two of your sentences.

Review Exercise B   *Quiz a Classmate*

Work with this list of subordinators:

although

when

because

if

- Choose one subordinator.
- Create two sentences that could be logically joined by that subordinator.
- Write the two sentences down, but keep the subordinator a secret.
- Repeat this procedure until you have created sentence pairs for each subordinator listed earlier.
- Exchange your sentence pairs with a classmate.
- Did he or she join the sentences correctly?
- Did he or she punctuate correctly?

Computer Note

Remember to take advantage of your computer. Print your draft at any time. At the editing stage, print a copy to see if you have used any subordinators. Highlight them. Would your draft be clearer or stronger if you combined more sentences with subordinators?

Apply Your Knowledge

When you are drafting, don't think too much about using subordinators. Focus, instead, on your ideas. Then, as you edit your writing assignment, look for places where you can combine independent clauses with subordinators. Reading your draft aloud will help you find places to do this.

Now, choose a piece of your writing and look to see if you used any subordinators. Find a place where you might join two sentences with a subordinator.

Transitions

Good writing is *coherent*. **Coherent** means all the pieces fit together and flow smoothly. Transitions help make writing coherent.

This chapter covers the following topics:

✦ Identifying transition words and phrases
✦ The power of transition words
✦ Punctuating correctly with transitions
✦ Transition words interrupting sentences
✦ Punctuating correctly with interrupting transitions

Identifying Transition Words and Phrases

Notes

Many words help readers move from one point to another. Coordinators and subordinators, for example, can help a reader understand how ideas relate to one another. However, this chapter focuses on *transitions*—words and phrases that act like bridges between ideas but that cannot join sentences with simply a comma. (See Chapters 23 and 24 for a discussion of coordinators and subordinators.) Here is a list of transitions and their meanings.

- *also, furthermore, next, similarly, in addition:* express addition of similar ideas
- *consequently, therefore, thus:* express cause-effect
- *however, otherwise, on the other hand, in contrast:* express opposites
- *then, next, finally, now:* express time
- *for example:* tells the reader an example is coming

The transitions are highlighted in these sentences:

- I explained my point for the third time. Finally, he understood the problem.
- He didn't want to quit his job; however, he knew the company was wrong for dumping chemicals into the river.

Notes

> **Practice #1** *Social Causes (identifying transition words)*
>
> Underline the transitions in the following sentences.
> Example: Professor Dunsmore always seems to take the sides of liberals. On the other hand, Professor Sutton seems to consistently support the conservatives.
>
> - Professor Dunsmore always seems to take the sides of liberals. <u>On the other hand,</u> Professor Sutton seems to consistently support the conservatives.
>
> 1. I am concerned about the people starving in Afghanistan; however, I am also aware that over 2,000 children live on the streets in my own city.
> 2. I want our country to send humanitarian aid to several countries. In addition, I want to see our own homeless problem dealt with effectively.
> 3. There are new studies that suggest that people may be "preprogrammed" to become drug addicts. Consequently, many people are suggesting that drug use is not simply a result of bad decision making.
> 4. Drug addiction costs this country a lot of money in terms of crime and hospital bills; furthermore, worker productivity is harmed.
> 5. We need to educate people about why people become addicts. Then, we need to use our knowledge to prevent people from becoming drug addicts.

The Power of Transition Words

As a writer, you might do a good job of focusing and organizing your ideas, but you can't always be certain that your reader will see how your information fits together. Transition words help your reader see how one idea relates to or leads to the next. Transition words act like bridges, improving the flow and coherence of your writing. Consider how odd these sentences sound together:

> Mr. Finney wasn't sure if this version of "Cinderella" was appropriate for his first-grade students. He loved the story.

Now consider how these sentences sound when they have a transition acting as a bridge between them:

> Mr. Finney wasn't sure if this version of "Cinderella" was appropriate for his first-grade students; however, he loved the story.

The *however* warns the reader that an opposite idea is coming. The writer is acknowledging two opposing ideas.

Here's another example. Without a transition, the following sentences might appear to be an unrelated list of ideas:

> I have always supported the idea that we shouldn't ban books. I don't think music should be censored.

In the following sentences, the relationship between the ideas is much clearer. The transition tells the reader that a similar idea is coming. Note that the transition comes at the beginning of a sentence.

> I have always supported the idea that we shouldn't ban books. <u>Similarly,</u> I don't think music should be censored.

Transitions can also come between two sentences.

> I have always supported the idea that we shouldn't ban books; <u>similarly,</u> I don't think music should be censored.

Punctuating Correctly with Transitions

If you have two complete sentences with a transition between them, you have two options for punctuating.

Put a period between the two sentences and a comma after the transition word:

> I think Americans focus too much on beauty<u>. Furthermore,</u> we spend too much time expecting other people to fix our problems.

Or, put a semicolon between the two sentences and a comma after the transition word:

> I think Americans focus too much on beauty<u>; furthermore,</u> we spend too much time expecting other people to fix our problems.

Computer Note
If you accidentally use a comma when you need a semicolon, your computer will probably underline your error. However, your computer could make a mistake, so know your punctuation rules and check your own work.

Practice #2   *My Writing (using transitions)*
On a separate piece of paper, add the transition words as directed.
Continued

Notes

Example: Use *thus* with a semicolon and a comma between the two sentences.
I used to think that writing a paragraph should take me one draft and about half an hour. You can imagine my surprise when I was asked to write a third draft!

- I used to think that writing a paragraph should take me one draft and about half and hour; thus, you can imagine my surprise when I was asked to write a third draft!

1. Use *however* with a semicolon and a comma between the two sentences.
   I thought my story was finished. My tutor pointed out some major weaknesses.

2. Use *then* with a semicolon and a comma between the two sentences.
   I added more detail and explained the events more clearly. I went back and edited.

3. Use *consequently* with a semicolon and a comma between the two sentences.
   I was very interested in this assignment. I put in more time than usual.

4. Use *next* and a comma to begin the second sentence.
   First I will freewrite on the new topic. I will begin drafting topic sentences.

5. Use *furthermore* and a comma to begin the second sentence.
   The tutor has helped me think through the topic in the beginning. He has aided me during the revising stage.

Practice #3 *Analyzing Fairy Tales (using transitions)*

- On a separate piece of paper, use one of the transitions listed to make the relationship between these sentences clearer.
- Use each transition once.
- Separate some sentence pairs with a period.
- Separate others with a semicolon.

finally	consequently
then	in addition
however	

Continued

1. I used to love fairy tales. As an adult, I worry about the violence and some of the messages in these tales.

2. In "Hansel and Gretel," the witch wants to eat Hansel. At the end of the story, it's the witch that gets cooked.

3. In the traditional version of "The Frog Prince," the princess throws the frog against a wall. The frog turns into a prince.

4. The princess gets her prince. The message must be that causing bodily harm to someone is okay.

5. I don't like the violence in these tales. I don't like the emphasis on beauty in some of the others.

Practice #4 *Working with a Classmate (using transitions)*

• On a separate piece of paper, use one of the transitions listed to make the relationship between these sentences clearer.

• Use each transition once.

• Separate some sentence pairs with a period.

• Separate others with a semicolon.

also

next

similarly

otherwise

thus

1. I suggested that my classmate make his topic sentence clearer.
   I recommended that he add some examples.

2. He saw some areas in mine where I could use transitions.
   He found a couple of places where I can easily add detail.

3. He's going to have to do a lot of editing work.
   The reader will be very confused by the run-ons and comma splices.

4. He really wants to do well on this assignment.
   He is committed to make all of these changes.

5. He works really hard on his writing.
   He spends a lot of time on each reading assignment.

Continued

Notes

Practice Review *Original Sentences (using transitions)*
On a separate piece of paper, create the sentences described.

1. Write an original sentence that uses *however* (with a comma and a semicolon).
2. Write an original sentence that uses *therefore* (with a comma and a semicolon).
3. Write an original sentence that uses *consequently* (with a comma and a semicolon).
4. Write two original sentences. The second should start with *similarly.*
5. Write two original sentences. The second should start with *then.*

Transition Words Interrupting Sentences

Transitions can interrupt a single sentence.

My fairy godmother, however, has never appeared.

This sentence structure adds interesting variety to your writing.

Punctuating Correctly with Interrupting Transitions

If you interrupt a single sentence with a transition word, you should put a comma before and after the transition word.

I, therefore, dramatically changed the plot line and the main characters in my story.

Mrs. Fitzbaum, consequently, bought three of my books.

Practice #5 *Different Skills (using interrupting transitions)*
- Read these sentence pairs carefully.
- Insert an appropriate transition word or phrase in the second sentence in each pair.
- Use each of these transitions once:
    therefore
    however

Continued

consequently
on the other hand

1. My father read to me every night.
   My mother, _____, was more interested in encouraging my drawing and painting.
2. My sister became an attorney.
   I, _____, decided to become a children's book author.
3. Each child has his or her own talents.
   Parents, _____, should pay attention to what their children do well and encourage those skills.
4. Too many children think that they are not "smart."
   Parents and teachers, _____, need to help children find what is special inside each child.

Practice #6

Interrupt the second sentence in each pair with a transition word. Write your new sentence on a separate piece of paper.

Example: Everyone in class did the homework
The class discussion was excellent.

- The class discussion, <u>consequently,</u> was excellent.

   Hint: The interrupting transition word often fits most smoothly right after the subject and before the verb.

Part 1 *A Class Discussion* (using interrupting transitions)

on the other hand
however
therefore
for example
consequently

1. Kim explained the lessons in the fairy tale as if everyone shared her analysis. My analysis was very different.
2. The instructor said we should speak up if we had different opinions. A number of students raised their hands.

Continued

Notes

3. Almost everyone had something to say. The discussion went on for quite a while.

4. Most students expressed their opinions respectfully. Julia got mad when someone disagreed with her.

5. The instructor reminded all of us that it is important to feel free to express ourselves honestly in this class. We shouldn't raise our voices to one another. (*Hint:* In this sentence, put the interrupting word after *shouldn't*.)

Part 2 *Cinderella on Film*

consequently

in contrast

furthermore

otherwise

therefore

1. For an extra credit assignment, our instructor suggested seeing two Cinderella films and explaining the contrasts. My friend and I spent Friday night watching almost 4 hours of Cinderella.

2. I thought that the storyline in *Ever After* was great. The storyline in Disney's version was not as interesting.

3. I liked Barrymore's love of books. Her self-confidence was inspiring.

4. I didn't think she should be wearing sparkle makeup in the last scene, but I guess it was necessary. The younger, romantic moviegoer might have been disappointed.

5. The overall movie was quite good. I recommend seeing it.

Create Your Own Sentences

Review Exercise A *Using Transitions in Original Sentences*

- Create three sentence pairs of your own. (You'll be writing a total of six sentences.)
- A transition word must fit smoothly between the two sentences.
- One sentence pair should be joined with a semicolon. *Continued*

- Two sentence pairs should be separated with a period.
- The sentences must connect in topic to your current reading and writing assignments.
- Use new vocabulary words in at least two of your sentences.

Review Exercise B   *Using Interrupting Transitions in Original Sentences*

- Create three sentence pairs of your own. (You'll be writing a total of six sentences.)
- The second sentence in each pair must be interrupted by a transition word or phrase.
- The sentences must connect in topic to your current reading and writing assignments.
- Use new vocabulary words in at least two of your sentences.

Apply Your Knowledge

Apply what you've learned about transitions to your current writing assignment.

- Look for places where you can improve the coherence of your writing by building bridges with transition words.
- Put a transition at the beginning of a sentence.
- Use a transition and a semicolon to connect two sentences.
- Interrupt a sentence with a transition.

Hint: Reading your work aloud will help you find places to use transitions.

Parallelism

Certain sentence structures are easier for readers to read, and these structures deliver your message more clearly. This chapter focuses on *parallel structure*.

This chapter covers the following topics:

✦ Understanding and identifying parallel structure
✦ Creating parallel structure

Notes

Understanding and Identifying Parallel Structure

Parallel structure is having two or more items in a sentence in similar form. For example, having a list of three *–ing* words in your sentence demonstrates parallel structure. Having two infinitives in your sentence would also demonstrate parallel structure. Study the following examples.

Not Parallel	Parallel
Children should spend their time playing, studying, and in extra curricular activities.	Children should spend their time *playing*, *studying*, and *participating* in extra curricular activities. (a parallel list of three *–ing* words)
She wrote a letter protesting child labor and to insist that new laws be written.	She wrote a letter *to protest* child labor and *to insist* that new laws be written. (a parallel pair of infinitives)
The men in my community always seemed tired, dealing with frustrating work situations, and depressed.	The men in my community always seemed *tired*, *frustrated*, and *depressed*. (a parallel list of three descriptive words)

Practice #1   *Find the Parallelism*
Underline the words or phrases that are parallel (similar in form).

1. I called, e-mailed, and faxed the information, but they still said they didn't know anything about my leaking roof.
2. Philomene loves to travel, to dance, and to cook.
3. I explained that they would be swimming, playing tennis, and hiking.
4. Please go to the store, buy the food, and deposit the check.
5. Mr. Jefferson told the children that there would be no gum chewing, screaming, or running.
6. Frank had a perfect day; he slept, read his book, and watched television.

Creating Parallelism

When you are editing your writing, read your work aloud. Listen for awkward places, and look for groups of words that you think should be similar in form.

Practice #2   *Make Items in Group Parallel*
Make the items in each group parallel in form. Discuss different solutions with classmates.

Example: ill-ventilated, dark, smelling like mold

• ill-ventilated, dark, moldy

1. to work, learning, to succeed
2. struggling, dreams, fights
3. waged, maimed, to labor
4. becoming ill, survival
5. keeping the goal in her sight, to fight those who stood in the way
6. asking for help, looking for guidance, to think of the future
7. to smell bad, scary, contagious
8. written, spoken, hear
9. hoped, promise, fought

Practice #3

On a separate piece of paper, rewrite the following sentences, correcting the parallelism error that is in italics.

Example: Her dream was to make beautiful paintings, entertain interesting people, and *watching her children grow up*.

- Her dream was to make beautiful paintings, entertain interesting people, and watch her children grow up.

Part 1 *Their Dreams, My Dreams* (creating parallelism)

1. My great grandparents dreamed of starting their own business and *to own* a house.
2. They made many financial sacrifices, worked long hours, and *had to wait* patiently for their business to take off.
3. The result was a restaurant that the whole community loved because the food was tasty, the prices were fair, and *good service was always the rule*.
4. My dream is to earn a degree in psychology, to compete in college basketball, and *finding* an occupation that mixes my interests in sports and the human mind.
5. Making good money is important to me, but I'm also interested in setting my own hours, being my own boss, and *to have* the freedom to travel.

Part 2 *The Computer Guy*

1. He dreamed of designing computer software, *built* his own house, and having a family.
2. Then something unbelievable happened, and he dropped out of school, *telling* his parents goodbye, and bought a Ferrari.
3. He had won the lottery and wouldn't have to work, save, or *borrowing* any money ever again.
4. He traveled the world, *meeting* new people, and felt unfulfilled.
5. What had gone wrong? He had climbed mountains, surfed 20-foot waves, and even *parachuting* off a cliff in Hawaii.
6. He thought, cried, and *began praying* when he suddenly realized what was wrong. He missed his computer.

Continued

Computer Note
The computer didn't notice any errors in Practice #3, so keep in mind that your computer may not identify parallelism errors. You will have to check for these yourself.

Practice Review *Add a Parallel Item*
Rewrite the following sentences, inserting parallel items.

Example: I *acknowledged* my friends' good intentions and then _____ how India was different from the United Sates.

- I acknowledged my friends' good intentions and then <u>pointed out</u> how India was different from the United States. (The word *explained* would also have worked. In fact, there are several ways to complete this sentence.)

1. I began to see an entirely different viewpoint and _____ my own beliefs.
2. I asked her about her work, _____, and hobbies.
3. The child seemed so frail, reluctant, and _____.
4. Wanting to help, I gathered signatures and _____ my senator for support.
5. I wrote the letter, mailed it, and _____ for the best.

Create Your Own Sentences

Review Exercise A
- Create five sentences that demonstrate your knowledge of parallelism. (The sentences should be on the same topic as your current writing assignment.)
- Use new vocabulary words in at least two of your sentences.

Apply Your Knowledge

Study a piece of your writing, and find places where parallel structure could make your ideas easier to read and understand. Pay close attention to any sentences that have two or more items in a series.

Beginning Sentences with Participal Phrases

Earlier chapters in this book explain the many roles an *–ing* word can have in a sentence. An *–ing* word can be

a verb (if it has a helper, see Chapter 12):

The student <u>is writing.</u>

a noun (and sometimes a subject, see Chapter 14):

<u>Writing</u> is an important tool for success.

a descriptive word (see Chapter 22):

The <u>laughing</u> student explained the joke.

This chapter is going to focus on *–ing* words that begin *descriptive participal phrases*. This chapter covers the following topics:

✦ Understanding and identifying the sentence pattern
✦ Creating the sentence pattern

Notes

Understanding and Identifying the Sentence Pattern

While there are many ways to use these descriptive phrases, this chapter focuses only on *participal phrases that begin sentences*. In these examples, the participal phrases are highlighted

Speaking with great enthusiasm, she convinced the workers to go on strike.
(The participal phrase is describing *she.*)

Listening to the protest songs, I felt moved to participate.
(The participal phrase is describing *I.*)

Ignoring the officer's warning, the protesters did not leave the building.
(The participal phrase is describing *the protesters.*)

Practice #1 *The Civil Rights Movement (identifying participal phrases)*
• In the following sentences, highlight the participal phrase.

Continued

- Circle the comma that follows the phrase.
- Find the noun being described and underline it.

Example:

- Hoping to be inspired, I read about the civil rights movement.

  1. Defying the segregation laws, Rosa Parks didn't give up her seat in the front of the bus.
  2. Wanting to have a career outside of the home, Ann Clark went to college.
  3. Having fought for their country, black soldiers returned to the United States wanting equality with whites.
  4. Barring discrimination in federal jobs, Truman insisted that blacks be treated with fairness in the military.
  5. Seeking to send his child to a school close to home, Oliver Brown sued the school board of Topeka, Kansas.

Creating the Sentence Pattern

There are four rules for creating sentences with this sentence pattern.

- The first word is a present participle (an *–ing* word).
- The participle is part of a phrase.
- There is a comma after the participial phrase.
- The first word after the participial phrase must be the noun that the phrase is describing.

Practice #2   *The Clown (combine the phrase and the
                       independent clause)*

In the following exercises, add the participial phrase to the beginning of the complete sentence. Write out the new, complete sentences on a separate piece of paper.

Example: Knocking down the "separate but equal" doctrine
The Supreme Court ruled in favor of the Browns.

- Knocking down the "separate but equal" doctrine, the Supreme Court ruled in favor of the Browns.

Continued

Notes

1. Surprising the children
   The clown pulled a rabbit out of a soda can.

2. Feeling nervous
   The clown stumbled over his own large feet.

3. Thinking he tripped on purpose
   The children laughed and laughed.

4. Hoping to regain his composure
   The clown did one of his safest tricks.

5. Realizing the kids were having fun
   The man in the clown suit felt like he had achieved his dream in life.

Practice #3   *Add the Independent Clause*
In the following exercises, you are given a participial phrase.

- Add an independent clause. (Remember an independent clause is a sentence that can stand on its own. See Chapter 16 for a review.)
- Make sure your independent clause begins with a noun the participial phrase is capable of describing.
- Write your new, original sentence on another sheet of paper.

Example: Working overtime at campaign headquarters

- Working overtime at campaign headquarters, Eli showed his commitment to politics.

1. Hearing that the striped frog was nearly extinct,
2. Knowing his solution was imperfect,
3. Realizing that she'd been relegated to secretarial work because she is a woman,
4. Ignoring the instructions he was given,
5. Thinking that the project was too big for one person,
6. Feeling the job was too mundane,
7. Fearing the disease was contagious,
8. Hoping this was more than a fleeting moment of passion,

Continued

9. Looking back at her years in college,
10. Seeking his dream,

Practice #4   *Social Causes (add the participial phrase)*

In the following exercise, find the participial phrase that appears in the first sentence. Add that phrase to the beginning of the second sentence. Write the new sentences on a separate piece of paper.

Example: Geoff was <u>speaking in slang.</u>
Geoff appeared to be an inarticulate person.

• Speaking in slang, Geoff appeared to be an inarticulate person.

1. The man was explaining his fervent desire to help abandoned animals.
   The man hoped to be put in charge of raising funds for the new shelter.
2. Timothy was listening to the testimony of both men.
   Timothy realized that the elections had probably been rigged.
3. The group was holding a sit-in at the state capitol.
   The group was hoping to draw attention to their fight to eradicate racism in the local schools.
4. Mr. Luigi was reading about the specific accomplishments of the charitable group.
   Mr. Luigi was impressed with the great strides the organization had made in cleaning up the neighborhood.
5. Maya was researching the recent influx of immigrants from Serbia.
   Maya realized that the school needed some teachers who spoke Serbian fluently.

Create Your Own Sentences

Review Exercise A   *Achievements (add an original –ing phrase)*

In the following exercise, add a participial phrase to the beginning of the sentence to create a more expressive sentence. Write the new sentences on a separate piece of paper.

Continued

Notes

1. Margaret practiced for four hours every day.
2. Cole felt proud and took the trophy home.
3. Cecilia was named best teacher of the year.
4. Max used his brilliant speaking skills to explain.
5. Ken and Kathleen were featured in the newspaper.

Review Exercise B   *Original Sentences*

- Create five original sentences that begin with participial phrases. Don't forget to punctuate correctly.
- Use new vocabulary words in at least two of your sentences.

Computer Note

Get to know your own writing. At the editing stage, print out a copy of your draft. Highlight all *–ing* words you find. Are you using them as nouns? Verbs (with helpers)? Adjectives? Variety is important to good writing. Use a participial phrase to begin a sentence.

Apply Your Knowledge

When you reach the editing stage of your writing process, look for sentences that might become clearer and more expressive if they began with a participial phrase. Use the participial phrase pattern to add interest, variety, and information to your writing.

Now, review a piece of your writing that you completed earlier. Find at least one sentence that would be better if it started with a participial phrase.

Editing Essentials

This section of *Expressions* offers you seven chapters that review rules for editing effectively.

In each chapter, you'll find rules and then practice exercises.

End Marks

This chapter covers the three punctuation marks used to end sentences:

✦ Periods
✦ Question marks
✦ Exclamation points

Notes

Periods

Periods are used to end sentences that are stating information:

I do not care for "real" TV.
Stephen enjoys documentary films.
Grandma doesn't even own a television.

Computer Note
Your computer will probably let you know if you forget to put a question mark at the end of a question. However, you'll have to make the decision about whether to use a period or an exclamation mark.

Question Marks

Question marks are used at the end of questions:

Do you think they really ate rats?
Would you swallow a live gold fish?
Why doesn't the president like green beans?

Exclamation Points

Exclamation points are used to end sentences that express surprise or other strong feelings:

I ate fried worms!
You're fired!
I will win the competition!

Practice #1 *Guns (end marks)*
Insert the correct end marks. (You and your classmates may not agree on each answer. Discuss any disagreements you have.)

Continued

1. Do you believe in gun control
2. Barry stated that too many people are killed by their own guns
3. Don't take my rights away
4. I learned how to shoot a gun when I was 16 years old
5. Will you show me how to clean this gun
6. You may not play at their house because they own guns
7. Did you hear me
8. You should do some research on this topic
9. I think both sides have some very good points
10. Does the Constitution really say that we have a right to own semiautomatic handguns

Practice #2   *The Peanut Game (end marks)*
Review diary entry #15 from *The Freedom Writers Diary* in Section VIII (pp. 406–407). On a separate piece of paper, complete the work described here.

1. Find two sentences that end with periods. Copy them down.
2. Find two sentences that end with question marks. Copy them down. Find sentences that are longer than just two words.
3. Find two sentences that end with exclamation points.
   a. Copy them down.
   b. Explain why it is important for these sentences to end with exclamation points and not periods.

Create Your Own Sentences

Review Exercise A   *Original Sentences (end marks)*
Create original sentences that fit the following descriptions. Use new vocabulary words in at least two sentences.

1. Create two sentences that require periods.
2. Create two sentences that require question marks.
3. Create two sentences that require exclamation points.

Apply Your Knowledge

Choosing the correct end marks will help you express your ideas more clearly and powerfully. Review one of the paragraphs you have written. Do any sentences need an exclamation point to help you show strong emotion? Do all of your questions end with question marks?

Note: Be careful. Use exclamation points selectively. If you have too many in a paragraph, you will sound like you're yelling at your reader. Also, don't end any statement or question with more than one end mark.

29

Commas, Semicolons, and Colons

Correctly punctuating sentences is important for two reasons:

✦ clarity
✦ a professional image

This chapter covers the following topics:

✦ The comma rules
✦ The semicolon rule
✦ The colon rule

The Comma Rules

Notes

You may have been taught that you should use commas whenever you "hear" a pause in your writing. This is not good advice because you will probably end up with many unnecessary commas and confuse your readers.

There are specific rules for using commas. Don't use commas unless you can point to the rule that says you need one.

Comma Rule #1

Put commas between items in a series.

• The exhausted, confused, and frustrated writer leaned back in his chair. (The comma before the *and* is optional with a list like this.)

Practice #1   *Fairy Tales (using Comma Rule #1)*
Apply Comma Rule #1 and add commas when necessary.

1. I read the Grimm story the Native American story and the modern story.
2. The Grimm story was old-fashioned violent and a little scary.
3. The bloody scenes the missing godmother and the punishment of the older sisters were all surprising to me.

Continued

Notes

4. I read fairy tales to my brothers my nieces and even my grandmother.
5. I'm looking for tales that teach courage honesty and determination.

Comma Rule #2

When you begin a sentence with a subordinated or dependent clause, you must put a comma after the subordinated (or dependent) clause.

- If he could just remember that great opening line, the rest would flow.

See Chapter 16 pp. 228–232 and Chapter 24 for a review of subordinators and subordinated clauses.

Here is a list of common subordinators:

if
since
while
thought
although
even though
because
when

Comma Rule #3

If the subordinated clause comes after the independent clause, you do not need a comma.

- The rest would flow if he could just remember that great opening line.

Practice #2   *Lessons (using Comma Rules #2 and #3)*
- Highlight the subordinated (or dependent) clause in each sentence.
- Apply Comma Rules #2 and #3. Add commas when necessary.
  Some sentences will not need any commas.

Continued

1. Since the stepsisters are blinded at the end of the story I believe that there is a lesson in this tale about treachery and punishment.
2. I think my story would be more interesting if it included a lesson modern readers could relate to.
3. Although I think people should be punished for their crimes I decided to focus on a lesson of forgiveness.
4. Because I was writing to a modern audience I used a little modern slang.
5. I was worried that the kids might not understand the lesson in my tale when I read it aloud to them.

Comma Rule #4

Put commas around interruptive words and phrases in a sentence.

- For two long hours, however, no words came to his mind.

Note that Comma Rule #4 deals with *a single sentence*. The word *however* is interrupting *a single sentence*.

- For two long hours, no words came to his mind.
  (a single sentence)

"However" is then inserted into the middle of the single sentence.

- For two long hours, *however,* no words came to his mind.

If there were two sentences, *however* could not join them with commas.

- *For two long hours, he typed. However, no words came to his mind.*
  (two sentences separated by a period)

Or

- For two long hours, he typed; however, no words came to his mind.
  (two sentences separated by a semicolon)

See Chapter 25 for more on transition words.

Practice #3   *Shakespeare (using Comma Rule #4)*
Apply Comma Rule #4 and add commas when necessary.

1. Shakespeare's play however was written in the 16th century.

Continued

Notes

2. The reader therefore might want to read that play out loud.
3. The movie based on that play however is easy to follow.
4. My brother on the other hand says he must see a live performance.
5. My sister therefore bought him season tickets to the local theater.

Comma Rule #5

See Chapter 23 for more on coordinators.

When you join two complete sentences with a coordinator (FANBOYS), you must put a comma after the first sentence.

- At midnight he finally remembered his thrilling opening line, and he began to type.
  ("Once upon a time. . . .")

The seven coordinating conjunctions (FANBOYS) are as follows:

For   And   Nor   But   Or   Yet   So

Practice #4   *Writing an Analysis (using Comma Rule #5)*
Apply Comma Rule #5 and add commas when necessary.

1. I read the stories carefully and I compared the differences between the two tales.
2. His analysis of the two stories made sense but he needed to give more evidence in his paragraph.
3. His tutor told him the same thing so he reread the story and found more evidence to include in the paragraph.
4. I will do my research on the Internet or I may interview a couple of people.
5. I am going to ask my instructor to look at my draft for he always offers useful advice.

Comma Rule #6

When you begin a sentence with an introductory phrase, put a comma after the introductory phrase.

- With feelings of great disappointment, the writer began to look for a new job.

Continued

Practice #5   *Discovery in Arizona (using Comma Rule #6)*
Apply Comma Rule #6 and add commas when necessary.

1. On his trip back from Arizona Spencer found some amazing rock specimens.
2. After showing his professor the unique rocks Spencer wrote a paper on his find.
3. Working with two senior researchers he gathered some terrific information.
4. Throughout his time in college Spencer had been hoping for a break like this.
5. Due to his brilliant paper he was quickly accepted into an excellent graduate program.

The Semicolon Rule

The semicolon is the mark that looks like a comma with a period over it. Its main purpose is to separate independent clauses (complete sentences.)

The Semicolon Rule

You may use a semicolon to separate two complete sentences.

- He liked his old job; he didn't want to go looking for a new one.

Note: Transition words like *however, therefore, of course,* and *then* cannot join sentences with a comma. If you want to use these words to build a bridge between two complete sentences, you must separate the sentences with a *semicolon* or period. Generally, the transition word is followed by a comma.

- He liked his old job; therefore, he didn't want to go looking for a new one.

Or

- He liked his old job. Therefore, he didn't want to go looking for a new one.

Practice #6   *Books Worth Reading (using the Semicolon Rule)*
Apply the Semicolon Rule and add semicolons when necessary.

1. I enjoyed the book *Into Thin Air* I couldn't put it down until I learned what happened to the climbers.   *Continued*

2. Helen Keller's autobiography is worth reading it's fascinating to see how hard she worked to read, write, and speak.
3. I was looking for a copy of *Midwives* in the secondhand bookstore a new copy costs too much.
4. My friend loves books therefore I recommended Denis Leary's new book.
5. My favorite book about volcanoes disappeared the day before my sister's trip to Mt. St. Helen's I believe she took it.

The Colon Rule

Computer Note
When typing, put one blank space after a colon. Other spacing rules: put one blank space after a period; leave five blank spaces or press your Tab key before the first sentence of any paragraph.

The colon is the mark that looks like two periods stacked on top of one another. Its main use is to introduce a list.

The Colon Rule

When you offer a list after a complete sentence, use a colon to separate the sentence and the list.

- In the newspaper, he saw a number of promising ads: creative writer needed for comic book company, writer needed in advertising firm, and editor needed for large publishing company.

Caution: Use a colon only when the list follows a *complete* sentence. Here is a sentence that should not have a colon:

- I wanted to: dance, sing, and twirl the baton.
  (incorrect: *I wanted to* is not a complete sentence.)

Practice #7 *Majors and Careers (using the Colon Rule)*
Apply the Colon Rule and add colons when necessary. If a sentence does not need a colon, write *C* to show that the sentence is correct as it stands.

1. I am considering three different majors anthropology, sociology, and psychology.
2. In the career class we watched a film, did some Internet research, and took an interest survey.

Continued

3. Instructor Jones has tried a few different career areas in the last twenty years clinical social work, law enforcement, and retail sales.
4. Consider three things when choosing a major your interests, future job availability, and salary.
5. The interview has three parts an information questionnaire, an oral interview, and a writing sample.
6. When I did that internship, I found out what tasks I like to do, discovered what I hate to do, and met some good contacts.

Review

Here is a review of the six Comma Rules, the Semicolon Rule, and the Colon Rule.

Comma Rule #1

Put commas between items in a series.

- The exhausted, confused, and frustrated writer leaned back in his chair.

Comma Rule #2

When you begin a sentence with a subordinated or dependent clause, you must put a comma after the subordinated (or dependent) clause.

- If he could just remember that great opening line, the rest would flow.

Comma Rule #3

If the subordinated clause comes after the independent clause, you do not need a comma.

- The rest would flow if he could just remember that great opening line.

Comma Rule #4

Put commas around interruptive words/phrases in a sentence.

- For two long hours, however, no words came to his mind.

Comma Rule #5

When you join two complete sentences with a coordinator (FANBOYS), you must put a comma after the first sentence.

- At midnight he finally remembered his thrilling opening line, and he began to type. ("Once upon a time. . . .")

Comma Rule #6

When you begin a sentence with an introductory phrase, put a comma after the introductory phrase.

- With feelings of great disappointment, the writer began to look for a new job.

Continued

Notes

The Semicolon Rule
You may use a semicolon to separate two complete sentences.
- He liked his old job; he didn't want to go looking for a new one.

The Colon Rule
When you offer a list after a complete sentence, use a colon to separate the sentence and the list.
- In the newspaper he saw a number of promising ads: creative writer needed for comic book company, writer needed in advertising firm, and editor needed for large publishing company.

Review Exercise A *Kids and Video Games (all eight punctuation rules)*
Study each sentence. Decide which punctuation rule is being applied. (There are no punctuation errors here.) Write the number of the Comma Rule, or write Semicolon Rule, or write Colon Rule.

Example: Bryan loves the action on video games, and he enjoys the challenge.
- Bryan loves the action on video games, and he enjoys the challenge.
  Comma Rule #1

1. I'm not sure I want my kids to play those video games because the violence seems too graphic.
2. At Christmas my oldest child had a one-track mind: video games, video games, and more video games.
3. My kids are smart and well-adjusted, but I believe games like that just add garbage to their developing minds.
4. I want to show them respect and trust; therefore, I'm going to discuss my concerns with them and work out a plan with their input.
5. Considering their good grades and how much they help out around the house, I don't want to be too hard on them.
6. When summer comes, they will have a lot of other distractions.
7. They will be swimming, camping, and playing tennis.
8. They might not, however, totally give up their video games.

Review Exercise B *Jazminka (all eight punctuation rules)*
- Correctly punctuate the following sentences.
- Write the number of the Comma Rule you are applying, or write that you are applying the Semicolon or Colon Rules.

Continued

Note: One sentence is already correct.

1. Jazminka's life had been ruined by four people her mother, her stepfather, and her two hateful stepsisters.
2. Jazminka cried because she did not want to sleep on the pallet in the garage.
3. The pallet was made of smelly straw and it was covered with a scratchy burlap.
4. Jazminka dreamed of sleeping in a sumptuous bed with silk sheets a down comforter and feather pillows.
5. When her treacherous sisters became debutantes the family had an incredible coming-out party.
6. Jazminka of course was told to stay in the garage with the cat.
7. Wanting to see how people were dressed and how they danced Jazminka sneaked into the kitchen and spied on the party.
8. She saw the man of her dreams he was sitting alone reading a book of poetry.

Review Exercise C   *John's Dream*

- Correctly punctuate the following sentences.
- Write the number of the Comma Rule you are applying, or write that you are applying the Semicolon or Colon Rules. *Note:* One sentence is already correct, and one rule should be applied twice.

1. John wanted so much to start his own business he had a well-formulated plan.
2. He worried however that being self-employed could put a financial strain on his family for a while.
3. He worked all day making other people a lot of money but he dreamed about being somewhere else.
4. One cold winter's day near Christmas he inherited money from a distant great uncle.
5. The next day he quit his job put together a home office and began contacting some associates.
6. He was excited about this new beginning even though he was nervous.
7. Because he was a very intelligent man with a lot of determination he had an excellent chance of succeeding.

Continued

8. His excellent reputation helped him in a number of ways getting customers, acquiring a line of credit, and attracting excellent employees.
9. Although he had to work long hours he had never been happier.

Create Your Own Sentences

Review Exercise D   *Original Sentences*
• On a separate piece of paper, write each Comma Rule and the Semicolon and Colon rules. Then create an original sentence of your own that can serve as an example of each rule.
• Use new vocabulary words in at least two of your sentences.

Apply Your Knowledge

Review one of the paragraphs you have written. Can you find any places where you did not use commas, semicolons, or colons correctly? Be prepared to share sentences with classmates.

When you are writing paragraphs (or other formal writing assignments), wait until the editing stage before worrying too much about punctuation. First get your ideas down and revise them to make an interesting, thoughtful piece of writing. Then carefully, sentence by sentence, review your work and apply the eight punctuation rules given in this chapter. You may find it helpful to refer to the rules chart in Appendix C (pp. 449–450).

Quotation Marks

In this chapter you will focus on how to use double quotation marks. This chapter covers the following topics:

+ Using quotation marks with titles
+ Using quotation marks with direct quotes

Using Quotation Marks with Titles

When you mention the title of someone else's *short* work in your own writing, you must put the title in quotation marks. Titles of *long* works are underlined or put in italics.

Short Works (use quotation marks)	Long Works (underline or use italics)
chapters	books
songs	CDs or albums
newspaper and magazine articles	magazines and newspapers
poems	movies
essays	

These sentences mention short works:

My friend's essay, "Say No to the Death Penalty," was really good.

My favorite song is "Let It Be" by the Beatles.

In the recent news article "Graffiti in Our Neighborhoods," the mayor says he wants stiffer punishments for people caught spray painting public property.

Here are some sentences that refer to long works:

I just read John Sanford's latest novel called *Easy Prey*.

Did you see *Saving Private Ryan*?

I read the *New York Times* every morning.

Notes

Computer Note

If you want to underline a title, type it. Then highlight it and click on the <u>U</u> on your menu, or go to Format on your menu and then to Font. Under Underline style, click on the single underline.

Computer Note

If you want a title to be in italics, type it. Then highlight it and click on the *I* on your menu, or go to Format on your menu and then to Font. Under Font Style, click on Italic.

Notes

> **Practice #1** *Books, Chapters, Magazines, and Articles (underlining and quotation marks)*
>
> Put quotation marks around the titles of short works. Underline the titles of longer works.
>
> Example: The Chicago Sun printed the article Scandalous Presidents.
>
> • The <u>Chicago Sun</u> printed the article "Scandalous Presidents."
>
> 1. Last month, our book club read The Autobiography of Malcolm X.
> 2. In the chapter called Hustler, Malcolm X describes some of the illegal activities he was involved in when he was young.
> 3. Since it is supposed to help me focus while studying, my sister bought me a CD called The Four Seasons.
> 4. In Time magazine I read the article Surviving Parenthood.
> 5. In Biology 56, we had to read the chapter called Germs in Our World from our textbook Biology Today.

If a comma or period immediately follows a title that is in quotation marks, put the comma or period inside the quotation marks:

When I reread "Once More to the Lake," I understood it better.

My husband just wrote a poem called "Whispering Pines."

If a question mark or exclamation point is part of a title that is in quotation marks, put the question mark or exclamation point inside the quotation marks. If, however, the question mark or exclamation point is part of the sentence *but not part of the title,* put the mark outside the quotation marks.

Here are some examples:

• I didn't like the article "Why Can't Johnny Read?" (The question mark is part of the title.)

• Did you like the essay Mike wrote called "On the Other Hand"? (The question mark is not part of the title. It is part of the sentence.)

• You've got to hear "My Only Baby"! (The exclamation mark is not part of the title.)

• Read this poem called "Gold!" (The exclamation mark is part of the title.)

Practice #2   *What's in a Title? (putting quotation marks in the right places)*

On a separate piece of paper, rewrite the following sentences and add quotation marks where necessary. Be prepared to explain the placement of your quotation marks. (You and your classmates may not always agree about the answers in this exercise. That's okay as long as you can defend your choices.)

Example: Have you read the chapter called Growing Up?

• Have you read the chapter called "Growing Up"? (The question mark is not part of the title.)

1. Why didn't you read the article called The Economy is Shifting?
2. For the encore, they will do a fantastic version of your favorite song Quiet Child!
3. I read her poem called Why Me?
4. Can you sing The Star Spangled Banner?
5. He made me so angry when he changed the words to Silent Night!
6. My essay Do You Know Where Your Dog Is? will be printed in this week's Time magazine.
7. For History 45, we have to read the chapter called The Gold Rush!
8. Will you sing Rock-a-Bye-Baby to the kids?

Using Quotation Marks with Direct Quotes

If you want your reader to know that you are giving the exact words of a speaker or writer, you'll need to put those words in quotation marks. Here's an example:

> As they were cleaning the room, the 7-year-old girl kept asking her mom what things she could throw away. Finally, her mom said, "Throw out whatever you want!" With a puzzled expression, the girl looked at her mom and said, "Why would I want to throw out things I want? Shouldn't I throw out things I *don't* want?"

The sentences in the quotation marks that represent the exact words spoken are called **direct quotes.**

Following is an example of a direct quote that comes from a reading:

In "The Library Card" Richard Wright explains his feelings about reading and writing when he says, "I had once tried to write, had once reveled in feeling, had let my crude imagination roam, but the impulse to dream had been slowly beaten out of me by experience. Now it surged up again and I hungered for books, new ways of looking and seeing." I can relate to Wright's experience. . . .

Here are the rules for punctuating direct quotes:

Direct Quote Rule #1

Most direct quotes are introduced by a phrase that is followed by a comma or a colon.

- The speaker said, "Please sit down."
- In her article she explained the procedures: "Everyone had to take a written exam and then a fitness test."

Direct Quote Rule #2

The first word in the direct quote is capitalized unless the quote is introduced by a word **like** *that.*

- The students said, "The regulations are too strict."
- He said that "the scores were excellent."

Direct Quote Rule #3

If a sentence ends with a direct quote, use the punctuation that belongs to the quote.

- Fred stood up and asked, "Why hasn't this been brought to our attention before?" (Fred asks a question, so the final piece of punctuation should be a question mark inside the quotation marks.)
- Josephine yelled out, "We wrote you letters and phoned your office at least five times!" (Josephine is yelling, so the final piece of punctuation should be an exclamation point inside the quotation marks.)
- I whispered, "I think this actor is pretty good."

Direct Quote Rule #4

If a direct quote comes in the middle of a sentence, put a comma or other appropriate punctuation for the quote inside the quotation marks, and then end the sentence according to what the sentence requires.

- When the speaker exclaimed, "We have four dogs for every person in this country!" I thought he was exaggerating.
- Why did the man say, "Phooey!" when I said that the pay was too low?
- That unusual woman said, "Have a groovy day," to every single person in line!

Practice #3   *A National Tragedy (using the direct quote rules)*

- On a separate piece of paper, rewrite these sentences and carefully punctuate them.
- Each sentence has a direct quote in it. You'll have to add quotation marks in every sentence.
- Some sentences will also need commas, colons, and capital letters.

Example: The man suddenly began singing my country 'tis of thee.

- The man suddenly began singing, "My country 'tis of thee." (A comma is added after *singing. My* is capitalized, and quotation marks are added.)

1. I was astounded when the news anchor exclaimed America is under attack by terrorists!
2. My roommate yelled how could this be?
3. The man screamed run as the smoke came billowing down the street.
4. In the news article, the writer stated that Americans must be vigilant against racism.
5. The writer said America stands for freedom and tolerance.
6. The sign in the store stated no more American flags available. Try back next week.
7. The magazine article stated that Americans should educate themselves about the Middle East.
8. The author has some specific recommendations so that people can begin to understand the history of that area listen to public radio. Read news articles from a variety of newspapers. Watch your public television station.

Create Your Own Sentences

Review Exercise A   *Original Sentences (using quotation marks)*

On a separate piece of paper, create the sentences described. Refer to rules given earlier in the chapter and use quotation marks, underlining, commas, exclamation points, questions marks, and capital letters correctly.   *Continued*

Notes

1. Create a sentence that has the name of a long work in it.
2. Create a sentence that has the name of a short work at the end of the sentence.
3. Create a sentence that has the name of a short work in the middle of the sentence. (You can make up the title, but the title must end with an exclamation point.)
4. Create a sentence that has a direct quote at the end of it. The direct quote must be introduced by a phrase that is followed by a comma.
5. Create a sentence that has a direct quote at the end of it. The direct quote must be introduced by a phrase that is followed by a colon.
6. Create a sentence that has a direct quote in the middle of the sentence.
7. Create a sentence that has a direct quote that is a question.

Apply Your Knowledge

Review one of the paragraphs you have written.

- Have you used quotation marks and underlining correctly when mentioning titles?
- Are the punctuation marks in the correct positions?
- Can you add direct quotes to your writing to make your paragraph more specific, believable, and interesting? Readers enjoy hearing the exact words of a speaker or a writer. Keep in mind, however, that most of the ideas and sentences in your paragraph should come from you—not from other speakers or writers.

Spelling

Learning to spell well is an important part of your progress as a student, writer, and employee. This chapter covers the following topics:

+ Why spelling can be tricky
+ Read and write to be a better speller
+ More spelling strategies
+ Common trouble spots in spelling

Why Spelling Can Be Tricky

Before books were common and when there were no dictionaries, people spelled words according to how they pronounced them. Unfortunately, not everyone pronounced words the same way. Consequently, not everyone spelled words the same way, which caused quite a bit of confusion. Today we still have some of the unique spellings that were created many years ago. Also, because English is a blend of many languages, some words that we borrowed are spelled in ways that we don't expect.

The result is that English contains at least forty sounds, but there are over 200 different spellings of these sounds. For example, consider the different spellings of the sound *sh* in *shoe, sugar, passion, ambitious, ocean,* and *champagne.* Think about the *k* in *knife* as opposed to *kite,* or the *p* in *psychology* as opposed to *party.*

English also contains many words that sound alike but have different spellings and meanings. Consider the differences in meaning between *here* and *hear,* or *one* and *won.*

Spelling, obviously, can be quite a challenge. However, there are some strategies you can use to become a better speller.

Read and Write to Be a Better Speller

Reading and writing are crucial to improving your spelling skills:

- **Read on a regular basis.** You'll become familiar with how words should *look.*

Notes

Computer Note
Try visiting these
websites if you are
looking for unabridged
books on tape:
www.booksontape.com
www.audiobookcollecti
on.com

- **Read a book while listening to it on an audiotape.** You'll learn how words are pronounced and spelled. You can rent or buy books on tape. To rent, go to your local video store or library. To buy, go to a bookstore. Look for tapes that are *unabridged*. Unabridged means that the entire story is read—and you can follow along. An abridged version is a shortened version, and it would be hard to read along with such a tape.
- **Write regularly.** Writing helps you memorize correct spellings.
- **Read a book that teaches *phoneme awareness*.** You'll learn how different sounds can be created and spelled with different combinations of letters.

More Spelling Strategies

While reading and writing more regularly, you may want to try out some of the strategies mentioned here.

Strategy #1 The Spelling Log

Carry a small 3 × 5 spiral notebook with you. In it, you can keep a list of problem words—words that cause *you* trouble—spelled correctly. When faced with a situation in which you must write, you will have your personal spelling list with you.

Of course, you need to add to this list as you begin to be more aware of your spelling and the kinds of spelling errors you're consistently making. Here are some good times to add new words:

- When editing a paragraph, add any misspelled words you catch to your list.
- When your instructor returns a paragraph, check for any misspellings he or she caught and then add them to your list.
- As you're reading, if you notice a word that you realize you've been misspelling, add it to your list.

Keeping a personal spelling list means that you're taking responsibility for your spelling and becoming more aware of your own repeated spelling errors.

Though it is best to carry a small 3 × 5 spiral notebook with you to classes (and to work), you will find a chart on p. 345 of this chapter.

You can use it to begin building your personal spelling list. While using this textbook, you can easily refer to this list during the editing stage of your writing process.

Strategy #2 Use Spell Check

Most computer writing programs today come with spell check, a program that identifies possible misspellings in papers and documents. Spell check works by searching the computer's dictionary and highlighting any words that don't appear in the dictionary.

In most cases, when spell check highlights a word, it offers a list of suggested spellings. Probably, the correctly spelled word is on that list. If so, just select the correct spelling, and the computer will replace the incorrect spelling in the paragraph.

Use spell check whenever you're writing on a computer, especially during the editing stage of the writing process. If your spelling skills are particularly weak, type all of your homework on the computer and then use spell check before turning it in. Add words to your own spelling list.

Spell check does have a few drawbacks, however. When a misspelling is highlighted, and you've been given a list of suggested spellings, don't assume the correct spelling for the word will *always* be on the list. It may not be. If it isn't, you'll need to go to the dictionary to find that word.

Spell check cannot catch words that sound alike but have different meanings. For example, if you use *to* when you should use *too*, the spell check program won't alert you—because the word is spelled correctly. (It just isn't the right word.) If you realize on your own that you might not have the right word, you will have to go to the dictionary or Chapter 34, "The Right Word," and check the meaning.

Finally, spell check does not identify errors in proper names and places. When editing your paper, be sure to check these spellings yourself.

Computer Note

There are many variations of spell check. If you are working in a computer lab, ask the computer technician to show you how to use it the first time.

Strategy #3 Use the Dictionary

The dictionary not only gives you the spelling of a word, but it offers the plural of the word, and for verbs, the basic tenses. When in doubt about how to spell a word, you can always look it up in the dictionary. You can use a dictionary in book form, a dictionary that is part of your

Notes

word processing program, or a dictionary on the Internet (for example, www.m-w.com/dictionary.html).

But how do you look up a word if you don't know how to spell it? Usually you do so through trial and error, looking up the word by pronunciation and then trying slightly different variations of spelling until you find the word. (A dictionary in book form is best for this kind of search.) If you find looking up words in the dictionary nearly impossible, however, you might benefit from a misspeller's dictionary.

The Misspeller's Dictionary

A misspeller's dictionary contains two columns of words: one column lists words as they are typically misspelled, and a corresponding column lists the same words spelled correctly. For instance, in such a dictionary, you might see the following entries:

Incorrect	Correct
eco	echo
eightteen	eighteen

Often this type of dictionary also contains a section on homophones (words that sound alike but have different meanings) and their meanings such as *find* (locate) and *fined* (given a penalty).

A Spelling List

Another speller's tool that you can purchase is a pocket-size spelling list. In it, words have been broken into syllables so that they're easier to look up according to pronunciation:

bi-og-ra-phy

re-cant

ty-po

Such spelling lists include the correct spellings for the most commonly misspelled words.

Both the misspeller's dictionary and the spelling list are light and compact enough to carry with you everywhere.

Common Trouble Spots in Spelling

The spelling log, spell check, dictionary, misspeller's dictionary, and spelling list dictionary will certainly help you cut down on the number of spelling errors in your writing. However, there are a few areas of spelling that students find particularly troublesome. In this section you'll review the spellings of plurals, past-tense and *have* forms of verbs, homonyms, and possessives.

Plurals

Change a noun from singular to plural according to the following rules:

Do not add an apostrophe when you simply want to make a word plural. See Chapter 32 for more on apostrophes.

- To form the plural of most nouns, add *–s* to the word: *tree* to *trees*, *action* to *actions*.
- To form the plural for nouns ending in *–s, –ss, –sh, –ch, –x, –z* (a hissing sound called a sibilant sound), add *es* to the word: *church* to *churches, hush* to *hushes, box* to *boxes, kiss* to *kisses.*
- To form the plural of a noun that ends in *–y* when preceded by a vowel, add *–s: toy* to *toys, monkey* to *monkeys.*
- To form the plural of a noun that ends in *–y* when preceded by a consonant, change the *y* to *i* and add *–es: party* to *parties, rally* to *rallies.*

Not all plurals are formed by adding *–s* or *–es.* Some are words adopted from other languages that maintain their original plural spellings. Others are simply irregular plurals and are exceptions to the rules mentioned earlier. Here are some examples of irregular plurals:

Singular	Plural
child	children
foot	feet
goose	geese
man	men
moose	moose
mouse	mice
ox	oxen
tooth	teeth

Practice #1   *Spelling Plurals Correctly*
- Write the correct plural form of these words. Use a dictionary or spell check as necessary—to check both meanings and plural forms.
- On a separate piece of paper, create an original sentence for each word.
- Use new vocabulary words in at least two of your sentences.
Continued

Notes

• Add words to your own spelling list as appropriate.

	Singular	Plural
1.	analysis	
2.	criterion	
3.	datum	
4.	medium	
5.	woman	

Verb Tense

The past-tense form and the *have* form of verbs pose spelling problems for students only when these forms are irregular. In most cases, the past-tense form and *have* form are easy to spell. Simply add –*ed* to the end of the base form, or just add –*d* if the base word ends in *e*. Here are some regular verbs:

Base	Past	Have
generate	generated	generated
talk	talked	talked

Irregular verbs, however, don't follow the –*ed* rule. Here are some irregular verbs:

Base	Past	Have
drive	drove	driven
sing	sang	sung

See Chapter 13 (pp. 191–192) for a chart of irregular verbs.

When you have questions about verb forms, you can look up the base form in the dictionary. After the base form, you'll find the past-tense form, the *have* form, and finally the -*ing* form. If the past-tense form and *have* form are the same, the dictionary will list that form once.

Practice #2   *Spelling Different Verb Forms Correctly*
• Find the correct form of each verb.
• On a separate piece of paper, create a sentence for each word.
• Use new vocabulary words in at least two of your sentences.

Example: Drive (*have* form)

• I have driven this car for seventeen years.   *Continued*

1. awake (past tense)
2. be (*have* form)
3. begin (past tense)
4. cut (*have* form)
5. see (*have* form)

Homophones

Homophones are words that sound alike but are spelled differently and have different meanings. Homophones cause problems for students, who may believe they're spelling words correctly—when in fact they're spelling the *wrong* words correctly. This is another time your dictionary is a valuable tool. When in doubt about which spelling to use, look it up. Another resource in this text is Chapter 34, "The Right Word," which contains a list of words that are often confused (p. 359).

Here are examples of correct use of the homophones *to*, *too*, and *two:*

- *To* means "toward a particular direction," or it may be part of an infinitive like "to see." *I traveled to Paris to see the Mona Lisa.*
- *Too* means *"also." My husband went too.*
- *Two* is the number. *We discovered two can travel for the price of one.*

Practice #3   *Spelling Homophones Correctly*
- On a separate piece of paper, create original sentences using each of these words in a sentence.
- Use new vocabulary words in at least two of your sentences.

Examples:

to
- I went to the store.

too
- The elephant was too big to fit through the door.

1. its
2. it's
3. which
4. witch

Continued

Notes

> 5. their
> 6. they're
> 7. there

Apply Your Knowledge

At the editing stage of your writing process, check for spelling errors.

- Take out your personal spelling list, or refer to your personal list in this book, and use the dictionary or other resources as necessary.
- When in doubt about the spelling of a word, always check the word. This takes patience, but it is worth it to maintain your professional image.

Personal Spelling List

(List the correct spelling for words you have previously misspelled.)

1. _____
2. _____
3. _____
4. _____
5. _____
6. _____
7. _____
8. _____
9. _____
10. _____
11. _____
12. _____
13. _____
14. _____
15. _____
16. _____
17. _____
18. _____
19. _____

20. _____
21. _____
22. _____
23. _____
24. _____
25. _____
26. _____
27. _____
28. _____
29. _____
30. _____
31. _____
32. _____
33. _____
34. _____
35. _____
36. _____
37. _____
38. _____

Apostrophes

The apostrophe is used in two different ways in English. It's used to form contractions and possessives. This chapter covers both uses:

✦ Contractions
   Stephanie *didn't* cause the accident.
✦ Possessives
   Stephanie's new car is spectacular.

Notes

Contractions

A **contraction** is a condensed form of two words with an apostrophe replacing one or more letters. Here are some examples:

it + is = it's
- *it's* is a contraction of the words *it* and *is*. The apostrophe indicates where the letter *i* has been left out.

had + not = hadn't
- *hadn't* is a contraction of the words *had* and *not*. The apostrophe indicates where the letter *o* has been left out.

Apostrophe Rule #1

To create a contraction, use an apostrophe to replace one or more letters.

- she + would = she'd
  she'd can be a contraction of *she* and *would* with the apostrophe replacing the letters *w, o, u,* and *l. she'd* can also be a contraction of *she* and *had.*

Practice #1   *Creating Contractions*
Change the following word combinations into contractions. If you're unsure about any contractions you create, look them up in the dictionary.

Continued

Example: I + will =

- I + will = I'll

1. he + would =
2. can + not =
3. will + not =
4. should + have =
5. could + have =

6. I + have =
7. you + are =
8. do + not =
9. it + will =
10. we + are =

Practice Review   *Use Contractions in Original Sentences*

- On a separate piece of paper, create original sentences using the contractions you created in items 1–5 of Practice #1.
- Use new vocabulary words in at least two sentences.

Possessives

A **possessive** is a word that shows ownership. In English we often use the apostrophe to form possessives of nouns and pronouns.

The *stepmother's* jewelry box was full of diamonds.
Fred *Jones's* car broke down on the way to the ball.
Somebody's slipper was left behind.
The *girls'* chatter stopped when the prince walked by.

Forming Possessive Nouns

Apostrophe Rule #2

To make a singular noun possessive, add an apostrophe and an –s.

- stepmother to stepmother's
- Cinderella to Cinderella's
- Fred Jones to Fred Jones's

Apostrophe Rule #3

To make most plural nouns possessive, add only an apostrophe.

- boys to boys'
- kites to kites'

Notes

Apostrophe Rule #4

To make some irregular plural nouns possessive, add an apostrophe and an –s.

- children to children's
- people to people's

Practice #2 Creating Possessives

Write the possessive form of each noun in the blank.

Examples:
clerk to _____

- clerk to <u>clerk's</u>

  clerks to _____

- clerks to <u>clerks'</u>

  1. sister to _____
  2. sisters to _____
  3. father to _____
  4. fathers to _____
  5. man to _____
  6. men to _____
  7. child to _____
  8. children to _____

Don't Confuse Simple Plurals with Possessives

Do not use an apostrophe to make a word plural. Here are some examples of plurals that are not possessives:

I bought two <u>dogs.</u>
He has been in two car <u>accidents</u> this year.
Do you have five <u>classes</u> this year?
Professor Burns has two <u>children.</u>

If you think you need an apostrophe to show possession, ask yourself if the sentence has a noun (a person, thing, place, or idea) that belongs to someone or something:

- The <u>musicians'</u> instruments need to be tuned. (The instruments belong to the musicians, so *musicians* needs an apostrophe.)
- The <u>alligators'</u> cages were not big enough. (The cages belong to the alligators, so *alligators* needs an apostrophe.)

Practice #3   *Plurals or Possessives?*
In the following sentences, decide if you need a simple plural form or a possessive form of a plural. Write the correct form in the blank.

Example:
I saw the two _____ (boy) toys scattered everywhere.

- I saw the two <u>boys'</u> toys scattered everywhere.

  I helped the _____(boys) clean up.

- I helped the <u>boys</u> clean up.

  1. I borrowed one of my _____ (friends) car.
  2. Both of her _____ (cars) are new.
  3. His two new music _____ (videos) are true _____ (pieces) of art.
  4. They are unusual _____ (videos) because the _____ (women) are all fully clothed.
  5. In fact, the _____ (videos) are about the two _____ (girls) determination to become basketball stars.
  6. The _____ (boys) father didn't understand modern music.
  7. The _____ (lyrics) are hard to understand.
  8. The _____ (bands) performance was fantastic.
  9. The two backup _____ (singers) were terrific.
  10. I was looking for the _____ (supervisors) donut and coffee.

Forming Possessive Pronouns

There are two basic types of pronouns, *personal* and *indefinite*. *Personal pronouns*—which refer to specific persons, places, or things— *do not need* apostrophes to show ownership. Here are some examples of possessive personal pronouns:

her
That is *her* slipper.

hers
That is *hers.*

his
She stepped on *his* foot during the dance.

its
The royal dog ate *its* bone.

my
My father is the king.

mine
The decision is *mine* to make.

your
The queen left a message on *your* machine.

yours
This ring is *yours.*

our
Our father should not have married that treacherous woman.

ours
This house is *ours.*

their
Their new stepmother was a wonderful person.

theirs
The jewelry is *theirs.*

Apostrophe Rule #5

Do not use an apostrophe to make a personal pronoun possessive.

- his
- its
- mine

Indefinite pronouns, which refer to nonspecific persons or things, *do need* apostrophes to indicate ownership. Here are some examples of possessive indefinite pronouns:

anybody's
It is *anybody's* guess.
anyone's
She would take *anyone's* advice.
everybody's
Everybody's carriage got stuck in the snow.
nobody's
Nobody's cell phone worked.
somebody's
I found *somebody's* earring on the dance floor.

Apostrophe Rule #6

***To make an indefinite pronoun possessive, add an apostrophe
and an –s.***

- everyone's
- someone's

Practice #4   *Using Possessive Pronouns*
Use possessive personal pronouns and possessive indefinite pronouns
to complete the following sentences.

1. _____ grade has been posted yet.
2. I washed _____ car.
3. They hid _____ hands behind _____ backs.
4. The book we found last night is _____.
5. I haven't seen _____ drawing yet.
6. I think the tickets are _____.
7. Frank saw _____ dog run out of the veterinary hospital.
8. I explained to them that the videos are _____.
9. Will you grab _____ key to the mailbox?
10. That job will be _____.

Practice Review   *Creating Sentences with Possessive Nouns*
On a separate piece of paper, create original sentences using these
words in the possessive forms.   *Continued*

Example: Student

- The student's final exam was on Tuesday.

1. nurse
2. people
3. grandparents
4. shark
5. birds

Practice Review *Creating Sentences with Possessive Personal Pronouns*

- On a separate piece of paper, create five original sentences that include possessive personal pronouns (no apostrophes.)
- Use new vocabulary words in at least two of your sentences.

Practice Review *Creating Sentences with Possessive Indefinite Pronouns*

- On a separate piece of paper, create five original sentences that include possessive indefinite pronouns (with apostrophes).
- Use new vocabulary words in at least two of your sentences.

Review

Here is a review of the apostrophe rules.

Apostrophe Rule #1
To create a contraction, use an apostrophe to replace one or more letters.

Apostrophe Rule #2
To make a singular noun possessive, add an apostrophe and an –s.

Apostrophe Rule #3
To make most plural nouns possessive, add only an apostrophe.

Apostrophe Rule #4
To make some irregular plural nouns possessive, add an apostrophe and an –s.

Apostrophe Rule #5
Do not use an apostrophe to make a personal pronoun possessive.

Apostrophe Rule #6
To make an indefinite pronoun possessive, add an apostrophe and an –s.

Note: Do not use apostrophes to create the plural forms of words. Use apostrophes according to the rules listed here.

Notes

Review Exercise A *Sally and Her Sisters*

On a separate piece of paper, rewrite the following sentences inserting apostrophes where necessary. Some sentences may not need apostrophes.

1. Sallys sisters wanted to go to the singles dance at the community center down the street.
2. Sally wasnt interested in the dance.
3. She was thinking about her local colleges peace corps meeting.
4. The sisters yelled and screamed about wanting the earrings that Sally had just bought.
5. Sally said, "Theyre yours, but I get to use the car."

Computer Note

For another look at apostrophes (and other punctuation marks), go to this website: www.grammarbook .com/ A few exercises are available at this site too.

Create Your Own Sentences

Review Exercise B

- Create original sentences to demonstrate your understanding of each apostrophe rule. You will write six original sentences. Before each sentence, write out the rule you are demonstrating.
- Use new vocabulary words in at least two of your sentences.

Apply Your Knowledge

Have you been using apostrophes when they are not necessary? Have you been forgetting to use apostrophes when you do need them? Review your work and your Tracking Sentence Errors Chart (p. 452). Then, before turning in your work, look at your sentences line by line and watch for the type of apostrophe error you have made in the past.

Capitalization

Capitalizing words correctly is another key to projecting a professional image. This chapter covers the following topics:

✦ Thirteen rules for capitalization
✦ Exercises for practice

Notes

Capitalization Rules 1 through 6

You can probably memorize most of these rules. But keep in mind that you may need to refer to this chapter when editing your work to make sure you have followed all of the capitalization rules.

Capitalization Rule #1
Capitalize the first word in a sentence.
- *He* got to the island by boat.

Capitalization Rule #2
Capitalize the first word of a quoted complete sentence.
- The ranger said, "*You* need to be back before nightfall."

(When an incomplete quote is introduced by the word *that,* you do not have to capitalize the first word of the quote: *In the phone message, she said that "she has not returned yet."*)

Capitalization Rule #3
Capitalize I when used as a personal pronoun.
- After he failed to return, *I* called the Coast Guard.

Capitalization Rule #4
Capitalize proper nouns—nouns naming specific *people, places, or things:*
- Maya Angelou
- San Francisco
- Ford Expedition

But do not capitalize common nouns: *writer, city, sports utility vehicle.*

Continued

Capitalization Rule #5
Capitalize the names that show family relationships.
- Mother
- Uncle Fred

But do not capitalize when the name is preceded by a possessive pronoun: *my mother, your sister, his uncle,* and so on.

Capitalization Rule #6
Capitalize the title of a person when the title is used with the person's name.
- Professor Bell
- Doctor Adams
- President Roosevelt

But do not capitalize the titles when they appear by themselves: I saw the *professor* buy that book.

Practice #1   *Co-Authors (using Capitalization Rules 1–6)*

This exercise will help you practice using Capitalization Rules 1 through 6. Capitalize words as necessary.

1. the mother wrote an essay called "Surviving Parenthood."
2. She told her daughter, "this is an essay that tells parents that they need to take good care of themselves—not just the kids. When my first draft is done, i'll show it to you."
3. Their neighbor, professor flitwick, read the essay and loved the vivid details.
4. For example, the professor liked how the writer mentioned how one mom went a whole year without buying herself new clothes but made almost weekly trips to baby gap and toys 'r us.
5. The daughter loved helping her mom revise and said, "mother, thank you for including me in this project."

Capitalization Rules 7 through 9

Capitalization Rule #7
Capitalize titles of specific courses.
- Art 101
- Biology lA

But do not capitalize subject areas: *history, geography.*

Continued

Notes

Capitalization Rule #8
Capitalize the names of commercial products.
- Pepsi
- Big Mac

Capitalization Rule #9
Capitalize the first and last words and other significant words in titles of books, essays, stories, films, movies, television series, compact discs, magazines, journals, poems, songs, and news articles.
- "Cinderfella Is Alive" (an essay)
- *Sociology in the Modern Age* (a textbook)
- *Ever After* (a movie)
- *New York Times* (a newspaper)

Do not capitalize *a, an, the,* coordinating conjunctions, or prepositions unless they are first or last in a title.

Practice #2   *A Song for Sociology 21 (using Capitalization Rules 7–9)*
This exercise will give you practice using Capitalization Rules 7 through 9. Capitalize words as necessary.

1. Simon decided he wanted to major in sociology, and so he signed up for sociology 21: the study of folktales and fairy tales.
2. For his midterm, Simon wrote an autobiographical song called "i was a male cinderella."
3. Since he mentions many cleaning products—comet, ivory soap, and tide—he thought he might get a corporate sponsor to produce his song.

Capitalization Rules 10 through 13

Capitalization Rule #10
Capitalize names of languages, nations, nationalities, and ethnicity.
- Germany
- Spanish
- Vietnamese

Capitalization Rule #11
Capitalize names of government agencies, unions, corporations, institutions, and religious and political organizations.
- Bank of America
- Microsoft

Continued

- Department of Defense
- Methodist

Capitalization Rule #12
Capitalize names of wars and historical events.
- the Vietnam War
- the American Revolution

Capitalization Rule #13
Capitalize the days of the week, months, and holidays.
- Monday
- November
- Thanksgiving

Do not capitalize the names of seasons: *summer, fall, winter, spring.*

Do not capitalize centuries: *the twentieth century.*

Practice #3   *Godmothers to the Rescue (using Capitalization Rules 10–13)*

This exercise will give you practice with Capitalization Rules 10 through 13. Capitalize words as necessary.

1. Many years ago, while stationed overseas during the korean war, I read a fairy tale by a russian writer who took a critical look at american capitalism.
2. The tale focused on how levi's — the jean manufacturing company— was creating thousands of cinderellas by working its employees too hard.
3. At the end of the story, on christmas day, an entire squadron of socialist godmothers swooped down and showered gold coins on the workers, who took over the factories and began to live better lives.

Review Exercise A   *Materialism, Reality*

This exercise reviews most of the thirteen capitalization rules. Capitalize words as necessary. Eighteen words need to be capitalized.

I read a newspaper column in the *sacramento bee* that compared the tv show *who wants to marry a millionaire* to common themes found in fairy tales. The writer, jacquelyn mitchard, was concerned that the man in the show and the men in most fairy tales have all the power. The writer says, "the prince holds all the cards." It is the woman

Continued

Computer Note
For a quick discussion and another set of review exercises, go to www.funtrivia.com and look under "education."

who must parade around in a swimsuit or spin straw into gold in order to win the man's hand. He makes the choice. The writer wants to know how these women will feel about such men after the wedding. She asks, "how do you think the princess who was expected to spin straw into gold felt about the prince who made her his bride after six months? After a year? How could you feel about someone who bought you on a shopping channel?"

Another article i read takes a different view of these arranged fairy tale weddings. donna britt, another newspaper columnist, points out that what happened on the television show isn't really very different from the "civilized" arranged marriages common in many countries (in the past and still today). The bride's parents look for a wealthy husband. (And looks are always a plus.) the husband's parents look for a good-looking, wealthy wife. britt seemed to suggest that we are not really more shallow or more materialistic now. Marriages have often been based on money and looks. People want their chevrolet suburbans, their diamonds from cartier, and they want to look at good-looking faces.

Create Your Own Sentences

Review Exercise B *Create Original Sentences*
- On a separate piece of paper, write each of the thirteen capitalization rules.
- Then write an original sentence for each rule to demonstrate that you understand the rule.
- Use new vocabulary words in at least two of your sentences.

Apply Your Knowledge

Refer to the rules listed in this chapter when you are editing your paragraphs. If you frequently review and apply these rules, you'll soon find that you have memorized most of them.

The Right Word

Clear communication requires that you use the correct word in the correct place. This chapter covers words that are easy to mix up.

✦ Homophones. These are words that sound the same but have different spellings and meanings.

✦ Similar words. These are words that are often confused with one another. They don't sound the same, but they do have similar spellings and sometimes similar meanings.

Homophones

Notes

Homophones are words that sound exactly alike but have different meanings.

Its: the possessive form of *it. The horse stomped <u>its</u> foot.*

It's: a contraction of the words *it* and *is. <u>It's</u> time to go to the racetrack.*

To: means "toward." *The man went to the park.* May also be part of an infinitive. *He wanted <u>to</u> jog.*

Two: is the number. *He ran <u>two</u> miles.*

Too: means "also" or "in excess." *He wanted to ride his bicycle <u>too</u>.*

Their: the possessive form of *they. They got in <u>their</u> car.*

They're: a contraction of the words *they* and *are. <u>They're</u> going to the church.*

There: means "the opposite of here." *The church is <u>there</u>.* May also be used to introduce a sentence. *<u>There</u> were many people at the church.*

Your: the possessive form of *you. <u>Your</u> dinner was sumptuous.*

You're: a contraction of the words *you* and *are. <u>You're</u> going to be a great househusband.*

359

Notes

Practice #1 *Cinderella on Wheels (using homophones correctly)*
Insert the correct word in the following sentences. You will use each of the homophones once.

Example: Put your book of fairy tales over _____.

• Put your book of fairy tales over <u>there.</u>

1. The young prince wanted _____ ride his Harley Davidson motorcycle to the ball, but it was snowing _____ hard.
2. "_____ a terrible night to be going out," said his mother.
3. "_____ such a worrywart, Mother," said the prince.
4. "Now that is no way to speak to _____ mother! You get your precious self home by _____ o'clock."
5. _____ was a great band at the ball.
6. When the prince saw Cinderella, he ran up to her and said, "_____ playing our song!"
7. After a few more songs, the band took _____ break, and Cinderella and the prince sat down, talked, and got to know each other.
8. Two years later, Cinderella and the prince got married and rode off on _____ Harleys into the sunset.

Practice Review *Create Original Sentences with Homophones*
On a separate piece of paper, create original sentences, using all of the ten homophones listed in this chapter at least once. Use new vocabulary words in at least two sentences.

Similar Words

The words in this section do not sound the same. Practice saying them with your classmates to review the differences in pronunciation.

Accept: a verb meaning "to receive." *I will <u>accept</u> your invitation to the concert.*

Except: indicates exclusion. *Everyone can go <u>except</u> her.*

Advice: an opinion about a problem or issue. *Dear Abby gave the woman useful <u>advice</u>.*

Advise: a verb meaning "to suggest." *I <u>advise</u> you to listen to Abby.*

Affect: a verb meaning "to influence." *The mother's abuse affected the little child.*

Effect: a noun meaning "result." *The effect of the abuse was not clear for many years.*

Choose: a present-tense verb. *Today, I choose to take my sisters to the party.*

Chose: a past-tense verb. *Yesterday, I chose to bring my sisters to the party.*

Lose: a present-tense verb. *Don't lose my new earrings.*

Loose: an adjective meaning "not tight or restricted." *The wild horses ran loose on the ranch.*

Then: suggests a moment later in time. *They kissed and then said goodbye. Then can also suggest the effect in a cause-effect situation. If you kiss the frog, then he will turn into a prince.*

Than: is used to compare two items. *Cinderella was stronger than the prince.*

Practice #2   *Money Therapy (using the right word)*

Insert the correct word in the following sentences. You will use each of the words from this section once.

1. I'm not sure why you _____ to come see me yesterday and ask for my _____.
2. Wouldn't you rather have a professional therapist_____ you?
3. I would say that you should take all of your _____ change and go to a casino.
4. If you _____ all of your coins in the slot machines, _____ you can dip into your savings and use that money to play high-stakes poker.
5. If you _____ my advice, you will have a very exciting time and a little vacation!
6. I would go with you _____ I have to try and explain my recent gambling debt to my husband, the prince.
7. He seems to think that I have let my new role as princess _____ my usually conservative spending habits.
8. I don't see the _____ that he is talking about.   *Continued*

Notes

Computer Note
For a longer list of
homophones and other
words that are often
confused, go to
www.webgrammar.com/
grammar.html

9. However, since I'm not an expert on money issues and investing, perhaps you should _____ someone else to help you.
10. You may actually find someone who is smarter _____ me.

Create Your Own Sentences

Review Exercise A
Create original sentences, using all of the 22 words from Chapter 34 at least once.

its	it's	
to	two	too
their	they're	there
yours	you're	
accept	except	
advice	advise	
affect	effect	
choose	chose	
lose	loose	
then	than	

Use new vocabulary words in at least two of your sentences.

Apply Your Knowledge

When editing your paragraphs, check for the words mentioned in this chapter. Have you mixed up any of these words? Are there other words that you mix up sometimes? Keep a list of words that you frequently mix up, and refer to that list as you edit. You may want to add these words to your personal spelling list on page 345.

College Survival Skills

This section offers you four chapters that will help you develop stronger writing, test-taking, and study skills.

Chapter 35 explains how *reading aloud* is an important strategy for writers.

Chapter 36 helps you discover what your *preferred learning style* is and how you can make the most of your style. It includes a paragraph assignment.

Chapter 37 helps you strengthen your *note-taking skills* so that you can get the most out of your lectures. It includes a presentation assignment.

Chapter 38 offers you strategies for doing well in *timed-writing* situations. It includes sample reading and writing assignments.

35

Reading Aloud

Most professional writers routinely read their own writing aloud. They know that reading aloud will help them identify weaknesses in their writing.

After a brief introduction, this chapter covers the following topics:

✦ Reading aloud helps you revise
✦ Reading aloud helps you edit
✦ Reading aloud helps you develop a "writer's ear"
✦ Some final notes about reading aloud

Notes

Introduction to Reading Aloud

Consider the following scene:

> After working hard on a paragraph and following all of the steps of the writing process, Lucia turns in her assignment.
>
> Her instructor reads the paragraph, offers suggestions about focus and development, and marks *many* spelling, grammatical, and typographical errors.
>
> Lucia appreciates the instructor's writing suggestions, and wonders why she didn't see those spots that clearly need improvement. And Lucia is shocked at the number of minor errors in what she thought was a perfect paragraph: How did she miss all those spelling, grammatical and typographical errors? Lucia feels discouraged.

This scenario is common. Sometimes writers are surprised that they didn't see the weak spots in their focus, development, or organization. Mostly, this is a normal part of acquiring good writing skills, but it can also be a sign that the writer hasn't been able to see her paper objectively.

Now, the mechanical errors (spelling, typing, and grammar errors) may seem minor. But they can confuse the reader, and they certainly ruin a professional image.

Being a good reviser and proofreader takes time and practice. The more you read and write, the better you will get. However, there are a few ways to acquire good revising and proofreading skills *more quickly*. One method is to *read aloud*.

Reading Aloud Helps You Revise

One semester at California State University, Sacramento, students were required to read all their essays aloud into tape recorders. Students were surprised by the many problems and errors they found in their essays. One student discovered that he needed to develop his ideas more in his essay on education. He read his essay aloud, and he made the following comment: "American students don't study enough. That's why they score lower than students in other countries. Hmm . . . I bet I need some proof here." With another assignment, a student noticed that she wasn't connecting her thoughts clearly: "The man murdered her husband. She is against capital punishment. Oh, that sounds funny. That doesn't flow." Reading aloud helped these students see their writing more clearly, more objectively.

There are, in fact, many benefits to reading aloud frequently. As you read, you may decide to

- add information
- delete unnecessary information
- add transitions
- move information

Reading aloud while writing your paragraph can also help you get going again if you lose focus or run out of things to say. Reading aloud is a tool professional writers rely upon:

> We know our language best by hearing it and speaking it. Writing is an **oral/aural** act and we do well to edit out loud, hearing the text as we revise and polish it. Should we add this, slow that down, speed it up here, take time to define this term, use this word, this construction? What is traditional and expected by the reader? What best supports and communicates the meaning of the draft? These questions can often be answered by reading the line out loud, taking something out and reading it out loud, putting something in and reading it out loud. Hand, eye, and ear, a constant interplay.
>
> Donald Murray
> American novelist, poet, Pulitzer Prize–winning journalist, writing instructor

Oral means relating to speech or the mouth. **Aural** means relating to hearing or the ear.

Reading Aloud Helps You Edit

Finally, when you are proofreading (editing) your paragraph, read aloud frequently. Don't leave this step to the last minute, because you may find areas where you left out a whole sentence, or you may find minor errors that you want to fix on the computer or typewriter before handing in your work.

Look for these kinds of errors:

- misspelled words
- missing words or sentences
- wrong words
- words repeated or used too often
- punctuation errors
- subject-verb agreement errors
- verb tense errors
- run-ons, comma splices, fragments

Reading Aloud Helps You Develop a "Writer's Ear"

Experienced writers like Donald Murray, quoted earlier in this section, have what we call an "ear" for language. They know what *sounds* good. By reading material aloud, they can easily hear punctuation errors, awkward sentences, weak spots in focus, development, and organization. You can improve your ear for language by finding good pieces of writing and reading them aloud.

Here are some recommendations:

- Choose a paragraph or essay out of this textbook each week and read it aloud at home.
- Participate in class when your instructor wants to read a paragraph or essay aloud.
- Choose something you really like to read (newspaper, magazine, novel, poem) and read aloud to your spouse, significant other, or children.
- Listen to books on tape (available at video stores and libraries.)

If you do some or all of these activities, you will

- Improve your vocabulary.
- Improve your sense of how sentences should flow.
- Improve your sense of how writers can focus, develop, and organize writing.

Some Final Notes about Reading Aloud

When a piece of reading is particularly difficult to understand, try reading it aloud. Students find it especially helpful to read aloud such things as famous speeches, poetry, and works by Shakespeare because these readings were meant to be heard.

Read to your children. Your ear for language will improve. Besides, reading to children helps them build their vocabularies, their ear for language, their problem-solving skills, and their knowledge of focus, development, and organization.

In addition, when you read aloud in private, you will be preparing yourself for those situations at school and work when you must present oral reports.

Finally, when you read aloud, note words that you are unsure about pronouncing. Look in a dictionary and study the pronunciation information. Ask a tutor or instructor how to pronounce these words—they are bound to show up again, perhaps when you need to make an oral report.

Skill Spotlight

Reading Aloud, with Passion

When you read aloud, you can learn more about sentence structure and punctuation if you pay attention to the punctuation you see. Working with two friends, imagine yourselves as dramatic actors and read these lines, emphasizing the punctuation marks you see. Have fun—go ahead and exaggerate the emotions these characters are feeling.

[Scenes from a soap opera.]

Narrator: Yesterday, on *Someone's Heart Is Always Breaking*, Frank Hubbard lost control of his refurbished Ford Pinto and went off a cliff. Mr. Carlisle, riding his bike home from the widower's ball, was the first on the scene. He cried hysterically over Frank's lifeless (but still perfectly handsome) body. Then he pedaled as fast as he could to Jessica's house, for he knew Jessica would want to know that her husband, Frank, was dead.

[Jessica has just opened her front door to find her father, Mr. Carlisle, staring at her with tears in his eyes.]

Mr. Carlisle: Jessica! Frank is dead!

Continued

Notes

Jessica: No! No! What will I do?

Mr. Carlisle: Hmm . . . perhaps we should go see your great Aunt Fiona. She could use her herbs to bring him back to life.

Jessica: Yes. Yes. Let's do that. Oh! But remember what Aunt Fiona did when Jimmy wanted Susie to fall in love with him?

Mr. Carlisle: No. Tell me.

Jessica: Oh! It was horrible! She used her herbs and turned Jimmy into a frog! Susie was supposed to kiss the frog and see Jimmy turn into a prince. But . . . little did Aunt Fiona know . . . Susie had a fear of frogs, so Susie never kissed him. Three years later, Jimmy was killed trying to cross the highway. At least I think it was Jimmy. The frog had a tattoo that read "Kiss Me!"

Mr. Carlisle: Well, maybe we should think about this some more. After all, there has been a rumor going around that Frank's body was recently taken over by aliens. Maybe you don't want him back.

For more work on sharpening your ear for English, read the parts of this book (and others) aloud.

Discovering Your Learning Style

Each person has his or her own learning style—a method of absorbing information that makes learning easier. This chapter covers the following topics:

✦ Understanding the four learning styles
✦ Discovering your learning style
✦ Paragraph assignment: Interview and report

Understanding the Four Learning Styles

Notes

Researchers have found that there are basically four styles: visual, auditory, tactile, and kinesthetic.

- Visual learners learn best when they see the material.
- Auditory learners learn best when they hear the material.
- Tactile learners learn best when they can touch the material.
- Kinesthetic learners learn best when they can involve their bodies in learning the material.

If you know what your learning style is, you will have an advantage in college, for then you can approach studying in the way that is best for you. For example, if you are a visual learner, you will want to use charts, study cards, and pictures when you are studying.

However, if you know that you are an auditory learner, you know that lecture classes will be easier for you, and you might even tape record information to play back to yourself.

If you are a tactile learner, you will want to write or trace information you must learn.

If you are a kinesthetic learner, you will want to find ways to learn information that involves physical movement—studying notecards while taking a walk.

Now, no one learns in *only* one way. You may learn best with visual techniques, second best with auditory techniques, third best with tactile techniques, and fourth best with kinesthetic techniques. The key

Notes

is knowing how you best learn, making the most of that method, and strengthening your other styles as you go along. In the next section you'll complete a learning style inventory and find out what your preferred learning style is. The last section of this chapter offers you a chance to write a paragraph about learning styles.

Discovering Your Learning Style

Jeffrey Barsch, a researcher with his PhD in education, created the following highly respected inventory. This is not a test with right and wrong answers. Rather, you should assume that you and your classmates will answer questions differently because you do not all have the same learning style. Read the following introduction, and then answer the inventory questions.

The Inventory

Barsch Learning Style Inventory
Jeffrey R. Barsch, EdD

To gain a better understanding of yourself as a learner you need to evaluate the way you prefer to learn. We all should develop a style which will enhance our learning potential. The following evaluation is a short, quick way of assessing your learning style.

This is not a timed test. Try to do as much as you can by yourself. You surely may, however, ask for assistance when and where you feel you need it. Answer each question as honestly as you can. There are thirty-two questions.

When you are finished, transfer each number to its proper place on the last page. Then, total each of the four columns on that page. You will then see very quickly what your best method of learning is, i.e., whether you are a **visual, auditory, tactile** or **kinesthetic** learner. By this we mean, whether you as an individual learn best through seeing things, hearing them, through the sense of touch, or through actually performing the task.

For example:

• If you are a visual learner, that is, if you have a high visual score, then by all means be sure you *see* all study materials. Use charts, maps, filmstrips, notes, and flashcards. Practice visualizing or picturing spelling words, for example, in your head. Use brightly colored markers to highlight your reading assignments. Write out everything for frequent and quick visual review.

• If you are an auditory learner, that is, if you have a high auditory score, then be sure to use tapes. Sit in the lecture hall or classroom where you can hear lectures clearly. Tape your class or lecture notes so that you can review them frequently. After you have read something, summarize it on tape. Verbally review spelling words and lectures with a friend.

- If you are a tactile learner, that is, have a high tactile score, you might trace words, for example, as you are saying them. Facts that must be learned should be written several times. Keep a supply of scratch paper just for this purpose. Taking and keeping lecture notes will be very important.
- If you are a kinesthetic learner, that is, if you have a high kinesthetic score, it means you need to involve your body in the process of learning. Take a walk and study your notes on flashcards at the same time. It is easier for you to memorize school work if you involve some movement in your memory task.

If several of your scores are within 4 or 5 points of each other, it means that you can use any of those senses for learning tasks. *When you are in a hurry, use your best learning styles. When you have extra time, improve your weak sensory areas.* Discuss the results of this test with your teacher or counselor. You will develop through conversation other helpful ways to study more efficiently. Good luck in your efforts to identify and use a more effective study pattern.

Place a check in the appropriate box after each statement.

	Often	Sometimes	Seldom
1. I can remember more about a subject through listening than reading.			
2. I follow written directions better than oral directions.			
3. Once shown a new physical movement, I perform it quickly with few errors.			
4. I bear down extremely hard with pen or pencil when writing.			
5. I require explanations of diagrams, graphs, or visual directions.			
6. I enjoy working with tools.			
7. I am skillful with and enjoy developing and making graphs and charts.			
8. I can tell if sounds match when presented with pairs of sounds.			
9. I can watch someone do a dance step and easily copy it myself.			

Notes

	Often	Sometimes	Seldom
10. I can understand and follow directions on maps.			
11. I do better at academic subjects by listening to lectures or tapes.			
12. I frequently play with coins or keys in pockets.			
13. I enjoy perfecting a movement in a sport or in dancing.			
14. I can better understand a news article by reading about it in the paper than by listening to the radio.			
15. I chew gum, smoke or snack during studies.			
16. I feel the best way to remember is to picture it in your head.			
17. I enjoy activities that make me aware of my body's movement.			
18. I would rather listen to a good lecture or speech than read about the same material in a textbook.			
19. I consider myself an athletic person.			
20. I grip objects in hands during learning period.			
21. I would prefer listening to the news on the radio rather than reading about it in a newspaper.			
22. I like to obtain information on an interesting subject by reading relevant materials.			
23. I am highly aware of sensations and feelings in my hips and shoulders after learning a new movement or exercise.			

	Often	Sometimes	Seldom
24. I follow oral directions better than written ones.			
25. It would be easy for me to memorize something if I could just use body movements at the same time.			
26. I like to write things down or take notes for visual review.			
27. I remember best when writing things down several times.			
28. I learn to spell better by repeating the letters out loud than by writing the word on paper.			
29. I frequently have the ability to visualize body movements to perform a task, e.g., correction of a golf swing, batting stance, dance position, etc.			
30. I could learn spelling well by tracing over the letters.			
31. I feel comfortable touching, hugging, shaking hands, etc.			
32. I am good at working and solving jigsaw puzzles and mazes.			

Scoring Procedures

Often = 5 points
Sometimes = 3 points
Seldom = 1 point

In the chart on the next page, place the point value on the line next to its corresponding item number. Next, add the points to obtain the preference scores under each heading.

How to Use This Information

This form is to be used in conjunction with other diagnostic tools to help you determine some of the ways you are best able to learn. Discuss your scores with someone who is qualified to interpret them in order to make the best use of the time and effort you have invested.

Example: If you answered "often" for question #2, put a 5 on the blank next to 2. If you answered "sometimes" to #1, put a 3 on the blank next to 1.

373

Notes

Visual		Auditory		Tactile		Kinesthetic	
No.	Pts.	No.	Pts.	No.	Pts.	No.	Pts.
2	____	1	____	4	____	3	____
7	____	5	____	6	____	9	____
10	____	8	____	12	____	13	____
14	____	11	____	15	____	17	____
16	____	18	____	20	____	19	____
22	____	21	____	27	____	23	____
26	____	24	____	30	____	25	____
32	____	28	____	31	____	29	____
VPS =		APS =		TPS =		KPS =	

VPS = visual preference score
APS = auditory preference score
TPS = tactile preference score
KPS = kinesthetic preference score

Study Tips for Different Learning Styles

Directions: Use the study tips outline for your first learning preference, and then reinforce what you are learning with tips from your second preference.

I. Tips for Visual Learners (Print, Pictorial)

1. Write down anything you want to remember, such as a list of things to do, facts to learn for a test, etc.
2. Try to write down information in your own words. If you don't have to think about the material and restate it in your own words, you won't really learn it.
3. Underline or highlight important words you need to learn as you read.
4. When learning a new vocabulary word, visualize the word.
5. When you have a list of things to remember, keep the list in a place where you will be sure to see it several times a day. Suggestions: bulletin board by your desk at home, in your notebook, on the mirror in the bathroom, etc.
6. Try drawing a picture of any information you want to learn. Try making a diagram, a chart, or actually drawing people, things, etc.
7. Always read any material in the textbook before going to class so you have a chance to visually connect with the information before hearing it.

II. Tips for Auditory Learners (Oral, Interactive)

1. Use a tape recorder to record notes when reading instead of writing facts down. Play it back while you are riding in the car, doing dishes, washing the car, jogging, etc.
2. Subvocalize—that is, talk to yourself about any information you want to remember. Try to recite it without looking at your notes or the book.

3. Discuss with others from your class and then quiz each other on the material. Really listen to yourself as you talk.

4. When learning a new vocabulary word, say it out loud. Then spell it out loud several times. See if it rhymes with a word you know. You could even try singing the word in a song.

5. To learn facts, say them out loud, put the facts to music, or read them into a tape recorder. Then listen often to what you have recorded.

6. When writing, talk to yourself. First, tell yourself what you will write, say it out loud as you write it, and then read aloud what you have written or tape record it.

7. Always read material in your textbook to be learned after hearing the information first in the class lecture (unless the instructor assigns the reading first before class so you can participate in class discussions).

III. Tips for Physical Learners (Haptic, Tactile, Kinesthetic)

1. Try to study through practical experiences, such as making models, doing lab work, or role playing.

2. Take frequent, short breaks (5–10 minutes) in study periods.

3. Trace words and letters to learn spelling and to remember facts.

4. Use the computer to reinforce learning through the sense of touch.

5. Memorize or drill while walking, jogging, or exercising.

6. Try expressing your abilities through dance, drama, or sports.

7. Try standing up when you are reading or writing.

8. Write facts to be learned on 3" x 5" cards with a question on one side and the answer on the other. Layout the cards, quiz yourself, shuffle them, lay them out again and quiz yourself again.

9. When working with a study group, think of T.V. quiz games (Jeopardy, etc.) as ways to review information.

IV. Tips for Multisensory Learners (Any Combination of the Above Styles)

Use any combination of the above study tips. It may take some experimentation before you find the best techniques for you.

Paragraph Assignment: Interview and Report

In this chapter, you have identified your preferred learning style. In the following assignment, you'll learn more about one of your classmates as you interview him or her about learning style and studying habits.

Here is the writing assignment you are preparing for:

Write a paragraph in which you explain what a classmate's preferred learning style is and how this should affect his or her studying techniques in college.

Notes

Notes

Interview

You'll need to interview one of our classmates to complete this assignment. Plan your interview questions ahead of time so that you get the information you need. Here are some questions you might ask. Add your own questions as well. Take careful notes. Your instructor may want you to turn in your interview notes with your final paragraph.

- What is your preferred learning style?
- What classes are you taking now?
- What learning styles do your teachers seem to teach to? Do they lecture? Do they have you work with your hands? What learning styles are being used?
- What classes might you take in your future?
- What kind of work do you do in these classes? Reading? Writing? Scientific experiments?

Can you think of other questions that will help you understand how this student is currently studying and performing in class? What questions should you ask to find out about this student's future in college? Can you form any other interview questions based on the information in the study skill tips that follow the learning style inventory?

Have your interview questions written out before interviewing your classmate. Be prepared to take notes. Remember that it is okay to drift away from your list of questions if you are discussing information that will help you write your paragraph.

It is a good idea to complete your interview as soon as possible. Then you may have time to go back and do a second interview after you begin writing your paragraph. You may realize that you need a few more pieces of information.

Pre-Drafting

Reread the study skill tips from the learning inventory, and consider these questions:

- Is this student making the most of his or her preferred learning style?
- Are there other study strategies that he or she should take advantage of?
- Does the student need to strengthen other learning styles in order to succeed in current or future classes? Explain.

- Does the student seem to feel that he or she is doing a good job studying now? Do you agree?

Notes

After considering these questions and making notes in response, you may want to go back to the student and ask more questions.

Here, again, is your writing assignment.

Write a paragraph in which you explain what a classmate's preferred learning style is and how this should affect his or her studying techniques in college.

Notice that this assignment has two parts:

- What is the student's learning style?
- How will this affect his or her studying techniques in college?

Considering what you've learned about learning styles and your classmate, write freely for 15 minutes or more. Let your thoughts flow freely. Think about the student's current habits and the student's future.

Drafting

Experiment with topic sentences until you create one that answers *all* of the writing assignment. There is room for creativity here.

- You may choose to focus on this student and his or her current class load, or you may choose to focus on the classes this student intends to take in the future.
- On the other hand, you may want to make a statement about how well he or she is using the preferred learning style.
- Or you may want to write your paragraph as a recommendation paragraph in which you outline changes the student should make in his or her study habits.

Here is one caution: Stick with the topic of learning style and how that learning style affects studying habits. Don't wander off into other topics that are related to studying but not to learning styles. For example, the amount of time spent studying and the location for the studying can affect how well a student does in his or her classes. However, these issues don't necessarily connect to learning styles, so information on these topics probably would not fit in this paragraph.

Notes

Revising

Share your paragraph with a classmate, tutor, or your instructor. Consider these questions:

- Does the topic sentence focus on the writing assignment? Does it answer all of the writing assignment? A topic sentence that announces the student's name and learning style is not answering *all* of the prompt.
- Are there some interesting, specific examples or recommendations in the body of the paragraph?
- Does the writer stay focused on issues directly relating to learning styles?

Review your Evaluation Chart (p. 453) and consider what your instructor said about previous writing assignments.

Revise your paragraph as necessary.

Skill Spotlight

Remembering Your Audience

The writing you do in college will be written to an academic audience. That is, you should imagine a group of college students and instructors as your audience. Many writing instructors will ask that you introduce and explain your topic in such a way that students and instructors from other classes will understand what you are writing about. This means you must give some background information on your topic.

With this interview and report assignment, you should keep in mind that not everyone knows who Barsch is, or what the words *visual, auditory, tactile,* and *kinesthetic* mean. You will have to give a little background information to help your audience.

Since you are writing a paragraph, you do not have much space for long explanations. You'll need to look for places where you can add a few words of explanation.

Consider this topic sentence:

According to the Barsch test, Stephen is a kinesthetic learner, and he'll need to be creative to make good use of this learning style in his college courses.

This is a good topic sentence because

- It tells what Stephen's learning style is.

Continued

- It tells the reader that the writer will be discussing how Stephen can use his learning style in college.

When revising, this writer could make this a great topic sentence by showing he is aware of his audience. "Barsch test" probably won't mean much to the audience, and using just the first name Stephen might seem too informal. Here's a revised topic sentence:

> According to the Jeffrey Barsch EdD "Learning Style Inventory," Stephen Jones is a kinesthetic learner, and he'll need to be creative to make good use of this learning style in his college courses.

Though the audience may not know who Jeffrey Barsch is, the audience will know that he has a PhD in Education (because of the EdD next to his name), which will make Barsch seem more believable. In addition, the audience can look up further information using the other clues the writer gave: first name (Jeffrey) and "Learning Style Inventory." Also, the audience feels better informed to know the first and last name of the student. From this point on, the writer can refer to the student as Stephen or Jones or Mr. Jones.

In the next sentence or two, the writer will need to explain the word *kinesthetic* for the audience. This explanation does not need to be long. Something like this might work:

> A kinesthetic learner is a person who learns best through physical movement. Such a person might use flash cards or make models while studying. In Stephen's case. . . .

Now the writer could focus on what Stephen's classes are (and will be) and how he can adapt his learning style to those classes. This is where the writer will get specific—naming classes like "Introduction to Biology" and "American History." Note that saying "Biology 10" might not be helpful to the audience. The audience might wonder "What is Biology 10?"

As you revise your paragraph, think about your audience. Picture yourself speaking to them. What questions would they have for you?

Editing

Consider what types of errors you tend to make and look for these errors. (Look at your Tracking Sentence Errors Chart p. 452.) Also consider what you've been most recently studying in your sentence exercises. How can you put your knowledge into action?

Taking Notes

This chapter focuses on one very important study skill: taking notes. You will review the difficulties of taking notes, and then you'll consider some ways to overcome these difficulties.

    This chapter covers the following topics:

◆ Taking good notes is a challenge
◆ Strategy #1: Get prepared
◆ Strategy #2: Focus on the main points
◆ Strategy #3: Review your notes
◆ A presentation assignment

Notes

Taking Good Notes Is a Challenge

School, from the earliest grades through college, requires you to do a lot of listening. In some classes, you may also read, discuss, create models, work on the computer, or do experiments. However, instructors must rely on speaking as a primary method of giving information, and you, the student, must listen efficiently. Of course, people do not remember everything they hear, just as they do not remember everything they read. So students need to take good notes.

    Taking good notes draws on your skills as a reader and your ability to identify the main points. You cannot and should not write down every word the speaker says. Your goal, instead, is to record the main points. This is a challenging task, for several reasons:

• You must concentrate. If your mind wanders off, you cannot push a replay button or refer to an earlier page.

• In addition, your mind thinks faster than people speak, so it is easy to let your mind wander.

• Finally, you probably write slower than most people talk.

    So when you are taking lecture notes you must concentrate, resist the urge to wander off mentally, and do your best to write useful notes quickly. Wow. That could be tough. But there are some strategies you can use to make this job easier (and, as with other skills, practice will help you improve your note-taking skills.)

The rest of this chapter focuses on taking good notes during lectures. Most of the suggestions presented here can also be applied to taking notes during speeches, interviews, and discussions.

Notes

Strategy #1: Get Prepared

With the reading and writing processes, you have preparation steps that help you perform well. Taking good notes also requires some preparation.

You must get your mind ready to accept new information. If your mind is ready, you will understand more during the lecture, and you will find it easier to focus on and record the main ideas.

First, take a few minutes before the lecture to think about your current topic, what you covered in the last class meeting, and what you are reading about. In fact, you should review the course syllabus and then the previous reading by looking at titles, subtitles, your margin notes, highlighted words, and so on.

Then you can preview the next reading by looking at titles, subtitles, introductory paragraphs, and topic sentences. Also look at your previous lecture notes. What was covered in your last lecture and class discussion?

Then, as with the reading process, anticipate what your instructor might be covering this time. What will he or she talk about? What will be emphasized? What assignments might be given?

Of course, you will want to come to class with all of your class materials. You should also sit where there will be few distractions. Do you often get distracted by other students? Is the view out of the window calling to you? Sitting in the middle or front of class is often a helpful strategy for maintaining concentration. (If you do find that you have wandered off during a lecture, don't give up. Bring your mind back, and take notes. Taking notes helps you stick with the lecturer.)

Make eye contact with the lecturer. This will help you concentrate and feel involved.

Participate when appropriate. The more active you are in the lecture, the more you will learn and remember.

Strategy #2: Focus on Main Points and Connections

As mentioned earlier, you don't need to record everything the speaker says. Good notes will focus on the main points of the lecture and perhaps a few helpful examples.

As with reading, it may be a challenge to figure out what the main points are. Here are some strategies for finding the main points in a lecture:

- Listen at the beginning of the lecture for a plan. A speaker will often give a brief outline of what he or she will be speaking about and may list main points.
- Listen for ideas and terms that are repeated. Repetition may be a sign of a main point.
- Copy down what the speaker writes on the chalkboard or on an overhead projector. These are usually main points.
- Listen for key words. The speaker may use phrases that signal main points: "most importantly," "of great significance," and so on.
- Listen for a summary or conclusion. Often a speaker will wrap up a presentation by summarizing main points or making a conclusion that brings all the information together.

Understanding how significant facts fit together is also important. Instructors will not ask you to write lists on exams. They will ask you to make sense of the pieces of information.

- Listen for transition words like *similarly, in contrast, as a result, consequently,* and so on. Words like these will tell you when one piece of information is similar to other pieces of information, if one fact shows an opposite possibility, or if one action caused another.

Keeping up with the speaker is another challenge. Consider these suggestions for writing quickly.

- You may need to use abbreviations. For example, if your history teacher says "Emancipation Proclamation," you may want to write "Emanci. Proc."
- If your instructor goes back and repeats a point, don't write it again. Circle or highlight it so that you know it's an important point.
- Don't get distracted by spelling, capitalization, or grammar. It is important to pay attention to the lecture. You can go back later and

find the correct spelling if it is necessary. Circle or underline the word for later review.

- Leave a margin so that you can add notes later. When you are reading, you use the margin to record your reactions and questions. You can do the same with your lecture notes.

Strategy #3: Review Your Notes

Being present in class to hear a lecture is important, and taking notes is important. However, because your memory will fade and lecture notes are rarely perfect, don't stop there.

Most people need to come in contact with a piece of information at least three times before they remember it. Consequently, you must *review* your notes soon after the lecture. Your memory of the lecture will still be good enough that you can add additional information and ideas, and reviewing the information again will help the main points stick in your mind.

If lecture notes are particularly important to a course, you may want to form a study group that reviews the lectures. You will benefit from hearing what other students thought were the main ideas.

Whether you review your lecture notes on your own or with a study group, you can use the blank space and the margins that you left on your lecture notes to add information and comments. You may also want to look at your textbook to see if there is information there that will clarify your notes.

Here are some points to remember about taking notes:

- Don't try to record everything the speaker says.
- Concentrate on main ideas, important facts, and helpful examples.
- Remember to pay attention to transitions, and to how the information presented fits together.
- Review your lecture notes. Learning from lectures requires that you listen, write, and review.

A Presentation Assignment

This assignment will give you an opportunity to put your note-taking skills into action. You will choose a lecture, try out the strategies mentioned in this chapter, and make a presentation to your class.

Notes

First, review this chapter so that you can use all of the strategies covered.

Here is your assignment:

Attend a lecture, applying the note-taking strategies mentioned in this chapter.

Prepare a presentation, 2–4 minutes in length, on how you applied note-taking strategies during the lecture. You will share the following information with classmates in your writing class.

- *What preparation steps did you take? Give or show examples.*
- *Where did you sit in the lecture room? Did you move from a previous seat? Was this a good idea?*
- *Did you try to make eye contact with the speaker? Was this difficult? Did you do this for the entire class?*
- *Did you participate during the lecture? Explain. Was participating uncomfortable for you? Or do you usually participate?*
- *What did you write? Show your class your lecture notes. Which of the strategies on pages 382–383 were most useful to you? Explain.*
- *What follow-up steps did you take after the lecture?*
- *What is your assessment of these note-taking strategies, in general? Can you, or will you, make them a routine? Explain.*

Skill Spotlight

Giving an Effective Oral Presentation

We have all listened to presentations that are interesting. Some even make us sit on the edge of our seats. Then again, we have all listened to presentations that are boring or confusing and make us want to sleep.

You don't have to be a brilliant professional speaker to give an effective presentation. Interesting speakers follow a few important guidelines.

- Dress nicely.
- Stand up straight and look your audience in the eye. Don't stare at just one person. Look at different individuals—make them feel that you are speaking directly to them.
- For long presentations (more than 5 minutes), move around. Don't appear to be rooted to the floor. You may also want to offer visual props for these longer presentations.

Continued

- Speak clearly and loudly. Make sure that everyone can hear you.
- Prepare for your presentation. Know what your main points and goals are. Make notes that you can refer to, but do not prepare something to read word for word. Audiences often find "reading" boring.
- Practice your presentation aloud a few times. You want to be familiar with your notes so that you can make eye contact with your audience.

In-Class Writing

Many students find in-class writing to be nerve-wracking. "Can I write well and quickly?" they ask. The answer is yes. You may not produce as good a paragraph as you would if you had two weeks to work on it at home, but everyone can learn to write competently in a timed situation.

This chapter covers the following topics:

- ✦ Timed-writing situations
- ✦ The many purposes of in-class exams
- ✦ Using the reading and writing processes
- ✦ Preparing for in-class writing
- ✦ Additional pointers
- ✦ Understanding the writing prompt
- ✦ Writing Assignment #1: An in-class paragraph
- ✦ Writing Assignment #2: An in-class paragraph
- ✦ More writing assignment prompts

Notes

Timed-Writing Situations

Consider for a moment the situations in which you may have to do a timed writing:

- In your college classes: to test your knowledge, reading, critical thinking, and writing skills
- During the written portion of a job interview
- During a test to earn a teaching credential
- At work when someone needs a report in a hurry

Writing well in these situations comes down to being able to concentrate and use your reading and writing processes effectively. This chapter reviews some strategies for writing good in-class paragraphs.

The Many Purposes of In-Class Exams

Instructors require in-class writing so that they can get a clear picture of your writing skills. Instructors want to see what you can do on your own—with no outside help from tutors, classmates, or friends. Most in-class writing situations will begin with a reading, so, in this sense, instructors are also testing your ability to read well.

The writing **prompts** will ask you to think about the reading or your previous course material and your reactions to or thoughts about the issues raised in those materials. Your instructors are testing your ability to think critically and apply your factual knowledge and life experiences. Clearly, your instructors (and employers) are not asking you to simply write grammatically correct sentences. Even in timed-writing situations, you are expected to write thoughtful, interesting material. This chapter gives you some pointers on how to write in-class paragraphs that are interesting, focused, developed, organized, and clear.

Using the Reading and Writing Processes

It might seem that a timed-writing situation calls for the writer to dive right in and hurry through the exercise. However, hurrying is the worst thing you can do.

When writers dive in with no preparation, they often wander in many different directions in the paragraph. The result is an unfocused, undeveloped, unorganized piece of writing. And it may not even answer the writing prompt.

Use the processes that you have learned in this writing course. You will have to move through your usual steps more quickly, but you should still complete each step.

If you are given a reading to consider before writing, use your reading process. Preview the piece and anticipate what the reading may be about. Read and reread the piece, marking important or intriguing parts. Look up words in the dictionary that seem important but are unclear to you. Take a moment to summarize. What is the overall main point? What are the important supporting points? Make a list of ideas.

Then follow all the steps of the writing process. Explore the writing assignment, and underline key words. Change the prompt into a question if it isn't a question already.

Freewrite. You want to explore different possible responses. Usually the first idea to pop into your head isn't the best—it's just the most obvious. Think carefully. Look at the topic from different angles. Make a list, a cluster, or just write for a few minutes.

When you have a focus in mind, create a topic sentence and take some time to plan what you will say. You want to make sure you can

Copyright © 2003 by Addison Wesley Longman, Inc.

Notes

Prompt means writing assignment.

Notes   follow your idea through from beginning to end. This may be the most important step in your writing process.

Draft your paragraph. If you have a detailed plan, you may choose to write only one draft. Or you may plan to rewrite and create a final draft. Most instructors will require you to double-space your paragraph. This is a smart move even if it is not required because it lets you easily insert a word, phrase, or sentence if you need to later.

Read your draft and revise. If you want to make some significant improvements, then you may need to rewrite your draft. If you simply have to add one more example or a transition, you might be able to insert the new information without rewriting the entire piece.

Edit your work. Though instructors realize that you probably won't do your best work in class, they do expect you to catch *most* of your own sentence errors. The errors that trouble instructors (and readers) the most are listed here.

- Verb tense errors (see Chapter 15)
- Subject-verb agreement errors (see Chapter 15)
- Fragments (see Chapter 18)
- Run-ons (see Chapter 19)
- Comma splices (see Chapter 20)
- Spelling, especially when the reader cannot tell which word you want (see Chapter 31)

Using the reading and writing processes requires time management and, sometimes, preparation before the class begins. The next few sections will give you some specific strategies.

Preparing for In-Class Writing

There are many different kinds of in-class writing situations:

Situation A: You may be given the reading ahead of time and know what the question will be.

Situation B: You may be given a reading ahead of time but not know what the question will be.

Situation C: You may be given a list of possible paragraph questions that deal with the course material for the school term.

Situation D: You may know only the general subject area.

Situation E: You may not be given anything (not a reading, a question, or even a hint of the general subject matter).

Each of these situations requires slightly different preparation.

Situation A

When you are given the reading ahead of time and know what the question will be, then your job is to follow the reading process and familiarize yourself with the reading selection at home.

Then you should follow the writing process. You'll want to write (draft, revise, and edit) a practice paragraph at home. You'll want to read over your work many times before going to class to write a fresh copy.

Situation B

When you are given a reading but not a writing prompt (a writing assignment), your preparation is a little different. You'll want to follow your reading process and familiarize yourself with the reading at home. If it is okay with your instructor, you may want to form a study group with your classmates and discuss the interesting parts of the reading.

Then, perhaps with the help of classmates, you should guess what the writing prompt might be. Make a few guesses and write out these possible writing prompts. Even if you are wrong, you will have a method of practicing your writing process and exploring ideas. So study your "pretend" prompts and freewrite, plan, and perhaps draft your answers.

Situation C

If you are not given a specific reading, you may be told that the writing prompt will relate to the information you've been studying during the school term. This is a common situation in courses like history, psychology, and sociology. In this case, you will need to review your textbook and lecture notes as you prepare.

Since you have a list of possible writing prompts in this situation, apply your writing process to each of the prompts. Reread your textbook and class materials as you think about each question. Freewrite about each prompt, and write topic sentences for each prompt. You probably won't be able to write a complete practice answer for each prompt, but you can still plan your main points and find your examples and support ahead of time.

Notes

Situation D

If you know only the general subject area, you will need to combine the strategies for situations B and C.

First create some possible writing prompts. To do this well, you should think about what your instructor has been emphasizing in class. What is your instructor most interested in? What is he or she likely to ask you? You may need to review your lecture notes to find possible patterns in what your instructor has covered or emphasized.

Once you have written out a few possible writing prompts, you will want to sketch an answer to each prompt, using your regular writing process. This will require that you review your textbook and lecture notes.

Situation E

If you are not given any information about what the writing prompt will be, you may want to prepare by writing some practice in-class paragraphs. Make your writing situation as realistic as you can (with a time limit and no interruptions). Ask your instructor if you can have one or more writing prompts from previous years. If previous prompts are not available, you can use the material later in this chapter for practice. Use your reading and writing processes.

Additional Pointers

Do you get really nervous in timed-writing situations? You can reduce your nervousness by preparing carefully and thinking positively. In the days before your timed writing, picture yourself in your classroom writing with ease. Focus on this image.

- Do your best to eliminate any complications on your test day.
- Get plenty of rest.
- Make sure you have a reliable alarm clock and method of transportation.
- Plan on being early to class.
- Purchase or gather any test materials a few days ahead of time. (You'll want to find out from your instructor if you should write in pen or pencil. Do you need an exam book? Can you use a dictionary? Are electronic dictionaries okay? If you've been given a reading ahead of time, can you bring your marked-up copy to class?)

Plan your class time. If you have 1 hour to write a paragraph, how many minutes will you spend on reading? On brainstorming, drafting, revising and editing? (You should bring your own watch.) Write out a time schedule when you are allowed to begin writing and follow this schedule. Here is a sample schedule:

A 1-Hour Paragraph
(Reading was given ahead of time, but no prompt until class time.)

10:00–10:20:	Read prompt carefully; underline key terms; freewrite; create a topic sentence; think of examples and support.
10:20–10:45:	Write paragraph.
10:45–10:55:	Reread paragraph and revise.
10:55–11:00:	Edit paragraph.

This schedule, of course, wouldn't work for all students. Some students, for example, might need to spend more than 5 minutes on editing because they tend to have a lot of serious sentence errors in their drafts.

Understanding the Writing Prompt

The first key to writing well is understanding what you are to write about. This is always true, but it is particularly challenging with in-class writing because you have no tutors or other readers to alert you if you write off topic.

When you get your writing prompt, consider it carefully. Look for key words that tell you what to do. Consider how these prompts ask for very different responses:

Discuss the different viewpoints people have on legalizing marijuana.
Argue for or against legalizing marijuana.
In "Legalize Now," John Smith argues that marijuana should be legalized now. *Compare* his arguments for legalizing marijuana to your own beliefs on this issue.

The key words in each prompt are *discuss, argue,* and *compare.* Each of these words asks you to do something specific.

Discuss (or Explain): You should consider different aspects of a single topic. You must present a balanced, fair discussion.

Notes

Argue: You must take a position. You will have been given a controversial topic, and you will need to choose a side and then defend your position.

Compare (or Compare and Contrast): You must discuss the similarities and differences between two or more subjects.

There are other kinds of writing prompts. Remember to read your instructions carefully, so that you write "on topic." Next in this chapter, you will find writing prompts that connect to the first three timed-writing situations described earlier. Your instructor may use this material for an in-class writing exam, or you may want to use this material for practice.

Writing Assignment #1: An In-Class Paragraph

This assignment fits with situation A. You will find both a reading and a writing prompt here. Follow the situation A instructions given on page 389.

Winning at All Costs Is Costing Society Too Much

By Marjie Lundstrom

Sacramento Bee
May 18, 2000

Winning isn't everything, it's the only thing.
-Vince Lombardi

1   In the culture of winning—in the do-what-it-takes, win-at-all-costs, world that we live in—some lessons are never learned.

2   Lessons about truth. About honor. About the value of shame.

3   Some people just never get it.

4   Nowhere was that more evident than in Chicago last week, where a 1995 cheating scandal was back in the headlines.

5   Five years have passed since nine students and a teacher at Chicago's Steinmetz High School—members of the Academic Decathlon team—cheated their way to victory in the state competition. Last Thursday, the teacher and some of the former teammates were reunited for a bizarre kind of celebration: the sneak preview of the movie about their lives, "Cheaters," which premieres Saturday on HBO.

6   Now if this sounds a little dated, given the recent rash of cheating scandals around standardized testing, here's the rub:

Notes

7   They aren't even sorry. Five years after they shamed their city, their school, their families and themselves, some of the former teammates have no regrets.

8   "If I had to do it all over again, the only thing I would change is getting caught," said former team member Jolie Fitch, quoted in the *Chicago Tribune.*

9   Another teammate, Tom O'Donnell, shrugged it off as the way the world works.

10   "It wasn't the first time there was cheating," he told the *New York Times,* "and it won't be the last."

11   Said Jolie: "I would do it again."

12   Brash and offensive as they sound—and foolhardy, besides—there is a disturbing truth here: This *is* the way the world often works. In our zeal to succeed—to be at the top, to get an " A," to win the big game—the rules, for many, no longer matter.

13   From big business to sports to schools, there are poster children everywhere:

*   *San Francisco Examiner* Publisher Tim White was suspended this month after testifying that he had offered Mayor Willie Brown favorable editorial coverage in exchange for the mayor's support of the *San Francisco Chronicle*'s sale to the Hearst Corp., owner of the *Examiner.*
*   Indiana University basketball coach Bob Knight was suspended this week for three games, fined $30,000 and ordered to apologize for verbally and physically abusing players and colleagues.
*   Seven Woodland teachers, accused of cheating on a standardized achievement test, last month were ordered suspended without pay. The teachers allegedly copied portions of last year's test and gave it to students for practice.

14   And these people are supposed to be role models. Is it any wonder that Jolie Fitch—and 30 freshman engineering students at Boston's Northeastern University, accused last month of "cyber-cheating"—think it's fine to do whatever it takes?

15   "The lesson being sent is that whatever works is acceptable, simply because it works. The world has moved from ethics to expediency," said ethicist Michael Josephson, founder of the Josephson Institute of Ethics in Marina del Rey. "The concept of honor is becoming more foreign to a lot of people."

16   And that includes young people, who were surveyed by the Josephson Institute about their ethics. The 1998 survey found that 7 in 10 high school students admitted to cheating on an exam in the previous

Notes

12 months; nearly half said they steal; almost all teenagers admitted to lying.

17   Curiously, 91 percent said they were satisfied with their own ethics and character. "This report card shows that the hole in our moral ozone is getting bigger," Josephson said.

18   Like the ethicist, we all have to hope the HBO movie—starring Jeff Daniels as Chicago teacher Gerard Plecki—is a constructive look back at the 1995 scandal, not one that glorifies it.

19   In its promotion, HBO promises to take "a provocative look at the moral issues raised by the 'winning is everything' mentality." Its "Cheaters—Based on a True Story" Web page lets visitors test their own ethics and sound off on ethical questions. (Not to be accused of getting too serious, the page also urges folks to vote for the most infamous cheater—Charles K. Ponzi, Milli Vanilli, Rosie Ruiz, Hugh Grant, among them—and win a trip to New York.)

20   The real life teacher, Plecki, who returned last week for the gala premiere, did confess and apologize for the first time. It was he who led the so-called "Cinderella team" to victory—a group of students from a working-class neighborhood who miraculously upset the perennial favorites from a prestigious magnet school.

21   Except it wasn't a miracle; it was a scam. Teammates had stolen a copy of the test, and Plecki—who orchestrated the cheating—pressured students to keep quiet. The secret was exposed when officials questioned the unusually high scores, and one student revealed the deception in an essay.

22   Plecki, who was paid by HBO as an adviser, no longer teaches and runs a business in Chicago.

23   Jolie Fitch, portrayed by actress Jena Malone, reportedly also had her life rights optioned and is the only student whose real name is used in the film.

24   For a woman with no regrets, Fitch does have another starring role these days: the mother of a 3-month-old boy.

25   Looks like he'll have to wait for the reruns to catch Mom in all her glory.

In-Class Writing Prompt

In the article "Winning at All Costs Is Costing Society Too Much," Marjie Lundstrom gives five specific examples of people taking immoral actions in order to win or get what they want. (She also discusses an ethics poll.) In paragraph 14, Lundstrom quotes an ethicist who says, "The world has moved from ethics to expediency."

In a paragraph, explain what that quote means and give an example to support what you say. You may use an example from Lund-

strom's article, but you must say where you found the example. Or you may use an example from your own life.

Writing Assignment #2: An In-Class Paragraph

This assignment fits situation B. Here is a reading but no prompt. Follow the situation B instructions given on page 389.

Supermom Is the Wrong Role Model

By Barbara T. Roessner

1   Everybody looks tired today. Burnt. Fried. Beat. Rings around the eyes, taut little lines around the mouth. Routine salutations in the hallways are accompanied by the kind of grim, forced smiles that scream, "I need a nap." And I know why: Everybody's a superwoman now—even the men.

2   Welcome to our world, boys. Isn't it awful? Work, kids, work, kids. Home, office, home, office. It's never done. It never ends. The twin monsters can never be satiated. No matter how much you give the job, no matter how much you give the family, it's not enough. And as for time for yourself, forget it. You're not even in the picture.

3   I've long sensed that working fathers were getting more like working moms, and the other day a batch of affirming statistics emerged.

4   A widely publicized new study by the Families and Work Institute found that over the past 20 years, working dads have steadily picked up more of the child-rearing and household duties traditionally left to working mothers. Women still do more than their fair share on the home front, but the gap is narrowing dramatically. And as a result, children are getting more attention from their parents overall.

5   The news was generally hailed as progress in the fight for gender equality. Men are stepping up as nurturers; like women, they're bringing home the bacon and frying it up in the pan. Increasingly, they're doing it all, just like us.

6   But I've got to ask, as I look around at all those hollow eyes and tight lips: Is this really a good thing? Is the superwoman model really worth emulating? Haven't we learned anything?

7   Although they've received scant attention, other stats coming out of the new study—the ones related to male and female workloads on the job—further illuminate the current epidemic of gender-neutral exhaustion. Not only are we all spending more time with the kids, the laundry

Notes

and the floor mop, we are also spending more time at the office, the factory or the shop. We're all spending less time on ourselves.

8   Employees are working 3.5 hours a week longer than they did in 1977. Over the past five years, both male and female workers note a substantial decline in their sense of job security. Meanwhile, they say they're working harder and faster. They're much more likely to bring work home than they were 20 years ago. Sixty-three percent of men and women yearn to work fewer hours; that's up 17 percent from when the question was first asked in 1992.

9   The bottom line: Everybody's working harder—on the job and on the home front. Everybody's burning the candle at both ends, and in the middle. We're working too hard. We're parenting too hard. We're fried.

10   The bottom-line question, though, is whether men should continue to become more like us, or whether we might strive to be more like them. I am toying with the latter. One Saturday this month, I spent most of the day on a golf course with a compatriot working mom—just as men have done for years.

11   "We're guys," we gleefully announced to each other and ourselves, relishing the novelty of spending a non-workday out of the house. "We are guys." And guys wouldn't go home at noon after nine holes, we reasoned. They'd go have a beer, which we did. Now there's a modus operandi worth copying.

More Writing Assignment Prompts

In this section you'll find a list of prompts as described in situation C. Follow the situation C instructions on page 389 to prepare for your in-class writing situation.

Here are the four writing assignment prompts:

1. *Review your readings from this semester. In a paragraph, explain how purpose and audience affected one author's style in writing. Use examples from one or more of your readings in this book to support your topic sentence.*

2. *In a paragraph, discuss why one author had to use writing to express himself or herself because other options were limited or did not exist.*

3. *In a paragraph, explain one of the most important things to learn in this writing class. Your audience is a student who will be taking this class in the next school term.*

4. *In a paragraph, name the reading or writing assignment you liked best in the current semester of this course. Defend your choice with examples and explanations.*

In this section you will find readings to supplement the work you do in class. Your instructor may substitute some of these readings for readings found in Chapters 6 through 11, or you may choose to use these readings to practice your reading, vocabulary, and critical thinking skills. You may also want to read these selections to learn more about a certain type of writing or topic.

THE READING SELECTIONS
Listed by Coordinating Chapter

CHAPTER 6
Diaries and Journals
+ *The Diary of a Young Girl,* by Anne Frank. This diary records a young girl's experiences while she and her family hid from the Nazis during World War II.
+ *The Freedom Writers Diary,* by The Freedom Writers, with Erin Gruwell. These diary entries are by students at a Long Beach high school in California (1994–98).

CHAPTER 7
Academic Paragraphs
+ "Don't Want to Be a Dummy Writer" (draft and final version) by Calvin Mak (student writer)
+ "Singing My Heart Out" by Cecilia Miles

CHAPTER 8
Letters and E-mail
+ "Out of Silence," by Anne LeClaire. In this letter, Anne LeClaire writes to her mother to express her complex feelings about her mother and communication in their family.
+ *Now You Know* (e-mail from an AOL website). These e-mails were sent to an AOL website after the writers saw the movie *Saving Private Ryan.* (These e-mails were published as a book called *Now You Know.* The introduction to that book is also included.)

CHAPTER 9
Autobiographies
+ *The Art of the Deal,* Chapter 3, by Donald J. Trump, with Tony Schwartz. Trump, a real estate developer and multimillionaire, discusses how he got started in this chapter of his autobiography.

CHAPTER 10
Fairy Tales
+ "Cindy Ellie: A Modern Fairy Tale," by Mary Carter Smith. This modern African American tale takes a different approach to the story of Cinderella.

CHAPTER 11
Essays: An Introduction
+ "My Vision," by Ayanna Williams. This student essay responds to "Essay Assignment: Your Dream." The writer explains her personal American dream.

Notes

Diaries and Journals

Reading Assignment—The Diary of a Young Girl

Preview Read the introductory information in brackets. Then skim through the entries, reading a few sentences on each page.

Anticipate What do you expect Frank to write about? What would most thirteen-year-old girls write about? What is special about her situation?

_____

_____

_____

_____

Read Read the diary entries. Mark unknown words, but don't look up any meanings in the dictionary yet.

The Diary of a Young Girl

By Anne Frank

[Anne Frank was a Jewish girl who lived in Holland during the German occupation of that country during World War II. She was thirteen years old when she began writing in her diary. Less than a month after starting her diary, the Frank family was forced to go into hiding to avoid being sent to German concentration camps. In her diary, Frank recorded information about the time they spent in hiding (almost 2 years.) She wrote nearly every day in her diary. The complete diary can be found in book form in most libraries. Here, you will find a few of her most memorable entries. Pay attention to the dates so that you know when many entries have been left out. Four earlier entries appear in Chapter 6; "Diaries and Journals" pp. 50–54.]

Thursday, 9 July, 1942

Dear Kitty,

1   So we walked in the pouring rain, Daddy, Mummy, and I, each with a school satchel and shopping bag filled to the brim with all kinds of things thrown together anyhow.

2   We got sympathetic looks from people on their way to work. You could see by their faces how sorry they were they couldn't offer us a lift; the gaudy yellow star spoke for itself.

3   Only when we were on the road did Mummy and Daddy begin to tell me bits and pieces about the plan. For months as many of our goods and **chattels** and necessities of life as possible had been sent away and they were sufficiently ready for us to have gone into hiding of our own accord on July 16. The plan had had to be speeded up ten days because of the call-up, so our quarters would not be so well organized, but we had to make the best of it. The hiding place itself would be in the building where Daddy has his office. It will be hard for outsiders to understand, but I shall explain that later on. Daddy didn't have many people working for him: Mr. Kraler, Koophuis, Miep, and Elli Vossen, a twenty-three-year-old typist who all knew of our arrival. Mr. Vossen, Elli's father, and two boys worked in the warehouse; they had not been told. [. . .]

Yours, Anne

Chattels means belongings.

Friday, 9 October, 1942 [3 months later]

Dear Kitty,

4   I've only got dismal and depressing news for you today. Our many Jewish friends are being taken away by the dozen. These people are treated by the Gestapo without a shred of decency, being loaded into cattle trucks and sent to Westerbork, the big Jewish camp in Drente. Westerbork sounds terrible: only one washing cubicle for a hundred people and not nearly enough lavatories. There is no separate accommodation. Men, women, and children all sleep together. One hears of frightful immorality because of this; and a lot of the women, and even girls, who stay there any length of time are expecting babies.

5   It is impossible to escape; most of the people in the camp are branded as inmates by their shaven heads and many also by their Jewish appearance.

6   If it is as bad as this in Holland whatever will it be like in the distant and barbarous regions they are sent to? We assume that most of them are murdered. The English radio speaks of their being gassed. [. . .]

Yours, Anne

Monday, 23 August, 1943 [1 year later]

Dear Kitty,

7   Continuation of the "Secret Annexe" daily timetable. As the clock strikes half past eight in the morning, Margot and Mummy are jittery:

"Ssh . . . Daddy, quiet, Otto, ssh . . . Pim." "It is half past eight, come back here, you can't run any more water; walk quietly!" These are the various cries to Daddy in the bathroom. As the clock strikes half past eight, he has to be in the living room. Not a drop of water, no lavatory, no walking about, everything quiet. As long as none of the office staff are there, everything can be heard in the warehouse. [. . .]

Yours, Anne

Wednesday, 29 March, 1944 [6 months later]

Dear Kitty,

M.P. stands for Member of Parliament.

8   Bolkestein, an **M.P.**, was speaking on the Dutch News from London, and he said that they ought to make a collection of diaries and letters after the war. Of course, they all made a rush at my diary immediately. Just imagine how interesting it would be if I were to publish a romance of the "Secret Annexe." The title alone would be enough to make people think it was a detective story.

9   But, seriously, it would seem quite funny ten years after the war if we Jews were to tell how we lived and what we ate and talked about here. Although I tell you a lot, still, even so, you only know very little of our lives. [. . .]

Yours, Anne

Tuesday, 4 April, 1944 [1 month later]

10   [. . .] And now it's all over. I must work, so as not to be a fool, to get on, to become a journalist, because that's what I want! I know that I can write, a couple of my stories are good, my descriptions of the "Secret Annexe" are humorous, there's a lot in my diary that speaks, but—whether I have real talent remains to be seen.

11   "Eva's Dream" is my best fairy tale, and the queer thing about it is that I don't know where it comes from. Quite a lot of "Cady's Life" is good too, but, on the whole, it's nothing.

12   I am the best and sharpest critic of my own work. I know myself what is and what is not well written. Anyone who doesn't write doesn't know how wonderful it is; I used to bemoan the fact that I couldn't draw at all, but now I am more than happy that I can at least write. And if I haven't any talent for writing books or newspaper articles, well, then I can always write for myself.

13   I want to get on; I can't imagine that I would have to lead the same sort of life as Mummy and Mrs. Van Daan and all the women who do their work and are then forgotten. I must have something besides a husband and children, something that I can devote myself to!

14   I want to go on living even after my death! And therefore I am grateful to God for giving me this gift, this possibility of developing myself and of writing, of expressing all that is in me.

15   I can shake off everything if I write; my sorrows disappear, my courage is reborn. But, and that is the great question, will I ever be able to write anything great, will I ever become a journalist or a writer? I hope so, oh, I hope so very much, for I can recapture everything when I write, my thoughts, my ideals and my fantasies. [. . .]

Yours, Anne

Reread Reread the diary. As you read, try to use context clues to figure out the meanings of unfamiliar words. Look up the meaning of any words that remain unclear. Use the margins to mark important and interesting points. Record any questions or comments in the margins. Mark the places where Frank discusses writing.

Vocabulary cards: Make a definition and a sentence card for the word listed here.

• *dismal*, paragraph 4

Think Critically and Summarize On another sheet of paper, answer these questions in writing.

1. As you reread the diary entries, you marked the places where Frank discusses writing. In your own words, why does Frank keep a diary? Why is the skill of writing so important to her?
2. What do you think readers might gain from reading Frank's diary? Discuss different kinds of readers—readers of different ages and interests.
3. Make a list of important events and information that Frank records in her diary.

✦ ✦ ✦

Reading Assignment—The Freedom Writers Diary

Preview Read the title, the authors' names, and the introductory information. Then quickly read a few of the paragraphs.

Anticipate What do you know about the authors? What do you expect to read about in their diary entries? What topics may come up?

_____

_____

_____

_____

Read Though the first entry by Ms. Gruwell may have some challenging vocabulary, most of the entries are written in a casual, almost conversational tone. (As you know, journals are generally casual in style and vocabulary.) Consequently, you may need to read these entries only once. If you are able to understand the entries easily, then go ahead and begin making your comments in the margins when you read for the first time.

The Freedom Writers Diary
How a Teacher and 150 Teens Used Writing to Change Themselves and the World around Them

By The Freedom Writers with Erin Gruwell

[These diary entries were written by high school students and their teacher, Ms. Gruwell. Later these entries were published in a book called *The Freedom Writers Diary.* Here is the introductory information printed on the back of their book.]

As an idealistic twenty-three-year-old English teacher at Wilson High School in Long Beach, California, Erin Gruwell confronted a room of "unteachable, at-risk" students. One day she intercepted a note with an ugly racial caricature, and angrily declared that this was precisely the sort of thing that led to the Holocaust—only to be met by uncomprehending looks. So she and her students, using the treasured books *Anne Frank: The Diary of a Young Girl* and *Zlata's Diary: A Child's Life in Sarajevo* as their guides, undertook a life-changing, eye-opening, spirit-raising odyssey against intolerance and misunderstanding. They learned to see how the events in these books paralleled their own lives, recording their thoughts and feelings in diaries and dubbing themselves the "Freedom Writers" in homage to the civil rights activists "The Freedom Riders."

With funds raised by a "Read-a-thon for Tolerance," they arranged for Miep Gies, the courageous Dutch woman who sheltered the Frank family, to visit them in California where she declared that Erin Gruwell's students were "the real heroes." Their efforts have paid off spectacularly, both in terms of recognition—appearances on "Prime Time Live" and "All Things Considered," coverage in *People* magazine, a meeting with U.S. Secretary of Education Richard Riley—and educationally. All 150 Freedom Writers have graduated from high school and are now attending college. [. . .]

[The diary writers do not give their names. Each entry (except for Ms. Gruwell's) is simply given a number. As you read, remember that the entries are written by different students. Also keep in mind that the book *The Freedom Writers Diary* has 142 entries that cover 4 years. Only 12 entries are included here. Noting how the entries are numbered will help you remember that many entries have been left out.]

Entry 1—Ms. Gruwell [freshman year, fall 1994]

Dear Diary,

1   Tomorrow morning, my journey as an English teacher officially begins. Since first impressions are so important, I wonder what my students will think about me. Will they think I'm out of touch or too preppy? Or worse yet, that I'm too young to be taken seriously? Maybe I'll have them write a journal entry describing what their expectations are of me and the class.

2   Even though I spent last year as a student teacher at Wilson High School, I'm still learning my way around the city. Long Beach is so different than the gated community I grew up in. Thanks to MTV dubbing Long Beach as the "gangsta-rap capital" with its depiction of guns and graffiti, my friends have a warped perception of the city, or LBC as the rappers refer to it. They think I should wear a bulletproof vest rather than pearls. Where I live in Newport Beach is a utopia compared to some of neighborhoods seen in a Snoop Doggy Dogg video. Still, TV tends to blow things out of proportion.

3   The school is actually located in a safe neighborhood, just a few miles from the ocean. Its location and reputation make it desirable. So much so that a lot of the students that live in what they call the "'hood" take two or three buses just to get to school every day. Students come in from every corner of the city: Rich kids from the shore sit next to poor kids from shore projects . . . there's every race, religion, and culture within the confines of the quad. But since the Rodney King riots, racial tension has spilled over into the school.

4   Due to busing and an outbreak in gang activity, Wilson's traditional white, upper-class demographics have changed radically. African Americans, Latinos, and Asians now make up the majority of the student body.

5   As a student teacher last year, I was pretty naïve. I wanted to see past color and culture, but I was immediately confronted by it when the first bell rang and a student named Sharaud sauntered in bouncing

a basketball. He was a junior, a disciplinary transfer from Wilson's crosstown rival, and his reputation preceded him. Word was that he had threatened his previous English teacher with a gun (which I later found out was only a plastic water gun, but it had all the makings of a dramatic showdown). In those first few minutes, he made it brutally clear that he hated Wilson, he hated English, and he hated me. His sole purpose was to make his "preppy" student teacher cry. Little did he know that within a month, he'd be the one crying.

6   Sharaud became the butt of a bad joke. A classmate got tired of Sharaud's antics and drew a **racial caricature** of him with huge, exaggerated lips. As the drawing made its way around the class, the other students laughed hysterically. When Sharaud saw it, he looked as if he was going to cry. For the first time, his tough façade began to crack.

> A **racial caricature** is a drawing that exaggerates specific features that people associate with a race.

7   When I got a hold of the picture, I went ballistic. "This is the type of propaganda that the Nazis used during the Holocaust," I yelled. When a student timidly asked me, "What's the Holocaust?" I was shocked.

8   I asked, "How many of you have heard of the Holocaust?" Not a single person raised his hand. Then I asked, "How many of you have been shot at?" Nearly every hand went up.

9   I immediately decided to throw out my **meticulously** planned lessons and make tolerance the core of my curriculum.

> **Meticulously** means very carefully.

10   From that moment on, I would try to bring history to life by using new books, inviting guest speakers, and going on field trips. Since I was just a student teacher, I had no budget for my schemes. So, I moonlighted as a **concierge** at the Marriott Hotel and sold lingerie at Nordstrom. My dad even asked me, "Why can't you just be a normal teacher?"

> A **concierge** is a person who helps hotel guests with their questions, complaints, mail, and so on.

11   Actually, normalcy didn't seem so bad after my first snafu. I took my students to see *Schindler's List* in Newport Beach, at a predominately white, upper-class theater. I was shocked to see women grab their pearls and clutch their purses in fear. A local paper ran a front-page article about the incident, describing how poorly my students were treated, after which I received death threats. One of my disgruntled neighbors had the **audacity** to say, "If you love black people so much, why don't you just marry a monkey?"

> **Audacity** is nerve or confidence, with a sense of rudeness and insensitivity.

12   All this drama and I didn't even have my teaching credentials yet. Luckily, some of my professors from University of California-Irvine read the article and invited my class to a seminar by the author of *Schindler's List*, Thomas Keneally. Keneally was so impressed by my students that a few days later we got an invitation to meet Steven Spielberg at Universal Studios. I couldn't believe it! The famous director wanted to meet the class that I had dubbed "as colorful as a box of Crayola crayons" and their "rookie teacher who was causing waves." He marveled at how far

these "unteachable" students had come as a junior class and what a close group they had become. He even asked Sharaud what "we" were planning to do next year as an encore. After all, if a film does well, you make a sequel—if a class surpasses everyone's expectations, you . . .

13 . . . dismantle it! Yep, that's exactly what happened. Upon my return from Universal, the head of the English department told me, "You're making us look bad." Talk about bursting my bubble! How was I making them look bad! After all, these were the same kids that "wouldn't last a month" or "were too stupid" to read advanced placement books.

14 She went on to say, "Things are based on seniority around here." So, in other words, I was lucky to have a job, and keeping Sharaud and his posse another year would be pushing the envelope. Instead, I'd be teaching freshmen—"at risk" freshmen. Hmm . . . not exactly the assignment I was hoping for.

15 So, starting tomorrow, it's back to the drawing board. But I'm convinced that if Sharaud could change, then anyone can. So basically, I should prepare myself for a roomful of Sharauds. If it took a month to win Sharaud over . . . I wonder how long it's gonna take a bunch of feisty fourteen-year-olds to come around?

Diary 2 [freshman year, fall 1994]

Dear Diary,

16 What the h— am I doing in *here*? I'm the only white person in this English class! I'm sitting in the corner of this classroom (if that's what you want to call this chaos), looking at my schedule and thinking, "Is this really where I'm supposed to be?" Okay, I know in high school I'm supposed to meet all kinds of different people, but this isn't exactly what I had in mind. Just my luck, I'm stuck in a classroom full of troubled kids who are bused in from bad neighborhoods. I feel really uncomfortable in here with all these rejects. There aren't even enough seats. My teacher, Ms. Gruwell, is young and determined, but this class is out of control and I bet she won't last very long.

17 This school is just asking for trouble when they put all these kids in the same class. It's a disaster waiting to happen.

18 I had lunch before class in the high school quad and noticed that, like everywhere else, it was really separated by race. Each race has its own section and nobody mixes. Everyone, including me, eats lunch with their own kind, and that's that. There is a section known as "Beverly Hills" or "Disneyland" where all of the rich white kids hang out. Then there's "China Town" where the Asians hang. The Hispanic section

Did students at your middle school or high school divide themselves this way?

Notes

is referred to as either "Tijuana Town" or "Run to the Border." The Black section is known as "Da Ghetto." Then there's the freak show in the middle of the quad that's reserved for the druggies, also called "Tweakers," and the kids who are into the Goth scene. From what's going on around me, it's obvious that the divisions in the quad carry into the classroom. [. . .]

Diary 15 [freshman year, spring 1995]

Dear Diary,

19   Ms. Gruwell's always trying to give meaning to everything. Like today, we were supposed to read this play, *Romeo and Juliet,* by some guy who talks funny—"thou" this, and "thee" that—and out of nowhere, she busts out with, "The Capulets are like the Latino gang, and the Montagues are like the Asian gang." What? One minute, we're reading about a guy named Mercutio getting killed, and she sets us up with the question "Do you think this family feud is stupid?" Like a dumb-a—, I took the bait and said, "H—, yeah!" After all, they were biting their thumbs and waving their wanna-be swords. Then she couldn't leave it alone. The next thing I know, she's comparing these two families to rival gangs in this city. [. . .]

20   I didn't think she knew about all the s— that happened up in Long Beach. I just thought she left school and drove home to her perfect life. After all, what's it to her? All of a sudden she questioned things that had never crossed our minds before. Did we think it was stupid that the Latino gang and the Asian gang are killing each other? I immediately said "No!"

21   "Why?"

22   "Because it's different."

23   "How?" This woman just wouldn't give up!

24   "It just *is*!" I didn't want to look stupid in front of everybody. But the more I thought about it, I realized it *is* stupid.

25   It's stupid because I don't even remember why we're rivals. That's just the way it is. [. . .] She always tries to corner you into accepting that there's another side, when there really isn't. I don't even remember how the whole thing got started, but it's obvious that if you're from one family, you need to be loyal and try to get some payback. Just like it's obvious that if you're from a Latino gang you don't get along with the Asian gang, and if you're from the Asian gang, you don't get along with the Latino gang. All this rivalry is more of a tradition. Who cares about the history behind it? Who cares about any kind of history? It's just two sides who tripped on each other way back

Notes

when and to this day make other people suffer because of their problems. Then I realized she was right, it's exactly like that stupid play. So our reasons might be stupid, but it's still going on, and who am I to try to change things?

Diary 42 [sophomore year, spring 1996]

Dear Diary,

26   To a fifteen-year-old, the only heroes I ever read about ran around in tight, colorful underwear and threw buildings at each other for fun. But today, that all changed. A true hero leapt off the pages of a book to pay my class a special visit. Her name is Miep Gies and she is the lady Anne Frank wrote about in her diary. I can't believe that the woman responsible for keeping Anne Frank alive in the attic came to speak to us in person!

Who is Anne Frank?

27   As I entered the Bruin Den teen center, I could feel the excitement. Many of us stayed after school yesterday to make welcome signs to decorate the walls and several students got to school really early to help set up a big buffet. We wanted everything to be perfect.

28   After the proper introductions were made by Ms. Gruwell, she made her entrance. Everybody stood up and cheered as Miep made her way into the hall. I was thrilled to see her in person after seeing her portrayed in movies and reading about her in the book. No colorful underwear needed—she was a true hero.

29   After she settled in, Miep began to talk about how she was delighted to meet us. She described to us firsthand how she hid the Frank family from the Nazi soldiers and how she found Anne's diary. When she described how the Gestapo captured Anne and would not allow Miep to say good-bye, it make all of us emotional. She told us about how she tried to bribe the officers into letting her friends go, but they threatened to kill her.

30   My friend who was sitting next to me was crying. Since we've been studying the Holocaust, it has made him think about all the people he knows who have been killed. His best friend accidentally shot himself, and to this day, he still has nightmares about his death. Miep told everyone that not a day goes by where she doesn't think about Anne.

31   When she said this, my friend stood up and told her she was his hero. Then he asked her if she believed that she was a hero. We expected her to say yes, but I think she surprised us all. She said, "No. You, my friends, are the true heroes." Heroes? Us? Having her say that made me realize more than ever how special my classmates are. [. . .]

Notes

Diary 75 [junior year, spring 1997]

Dear Diary,

Who is Rosa Parks?

32   I feel like I finally have a purpose in this class and in life.

33   That purpose is to make a difference and stand up for a cause.

34   Ms. G. showed us a video during Black History Month, about a group of Civil Rights activists, in the 1960s, who were inspired by Rosa Parks. They decided to challenge segregation in the South. Rather than boycott buses, they took their challenge a step farther. They integrated their bus and traveled from Washington D.C., through the deep South.

35   There were seven whites and six blacks on the bus, most of them college students. The were called the Freedom Riders, and their goal was to change segregated interstate travel, along with everyone's life forever. [. . .]

36   At the end of the video, a fellow classmate asked the question, "They fought racism by riding the bus?" That was it! The bells were ringing, the sirens were sounding. It hit me! The Freedom Riders fought intolerance by riding a bus and pushing racial limits in the deep South. Then somebody suggested that we name ourselves the Freedom Writers, in honor of the Freedom Riders. [. . .]

Diary 107 [senior year, fall 1997]

Dear Diary,

37   Today at Butler Elementary School, the Freedom Writers mentored the kids. I feel so happy right now because we made a difference that will probably change some lives. These children are like lotus plants. A lotus flower doesn't grow in a swimming pool, but grows in a muddy pond. It lives in a dirty environment, but amid the muddy pond lies a beautiful flower emerging from the water. I hope with guidance, these kids can become as beautiful as the lotus flower.

38   Butler is located by the most dangerous, gang-infested park in Long Beach. In the past there have been shootings, drug dealings, and other illegal activities. . . . Most of these children live near the school and have witnessed a drive-by shooting by the age of ten.

39   One of the teachers from Butler read an article about the Freedom Writers in the *Los Angeles Times*. The article was inspiring and many teachers throughout the country responded by inviting us to speak at their schools. [. . .]

40   There we were in an auditorium in front of an audience of fifty kids. There were kids from every ethnic background [. . .].Today we were given the torch to carry our message of tolerance and education to

these kids. To start off the assembly we presented a video documentary of the Freedom Writers in Washington, D.C. After the video we answered their questions [. . .]. Later on we played an icebreaker game. The kids were on one side of the room and we were on the other, and down the center was a white line that divided us. Each one of the Freedom Writers had to go down the line and read a sentence from a piece of paper. Some of the questions asked were, "Who's wearing a green shirt?" or "Does anybody know what they want to do in the future?" If any of the questions applied to them, then they would have to stand on the white line. As we got toward the end there were some personal questions. We asked them, "Has anybody seen someone get shot before?" Almost everyone stepped on the white line. At that moment we decided to share some of our personal experiences with the kids.

41   One Freedom Writer told about his experience of being in a gang and living on the street. Another person shared his experience of quitting school and realizing that life isn't a fantasy world. [. . .]By the end of the day, all of the children were declaring that they would become "doctors, lawyers, and teachers!" but they also promised to come back to the community they lived in to fix the problems. We gave them hugs and words of encouragement to hold on to their dreams and goals and to always soar high.

42   It's amazing. I remember when we got back from Washington, D.C., Ms. G said that kids will think of us as heroes and will want to become Freedom Writers, too. We laughed at Ms. G's analogy, and did not take her seriously. We have come to learn not to doubt Ms. G.

Diary 108 [senior year, fall 1997]

Dear Diary,

43   I didn't realize writing was so hard. It's very tedious and overwhelming, but satisfying at the same time. The writing assignments I do for Ms. G's class require draft after draft until everything is perfect. I can't begin to imagine how hard Nancy Wride has it when she goes through everything over and over to finish a story. That is what she does, she tried to make her work perfect for the *Los Angeles Times*.

44   Nancy Wride is a wonderful reporter who just wrote a story about us. [. . .] She makes sure that what we say is reported accurately word for word in the newspaper.

45   When Nancy's story was published, it felt as if the entire world had read it and then decided to call Room 203. We've had to assign a student to act as receptionist in each class period. We've been receiving so

much mail from people all across the country, and we have no idea what to do with it all; the donations for our college fund are amazing and quite touching. People have thanked us for the work we have done in educating others and ourselves. [. . .]

Reread If you were unsure about some of the vocabulary words, go back and reread those sections to see if you can use context clues to the guess the meaning. You may also want to go back and reread any entries that seemed particularly interesting to you.

Vocabulary cards: Make definition and sentence cards for the words listed here.

- *utopia,* paragraph 2
- *naïve,* paragraph 5
- *façade,* paragraph 6
- *propaganda,* paragraph 7
- *timidly,* paragraph 7

Think Critically and Summarize Answer these questions on a separate piece of paper.

1. When these students begin the school year, they have similar attitudes and beliefs. What are some of these attitudes and beliefs?
2. What are the main topics, events, and people that are mentioned in these entries? Make a list.
3. As the years go by and Ms. Gruwell exposes the students to history lessons, literature, field trips, and guest speakers, their attitudes and visions of the world change. When do you see important signs of change in these diary entries? Explain in your own words and give paragraph numbers.
4. Which entry interested you most? Why?
5. In your own words, state what you think is the message of the Freedom Writers.

Academic Paragraphs

Reading Assignment—"Don't Want to Be a Dummy Writer" (Draft and Final Version)

Preview First you will read a draft of student Calvin Mak's paragraph. Read the title and the first three sentences.

Anticipate What do you expect to find in this draft? What do drafts often have?

_____

_____

_____

_____

Read Read this paragraph once and read the instructor's comments. Then read the final version.

"Don't Want to Be a Dummy Writer" (Draft)

By Calvin Mak

One of my writing goal is I can write an effective paragraph, because writting is an important elements to be suceed in college. If you want to write an effective paragraph, you must make sure that you can write a paragarph that is interesting, focused, developed, and organized. Even though is not enough, because you should know a paragraphs include topic sentence, body, purpose and wrap-up sentence. I know that my writhing is very boring, because i always used the same word in every sentences. So I need to learn more adjective to make the paragraphs more interesting. I hate to read a boring articles, that's why i don't like to write a boring articles too. To write an interesting paragraphs, just a part i want to learn. In addition, focused is also important, i always write somethings doesn't connect to main idea. That will make the reader very confused; what are you writing? After that i find out, we must stick to our main idea and leave out everything doesn't connect to the topic sentence. Another things is, when we got different kind of informations we should have a good organization and analysis to choose what informations we need. After that is developed. This is the weak part of me, because i can't find a way to explained and supported my main idea. The best way is to look back our informations and brainstorm. I'm sure that if my writing is honest and finished the steps i mentioned, my writhing will be effective.

Here are the instructor's comments:

Calvin, there's a lot of good information here. In fact, there's too much!

Notes

The topic sentence is too broad. Narrow your focus.

Choose a goal—one that you can develop into a full paragraph. Think about using examples.

Once you have a more focused, developed draft, you'll have to edit carefully. Areas to pay attention to: verb tense, plural versus singular word forms, subject-verb agreement.

Here is the final version:

Don't Want to Be a Dummy Writer (Final Version)

By Calvin Mak

One of my most important writing goals in this semester is learning to make my writing interesting and thoughtful. Every time when I'm writing the paragraphs, I always use the same patterns and the same words which make my writing boring and give me little confidence to write more paragraphs. For example, I always use the word "always" as an adjective. In addition, I use a subject followed by a verb for my pattern. For instance, I like the sentence "Don't give up on free writing after one exercise." I believe to be successful, I need to read more articles and write more paragraphs. I think this is the best way to improve my boring writing skill. I'm sure that I can write an interesting and thoughtful paragraph after this semester.

Reread   Reread the final draft and mark the sentences you like best.

Think Critically and Summarize   Answer these questions on a separate piece of paper.

1. How many goals does Mak mention in his draft? Highlight them.
2. When he revises, what does he do? What is the main point of his final draft?
3. Would you call his final draft well developed? Explain.
4. Does the paragraph have a wrap-up sentence?
5. Do you think Mak needs to do anything else with this piece? If so, what?

✦   ✦   ✦

Reading Assignment—"Singing My Heart Out"

Preview   Read the title, the author's name, and the topic sentence.

Anticipate What do you expect to read about? What ideas and feelings might be mentioned?

_____

_____

_____

_____

Read Read the paragraph.

Singing My Heart Out

By Cecelia Miles

Now and then, I express myself through song. I don't know if I have a good voice or not, but I love to sing. I discovered this after my children were born and I began singing to them. One time when two of my kids were real little, and they were both crying loudly, I began singing. Since they were so loud, I sang this lullaby louder and louder. Pretty soon they were quiet and I was belting out this lullaby and really enjoying myself. From then on, I began to sing to them at night, and I can feel myself lift right out of my own body as I sing about sleep and love and children. At those times, I am filled with love, and I am able to express all those tender thoughts for my kids through my songs.

Reread Reread the paragraph. Underline the topic sentence and the parts of the paragraph that you like best. Make notes in the margins about any areas you would change or improve.

Vocabulary cards: Make a definition and a sentence card for the word listed here.

• *belting*

Think Critically and Summarize Answer these questions on a separate piece of paper.

1. What complements would you give to Miles?

2. What suggestions might you give her about making her paragraph stronger?

3. Do you enjoy singing, dancing, art, photography, making music? In what ways are your interests similar to those of Miles?

Letters and E-mail

Reading Assignment—"Out of Silence"

Preview This letter comes from a book of letters. The editor of the book asked women writers to write letters to their moms. Read the biographical information that comes before the letter, the title, and the first few paragraphs of the letter.

Anticipate What kinds of moods and emotions do you think you'll find in the letter? What might LeClaire write about? Make specific guesses.

_____

_____

_____

_____

_____

Read Read the letter quickly. Mark unknown words, but don't look up any meanings in the dictionary yet.

Anne D. LeClaire was born in Ware, Massachusetts, in 1942, and educated at the MacDuffie School in Springfield, Massachusetts, and at Miami University in Oxford, Ohio. The mother of two children, she is married to Hillary LeClaire and lives on Cape Cod. A news reporter and op-ed columnist before turning to fiction, she is the author of four novels, the most recent of which are *Grace Point* (1992) and *Sideshow* (1994).

Louise E. Dickinson was born in Chelsea, Massachusetts, in 1915. A classically trained pianist, she was educated at the New England Conservatory and Perry Normal School. She was a teacher for 30 years. The mother of three daughters, she has nine grandchildren and eight great-grandchildren. She is now retired and lives on Cape Cod.

Out of Silence

Dear Mom,

1   You taught me to be silent.

2   And so the idea of writing anything about you—about us—immobilizes me. I encounter a writer's block stonier, blacker than any I have ever known. What words, I wonder, could I write to you that could fill me with such terror and so numb my mind?

3   Reason evaporates.

4   You taught me to be silent.

5   Days pass. Twice, I approach the computer, stumble into beginnings. Needing to be authentic, I struggle with truth, not pretty, but real. I write of anger. Of shame, confusion, and guilt. Of the regret and sorrow that **permeates** my relationship with you. I write of the misunderstandings and judgments that long clouded my perception of you. I write of growing older, raising a family, working through disappointments, all of which brought me closer to understanding you. But I cannot finish. I turn off the machine. Nothing is saved in the file.

> **Permeates** means to spread through and fill.

6   Another effort. This time I write of love, of my admiration for you, of my fierce gratitude and pride. I write of your formidable courage and strength, your beauty, your music, your sense of adventure. I write of healing and forgiveness. Again I stop. Even to record love feels forbidden. So anxious I feel ill, I erase everything from the screen.

7   Both of these attempts are true—or a melding of them—but another truth is stronger.

8   You taught me to be silent.

9   This was a lesson of my childhood and I am stunned to discover that even now, at a remove of many years, it still holds power, still rises from my gut, bringing fear. I thought I was finished with that, with having to push through.

> How does your family deal with problems?

10   "We're not like some of those families, like Italians," you said years ago, "families who scream horrible things at each other, things no one can ever forgive or forget." Obediently, I learned to curb my words lest they be unforgettable. Unforgivable.

11   By your example, the scholarship of your silence, I learned it was not safe to speak. Early I discovered, as you did before me, that to give voice to emotions, to tell the story of our family, was taboo, a lesson **perpetuated** by more than one generation of womanhood. Was this impulse born of a desire to protect and shield? Or a belief that there was safety in being invisible?

> **Perpetuated** means continued.

Notes

12   Gradually, year after year, pressing against the prohibited, I found my way out, encountered courage, discovered my voice. What did not feel safe to say aloud, I spilled onto paper.

13   The constraint—we must not give voice to love, to hate, to anger, to history—all this gave me something to push against and that's how we get born.

14   Out of pain comes life. And love. And passion.

15   You taught me to be silent. I learned to write.

Love, Anne

Reread Reread the letter. As you read, try to use context clues to figure out the meanings of unknown words. Also make guesses about replacement words for unknown words. Look up the meanings of any words that remain unclear. Mark important and interesting points. In addition to answering the question printed in the margin, record your own questions and your responses to the reading in the margins.

Vocabulary cards: Make definition and sentence cards for the words listed here.

- *formidable*, paragraph 6
- *curb*, paragraph 10

Think Critically In preparation for class discussion, be sure that you mark the text as suggested earlier. Also answer these questions in writing.

1. LeClaire seems to have mixed feelings about her mom. What are some of these feelings?
2. How did her mom play a role in LeClaire becoming a writer?
3. Why do you think LeClaire wrote this letter? Does she expect her mom to read it? She knows other people will read it. What do you think she hopes readers will get from her letter?

Summarize What main points would LeClaire want you to remember from her letter?

✦　✦　✦

Reading Assignment—Now You Know

Preview Read the title and the author's name. Since this piece has an introduction, use it as a preview tool. Read the introduction and then each of the major headings that follow.

Anticipate What will these e-mails be about? What ideas, concerns, issues, and feelings might be mentioned?

Notes

_____

_____

_____

_____

Read Read the four e-mails.

Now You Know

Compiled by America Online and DreamWorks
Edited by Jesse Kornbluth and Linda Sunshine

Introduction

1   Most major films get so much pre-release media coverage that by the
time they reach theaters you feel as if you've already seen them.
Steven Spielberg wanted *Saving Private Ryan* to be different. He
wanted it to be a pure and unexpected emotional experience, unaf-
fected by pre-release publicity. So for most of America, Spielberg's
film was very much like D-Day itself—towering, dramatic, and a near-
total surprise.

2   At America Online, we knew in advance that Spielberg had a big
new movie coming out. But no one at AOL knew just how powerful it
was until a picture-and-text book, *Saving Private Ryan: The Men, The Mission, The Movie* was delivered to us about ten days before the film
opened.

3   Looking at the pictures taken from the film was like stepping back
into time behind a photographer's lens on D-Day. There was one picture
of a soldier—an actor—being literally blown off his feet. The image was
so powerful and so real that it gave you the chills to look at it.

4   From the moment we got that book, it was clear that *Saving Private
Ryan* wasn't going to be just a film—it was going to be a profound and
personal experience for millions of Americans. More important, it was
clear that watching it would be only part of that experience. Afterward,
people were going to want to discuss it.

Notes

Cajole means to
encourage someone
with flattery or
soothing language.

5   That's where we knew AOL could play an important role. Every day, millions of AOL members come online to meet and talk, to exchange information and make friends, to laugh and yell and debate and **cajole.**

6   That daily dialogue has grown to astonishing proportions. On a typical day, AOL members now exchange nearly 50 million individual e-mails and a whopping 400 million Instant Messages. They take part in so many chat rooms and message boards that we need a small army of 14,000 volunteers just to keep track.

7   The day that *Saving Private Ryan* opened, we launched a special section of AOL devoted to the movie. Created by Jesse Kornbluth, AOL's Editorial Director of Channel Programming, the *Saving Private Ryan* area had links to reviews of the film, to historical accounts of D-Day, and to books about World War II. But the most significant link was to a message board about the film—and about that war.

8   "What soldiers have seen, others cannot imagine," was the introduction at the top of that message board. "*Saving Private Ryan* may spark an outpouring of painful, moving memories about war. We invite you to share them here."

9   And share our members did. That first weekend, you could visit that message board, note the number of messages posted there, go away and immediately return—and find a hundred new messages. All weekend, the messages came like that: in waves. You could almost picture our members stumbling out of the theaters and, with their eyes still damp and their emotions still raw, logging on to AOL to share their memories and feelings.

10   These messages were stunning in their intimacy. Children of veterans wrote to say how sad they were that their fathers had never spoken of the war—but now they understood why. Other children of veterans wrote to say they had seen the film with their fathers and had wept together. Some wrote to thank veterans for heroism on a scale they could hardly imagine, to wonder if today's young men could rise to such a challenge, or to ask if war could ever be stopped.

11   Five thousand messages, ten thousand, fifteen thousand. Within days, the *Saving Private Ryan* message board had become the center of a national conversation about this film and about war in general. Newspapers wrote about this phenomenon and what AOL members were sharing. That public exposure led to even more messages—and to this book.

12   In the end, about 30,000 AOL members posted their thoughts and opinions, their memories and emotions on the *Saving Private Ryan* message board. We've chosen a representative sampling of their posts here. To read them in one sitting is an intense and emotional experience.

13   I hope you will be as moved by the power and insight of what our members wrote as I was. And I also hope you will share my excitement

about how they have used our extraordinary interactive medium to share, to understand, and to grow. For both reasons, I'm immensely proud of this book and very grateful to the AOL members who are its true authors.

Notes

—Steve Case
Chairman and CEO, America Online
February, 1999

(E-mail messages from four different people.)

A father lost . . . a father found . . . (e-mail #1, p. 28)

14   My father was killed in World War II in 1945 when I was only 18 months old. His plane was shot down by a Japanese warship in the Pacific, and although I had a few snapshots and one treasured portrait of him in his flying uniform, I really never knew this man who helped bring me into the world. He was an idealized, almost mythic figure to me, and I accepted, as children do, the fact that I had no father.

15   My mother remarried in 1950, and my stepfather, who had been in the Navy at Pearl Harbor when it was bombed, was now in the Army. He was stationed in Germany starting in 1953, and there I saw, at the impressionable age of 10 years, bombed-out cities and people living in ruins. The war became real to me.

16   My stepfather had lost a brother in the D-Day invasion, so he very much wanted to go the cemetery at Omaha Beach to find his grave. We went, and to this day I can remember the sights, sounds, and feelings that overwhelmed me as we walked. I had seen war pictures and knew of the terrible battle that occurred during the invasion, but that day it was a silent, peaceful place . . . clear blue sky with a gentle breeze off the water. The rows and rows and rows of white crosses went on forever in every direction—I was stunned by that sight more than any pictures of the battle. It seemed there was now an army of white crosses forever guarding this coastline of France from any assaults on freedom ever again.

17   More than any ruins or museums or pictures I have ever seen, that sight had the greatest impact of the losses of lives that occurred—not just at that spot,

but during that whole, hellish war. I grew up with the greatest respect for my father and stepfather and all those men like them who went through such unimaginable horrors.

18 Thirty-five years later my husband and I went to Hawaii, and I had learned of the Punchbowl Cemetery in Honolulu and wanted to go there. It, too, seemed to be almost otherworldly in beauty and peace, and there was a simple but majestic monument to the servicemen who died in the Pacific during WWII. I was shaking with emotion as I saw the large columns with names engraved on them. Suddenly I found myself looking at my father's name and at that sight, there overlooking the Pacific where he died, I broke down and wept and wept for the father I had found at last. He had lived, and died so very young, but he was remembered.

19 "Saving Private Ryan" reminds us we must NEVER stop remembering them all and what they went through for all of us.

Response to: A father lost . . . a father found . . . (e-mail #2, p. 29)

20 I'm sorry you never knew your dad. But now, perhaps, you know how brave he was. And that others recognize his sacrifice. My dad made it out alive. He, too, was just a kid, when he crawled up on that red sand. An innocent boy who lived a lifetime of horror in just a few months. An angel sat upon his shoulder and carried him through two more major battles in France.

21 He came back home, met and married my Mom, and went on to a 30-year career in the Air Force. I remember seeing the shrapnel wounds on his old head (he wore a military crew cut). I never asked why they were there. We all lived our **idyllic** existence, totally unaware of what he had gone through.

Idyllic means simple and pleasant.

22 He didn't have the support groups that Vietnam Vets have now . . . he just went on and lived his life and put those vicious memories away somewhere. I'm sure they revisited him at times when he least expected. He didn't whine or complain, my dad. It pains me to know what horrors were swirling around in his battle-scarred head.

23   When I was a teenager, I remember thinking how clueless he was. After this movie, I can tell you: He is more man than anybody I know. He is 75 now, gray, and has grown smaller, now, and he totters. It is hard to imagine him, young, strong, and scared to death as he belly-crawled through the gore.

24   He has never talked about this experience in his life, but now I feel compelled to sit down with him and **prod** him. Gently, though, for I don't want to disturb the bad place inside him where the beastly sights, sounds, and smell lurk. I will love and honor my Dad, and in doing this, your Dad is honored.

Notes

Prod means encourage, urge.

25   God bless you and your family. You all paid a terrible price, but you can be proud of your Dad. I'm glad you found him and I know he felt your presence. I'm 44, and I thought I was pretty seasoned—how wrong I was. I'm still learning about life and death on this earth of ours, and the ghosts that **traverse** it.

Traverse means to travel across.

Why is this film important? (e-mail #3, p. 82)

26   It's obvious, given the testimonials posted here, that many of us had little idea how brutal war is, and consequently we have had a thin appreciation of the bravery and sacrifice of those who have served their country. Stories like the Normandy invasion must be told, but they also must be understood. By bluntly depicting the carnage of D-Day, Spielberg tells the story with a clarity and **resonance** that most Americans have never known, and in doing so he honors these men.

Resonance means a lasting meaning and interest.

27   Do not dismiss this enlightenment as insubstantial because it's inspired by cinema. The motion picture arts as a whole do not deserve the reputation that Hollywood has established. Great films have always, and will always, be produced, even as many Hollywood pictures continue to degrade humanity and insult our intelligence. Words do not reign supreme as a form of expression. We need pictures and music as well. (For centuries, Michelangelo's painting of "The Final Judgment" has impressed millions of viewers with the weight of words written by St. Paul.)

Notes

28   As a work of art, "Saving Private Ryan" may succeed as one of this century's most eloquent statements on the subject of war and its miseries. I think it is evident that the great majority of those who watched the film have gained a greater understanding of why we must honor our veterans, why we must honor the memory of the fallen, and why we must honor the debt that we owe them. Keep reading and listening to what people are saying. There already appears to be a transformation of consciousness happening on a mass scale, across generational lines. This is what cinema is meant to do.

Thank you (e-mail #4, p. 91)

29   To all the veterans out there, I just want to say "thank you" from all of us young, cocky American kids who take for granted every day the freedom that we have only because you and your friends and brothers put your lives on the line.

30   I have to admit that this movie really woke me up to the fact that people actually do get killed, and they cry for their mothers, and that war is horrible and scary. And I got these feelings from sitting in a padded chair in an air-conditioned movie theater with five of my best friends.

31   I can't even begin to fathom how it was to really be there. People who list a movie star or sports figure as their hero need to have their heads checked out. From what I saw, if the hype is true and that was really an example of the reality of war, all of you veterans should be the only heroes on this earth.

32   It's because of you that I can write this message, that I can freely express my opinion, that I can do as I please, be whatever I want, and lead my life the way I want. We all owe you our lives. Thank you to each of you brave men from the bottom of my heart.

33   It's just too bad that it took a movie to wake this country up, including myself. I know one thing's for sure—I will never experience Memorial Day the same way again. Thank you for my life.

Reread As you reread the introduction and the four e-mails, ask yourself why people chose to express their thoughts at this AOL website. Record your thoughts, questions, and reactions in the margins. Use context clues to figure out the meaning of unknown words. Use the dictionary for words that remain unclear.

Vocabulary cards: Make definition and sentence cards for the words listed here.

- *lurk*, paragraph 24
- *carnage*, paragraph 26
- *fathom*, paragraph 31

Think Critically and Summarize Write your answers on a separate piece of paper.

1. What did you learn from the introduction about the four e-mails that follow it? What did you learn about e-mail in general?
2. What do you think the main message is in the first e-mail (paragraphs 14–19)?
3. What was the purpose of the second e-mail (paragraphs 20–25)? Which paragraph most clearly explains that writer's reason for writing?
4. In your own words, what is the message in paragraphs 27 and 28? What is that writer expressing?
5. In your own words, what is the main point in paragraph 31? Do you agree?
6. Considering these four e-mail messages and the information in the introduction and your own ideas, why do people choose to express themselves through e-mail? Write down at least three different reasons for choosing e-mail.
7. Do you see any drawbacks to e-mail?

Autobiographies

Reading Assignment—The Art of the Deal, "Chapter 3: Growing Up"

Preview Read the first paragraph and the topic sentence for every other paragraph.

Notes

Anticipate What do you know about Donald Trump? What do you expect him to write about? What information did you learn in your preview step?

_____

_____

_____

_____

_____

Read You may find this chapter from Trump's autobiography easy to read. If you are able to identify main points during your first reading, mark them. Also record your reactions and questions in the margins. However, don't interrupt your reading to look up words in the dictionary. Mark any unfamiliar words and go back to them during the rereading step.

The Art of the Deal
Chapter 3: Growing Up

By Donald J. Trump with Tony Schwartz

1   The most important influence on me, growing up, was my father, Fred Trump. I learned a lot from him. I learned about toughness in a very tough business, I learned about motivating people, and I learned about competence and efficiency: get in, get it done, get it done right, and get out.

2   At the same time, I learned very early on that I didn't want to be in the business my father was in. He did very well building rent-controlled and rent-stabilized housing in Queens and Brooklyn, but it was a very tough way to make a buck. I wanted to try something grander, more glamorous, and more exciting. I also realized that if I ever wanted to be known as more than Fred Trump's son, I was eventually going to have to go out and make my own mark. I'm fortunate that my father was content to stay with what he knew and did so well. That left me free to make my mark in Manhattan. Even so, I never forgot the lessons I learned at my father's side.

Horatio Alger is an American writer who lived from 1832–99. He wrote books for boys, teaching kids that they can be successful if they work hard and are self-reliant.

3   His story is classic **Horatio Alger.** Fred Trump was born in New Jersey in 1905. His father, who came here from Sweden as a child, owned

a moderately successful restaurant, but he was also a hard liver and a hard drinker, and he died when my father was eleven years old. My father's mother, Elizabeth, went to work as a seamstress to support her three children. The oldest, also named Elizabeth, was sixteen at the time, and the youngest, John, was nine. My father was the middle child but the first son, and he became the man of the house. Almost immediately, he began taking odd jobs—everything from deliveries for a local fruit store to shining shoes to hauling lumber on a construction site. Construction always interested him, and during high school he began taking night classes in carpentry, plan-reading, and estimating, figuring that if he learned a trade, he'd always be able to make a living. By the age of sixteen, he'd built his first structure, a two-car frame garage for a neighbor. Middle-class people were just beginning to buy cars, few homes had attached garages, and my father was soon able to establish a very good new business building prefabricated garages for fifty dollars apiece.

4   He graduated from high school in 1922, and with a family to support, he couldn't even consider college. Instead, he went to work as a carpenter's helper for a home-builder in Queens. He was better with his hands than most, but he also had some other advantages. For starters, he was just a very smart guy. Even to this day, he can add five columns of numbers in his head and keep them all straight. Between his night courses and his basic common sense, he was able to show the other carpenters, most of whom had no education at all, shortcuts, such as how to frame a rafter with a steel square. [. . .]

5   Instinctively, my father began to think bigger. By 1929, aiming at a more affluent market, he started building much larger homes. Instead of tiny brick houses, he put up three-story Colonials, Tudors, and Victorians in a section of Queens that ultimately became known as Jamaica Estates—and where, eventually, he built a home for our family. When the Depression hit and the housing market fell off, my father turned his attention to other businesses. He bought a bankrupt mortgage-servicing company and sold it at a profit a year later. Next, he built a self-service supermarket in Woodhaven, one of the first of its kind. All the local tradesmen—butcher, tailor, shoemaker—**rented concessions** in the space, and the convenience of having everything available under one roof made the operation an immediate success. Within a year, however, eager to return to building, my father sold out to King Kullen for a large profit.

6   By 1934 the Depression was finally beginning to ease, but money was still tight and so my father decided to go back to building lower-priced homes. This time he chose the depressed Flatbush area of

Notes

Mark places where Trump points out what his father taught him. Make comments in the margin so that you can find these lessons easily.

To **rent concessions** is to rent parts of a building for businesses.

Brooklyn, where land was cheap and he sensed there was a lot of room for growth. Once again his instincts were right. In three weeks he sold 78 homes, and during the next dozen years, he built 2,500 more throughout Queens and Brooklyn. He was becoming very successful. [. . .]

7   Fortunately for me, I was drawn to business very early, and I was never intimidated by my father the way most people were. I stood up to him and he respected that. We had a relationship that was almost businesslike. I sometimes wonder if we'd have gotten along so well if I hadn't been as business-oriented as I am.

8   Even in elementary school, I was a very assertive, aggressive kid. In the second grade I actually gave a teacher a black eye—I punched my music teacher because I didn't think he knew anything about music and I almost got expelled. I'm not proud of that but it's clear evidence that even early on I had a tendency to stand up and make my opinions known in a very forceful way. The difference now is that I like to use my brain instead of my fists.

9   I was always something of a leader in my neighborhood. Much the way it is today, people either liked me a lot, or they didn't like me at all. In my own crowd I was very well liked, and I tended to be the kid that others followed. As an adolescent I was mostly interested in creating mischief, because for some reason I liked to stir things up, and I liked to test people. I'd throw water balloons, shoot spitballs, and make a ruckus in the schoolyard and at birthday parties. It wasn't malicious so much as it was aggressive. My brother Robert likes to tell the story of the time when it became clear to him where I was headed.

10   Robert is two years younger than I am, and we have always been very close, although he is much quieter and more easygoing than I am. One day we were in the playroom of our house, building with blocks. I wanted to build a very tall building, but it turned out that I didn't have enough blocks. I asked Robert if I could borrow some of his, and he said, "Okay, but you have to give them back when you're done." I ended up using all of my blocks, and then all of his, and when I was done, I'd created a beautiful building. I liked it so much that I glued the whole thing together. And that was the end of Robert's blocks.

11   When I turned thirteen, my father decided to send me to a military school, assuming that a little military training might be good for me. I wasn't thrilled about the idea, but it turned out he was right. Beginning in the eighth grade I went to the New York Military Academy in upstate New York. [. . .]

12   Almost from the time could walk, I'd been going to construction sites with my father. Robert and I would tag along and spend our time hunting for empty soda bottles, which we'd take to the store for deposit money. As a teenager, when I came home from school for vacation, I followed my father around to learn about the business close up—dealing with contractors or visiting buildings or negotiating for a new site.

13   You made it in my father's business—rent-controlled and rent-stabilized buildings—by being very tough and very relentless. To turn a profit, you had to keep your costs down, and my father was always very price-conscious. He'd negotiate just as hard with a supplier of mops and floor wax as he would with the general contractor for the larger items on a project. One advantage my father had was that he knew what everything cost. No one could put anything over on him. If you know, for example, that a plumbing job is going to cost the contractor $400,000, then you know how far you can push the guy. You're not going to try to negotiate him down to $300,000, because that is just going to put him out of business. But you're also not going to let him talk you into $600,000.

14   The other way my father got contractors to work for a good price was by selling them on his reliability. He'd offer a low price for a job, but then he'd say, "Look, with me you get paid, and you get paid on time, and with someone else, who knows if you ever see your money?" He'd also point out that with him they'd get in and out quickly and on to the next job. And finally, because he was always building, he could hold out the promise of plenty of future work. His arguments were usually compelling.

15   My father was also an unbelievably demanding taskmaster. Every morning at six, he'd be there at the site and he would just pound and pound and pound. He was almost a one-man show. If a guy wasn't doing his job the way my father thought it should be done, and I mean any job, because he could do them all—he'd jump in and take over. [. . .]

16   After I graduated from New York Military Academy in 1964 I flirted briefly with the idea of attending film school at the University of Southern California. I was attracted to the glamour of the movies, and I admired guys like Sam Goldwyn, Darryl Zanuck, and most of all Louis B. Mayer, whom I considered great showmen. But in the end I decided real estate was a much better business.

17   I began by attending Fordham University in the Bronx, mostly because I wanted to be close to home. I got along very well with the Jesuits who ran the school, but after two years, I decided that as long as I had to be in college, I might as well test myself against the best. I applied to the Wharton School of Finance at the University of Pennsylvania and I got in. At the time, if you were going to make a career in business, Wharton was the place to go. Harvard Business School may produce a

Notes

lot of CEOs—guys who manage public companies—but the real entre-preneurs all seemed to go to Wharton: Saul Steinberg, Leonard Lauder, Ron Perelman—the list goes on and on.

18   Perhaps the most important thing I learned at Wharton was not to be overly impressed by academic credentials. It didn't take me long to realize that there was nothing particularly awesome or exceptional about my classmates, and that I could compete with them just fine. The other important thing I got from Wharton was a Wharton degree. In my opinion, that degree doesn't prove very much, but a lot of people I do business with take it very seriously, and it's considered very prestigious. So all things considered, I'm glad I went to Wharton.

19   I was also very glad to get finished. I immediately moved back home and went to work full-time with my father. I continued to learn a lot, but it was during this period that I began to think about alternatives.

20   For starters, my father's scene was a little rough for my tastes—and by that I mean physically rough. I remember, for example, going around with the men we called rent collectors. To do this job you had to be physically imposing, because when it came to collecting rent from peo-ple who didn't want to pay, size mattered a lot more than brains.

21   One of the first tricks I learned was that you never stand in front of someone's door when you knock. Instead you stand by the wall and reach over to knock. The first time a collector explained that to me, I couldn't imagine what he was talking about. "What's the point?" I said. He looked at me like I was crazy. "The point," he said, "is that if you stand to the side, the only thing exposed to danger is your hand." I still wasn't sure what he meant. "In this business," he said, "if you knock on the wrong apartment at the wrong time, you're liable to get shot."

22   My father had never sheltered me, but even so, this was not a world I found very attractive. I'd just graduated from Wharton, and suddenly here I was in a scene that was violent at worst and unpleas-ant at best. For example, there were tenants who'd throw their garbage out the window, because it was easier than putting it in the **incinerator.** At one point, I instituted a program to teach people about using the incinerators. The vast majority of tenants were just fine, but the bad element required attention, and to me it just wasn't worth it.

An **incinerator** is a machine that burns trash.

23   The second thing I didn't find appealing was that the profit margins were so low. You had no choice but to pinch pennies, and there was no room for any luxuries. Design was beside the point because every build-ing had to be pretty much the same: four walls, common brick facades,

and straight up. You used red brick, not necessarily because you liked it but because it was a penny a brick cheaper than tan brick.

24   I still remember a time when my father visited the Trump Tower site, midway through construction. Our facade was a glass curtain wall, which is far more expensive than brick. In addition, we were using the most expensive glass you can buy—bronze solar. My father took one look, and he said to me, "Why don't you forget about the damn glass? Give them four or five stories of it and then use common brick for the rest. Nobody is going to look up anyway!" It was a classic, Fred Trump standing there on 57th Street and Fifth Avenue trying to save a few bucks. I was touched, and of course I understood where he was coming from—but also exactly why I'd decided to leave.

25   The real reason I wanted out of my father's business—more important than the fact that it was physically rough and financially tough—was that I had loftier dreams and visions. And there was no way to implement them building housing in the outer boroughs.

26   Looking back, I realize now that I got some of my sense of showmanship from my mother. She always had a flair for the dramatic and the grand. She was a very traditional housewife, but she also had a sense of the world beyond her. I still remember my mother, who is Scottish by birth, sitting in front of the television set to watch Queen Elizabeth's coronation and not budging for an entire day. She was just enthralled by the pomp and circumstance, the whole idea of royalty and glamour. I also remember my father that day, pacing around impatiently. "For Christ's sake, Mary," he'd say. "Enough is enough, turn it off. They're all a bunch of con artists." My mother didn't even look up. They were total opposites in that sense. My mother loves splendor and magnificence, while my father, who is very down-to-earth, gets excited only by competence and efficiency.

Reread Review this chapter from Trump's autobiography. Use context clues to figure out the meanings of unfamiliar words. Look up any words that remain unclear in the dictionary. Also, review the chapter to identify the main messages Trump is expressing in this chapter. Make notes in the margins.

Vocabulary cards: Make definition and sentence cards for the words listed here.

- *assertive*, paragraph 8
- *relentless*, paragraph 13

Notes   • *loftier,* paragraph 25

Think Critically and Summarize Answer these questions on another piece of paper.

1. Based on what you have read here, why do you think Trump wrote an autobiography? What does he expect his audience to gain from reading his autobiography?
2. Why does Trump spend so much time discussing his father?
3. List specific lessons or information that seem important in this chapter.
4. Would you recommend this autobiography to anyone? Whom? Why?

Fairy Tales

Reading Assignment—"Cindy Ellie: A Modern Fairy Tale"

An **anthology** is a book that has a variety of literary pieces written by different authors.

Preview This story comes from an **anthology** of African American storytelling. In this case, "Cindy Ellie" comes from a book that is a collection of fables, sermons, stories, tales, raps, and rhymes that are meant to be told aloud. Read the title, the author's name, and the first three paragraphs.

Anticipate What do the first three paragraphs tell you about the style of this story? What kind of language will the writer use? What is the time period? What do you think might be different in this version of Cinderella?

_____

_____

_____

_____

_____

Read Read the story. Mark unknown words, but don't look up any meanings in the dictionary yet.

Cindy Ellie:
A Modern Fairy Tale

By Mary Carter Smith

1   Once upon a time, over in East Baltimore, there lived a happy family: Sam Johnson, his wife Lula, and their daughter Ellie. Lula was good and kind; a quiet, church-going woman but mighty puny and sickly. One day Lula called Ellie to her bedside. "Child, Mama ain't feeling so well. One of these days I might leave you." "Oh, Mama, don't say that," Ellie said with tears in her eyes. "Don't cry, child. All of us go sometime, and I'd rather it be me than you. So there are a few things I want to tell you. Always mind your daddy. Stay in church, go to school, and learn that book. Remember what I'm telling you." "All right, Mama, I'll remember."

2   One day, not long after, the poor woman just up and died; <u>real peaceful-like</u> and quiet.

Why do you think Smith says "real peaceful-like" instead of "very peacefully"?

3   Honey, let me tell you, they had a beautiful funeral. Sam sure put her away nice. The Senior Choir turned out full force. The Junior Choir was there. And the Gospel Chorus just sung their hearts out! The church was crowded! Folks all on the outside, with loudspeakers going. Lula's lodge sisters was there in their white dresses, and them purple sashes all edged in gold. Ellie was on the front row beside her daddy. Just as cute as she could be in a white dress and her hair in a fine bush. Ellie was one purty young black sister, her skin like black velvet.

4   Child, let me tell you, that poor woman's body wasn't hardly cold before them church sisters was after Sam Johnson like flies after honey! 'Cause he had a good job down Sparrow's Point, with lots of seniority. And they had just paid for one of them pretty, big houses on Broadway, with them pretty white marble steps. It was a lovely block; won first prize in the AFRO Clean Block three years running!

5   That poor man, like so many good men, was weak for a pretty face and big legs and big hips. One huzzy, the boldest of 'em all, had a heart as hard as a rock. <u>The milk of human kindness had curdled in her breast.</u> But she did have a pretty face, big legs, and great big hips. Ooh-wee! She could put on! Made like she loved Ellie so, and was always bringing <u>good barbecued ribs, collard greens, cracklin' bread, and jelly-layer cake</u> to Ellie and Sam. Well, that fool man fell right into that woman's trap. She had that man cornered and married before you could say, "Jackie Robinson."

What does the underlined sentence mean?

Why does Smith mention these specific foods? Why doesn't she just say "good food"?

6   Then bless my soul. You ain't never seen such a change in nobody! First off that woman went down to Souse Car'lina for her two big-footed, ugly gals her Mama'd been keeping. Brought them back to

Baltimore, and put poor Ellie out of the pretty room with the canopied bed and let her ugly gals sleep in that pretty room. Made poor little Ellie sleep on a **pallet** in the cellar.

7 Now Ellie's mama had been wise. When everybody else was converting they furnaces to oil and gas, she said, "Uh-uh. One day they gone be hard to get." She had kept her coal furnace. Poor little Ellie had to do all the cooking, cleaning, washing, and ironing. She had to scrub them marble steps twice a day and wait on them ugly gals hand and foot. Not only that, but in the winter she had to keep the fire going and clean out the ashes and cinders. So they got to calling her Cindy Ellie.

8 Tell you the truth, I believe that woman had put some roots on that man! 'Cause no matter how she mistreated Cindy Ellie, he never said a word, just *crazy* 'bout that big-legged woman.

9 That November, the good white folks, the good Asian folks, and the good black folks all turned out and voted for a good black brother, running for mayor. And he won the election by a landslide! He was having his inauguration ball down at the convention center. So many folks voted for him that they had to hold it for two nights running. The mayor's son had come home from college to go to the ball.

10 Oh, them stepsisters was primping and buying designer gowns to go to the ball. Poor Cindy Ellie had to give one a perm, the other a jheri curl, and both of them facials; not that it helped much. Honey, them gals was ugly from the inside out!

11 "Cindy Ellie, don't you wish you could go to the ball?" they asked her.

12 "Oh, you are making fun of me," Cindy Ellie said.

13 So Cindy Ellie's daddy, her stepmother, and them two ugly gals all went to the ball and left poor Cindy Ellie home.

14 Now Cindy Ellie had a godma. She had been her dear mama's best friend, and she still had a key to the house. She came to the house, as she often did, to sneak food to poor Cindy Ellie and found the child lying on her hard pallet, just crying her heart out!

15 "Why are you crying, child?" she asked her.

16 "Be-because I want to go to the ball."

17 Now this godma had been born with a veil over her face, down in New Orleans. She knew a thing or two about voodoo and hoodoo. Besides that, she had a High John the Conqueror Root that she always used for good. The godma told Cindy Ellie, "Go upstairs to the kitchen, child. Look in the kitchen cabinet drawer and bring me the biggest white onion you can find." Cindy Ellie was an obedient child. She didn't ask, "Why?" She just did what her godma told her to do. Cindy Ellie brought her the onion. She gave it to her godma. Then they went out in the backyard. The godma laid that onion on the ground. Then she

stepped back and waved that root over that onion! And right before their eyes that onion turned into a long white Cadillac that parked itself in the back alley!

18   "Cindy Ellie go up on the third floor and bring me that mousetrap." Cindy Ellie brought it down. There were two little black mice trapped in a little cage. She told Cindy Ellie to open the door and them mice started out. But that godma waved that root over them and they turned into two six-foot-tall black chauffeurs dressed in shining white uniforms with fancy white caps! And they had on long black boots! And they was bowing and scraping. "All right, Cindy Ellie, you can go to the ball now."

19   "But, godma, look at me. I'm clean but I'm ragged."

20   "Don't worry 'bout it," her godma said. Then she stepped back and waved that root over Cindy Ellie. <u>Her rags turned into a dazzling dress of pink African laces! Her hair was braided into a hundred shining braids, and on the end of each braid were beads of pure gold! Her eyes were beautifully shaded and her skin was shining like polished ebony! Golden bracelets covered her arms clean up to her elbows! On each ear hung five small diamond earrings. On her tiny feet were dainty golden sandals encrusted with dazzling jewels!</u> Cindy Ellie was laid back!

21   As one of the chauffeurs helped her into the white Cadillac her godma told her, "Be sure you leave before midnight or you'll be as you was. Your Cadillac will turn back into an onion, your chauffeurs into mice, and your clothes into rags." Cindy Ellie promised her godma that she would leave before midnight. Away she went, as happy as could be.

22   The mayor's son heard that a beautiful girl had arrived who looked like an African princess. He came out to see and said to himself, "This sure is a fine fox!" He asked her, "May I escort you into the ballroom?" Cindy Ellie replied in tones soft and low, "I don't mind if you do." He helped her out of her limousine and escorted her into the ballroom and to the head table where he was sitting. Every eye was on Cindy Ellie. You could have heard a pin drop. Then voices could be heard "Gorgeous," "Lovely," "Devastating," "Elegant," etc. Even the mayor himself could not take his eyes off her. His wife agreed that she was indeed a charming young woman. The other ladies were looking at her clothes and wishing they had material in their gowns as beautiful as that in Cindy Ellie's.

23   Although the table was loaded with sumptuous food, Toussaint, the mayor's son, couldn't eat a bite! Just busy looking at Cindy Ellie. In her honor, the band played the Ghanian High-Life. Cindy Ellie and Toussaint danced it as if they had been dancing together all their lives. Cindy Ellie was friendly and courteous to everyone she met. She even sat beside her stepsisters (who had no idea who she was) and invited them to come

Notes

Highlight the words in this underlined passage that make the image of Cindy clear and colorful.

Notes

back the next night. For Toussaint had begged Cindy Ellie to return for the second night of the ball.

24   Then Cindy Ellie heard the clock strike forty-five minutes after eleven! She murmered to Toussaint, "Really, I must be getting home." And she rushed out as fast as she could go.

25   As soon as she was home Cindy Ellie called her godma and thanked her for such a splendid time. The doorbell rang and she heard her step-sisters' voices: "Hurry, stupid! Open the door!" Cindy Ellie came, yawning and rubbing her eyes, as if she'd been asleep. "Did you have a good time?" she asked. "Oh, it was all right, but we didn't get to dance with the mayor's son. He danced only with some new girl. No one had seen her before. She had on some old African clothes. But on her they did look good. She did have the good sense to recognize what quality people we are, and she had the mayor's son invite all of us tomorrow night. "What was her name?" asked Cindy Ellie. "No one knows. The mayor's son is dying to find out who she is." Cindy Ellie said, "You don't mean it. Oh, how I wish I could go to the ball tomorrow night. Lillie, won't you lend me your old blue gown so I can go also?" They almost split their sides laughing. "You, with your ragged self, going to the inauguration ball? Wouldn't that be something else! Of course not. Come and help us get undressed and turn back the covers on the bed so we can go to sleep."

26   As on the night before, poor little Cindy Ellie was left behind while the rest of them went to the ball again. Her godma came in and heard the child crying again. "Why you crying, child? You want to go to that ball again?" "Yes, ma'am." "I thought so. You've been a good child all your life, and you always respect your elders. So don't worry. You can go to the ball again. Now dry your eyes and get your face together. Look in that kitchen cabinet drawer and bring me the biggest yellow onion you can find." Cindy Ellie came back with the biggest yellow onion you ever laid your eyes on. Then they went out in the backyard. The godma laid that onion on the ground. Then she stepped back and waved that root over that onion! And right before their eyes that onion turned into a solid gold Mercedes-Benz about half a block long! And it parked itself in the back alley.

27   "Cindy Ellie, go up on the third floor and bring me that rat trap." Cindy Ellie brought it down. There were two big white rats trapped in a big wire cage.

28   That family lived so close to Johns Hopkins Hospital that mice and rats used to escape from them laboratories up there. They took that cage out in the backyard. She told Cindy Ellie to open the door and them rats started out. But that godma stood back and waved that High

John the Conqueror root over them, and they turned into two seven-foot-tall white chauffeurs dressed in shining gold uniforms with fancy gold caps! And they had on shining white boots! And they was bowing and scraping.

29   "All right, Cindy Ellie, you can go to the ball now."

30   "But godma, look at me. I'm clean but I'm ragged."

31   "Don't worry 'bout it," her godma said. Then she stepped back and waved that root over Cindy Ellie. Her rags turned into a dress made of pure silk kente, that royal cloth from Ghana! Worth thousands of dollars! On her head was a geelee of the rarest of taffeta, standing tall and stiff and just gorgeous! Her big pretty eyes were beautifully shaded, and her skin was shining like polished ebony. Golden bracelets covered her arms clean up to her shoulders! On each ear hung five small diamond earrings. On her tiny feet were dainty golden sandals encrusted with dazzling jewels. She was cool!

32   As one of the chauffeurs helped her into that gold Mercedes-Benz, her godma told her, "Be sure you leave before midnight or you'll be as you was. That Mercedes-Benz will turn back into an onion, your chauffeurs into rats, and your clothes into rags." Cindy Ellie promised her godma that she would leave before midnight. Away she went, as happy as could be.

33   As they drove up, Toussaint was waiting for her. She went into the ballroom draped on his arm. Oh, they was having such a good time laughing and talking and cha-cha-chaing and waltzing and boogeying! That poor child forgot all about time! Then she heard the clock as it began to strike twelve! She ran out of there as fast as her legs would carry her. She ran so fast, she ran out of one of those sandals. She put the other in her hand and ran on. Toussaint ran behind her, but he couldn't see where she had gone. He picked up the golden sandal.

34   He asked the security people, "Did you see an African princess run by you?" "No. We did see a girl dressed in rags run out of the door. We thought she had stole something. But that chick was gone!"

35   That night when the family came home from the ball they told Cindy Ellie, "Something mighty strange happened tonight. As the clock on city hall began to strike twelve that African princess began to run like crazy! She ran so fast, she ran out of one of her golden sandals. The mayor's son found it and kept it. He just kept looking at it. He's really upset over that sister."

36   Child, the next day the mayor's son came on television, came on the radio, and announced to every paper in Baltimore that he would marry the girl whose foot would fit that sandal he had picked up. Now a lot of folks who had supported the mayor lived in the places surrounding Baltimore. So first all them sorority girls and debutantes and folks like that tried to fit their foot in that sandal. Wouldn't fit none of them girls in Columbia,

Notes

Cockeysville, Randallstown, and places like that. Then they went to them rich folks' houses up on Cadillac Row and places like that. Wouldn't fit none of them girls neither. Then they went to all them condominiums downtown by The Inner Harbor and them fancy town houses. Wouldn't fit none of them neither. Finally they come to East Baltimore. Length and long they came to Broadway and knocked at the Johnsons' residence. The mayor's men came in with that golden sandal on a red velvet pillow. Them two stepsisters tried their best to put on that shoe! They pushed and they jugged. But their big feet would not get into that shoe. No way, Jose! "May I try?" asked Cindy Ellie. "No, stupid. It's not for the likes of you." "Yes, you may try on the sandal," the mayor's representative said. "For the proclamation issued by the mayor said that any girl in Baltimore and surrounding areas may try. He spoke kindly to Cindy Ellie. "Sit down, miss, and see if it fits you." And do you know, that sandal just slid on Cindy Ellie's little foot as smooth as silk. Then she pulled from the pocket in her clean but ragged dress the other sandal. As soon as she put it on her foot, right there before their very eyes, Cindy Ellie was transformed into the African princess they had seen the nights before! Them two step-sisters had a fit! "Oh, Cindy Ellie, we didn't mean no harm! Oh, Cindy Ellie, please forgive us!" They was on the floor rolling round and carrying on.

37   Cindy Ellie told them, "Get up off that floor and stop all that whooping and hollering. I forgive you."

38   Then Cindy Ellie was transported to the mayor's mansion in his private limousine. Toussaint was there waiting to welcome her with open arms. Cindy Ellie was true to her word, for she not only forgave her stepsisters in word but in deed. She found them two ugly councilmen for husbands. Toussaint and Cindy Ellie were married in the biggest Baptist church in East Baltimore, and the reception was held in the convention center. And they lived happily, happily forever after.

Reread Reread the story. Since this author uses a conversational style and tone, this would be a good story to read aloud. As you read, try to use context cues to figure out the meanings of unknown words. Look up the meanings of any words that remain unclear. Mark important and interesting points. In addition to responding to the questions and directions in the margin, make more notes in the margins to record your reactions to the story and to mark places where this story is different from the other two versions of "Cinderella."

Vocabulary cards: Make definition cards and sentence cards for the words listed here.

- *sumptuous,* paragraph 23
- *debutantes,* paragraph 36

Think Critically Answer these questions on a separate piece of paper.

1. As noted in the preview step of your reading process, this story is meant to be read aloud. Mary Carter Smith has written this story with a clear, strong voice. Highlight the places in the story where her voice can be heard most strongly. What kind of voice is it? (Casual? Serious? Formal?) From studying Smith's voice, what can you say about the audience of this tale? (Age? Interests? Values?) What evidence do you have?
2. List some similarities between the Grimm version and this version. Give paragraph numbers when listing similarities.
3. List some ways in which Smith modernized her tale. Give paragraph numbers when listing evidence. Do any of these modern touches tell you anything about the values, interests, or morals of Smith's audience?
4. How does this story handle the fairy godmother? Explain how the godma in this tale is similar to but also different from the fairy godmothers in traditional fairy tales? Why did Smith create this godma the way she did?
5. How does Cindy Ellie treat the stepsisters at the end of the story? Do you like this ending? Why or why not? What lesson are the stepsisters learning?
6. What does the author of this tale say about the father? What is your opinion of the father? Is he a good person? Is he similar to the father in the Grimm version of Cinderella? Explain.

Summarize
   List the major events in the story.

Essays

Reading Assignment—"My Vision"

Preview Since this is an academic essay, you can expect to find an introduction that ends with a thesis and body paragraphs that begin with topic sentences. Read the title, the introduction, and the topic sentences.

Anticipate What will this essay be about?

_____

_____

_____

_____

Read Read the essay once quickly.

My Vision

By Ayanna Williams

1   "The American Dream" is a hopeful and conscious vision of what one wants to achieve. For many people the "American Dream" is a house, car, two kids, a job and good income. I, for one, want that job to be very meaningful. I agree with the "American Dream" to a certain point, but I want it to be on my terms.

2   In the 1930's the "American Dream" was born. Back then for many people, the "American Dream" consisted of having a house, two kids and a dog of which the women took care. The job and bringing in the good income was the man's job. People also wanted stability in their lives, because they had just lost everything. Stability in the 1930's was knowing that everything you worked so hard for was on a solid foundation that couldn't be broken. Part of the dream was to get through a bleak period. At this time many people had no money, food or even a place to stay, which made them want the dream even more.

3   The "American Dream" for me is one of great passion. I want to own a travel agency. Being able to create a business of my own, will enable me to have a future that I will enjoy. I plan to get my business started by working in my office for about two years. Ultimately in the long run I want to travel and visit places. By doing this I will be able to give my clients advice about which hotels to stay in, to go shop, party, and dine. Traveling, exploring new places and being able to share this with my kids is part of my vision. In order for their education to come first, I will need to have a tutor that will travel with us.

4   As cliché as it seems, I also want financial stability in my personal dream although some might say that traveling all over the world at a moment's notice is not stable. Financial stability will help with my travel expenses, such as having a personal tutor. However, being a travel agent will give me plenty of perks and low cost opportunities.

5   The terms that I speak of are very simple. Being able to go to college, a business trade school, or learning from hands on experience. Unlike in the 1930's when women stayed home with the children, I want to take my children with me. My dream doesn't really consist of materialistic things like a house, car, dog, and husband. Being able to achieve my goals without the help of any man is on my terms.

6   In the end the "American Dream," while universal, is as individual as each person who dreams it. For me the "American Dream" becomes a conscious vision only when it's on my terms. Instead of being in the world I want to see the world.

Reread When you reread, highlight the topic sentence in paragraphs 2–5. In the margin next to each paragraph, make a note about what each paragraph focuses on.

Think Critically and Summarize Write your answers on a separate piece of paper.

1. Does the title fit the essay? Explain. A title is the author's first chance to give the reader a clue about the essay. What does this title tell you? What other titles might have worked?
2. What does Williams do in her introduction? How is she preparing you for her essay? Underline or highlight her thesis.
3. Would the essay be stronger if the order of the paragraphs was changed? Explain.
4. Which paragraph do you think was developed most effectively? (Look for a paragraph that answers your questions and that supplies details and examples.) Be prepared to defend your choice.
5. In paragraph 5, Williams accidentally created a fragment. Find it and correct it. (See Chapter 18 for a review of fragments.)
6. In paragraph 3, Williams accidentally creates a sentence with unparallel structure. Find it and correct it. (See Chapter 26 for a review of parallelism.)

Vocabulary Lists

Appendix A

Sentence Term Chart

Term	Definition	Examples
Verb (See Chaps. 12 and 13)	Expresses action or connects the subject to information in the sentence. • Can change tense • *–ing* word needs a helper to be a verb	He <u>dances</u>. The child <u>is</u> quiet. He <u>danced</u>. The child <u>was</u> quiet. She <u>is working</u>.
Noun (See Chap. 14)	A person, place, idea, or thing.	<u>Joe</u>, <u>house</u>, <u>freedom</u>, <u>cake</u>
Subject (See Chap. 14)	Does the action. Is being connected to information in the sentence.	The <u>frog</u> jumps. The <u>man</u> is happy.
Predicate (See Chap. 14)	The verb and everything that comes after the verb.	The child <u>reads well</u>.
Completer (See Chap. 18)	Finishes the idea.	I cut <u>the cake</u>.
Prepositional Phrase (See Chap. 12)	Shows position. Expresses a relationship. • Consists of preposition and object	<u>At the store</u> <u>By the river</u> (The preposition is highlighted. The object follows the preposition.)
Infinitive (See Chap. 12)	To + verb • Cannot be a verb.	<u>To walk</u> <u>To sing</u> <u>To think</u>
Clause (See Chap. 16)	Group of words with a subject and a verb. • Can be independent or dependent.	<u>The man is working.</u> <u>When the man is working</u>

Term	Definition	Examples
Phrase (See Chap. 17)	Group of words missing a subject, verb, *or* both.	<u>The tall man</u>
Pronoun (See Chap. 21)	A word that can stand in place of a noun.	<u>He</u> is tall. <u>She</u> works all night. <u>It</u> rose from the swamp. <u>They</u> ran all the way home.
Antecedent (See Chap. 21)	The noun that a pronoun refers to.	My <u>mom</u> told her story to the reporter.
Adjective (See Chap. 22)	A word that describes a noun.	The <u>rebellious</u> songwriter used foul language.
Adverb (See Chap. 22)	A word that describes a verb or an adjective.	The <u>incredibly</u> powerful dog <u>quickly</u> lunged at the cat.
Coordinator (See Chap. 23)	A word that can join two sentences.	I ran to the exit, <u>for</u> I smelled fire.
Subordinator (See Chap. 24)	A word that makes a clause dependent.	<u>If</u> we walk <u>When</u> <u>Because</u>
Transition (See Chaps. 16 and 25)	Creates a bridge between ideas. • Can interrupt sentences	I like seafood. However, he does not. I like seafood; however, he does not. The kids, however, went to school.

Appendix B

Editing Errors Chart

Error Name and Abbreviation	The Problem (and Examples)	How To Fix (and Corrected Examples)
Subject-Verb Agreement Error **(s-v agr)** (See Chap. 15)	Subject and verbs do not agree in number.	• Read sentences carefully. • Find verbs. • Check verb endings A present tense third-person singular verb must have an *s* on the end.
	He <u>eat</u> cake. (incorrect)	*He <u>eats</u> cake.*

Verb Tense Error **(vt)** (See Chap. 15)	Verb is not in the correct tense.	• Read sentence carefully. • Find verbs. • Check tenses. • Be consistent.
		
		Examples of tenses:
		  Present tense eat
		  Past tense ate
		  Future tense will eat

	Yesterday, he <u>eats</u> cake. (incorrect)	*Yesterday, he <u>ate</u> cake.*
Fragment **(frag)** (See Chap. 18)	A sentence that is incomplete. It may be missing a verb and/or a subject: *The man sitting behind me. Sits behind me. (incorrect)* It may actually be a subordinated clause: *If the man sits behind me. (incorrect)*	• Add a verb or a helper verb. *The man <u>is</u> sitting behind me.* *The man sitting behind me <u>laughs</u>.* • Add a subject. *He sits behind me.* • Delete the subordinator, or complete the idea. *The man sits behind me. If the man sits behind me, I'll have to listen to his complaining.*

Error Name and Abbreviation	The Problem (and Examples)	How To Fix (and Corrected Examples)
Comma splice **(cs)** (See Chap. 20)	Two complete sentences are incorrectly joined by a comma. This error usually occurs because ideas are closely related: *Journals seem important, they help us explore experiences. (incorrect)*	Separate the complete sentences with a semicolon or a period, or use a co-ordinating conjunction with a comma. *Journals seem important; they help us explore experiences.* *Journals seem important. They help us explore experiences.* *Journals seem important, for they help us explore experiences.*
Run-on (See Chap. 19)	Two complete sentences are combined as one sentence, with no punctuation separating them. *Journals seem important they help us explore experiences. (incorrect)*	Separate the complete sentences with a semicolon or a period, or use a coordinating conjunction with a comma. *Journals seem important; they help us explore experiences.* *Journals seem important. They help us explore experiences.* *Journals seem important, for they help us explore experiences.*
Wrong Word **(ww)** (See Chap. 34)	An incorrect word that probably sounds the same as the correct word has been used. *There discussing the reading. (incorrect)*	• Read sentences carefully. • Use dictionary to check words. • Keep a list of words you tend to mix up. Commonly confused words: to/too, there/they're/their, its/it's, your/you're *They're discussing the reading.*
Word form **(wf)**	The correct word is used but its form is incorrect. *Boxing is excited. (incorrect)*	• Read sentences carefully. • Use dictionary to check words. • Keep a list of words you tend to mix up. *Boxing is exciting.*
Spelling (sp) (See Chap. 31)	A word is misspelled. *You have to make a comitment. (incorrect)*	• Use a dictionary to look up any words you are uncertain about. • Use spell check on the computer. • Keep a list of words you commonly misspell. *You have to make a commitment.*

Error Name and Abbreviation	The Problem (and Examples)	How To Fix (and Corrected Examples)
Capitalization (cap) (See Chap. 33)	A word should be capitalized *or* it should not be capitalized.	• Read sentences carefully and refer to this list when you have a question about capitalization. • Refer to Chapter 33 for more information about each rule. 1. Capitalize the first word in a sentence. 2. Capitalize the first word of a quoted sentence. 3. Capitalize *I* when used as a personal pronoun. 4. Capitalize proper nouns (naming *specific* people, places, things.) 5. Capitalize the names that show family relationships. 6. Capitalize the title of a person when the title is used with the person's name. 7. Capitalize *specific* courses. 8. Capitalize the names of commercial products. 9. Capitalize the first and last words and other significant words in titles of books, essays, stories, films, movies, television series, compact discs, magazines, journals, poems, songs, and news articles. 10. Capitalize names of languages, nations, nationalities, and ethnicity. 11. Capitalize names of government agencies, unions, corporations, institutions, religious and political organizations. 12. Capitalize names of wars and historical events. 13. Capitalize the days of the week, months, and holidays.
	my Father, general booth, said i should join the *united states marine corps* next *september*. *(incorrect)*	*My father, General Booth*, said I should join the *United States Marine Corps* next *September*.

Error Name and Abbreviation	The Problem (and Examples)	How To Fix (and Corrected Examples)
Plural/Singular (pl or sl) (See Chap. 31)	A word should be plural *or* it should be singular. *Rivers and <u>ocean</u> need to be protected by our government. (incorrect)*	• Make the word plural or make it singular. *Rivers and <u>oceans</u> need to be protected by our government.*
Pronoun Reference (ref) (See Chap. 21)	The pronoun does not clearly refer to a noun. *I told the residents of the apartment building to write <u>them</u> down. (incorrect)*	Use a noun instead of the pronoun, or revise your sentences and supply a clear antecedent for your pronoun. *I told the residents of the apartment building to write their <u>complaints</u> down.* or *The residents told me about their <u>complaints</u>, and I suggested that they write <u>them</u> down.*
Apostrophe (apost) (See Chap. 32)	An apostrophe must be added, deleted, or moved. *The <u>childs</u> bike was missing.*	Add, delete, or move an apostrophe. *The <u>child's</u> bike was missing.*

Appendix C
Comma, Semicolon, and Colon Rules Chart

(See Chapter 29: Commas, Semicolons, and Colons for more information.)

Comma Rule #1 Put commas between items in a series.	**Example** *The exhausted, confused, and frustrated writer leaned back in his chair.* (The comma before the *and* is optional with a list like this.)
Comma Rule #2 When you begin a sentence with a subordinated or dependent clause, you must put a comma after the subordinated (or dependent) clause.	**Example** *If he could just remember that great opening line, the rest would flow.*
Comma Rule #3 If the subordinated clause comes after the independent clause, you do not need a comma.	**Example** *The rest would flow if he could just remember that great opening line.*
Comma Rule #4 Put commas around interruptive words and phrases in a sentence.	**Example** *For two long hours, however, no words came to his mind.*
Comma Rule #5 When you join two complete sentences with a coordinator (FANBOYS), you must put a comma after the first sentence.	**Example** *At midnight he finally remembered his thrilling opening line, and he began to type.* *("Once upon a time ...")*
Comma Rule #6 When you begin a sentence with an introductory phrase, put a comma after the introductory phrase.	**Example** *With feelings of great disappointment, the writer began to look for a new job.*

The Semicolon Rule	**Example**
You can use a semicolon to separate two complete sentences.	*He liked his old job; he didn't want to go looking for a new one.*
Note: Transition words like *however, therefore, of course,* and *then* cannot be used to join sentences with a comma. If you want to use these words to build a bridge between two complete sentences, you must separate the sentences with a *semicolon* or period. Generally, the transition word is followed by a comma.	*He liked his old job; therefore, he didn't want to go looking for a new one.* or *He liked his old job. Therefore, he didn't want to go looking for a new one.*
The Colon Rule	**Example**
When you offer a list after a complete sentence, use a colon to separate the sentence and the list.	*In the newspaper, he saw a number of promising ads: creative writer needed for comic book company, writer needed in advertising firm, and editor needed for large publishing company.*

Appendix D
Tracking Sentence Errors Chart

Your editing work will be easier if you know what kinds of errors you tend to make. Then you can focus your editing work on mostly looking for these types of errors.

Use the following chart to keep track of your sentence errors. In each box, write down how many of each kind of error you made in each writing assignment. You'll probably begin to see a pattern, and you'll know better how to focus your editing efforts.

Key to Abbreviations (See the "Editing Errors Chart" on pp. 444–447 for further explanation of each error.)

s-v agr	subject-verb agreement
vt	verb tense
frag	fragment
cs	comma splice
run-on	run-on
ww	wrong word
wf	word form
sp	spelling
cap	capitalization
pl	plural
sl	singular
ref	pronoun reference
apost	apostrophe

Tracking Sentence Errors Chart

Writing Assignment	S-V AGR	VT	FRAG	CS	RUN-ON	WW	WF	SP	CAP	PL (Change to Plural)	SL (Change to Singular)	REF	APOST
1													
2													
3													
4													
5													
6													
7													
8													
9													

Appendix E
Evaluation Chart

Along with tracking your sentence errors, you should also record your strengths and weaknesses in the following areas: focus, interest/thoughtfulness, development, and organization. After your instructor has evaluated your writing, make notes here that show what you did well and what you must continue to work on. Watch for patterns of strengths and weaknesses.

Writing Assignment	Focus	Interest and Thoughtfulness	Development	Organization
1				
2				
3				
4				
5				
6				

Writing Assignment	Focus	Interest and Thoughtfulness	Development	Organization
7				
8				
9				
10				
11				
12				
13				
14				

Glossary

action verb: a word that expresses activity or movement (179).

adjective: a word that describes a noun (277).

adverb: a word that describes verbs, adjectives, other adverbs, and whole groups of words (282).

analyze: to break down a complex concept into smaller, less complex pieces and then study the pieces (127).

antecedent: the noun a pronoun refers to (268).

anticipate: a step in the reading process when the reader guesses what the reading will be about based on his or her preview of the reading material. Readers also anticipate (or guess what will come next) while reading the entire piece for the first time (19).

base form: the form of a word with no special endings like –ed or –ly (40).

body (of the paragraph): the 5–10 sentences in the middle of a paragraph that support the topic sentence with examples, comparisons, personal experience, quotations, explanations, and so on (58).

body paragraph: a paragraph that appears after the introduction of an essay and before the conclusion. It contains information that helps support the thesis (159).

brainstorming: the act of writing without worrying about correctness. The purpose of a brainstorm is to let the writer explore ideas during the pre-drafting stage of the writing process (34).

clause: a group of words with a subject and verb (222).

clearly written: a term that refers to the sentences in paragraphs. In a final draft of a paragraph, sentences should be clear and varied (61).

coherent: in a coherent paragraph, all the ideas fit together and support the topic sentence (299).

comma splice: an error that is created when two complete sentences are joined as one with only a comma to separate them (257).

complete sentence: a group of words that includes a subject and a verb and that expresses a complete idea (178).

completer: a word or phrase that completes the meaning of the sentence (245).

conclusion paragraph: the final paragraph in an essay. It sums up the most important points, restates the writer's thesis, and draws the piece to an end (159).

contraction: a condensed form of two words with an apostrophe replacing one or more letters (346).

coordinating conjunction: a word that can join independent clauses: *for, and, nor, but, or, yet,* and *so* (223).

dependent clause: a group of words with a subject and a verb that cannot stand alone as a sentence (228).

developed: a term used to describe ideas that have been fully explained and supported (61).

direct quote: a sentence in quotation marks that represents the exact words spoken or written by another person (333).

drafting: a step in the writing process during which the writer creates a complete paragraph although the paragraph might be a little rough (30).

editing: a step in the writing process during which the writer works on sentence structure, usage, punctuation, and spelling. This is the "polishing" step (30).

essay: an organized, multiparagraph piece of writing in which the writer focuses on and develops a single, complex idea (156).

FANBOYS: the seven coordinating conjunctions: *for, and, nor, but, or, yet,* and *so* (223).

five qualities of effective writing, the: the characteristics readers expect from good writing: *interesting and thoughtful, focused, organized, developed,* and *clearly written* (59)

focused: a term used to describe writing that sticks to one point (60).

fragment: an incomplete sentence (244).

freewriting: the act of writing without worrying about correctness. The purpose of freewriting is to let the writer explore ideas during the pre-drafting stage of the writing process (34).

fused sentence: two sentences incorrectly joined as one with no punctuation separating them; also called a *run-on sentence* (250).

gerund: a verb form that ends in *–ing* but works as a noun in a sentence (201).

helping verb: a verb that works with another word to create a verb (181).

homophones: words that sound alike but have different spellings and meanings (343).

indefinite pronoun: a pronoun that does not name a specific person or thing (216).

independent clause: a group of words that can stand alone as a sentence (222).

infinitive: a phrase made of *to* + a verb form (182).

interesting and thoughtful: terms used to describe a paragraph that shows the writer has thought carefully about the topic and has found compelling information to include (59).

introduction: the first paragraph or two of an essay. Its function is to warm-up the reader and get the reader focused on the main point (158).

introduction paragraph: the first paragraph or two of an essay which explain what the essay will be about (157).

irregular verb: a verb that doesn't seem to follow any particular rule when it changes tense (191).

linking verb: a verb that does not express action. Instead, it acts as an "equals sign" between the subject and other information in the sentence (180).

multiword verb: a verb made up of more than one word (193).

narration: the act of telling a story (101).

noun: a word that names a person, place, thing, or idea (200).

organized: a term that describes a paragraph in which the ideas are presented in a logical order (60).

parallel: means having similar form (167).

parallel structure: a type of sentence structure in which the writer has put two or more items in a similar form (308).

participial phrase: a group of words consisting of a present or past participle and the words attached to that participle (239).

PARTS: The five stages of the reading process—*preview, anticipate, read and reread, think critically,* and *summarize* (19).

past participle: a verb form that often ends in *–ed*, but not always. This verb form is also called the *have* form (191).

phrase: a group of words that is missing a subject, a verb, or both (235).

plural: more than one (212).

possessive: a word that shows ownership (347).

predicate: in a sentence, the verb and all the words that are not part of the subject (199).

pre-drafting : a step in the writing process in which the writer talks about the assigned topic, reads, discusses readings, thinks critically, reviews the actual writing assignment, and brainstorms (30).

preposition: a word that suggests position, location, direction, condition, or time (183).

prepositional phrase: a group of words consisting of a preposition and its object (183).

present participle: a verb form that ends in *–ing* (181).

preview: the first step in the reading process in which the reader looks at author, title, length, topic sentences, headings, subheadings, charts, pictures, or diagrams in order to get a sense of what the reading will be about (19).

prompt: a writing assignment or question (387).

pronoun: a word that can be used instead of a noun (200).

read and reread: a step in the reading process in which the reader reads through a selection quickly (only marking unknown terms and interesting points) and then rereads a second time more carefully (responding to the text and looking up unknown terms) (19).

reading process: the five steps that experienced writers take when reading: *preview, anticipate, read and reread, think critically,* and *summarize* (19).

regular verb: a verb that changes form in a regular pattern (191).

revising: a step in the writing process in which the writer changes and improves his or her draft. The writer might rethink some of the ideas, add information, delete information, and move ideas around (30).

run-on sentence: two sentences incorrectly joined as one with no punctuation separating them; also called a *fused sentence* (250).

studying the context: the act of looking at the sentences that come before and after an unfamiliar word so that the reader can try and figure out the meaning of the word (38).

subject: the person or thing the sentence is about. The subject is performing the action expressed by the verb, or it is being linked to other information by the verb (178).

subordinator: a word that can attach to an independent clause and change it into a dependent clause (228).

subordinated clause: a group of words with a subject and verb that cannot stand on its own (228).

summarize: find the main points; the last step in the reading process (20).

synonym: a word that is similar in meaning to another word (42).

thesis statement: the main idea of an essay (158).

think critically: the fourth step in the reading process when the reader thinks about the techniques used in the reading, the message expressed, and his or her own reaction to the reading (20).

topic sentence: a sentence that expresses your main point in a paragraph (58).

transitions: words or phrases that help the reader move smoothly from one idea to the next (60).

verb: a word that expresses action or links the subject of the sentence to other information in the sentence (178).

verb tense: tells us what time the action (or the linking) takes place (188).

wrap-up sentence: the last sentence in an academic paragraph. It reminds the reader what the main point of the paragraph is (58).

writing process: the steps a writer takes when completing a writing assignment. There are four steps: *pre-drafting, drafting, revising,* and *editing* (30).

Bibliography

Preface for Instructors
Shaughnessy, Mina P. *Errors and Expectations: A Guide for the Teacher of Basic Writing.* New York: Oxford UP, 1977.

Chapter 1
Frank, Anne. *The Diary of a Young Girl.* Trans. from the Dutch by B. M. Mooyaart-Doubleday. New York: Doubleday & Company, 1967. 218.

Chapter 5
Merriam-Webster's Collegiate Dictionary. 10th ed. 1993.
The Merriam-Webster Dictionary. 1st ed. 1994.

Chapter 9
X, Malcolm, with Alex Haley. *The Autobiography of Malcolm X.* New York: Ballantine Books, 1992.

Chapter 17
Leakey, Richard. "Extinctions Past and Present." Spec. ed. of *Time* April–May 2000: 35.

Chapter 33
Mitchard, Jacquelyn. "After All, Who Wants To Marry a Prince Who's Acting Like a Frog?" *Sacramento Bee* 27 Feb. 2000: D2.
Britt, Donna. "Who Knows? Perhaps Two Wrongs Can Be Right for Each Other." *Sacramento Bee* 23 Feb. 2000: H3.

Text Credits

Page 21, Reprinted with permission of Scribner, an imprint of Simon & Schuster Adult Publishing Group, from *O Rugged Land of Gold* by Mary Martin. Copyright © 1952, 1953 by Macmillan Publishing Company; copyright renewed 1980, 1981 by Christina M. Niemi. Page 31, 401, From *The Freedom Writers Diary* by the Freedom Writers with Erin Gruwell, copyright © 1999 by The Tolerance Education Foundation. Used by permission of Doubleday, a division of Random House, Inc. Page 50, From *The Diary of a Young Girl; The Definitive Edition* by Anne Frank. Otto H. Frank & Mirjam Pressler, Editors, translated by Susan Massotty, copyright © 1995 by Doubleday, a division of Random House, Inc. Used by permission of Doubleday, a division of Random House, Inc. Page 57, Christine Burroughs, "Battle." Reprinted by permission of the author. Page 59, Lucky Le, "My Own Writing Goal." Reprinted by permission of the author. Page 61, Gloria Ayala-Partida, "How Not To Pop Your Top." Reprinted by permission of the author. Page 62, Christine Burroughs, "Why I Write Poetry." Reprinted by permission of the author. Page 64, Anonymous, "Writing Well Is a Step to My Goal." Reprinted by permission of the author. Page 71, Judy Hudson, "One Student's Writing Goal." Reprinted by permission of the author. Page 79, Mary Harris "Mother" Jones, "Mother Jones to President Theodore Roosevelt," *Letters of a Nation: A Collection of Extraordinary American Letters,* ed. Andrew Carroll. NY: Kodansha International, 1997, pp. 186–188. Reprinted by permission. Page 83, Diana Griego Erwin, "Nike: 'Sweatshop' Order Not Funny," *The Sacramento Bee,* February 20, 2001, p. B1. Copyright, The Sacramento Bee, 2002. Reprinted by permission. Page 98, Elizabeth Villar, "Student Sample—a Business Letter." Reprinted by permission of the author. Page 103, Alice Walker, "Beauty: When the Other Dancer is the Self," as appeared in *Dreams and Inward Journeys: A Rhetoric and Reader for Writers,* 3rd edition, Marjorie Ford and Jon Ford. NY: Addison Wesley Longman, Inc., 1998, pp. 140–145. Reprinted by permission. Page 130, Brothers Grimm, "Cinderella," *The Complete Illustrated Works of the Brothers Grimm.* London: Chancellor Press Michelin House, 1996, pp. 114–121. Reprinted by permission. Page 138, Bill Harbaugh, "The Truth About Cinderella and Her Evil Stepsisters," *from http://harbaugh.uoregon.edu/family/Cinderella.htm* Reprinted by permission of Bill Harbaugh and Daughters. Page 150, Theresa Michelini, "The Tale of Cindy Spirelli." Reprinted by permission of the author. Page 163, Ivana Kim, "Dreams as Concious Visions," from *Dreams and Inward Journeys: A Rhetoric and Reader for Writers,* 3rd edition, Marjorie Ford and Jon Ford. NY: Addison Wesley Longman, Inc., 1998, pp. 534–536. Page 170, Francis Vessigault, "My Personal Dream." Reprinted by permission of the author. Page 172, Lucky Le, "Good-bye American Dream." Reprinted by permis-

sion of the author. Page 370, Jeffrey Barsch, EdD, *Barsch Learning Style Inventory,* ©1996 Edition, Academic Therapy Publications, 20 Commercial Blvd., Novato, CA 94949 / Order #905–2. Reprinted with permission. Page 392, Marjorie Lundstrom, "Winning at All Costs is Costing Society Too Much," *The Sacramento Bee,* May 18, 2000, p. A3. Copyright, The Sacramento Bee, 2002. Reprinted by permission. Page 395, Barbara T. Roessner, "Supermom is the Wrong Role Model," as appeared in *The Sacramento Bee,* April 22, 1998, p. B7. Reprinted by permission. Page 411, Calvin Mak, "Don't Want to be a Dummy Writer." Reprinted by permission of the author. Page 412, Cecelia Miles, "Singing My Heart Out." Reprinted by permission of the author. Page 414, Anne D. LeClaire, "Out of Silence," from *Letters to Our Mothers: I've Always Meant to Tell You: An Anthology of Contemporary Women Writers,* ed. Constance Warloe. NY: Pocket Books, Simon & Schuster, Inc., 1997, pp. 275–276. Reprinted by permission of the author. Page 416, From *Now You Know: Reactions After Seeing Saving Private Ryan.* Copyright © 1999 Dream Works LLC and Paramount Pictures Corporation and Amblin Entertainment, Inc. All rights reserved. Reprinted by permission of Newmarket Press, 18 East 48th Street, New York, NY 10017. Page 423, From *Trump: The Art of the Deal* by Donald Trump, copyright © 1987 by Donald Trump. Used by permission of Random House, Inc. Page 430, Mary Carter Smith, "Cindy Ellie, a Modern Fairy Tale," from *Talk that Talk: An Anthology of African-American Storytelling,* eds. Linda Goss & Marian E. Barnes. NY: A Touchstone Book, Simon & Schuster, Inc., 1989, pp. 396–402. Copyright 1982 Mary Carter Smith. Reprinted by permission of the author. Page 437, Ayanna Willliams, "My Vision." Reprinted by permission of the author.

Photo Credits

Page 8: ©1997 M. McCarron/AP/Wide World Photos; 18: © Baker Furniture; 29: ©Matt Collins; 37: ©AP/Wide World Photos; 48: © John Steuart Curry, Tornado Over Kansas, Hackley Picture Fund Purchase, Muskegon Museum of Art; 77: © Freer Gallery of Art, Smithsonian Institution, Washington, D.C.; Gift of Charles Lang Freer, F1893.11; 101: © Robert Arneson/ Collection of the American Craft Museum, NY, Gift of the Johnson Wax Company, from OBJECTS: USA, 1977. Donated to the American Craft Museum by the American Craft Council, 1990; 125: © The Quigmans/ Tribune Media; 156: ©Dorthea Lange Collection, Oakland Museum of California, City of Oakland. Gift of Paul S. Taylor.

Subject Index

Index of Authors and Titles